ADVANCED database projects in ACCESS 2007

Suitable for users of Office 2010

Ian Rendell & Julian Mott

The Publishers would like to thank the following for permission to reproduce copyright material:

Photo credits: **p.268** © TNT Magazine/Alamy; **p.274** © Steve Bardens/Actionplus; **p.281** *l* © Kim Karpeles/Alamy, *r* © Mode Images Limited/Alamy; **p.291** *l* © ImageState/Alamy, *r* © Laurence Griffiths/Getty Images; **p. 292** © TNT Magazine/Alamy; **p. 293** *t* © Foodfolio/Alamy, *b* © Food, drink and diet/Mark Sykes/Alamy; **p.294** © ArkReligion.com/Alamy; **p.296** © Steve Bardens/Actionplus; **p.297** © Ron Evans/Alamy; **p.298** © Gary Roebuck/Alamy; **p.299** © The Photolibrary Wales/Alamy; **p.301** © Mode Images Limited/Alamy; **p.302** *tl* © Chris Jackson/Getty Images, *tr* © Stockdisc / Corbis, *br* © Niall McDiarmid/Alamy; **p.303** © Peter Titmuss/Alamy; **p.304** *l* © Isopix/Rex Features, *r* © Chris Ladd/Getty Images.

Every effort has been made to trace all copyright holders, but if any have been inadvertently overlooked the Publishers will be pleased to make the necessary arrangements at the first opportunity.

t = top, b = bottom, l = left, r = right

Although every effort has been made to ensure that website addresses are correct at time of going to press, Hodder Education cannot be held responsible for the content of any website mentioned in this book. It is sometimes possible to find a relocated web page by typing in the address of the home page for a website in the URL window of your browser.

Hachette UK's policy is to use papers that are natural, renewable and recyclable products and made from wood grown in sustainable forests. The logging and manufacturing processes are expected to conform to the environmental regulations of the country of origin.

Orders: please contact Bookpoint Ltd, 130 Milton Park, Abingdon, Oxon OX14 4SB. Telephone: (44) 01235 827720. Fax: (44) 01235 400454. Lines are open 9.00 – 5.00, Monday to Saturday, with a 24-hour message answering service. Visit our website at www.hoddereducation.co.uk

First published in 2008 by
Hodder Education
An Hachette UK Company
338 Euston Road
London NW1 3BH
Impression number 5 4 3 2 1

Year 2014 2013 2012 2011 2010

Cover photo Jupiter Images

Illustrations by Barking Dog Art

Typeset in Goudy Old Style 10/12pt by DC Graphic Design Limited, Swanley Village, Kent

Printed in Italy

A catalogue record for this title is available from the British Library

ISBN: 978 1444 117370

Contents

Part Four Project Ideas

Part Five Project Documentation

(all materials in Part Five are on the website that supports this book, www.dynamic-learning-student.co.uk)

Part Six Finding Project Ideas

(all materials in Part Six are on the website that supports this book, www.dynamic-learning-student.co.uk)

Introduction

Aims

The book is aimed at a number of Advanced courses of study within the National Qualifications Framework currently available in schools and colleges.

The book covers all the key software skills required in practical components of ICT and Computing specifications where a study of databases using Microsoft Access is required.

The materials and approach used in the book are also applicable to students on many Computing and ICT related courses in further and higher education where a study of databases through Microsoft Access is necessary.

Features of Access covered in this book

The main units take students through the following features in Access:

- tables and data types
- simple input masks and data validation
- related tables
- select, parameter and multi-table queries
- calculated fields
- data entry using fully customised forms
- list boxes or combo boxes to facilitate data entry
- basic reports
- macros to automate commonly used features
- switchboards and start-up screens
- subforms to display information in related tables
- update, append and delete queries
- forms and reports based on multi-table queries
- customised reports with use of logos, headers and footers to show grouped data and calculated totals
- customised menus and interfaces.

The **Tricks and Tips** section provides many further features in Access.

How to use this book

The book assumes students have a working knowledge of Microsoft Windows and Windows-based software. It is expected that students will be familiar with the concept of files, records and fields and will have practical experience of simple searching and sorting techniques.

It is also assumed that students will have studied the design of relational databases through a theory component in their course of study.

The book can be used as a formal teaching aid by lecturers and teachers, or students can work independently through the self-study units in class or away from the classroom.

Part One takes the student through the development of a system, with each unit building on the range of features in Access. The system is based around a driving school, is fictitious and has been designed to incorporate as many features as is possible for demonstration purposes only. The units are best worked through in sequence.

Units 1 to 15 set up a working system, using features which might be expected from students working at this level. The system at this point forms the basis for the support materials available on the net offering advice on documenting solutions. Units 16 to 20 show how to develop this system further.

Teachers and lecturers will clearly use the units in different ways and offer their own input during lessons. However, it is expected that the units will take no more than 15–20 hours of study time.

Part Two offers a range of useful tips and features in Access to support the units and should provide interesting reading. These could be used as further activities for students.

Part Three provides three 'Starting Points'. These are brief activities each of 1–2 hours' duration. The tables and data are downloadable from the net. Students set up the relationships and forms using just the Wizards. They are then taken through a key process or two in each activity.

- Cricket Bat Orders focuses on the IIf function, form referencing and producing customised output.
- Bouncy Castle Hire focuses on the hiring and returning processes. A common project at this level is DVD rentals. Many students forget that once you have taken a DVD/Video out, it has to come back! This involves more than just deleting its record from a loans table. This offers a starter but no more!
- Stationery Store deals with the situation where you need to order more than one item. It revises in detail the use of main form/subform approaches.

Each starting point offers good revision and new skills and hopefully will open up project potential and ideas for the student.

Part Four provides fifteen ideas for students' projects. Students could adapt a problem or undertake a similar problem to meet the demands of a real user.

Further ideas for projects are downloadable from the internet.

Submitting a Driving School as a coursework for an examination

A number of schools and colleges have steered students away from choosing a Driving School for their choice of project. This should not really be the case but students choosing this option should ensure that their database is not just a copy of the database in this book.

A student who sets about this type of project with a real user will very quickly come up with a significantly different solution. They will find that:

- the driving school may only have one instructor
- the user wants to keep progress records on students
- lessons are block-booked, with a variety of discounts on offer
- payments for lessons need to be managed
- different management reports are required
- the organisation of practical and theory tests needs to become part of the solution.

Database Projects in Access – differences between the 2nd and 3rd editions

The 3rd edition of this book was published in 2008 and based on Access 2003.

The support file called **DrivingSchoolData** now offers 105 lessons pre-set-up for students. This will not only save time entering data but enable students to explore reporting in greater detail. The file offers greater scope for sorting, grouping, forcing page breaks and producing meaningful management reports.

The **Tricks and Tips** section has been significantly added to in a way that offers extension work to the units and stretches the student wishing to move through the materials at pace.

Students, teachers and lecturers should find no significant differences in working with edition 2 alongside edition 3 in the classroom. A file called **Changes to Edition 3 from 2** is downloadable from the net. This outlines the differences in more detail.

Database Projects in Access 2007

Schools, colleges and universities are going through the process of upgrading from Access 2003 to Access 2007.

Database Projects in Access 2007 is the 4th edition of this book. It follows very closely the 3rd edition, based on Access 2003, but has been upgraded to use Access 2007. A file called **Changes to Edition 4 from 3 and 2** is downloadable from the net.

What's new in Access 2007?

Access 2007 introduces a completely new interface and many new functions and features, including:

- many template databases to get you started
- a new interface with the Ribbon, Navigation Pane and Create tab
- choice between Tabbed Documents and Overlapping Windows
- a new Layout View – redesign forms and reports while viewing them
- append only memo fields
- multi-value fields

- totals offered in Datasheet View
- attachment data types to easily display graphics in each record
- automatic calendar controls added to date/time fields
- improved sorting and grouping in reports.

There are many websites giving details of the new functionality in Access 2007. A starting point for further investigation is:

http://office.microsoft.com/en-us/access

Alternatively, load Access 2007 and click on the question mark in the top right-hand corner (**Microsoft Office Access Help**). Enter 'What's new in Microsoft Office Access 2007'.

Compatibility issues

Access 2007 is a significant upgrade to previous versions.

If you create a new database in Access 2007 it is saved with an **.accdb** file name extension unlike earlier versions of Access which used the **.mdb** format. It is recommended that users of Access 2007 use the new file format whenever possible.

If you use the **.accdb** file format for your database you will not be able to open it in earlier versions of Access. You can, however, save your database in an earlier format.

- Click on the **Office Button** and select the **Save As** option to select the required version. See Figure 1.0.1.

Figure 1.0.1 ▶

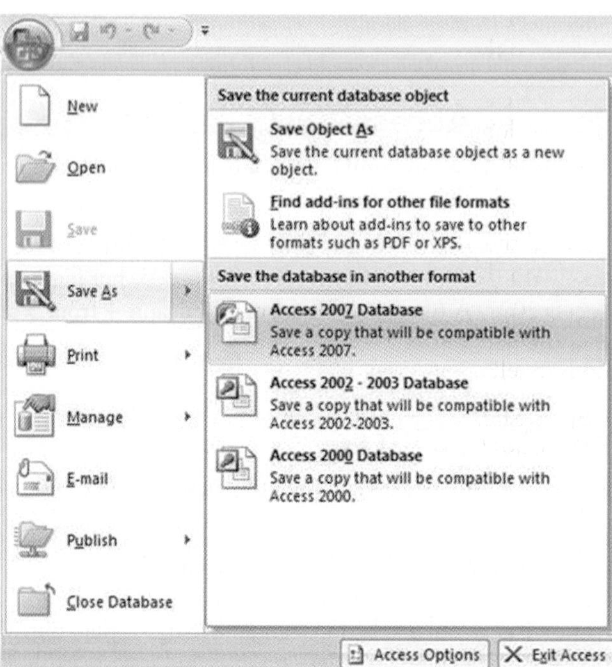

You can open earlier versions of Access databases in Access 2007. They will remain in the earlier format unless you choose to convert to Access 2007.

- Click on the **Office Button** and select the **Convert** option. Choose the location and name for the database and click on **Save**.

A note to students and lecturers using the materials for external examination

It is important to note that the system used in the text is not being put forward for a particular grade at any level. The system is fictitious and is aimed at showing the student the potential of Microsoft Access and how software features can be incorporated to produce a working ICT system.

All exam boards provide exemplar materials, support and training. It is vital that students, in conjunction with their tutors, are guided by the specifications.

A word of real caution. Students must on no account copy materials in text books and submit them for examination. Moderators, examiners and the exam boards are very aware of published exemplar materials.

Database Projects in Access Support at www.dynamic-learning-student.co.uk

A number of support files are available at www.dynamic-learning-student.co.uk

Units 1 to 20 are supported with an end-of-unit file. This will enable students to pick up the solution at any point in the development.

A file for each trick and tip is included, where appropriate. This hopefully will save development time, particularly for teachers/lecturers wanting to demonstrate a specific feature in Access.

A range of PowerPoint files offer advice and support to assist students in documenting the systems they have developed and also allow teachers/lecturers to explain the key issues.

Further files are available, offering ideas for project work.

Ian Rendell and Julian Mott have written two coursework books:

- Spreadsheet Projects in Excel for Advanced Level and
- Database Projects in Access for Advanced Level

The Development of a System

Unit 1: The Pass IT Driving School

The system covered by this book is based on a local driving school. The driving school caters for many students in the surrounding villages. The school has a number of full-time and part-time instructors.

The driving school offers different types of lesson: Introductory, Standard, Pass Plus or the Driving Test. Fees are charged depending on the type of lesson booked.

When a student starts a course of lessons they are issued with a student record card and allocated an instructor. The record card stores the personal contact details of the student driver and can be used by them to keep records of their lessons and the progress they are making.

Students can book lessons through their instructor or by phoning the driving school office. Students usually book lessons of one or two hours, though they can book longer sessions if they wish. The driving school organises the practical and theory test for the students; if successful they can go on to do the Pass Plus course.

The driving school office keeps contact detail record cards on each of its instructors. Each instructor is also issued with lesson record sheets on which are kept details of student progress. These are handed into the office at the end of each day.

The system implemented will allow the user to book, cancel and cost driving lessons. Details of all students and their test dates will be stored, enabling quick access and easy editing. Contact details for instructors working for the school will also be stored.

A range of search options will allow the user to quickly locate details of students and/or lessons. Full reporting menus will offer a range of management information, including weekly or daily lesson timetables for specified instructors. Further options will include the automatic:

- processing of students who leave the school after passing their test
- filing of all lessons taken for later reference
- analysis of lessons taken.

All user interfaces will be fully customised with user-friendly menus.

Individual student lesson progress and lesson payments will not be implemented, enabling the reader to research and develop that side of the solution. Further ideas are discussed in the Introduction.

The system will have four related tables: Student, Instructor, Lesson and Lesson Type. Details are shown in Figure 1.1.1.

Student Table
StudentID
Title
Surname
Forename
Address1
Address2
Address3
Address4
TelNo
DateOfBirth
Sex
TheoryTestDate
PassedTheoryTest
PracticalTestDate
PassedPracticalTest

Instructor Table
InstructorID
Title
Surname
Forename
Address1
Address2
Address3
Address4
HomeTelNo
MobileNo

Lesson Table
LessonNo
StudentID
InstructorID
DateOfLesson
StartTime
LengthOfLesson
CollectionPoint
DropOffPoint
LessonType

Lesson Type Table
LessonType
Cost

Figure 1.1.1 ▲

Unit 2: Getting started

Microsoft Access is a database management system. It allows the user to store and manipulate data.

The main components of an Access database are:

- tables
- queries
- forms
- reports
- macros.

Tables

Access stores data in tables. A table is organised in rows (called records) and columns (called fields).

For example, in a student table a row would store the information about one particular student. This is called a record. Each column would contain details about each student such as forename, surname, etc. These are called fields.

Figure 1.2.1 ▶

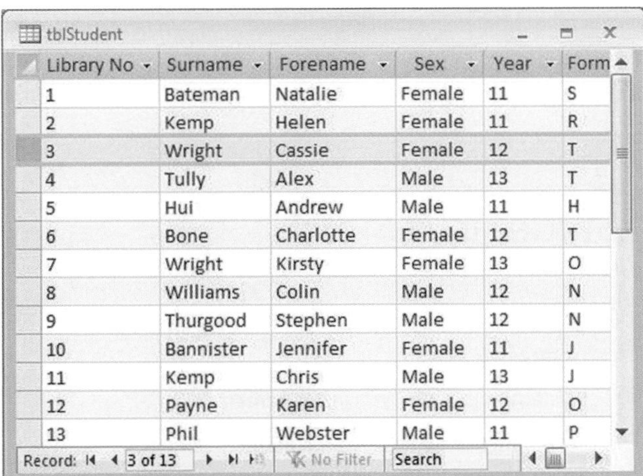

tblStudent

Library No	Surname	Forename	Sex	Year	Form
1	Bateman	Natalie	Female	11	S
2	Kemp	Helen	Female	11	R
3	Wright	Cassie	Female	12	T
4	Tully	Alex	Male	13	T
5	Hui	Andrew	Male	11	H
6	Bone	Charlotte	Female	12	T
7	Wright	Kirsty	Female	13	O
8	Williams	Colin	Male	12	N
9	Thurgood	Stephen	Male	12	N
10	Bannister	Jennifer	Female	11	J
11	Kemp	Chris	Male	13	J
12	Payne	Karen	Female	12	O
13	Phil	Webster	Male	11	P

Record: 3 of 13 No Filter Search

Typically a system will consist of more than one table. For example, in a school library the database might be made up of a student table, a book table and a loan table. The student table is shown in Figure 1.2.1.

Access is often referred to as a relational database. Relationships can be defined between tables and used to support the searching and processing of data. A relational database will have at least two tables that are linked together.

Queries

A query is a way of asking questions about the data in your tables according to certain criteria. The user may wish to display a list of appointments for a particular day or output customers who owe payments.

In the example shown in Figure 1.2.2 a query has produced a list of students in Year 11. This is known as a **Select Query**.

Figure 1.2.2 ▶

Library No	Surname	Forename	Sex	Year	Form
1	Bateman	Natalie	Female	11	S
2	Kemp	Helen	Female	11	R
5	Hui	Andrew	Male	11	H
10	Bannister	Jennifer	Female	11	J
13	Phil	Webster	Male	11	P

You will notice that there are five records in the output from this query. In the original table there were thirteen records. Five of the thirteen pupils are in Year 11.

Queries in Access offer a powerful processing tool. Later you will meet action and parameter queries. Queries can also be used to take data from more than one table and perform calculations on data.

Forms

Forms are used mainly to display the records in a table in a user-friendly way. Through a form you can enter and edit records more easily.

Figure 1.2.3 ▶

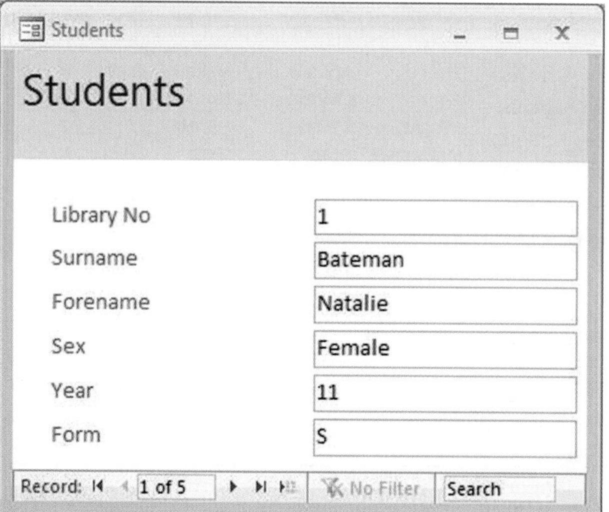

Forms are fully customisable. You can add buttons and controls, edit the appearance and include images (see Figure 1.2.3).

Reports

Reports are used to print information from your database. They provide professional looking output from a table or query. They can be fully customised and can display summary information (see Figure 1.2.4).

Figure 1.2.4 ▶

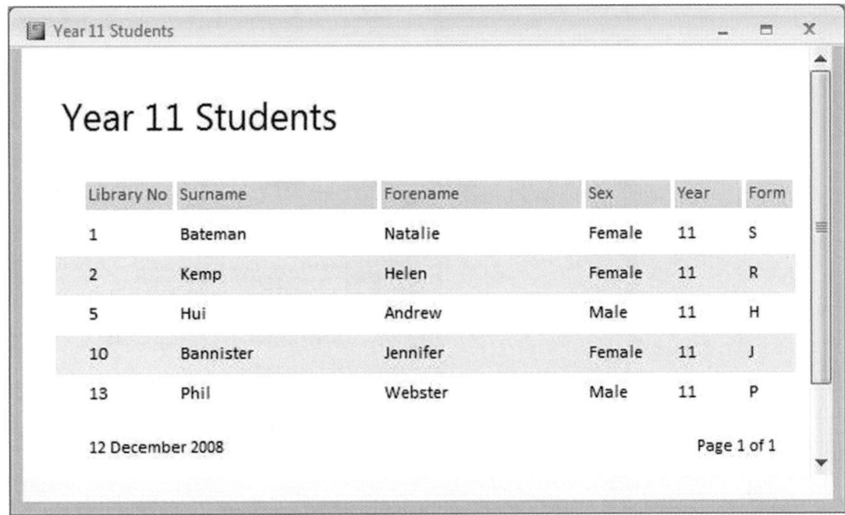

Year 11 Students

Year 11 Students

Library No	Surname	Forename	Sex	Year	Form
1	Bateman	Natalie	Female	11	S
2	Kemp	Helen	Female	11	R
5	Hui	Andrew	Male	11	H
10	Bannister	Jennifer	Female	11	J
13	Phil	Webster	Male	11	P

12 December 2008 Page 1 of 1

Macros

A macro is a set of one or more actions that perform a particular operation. You can use macros to add buttons to print a report, open a form and perform other commonly used tasks. Macros help you to fully automate and customise your system.

Starting Access 2007

When you launch Access 2007, it opens with the **Getting Started with Microsoft Office Access** screen shown in Figure 1.2.5.

From here you can choose to start working with one of the many pre-designed templates supplied with Access 2007. The left pane shows the categories available.

You can start a **New Blank Database** by clicking on the **Blank Database** icon. Alternatively, you can click on the **Office Button** and select **New**.

The right pane displays the most recently opened databases. You can select one or click on **More** to locate your database. Alternatively, you can click on the **Office Button** and select **Open**.

Figure 1.2.5 ▶

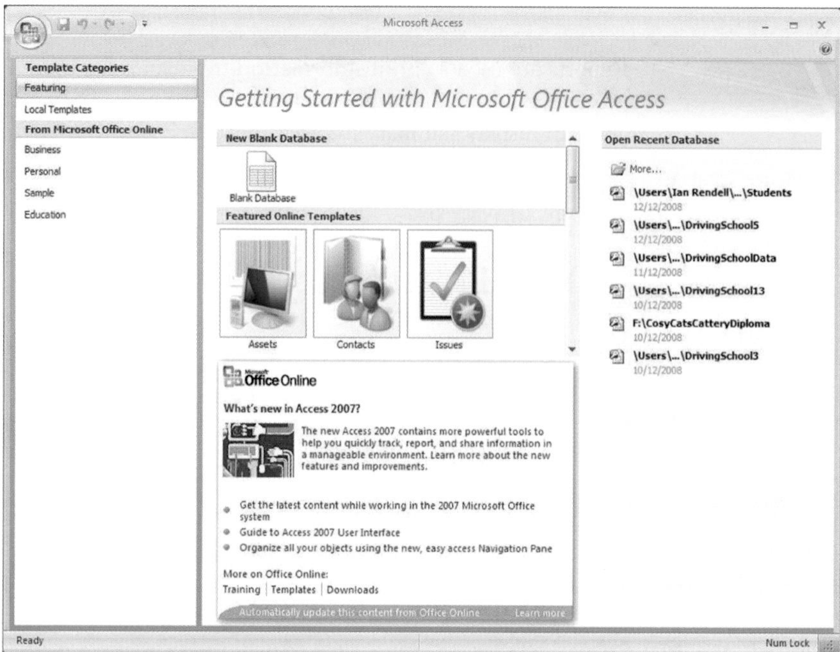

Finding your way round the Access 2007 window

Access 2007 shares a common theme with other Microsoft Office applications. A standardised layout across all Microsoft Office applications helps the user find functions quickly and easily.

A demonstration database called **Students** is available to download from the internet. It may be useful to load the file and explore the following options. To load the file:

Start **Access 2007** and click on the **Office Button**. Select **Open** and navigate to the folder where the **Students** database is stored. Double-click to open the file. The database loads as shown in Figure 1.2.6.

Figure 1.2.6 ▼

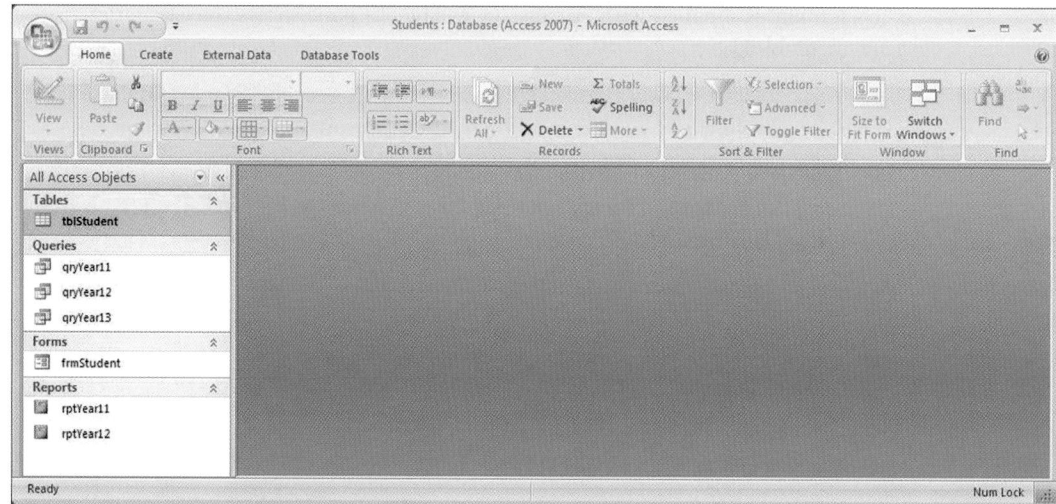

Note: When opening an existing database, Access 2007 may display a security warning in the Message bar. Click on **Options** and choose **Enable this content** in the Security Alert window. For more on this topic, see later in this unit.

The Navigation Pane

The **Navigation Pane** to the left of the window displays the objects that make up your database, such as Tables, Queries, Forms and Reports. This is the control centre of your application and replaces the Database Window in earlier versions of Access.

The **Navigation Pane** in Figure 1.2.7 shows the objects that make up our **Students** database. To open an object in the **Navigation Pane**, double-click its icon, for example, to open the Year 11 Student report, simply double-click the **rptYear11** icon.

Figure 1.2.7 ▼

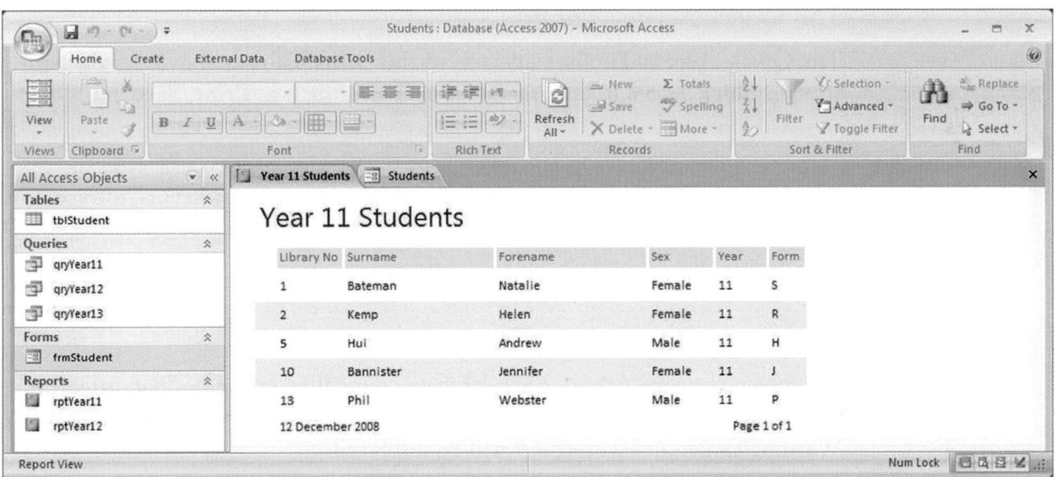

To open the **Student** form, double-click **frmStudent**. The objects are displayed as **Tabbed Documents**. Simply click the tab to toggle between them.

If you prefer to work the way you did in earlier versions of Access, you can switch to **Overlapping Windows**. For more on this topic, see later in this unit.

Right-clicking on the objects in the **Navigation Pane** or on the Tab offers further options which we will meet in the units ahead.

To hide the **Navigation Pane** click the **Shutter Bar Open/Close Button** in the top right of the pane. Click the **All Access Objects** drop-down to customise the **Navigation Pane**.

Hint Use **F11** to quickly Hide/Display the Navigation Pane.

The Office Button

The **Office Button** is found in the top left corner of the window and offers many of the options previously found under the **File** menu in earlier versions of Office, such as **New**, **Open**, **Save**, **Save As** etc.

Figure 1.2.8 ►

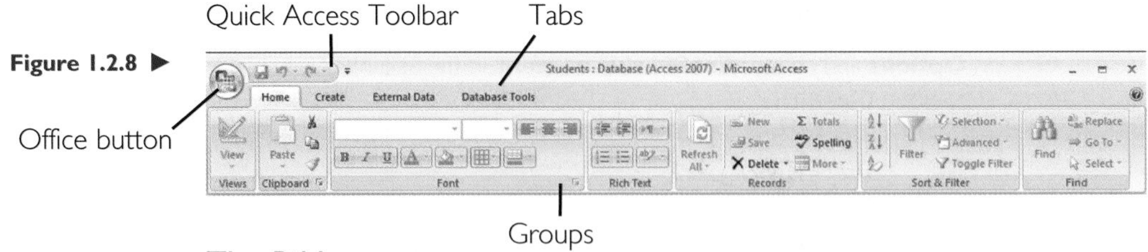

The Ribbon

The **Ribbon** in Figure 1.2.8 replaces the toolbars and menus found in earlier versions of Office. The **Ribbon** is divided into a series of Tabs. All the options in each Tab are sorted into Groups. As you work on your database, the **Ribbon** will change accordingly and display the options considered most useable.

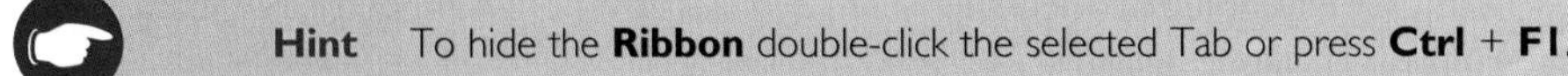

Hint To hide the **Ribbon** double-click the selected Tab or press **Ctrl** + **F1**.

The Quick Access Toolbar

The **Quick Access Toolbar** sits next to the **Office Button** above the **Ribbon**. It offers quick access to commonly used features such as **Print**, **Save** and **Undo**.

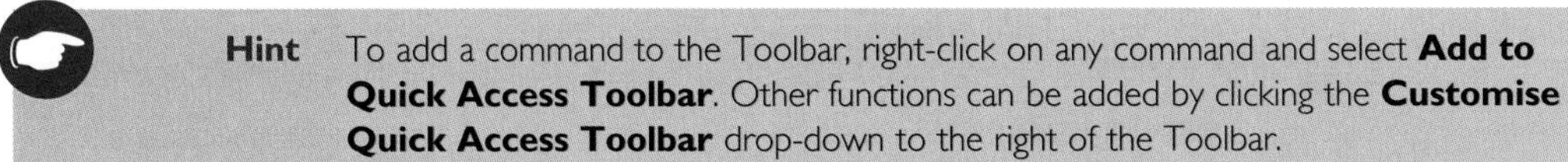

Hint To add a command to the Toolbar, right-click on any command and select **Add to Quick Access Toolbar**. Other functions can be added by clicking the **Customise Quick Access Toolbar** drop-down to the right of the Toolbar.

Database Security – the Trust Center

When you open an Access 2007 database you will be warned of potential security threats relating to macro code within the application. The **Security Warning** shown in Figure 1.2.9 will be displayed.

Figure 1.2.9 ►

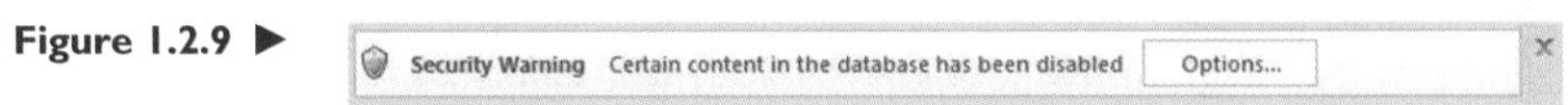

If you trust the content of this file then click on **Options** and select **Enable this content**. See Figure 1.2.10.

Figure 1.2.10 ►

To avoid this process every time you open your database, you can set up a folder to be a Trusted Location by using the Trust Center.

1 Open the file again to display the **Security Warning** and click on **Options**. At the bottom left corner of the **Security Options** dialog box, click on **Open the Trust Center**.
2 In the **Trust Center** dialog box, shown in Figure 1.2.11, select **Trusted Locations** and click on **Add new location**.

Figure 1.2.11 ▼

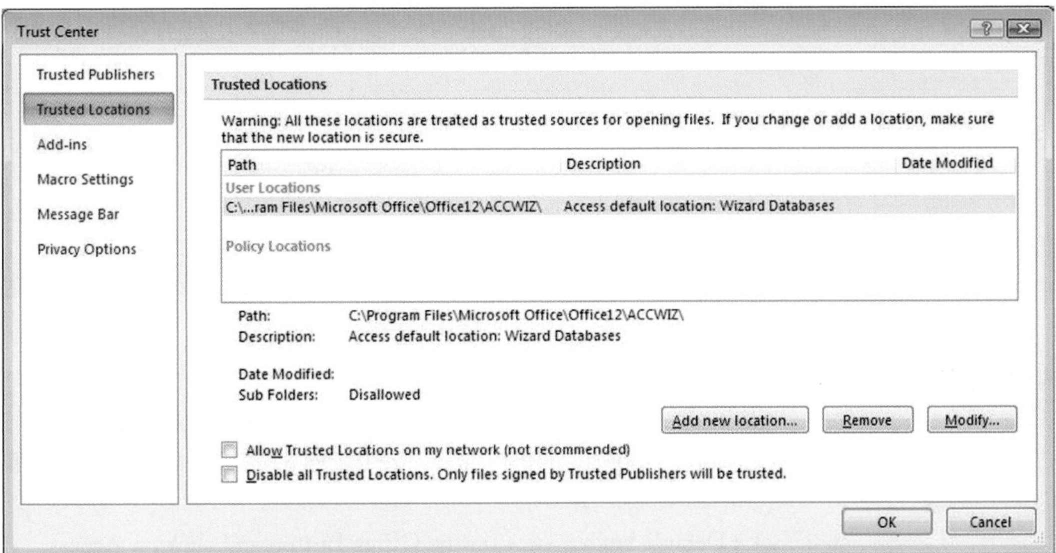

3 Click on the **Browse** button to select your trusted folder, in this case a folder called **Driving School** on the **Desktop**, figure 1.2.12. Click on **OK**.

Figure 1.2.12 ►

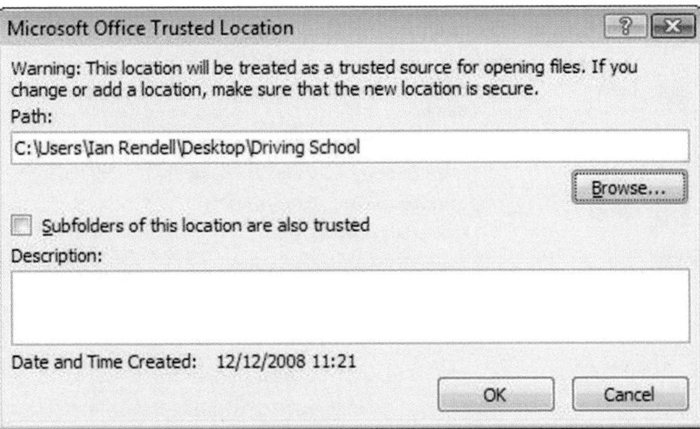

4 You will see your folder is now a **Trusted Location**, as shown in Figure 1.2.13. Click on **OK** to close the remaining dialog box.

Figure 1.2.13 ▼

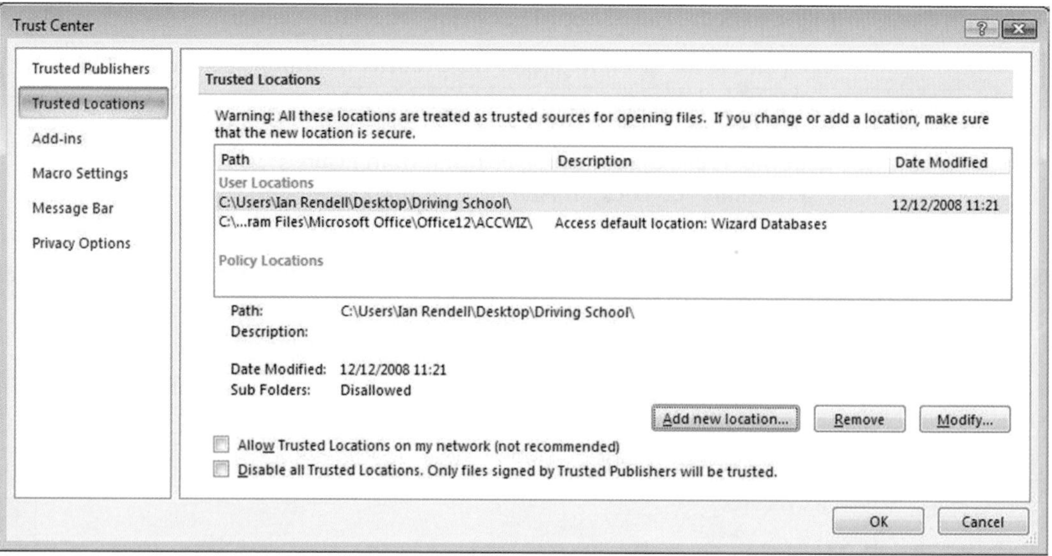

Setting a Default Folder for your work

When working in Access it is useful to set a default for a folder in which to store your work. This way, when you choose to Open or Save a file, Access will always look in the same place.

1 To set a **Default Folder**, click on the **Office Button** and click on **Access Options** at the bottom of the window. See Figure 1.2.14.

Figure 1.2.14 ▶

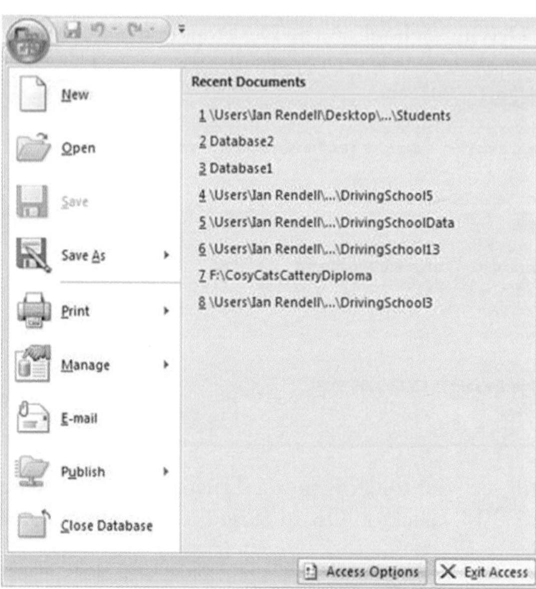

2 The **Access Options** window will be displayed. Click on **Browse** and choose your **Default database folder**. In this case, we have selected a folder called **Driving School** on the **Desktop**. See Figure 1.2.15.

Figure 1.2.15 ▼

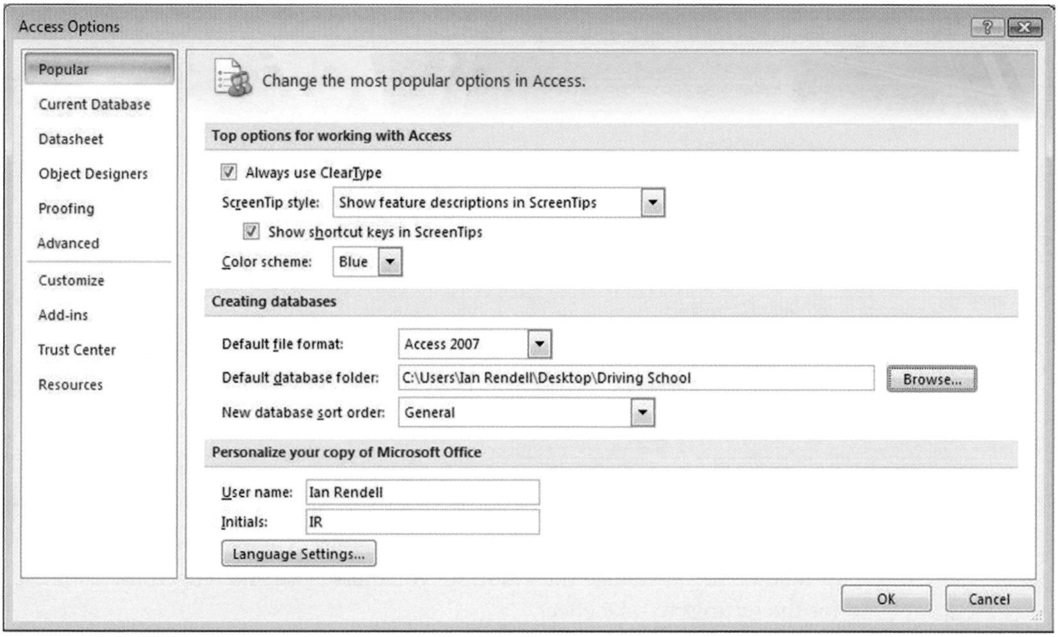

Using Tabbed Documents or Overlapping Windows

When working in Access you can choose to work with your objects, such as tables, forms and reports, either as **Tabbed Documents** or **Overlapping Windows**.

Figure 1.2.16 ▼

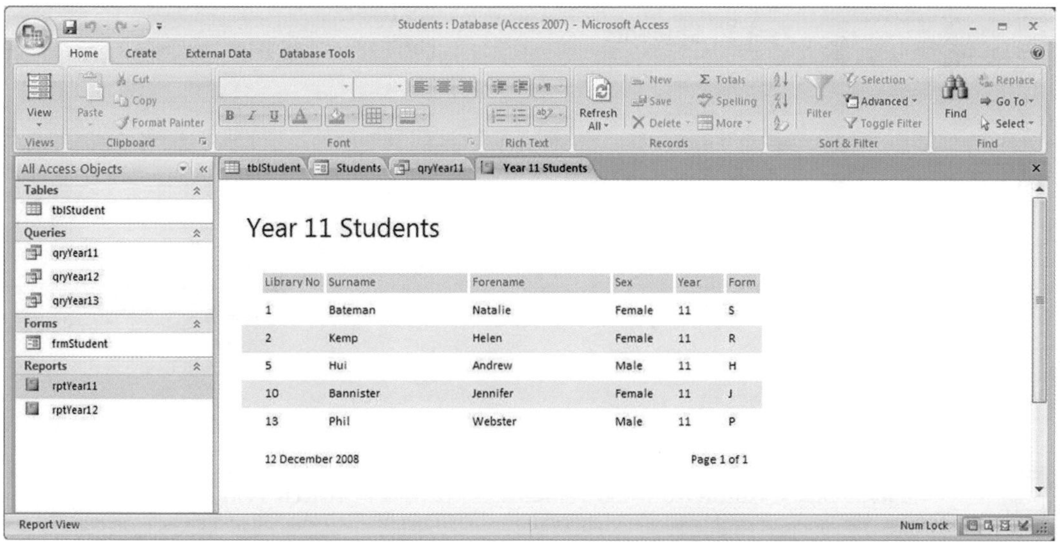

1 The window in Figure 1.2.16 shows Access using **Tabbed Documents**. To change this setting, click on the **Office Button** and select **Access Options**.
2 The **Access Options** window will be displayed. Click on **Current Database** and check **Overlapping Windows**, as shown in Figure 1.2.17.

Figure 1.2.17 ▼

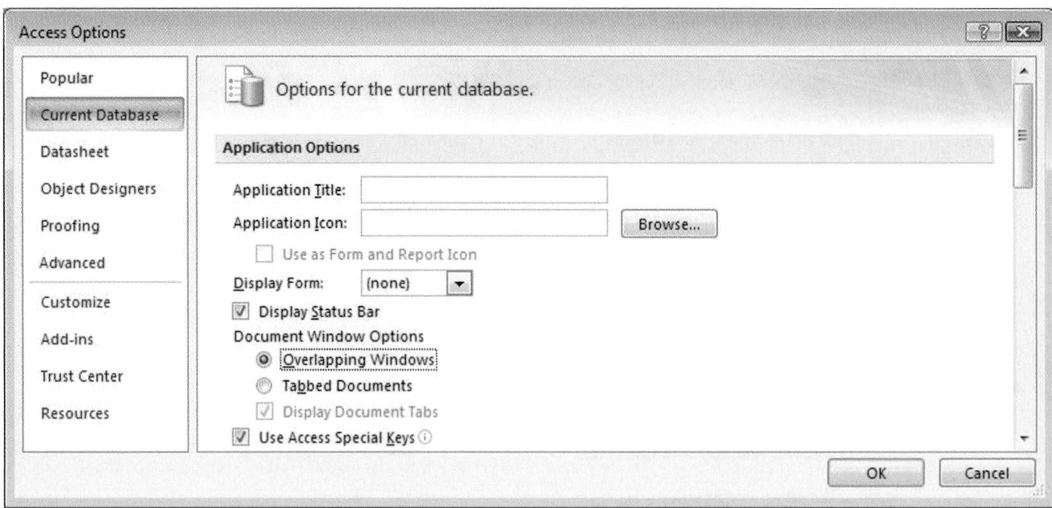

The window in Figure 1.2.18 shows Access set up to work with Overlapping Windows. If you change these settings you must close and reopen the database for the settings to take effect.

Figure 1.2.18 ▼

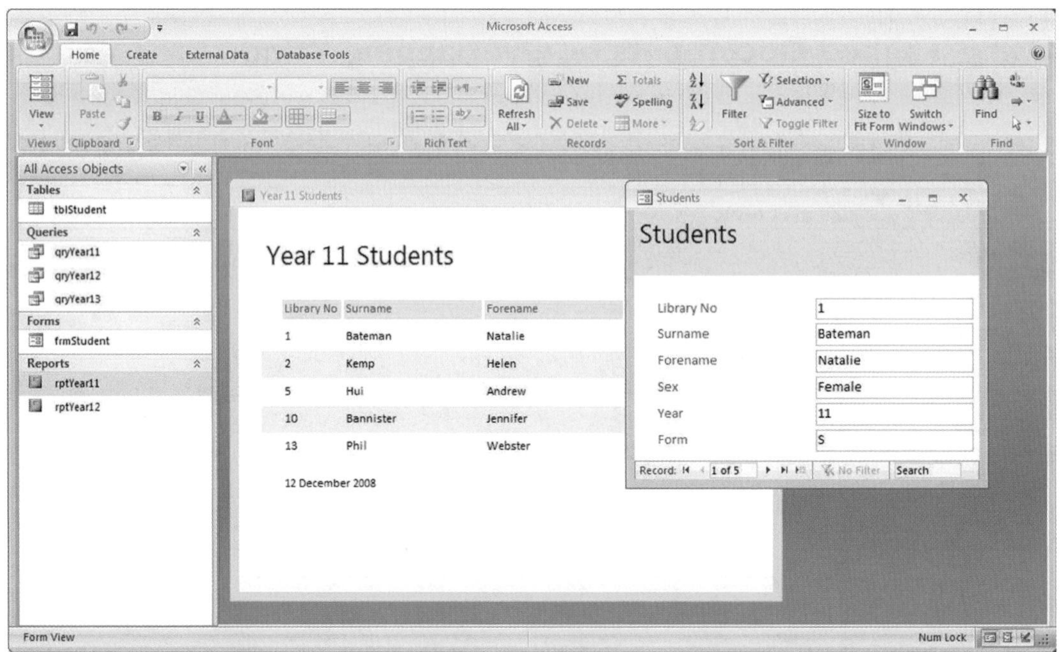

Hint On the **Home** tab, in the **Window** group, click on **Switch Windows** to tile your windows vertically or horizontally.

Unit 3: Setting up the Tables

In Units 3 and 4 you will learn how to set up the tables that are needed to store the data for the Pass IT Driving School. The Driving School system is based on four tables:

- Student
- Instructor
- Lesson
- Lesson Type.

In this unit, you will set up the **Student Table**. In Unit 4, you will enter the data and set up the remaining tables.

There are two stages to designing a table:

- Define the field names that make up the table and declare the data type for each.
- Set the field properties for each field name.

Defining the Field Names and Data Types

Access needs to know the name of each field in each table and what sort of data to expect. For example, in the Student table, the student's telephone number might have as its **Field Name**: TelNo. You also need to tell Access whether the **Data Type** is number, text, date/time, currency, etc. In this case it is text.

Setting the Field Properties

Once you have named the table and defined each field with its data type, you can control the fields further by setting **Field Properties**. These properties tell Access how you want the data stored and displayed. For example, a date could be displayed 19/06/2007, 19 June 2007 or 19-Jun-07.

Setting up the Student Table

1 Load **Microsoft Access 2007** and click on **Blank Database**.
2 In the lower right pane give the database a name, such as **DrivingSchool,** and click **Create**, see figure 1.3.1. Access saves your file in the default folder shown. You can navigate to another folder by clicking the **Browse** button.

Figure 1.3.1 ▶

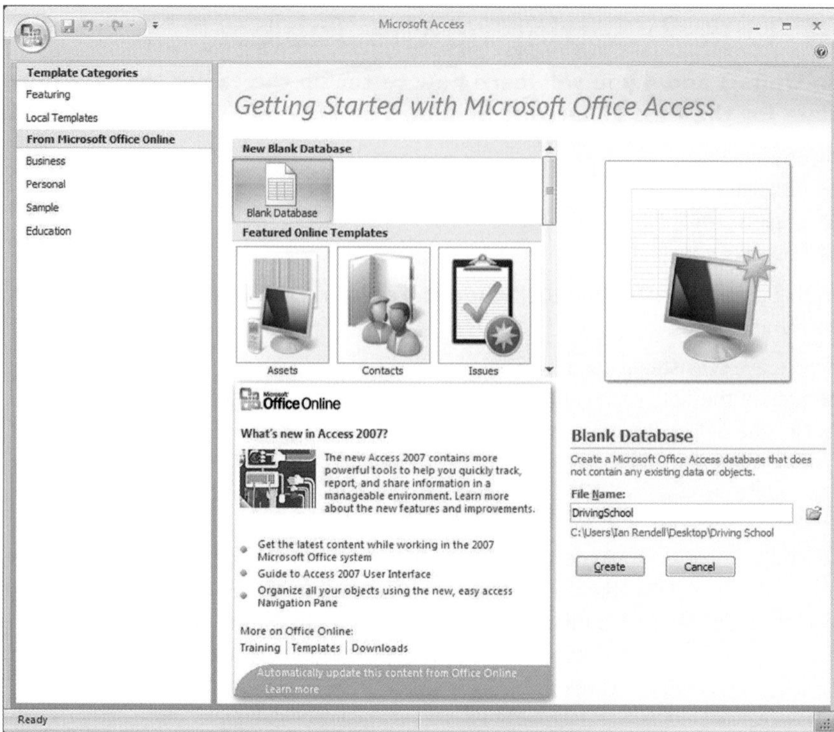

The **Access** window appears as in Figure 1.3.2. Access creates an empty database with a blank **Table1** shown in **Datasheet View**.

Datasheet View allows you to enter data into your table.

Figure 1.3.2 ▶

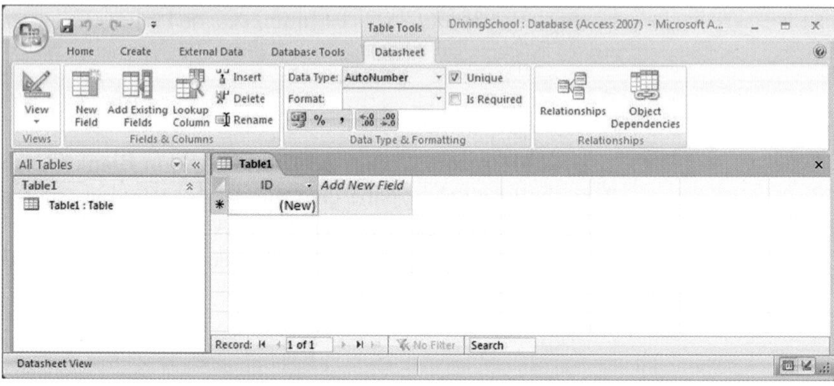

Note: Figure 1.3.2 is shown in Tabbed Documents mode. The screenshots in this book are generally displayed in Overlapping Windows mode as in Figure 1.3.4. For more on Overlapping Windows and Tabbed Documents see Unit 2.

3 Click the **View** button on the Ribbon. You will be prompted for a table name, call it **tblStudent.** You are now in **Design View**, as shown in Figure 1.3.3, and ready to set up the fields in our **Student** table. **Design View** allows you to add, delete and edit fields in your table.

Access automatically enters the first field as **ID** and sets the **Data Type** to **AutoNumber**. It also sets it as the **Primary Key** field shown by the key icon.

You will notice the **Field Properties** are displayed in the lower half of the window; we will enter these later in the unit.

Figure 1.3.3 ▼

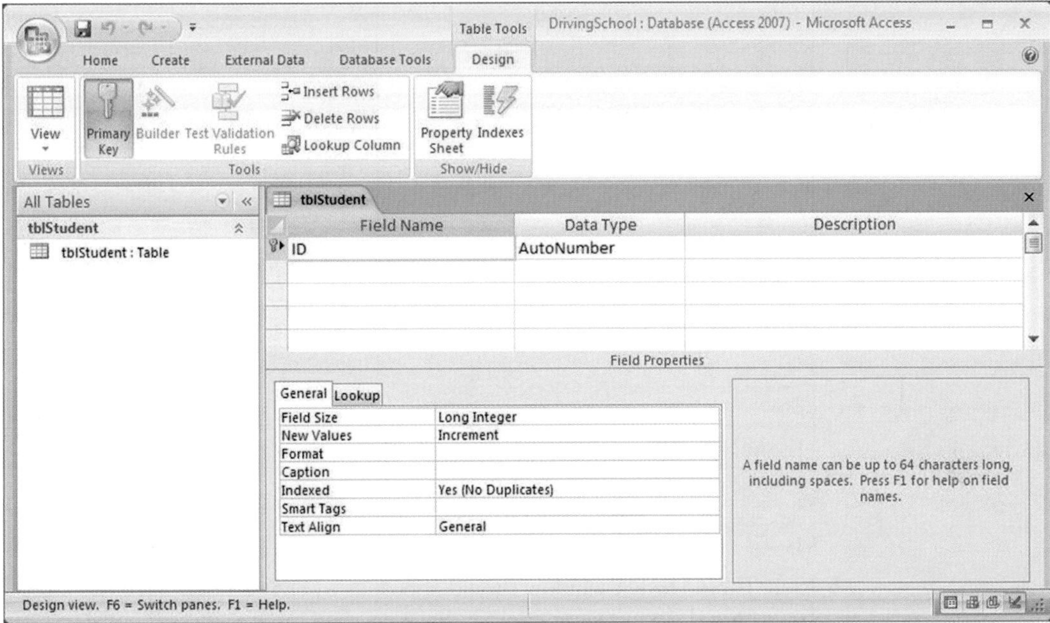

Defining the Field Names and Data Types

1 Edit the first **Field Name** to read **StudentID** and press **TAB** or **ENTER** to move to the **Data Type** column.

2 Click on the drop-down and view the choices, but ensure **AutoNumber** remains selected (see Figure 1.3.4).

Figure 1.3.4 ▶

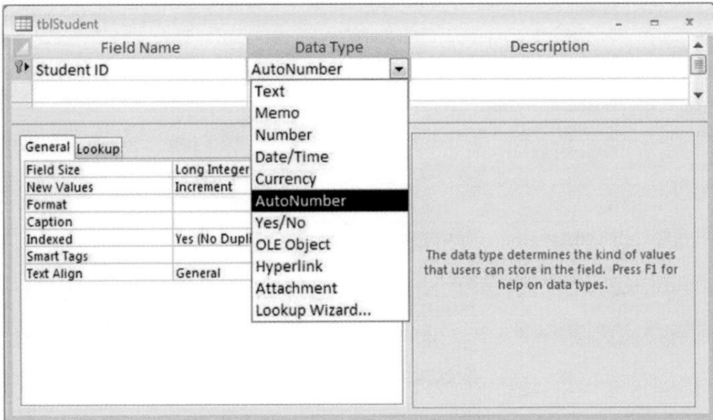

3 In the **Description** column, enter **Student's ID number**. This is optional and only for information.

4 Complete the Field Names and Data Types as shown below for the Student table.

Field Name	**Data Type**
StudentID	AutoNumber
Title	Text
Surname	Text
Forename	Text
Address1	Text
Address2	Text
Address3	Text
Address4	Text
TelNo	Text
DateOfBirth	Date/Time
Sex	Text
TheoryTestDate	Date/Time
PassedTheoryTest	Yes/No
PracticalTestDate	Date/Time
PassedPracticalTest	Yes/No

5 Your **Table Design** window should appear as in Figure 1.3.5. Save the table by closing the window or click on **Save** on the **Quick Access Toolbar.**

Figure 1.3.5 ▶

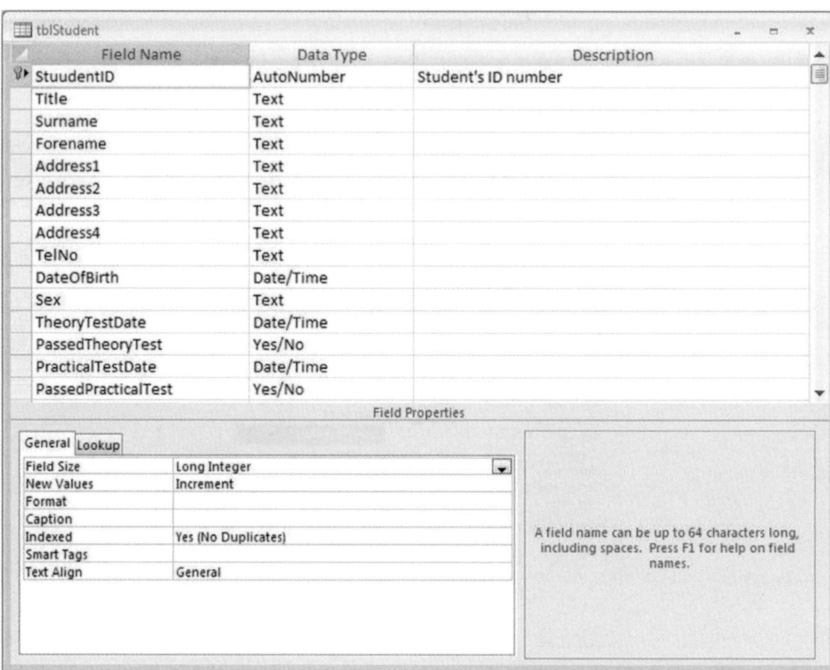

Note: When saving tables, some Access users like to start the name with **tbl**, e.g. **tblstudent**. They would start queries with **qry**, forms with **frm**, reports with **rpt** and macros with **mcr**. You may wish to consider using this naming convention.

Editing the Table Structure

During the course of setting up the table, it is probable you will make a mistake or decide to make a change to your table's structure. You have a number of editing options available.

Inserting a Field

1 Click on the row selector of the field below the insertion point.
2 Press the INSERT key on the keyboard or click the **Insert Rows** button on the Ribbon.

Deleting a Field

1 Click on the row selector of a field to delete it.
2 Press the DELETE key on the keyboard or click the **Delete Rows** button on the Ribbon.

Moving a Field

1 Click on the row selector of the field you wish to move.
2 Click again and drag it to its new position – a black line marks the insertion point.

Changing the Primary Key Field

You can only have one primary key. If you have set the wrong field as the primary key, remove it as follows:

1 Click on the row selector of the correct field.
2 Click the **Primary Key** button on the Ribbon.

Setting the Field Properties

When you click on a field in **Design View** its field properties are displayed in the lower half of the window. Field properties allow you to control the way information is stored and displayed.

We will go through each field in the Student table and set its field properties, including input masks where appropriate.

StudentID

1 In the Navigation Pane, double-click the **tblStudent** icon and click on the **View** button to open your table in **Design View**. Alternatively, right-click **tblStudent** and click on **Design View**.
2 The StudentID field should be the one selected. If not, click in the row selector for StudentID.
3 In the Field Properties set **Field Size** to **Long Integer** (it probably already is). See Figure 1.3.6.

Figure 1.3.6 ▶

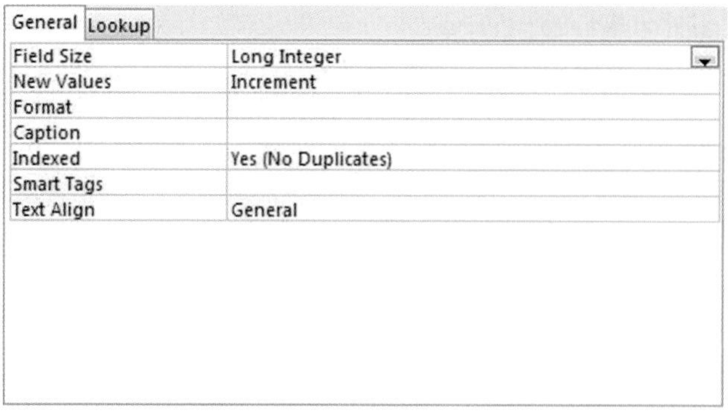

General	Lookup
Field Size	Long Integer
New Values	Increment
Format	
Caption	
Indexed	Yes (No Duplicates)
Smart Tags	
Text Align	General

Title

The Title field can only have the values Mr, Mrs, Miss and Ms. We can use the **Lookup Wizard** to restrict the data entered into a field to certain values.

1 Click on the **Title** field name and in the **Data Type** column, click on **Lookup Wizard**. See Figure 1.3.7.

Figure 1.3.7 ▶

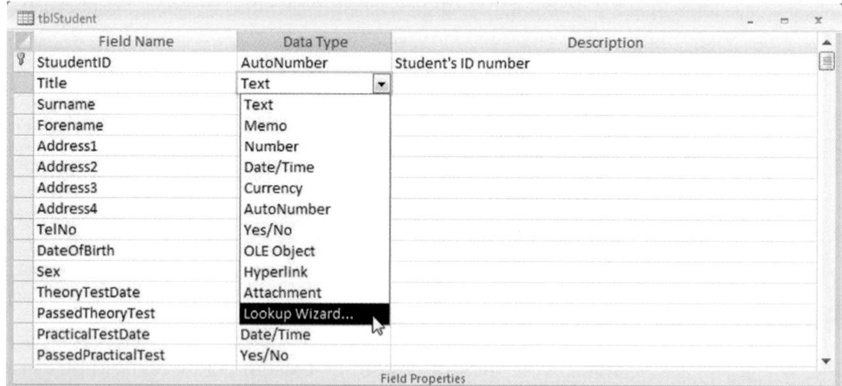

2 Click on **'I will type in the values that I want.'** and click on **Next**. See Figure 1.3.8.

Figure 1.3.8 ▶

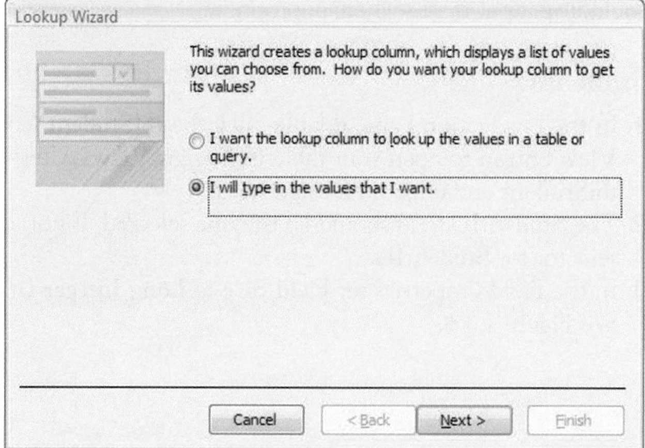

3 Enter **Mr**, **Mrs**, **Miss** and **Ms** into the column, press TAB to move to the next row. See Figure 1.3.9.

Figure 1.3.9 ▶

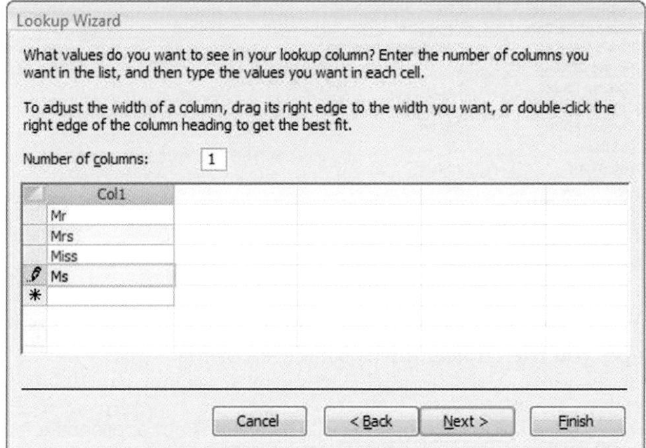

4 Click on **Next** and then click on **Finish**. See Figure 1.3.10.

Figure 1.3.10 ▶

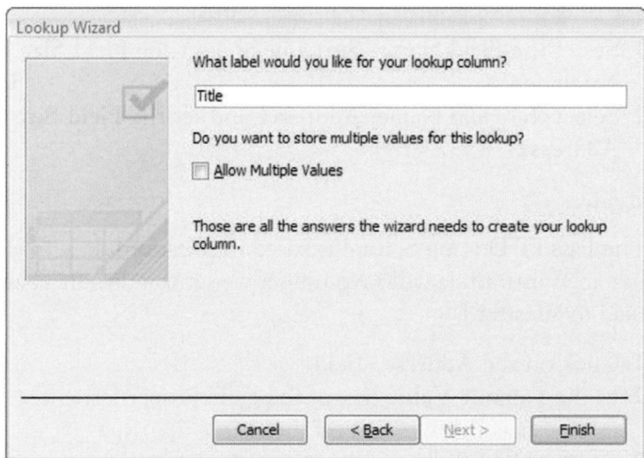

5 In the **Field Properties** set the **Field Size** to 6. See Figure 1.3.11.

Figure 1.3.11 ▶

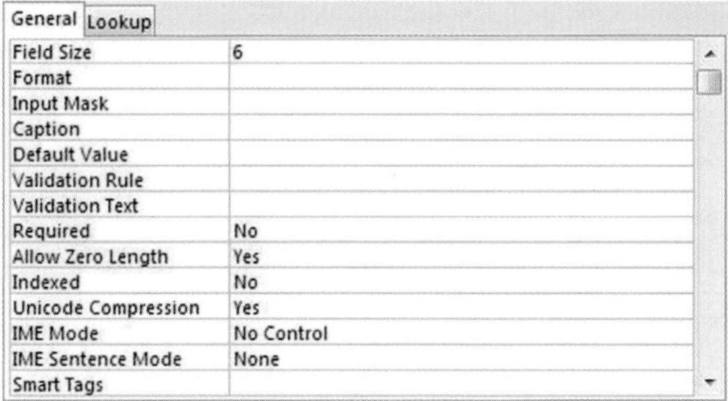

6 If you click on the **Lookup** tab you will see the screen shown in Figure 1.3.12.

Figure 1.3.12 ▶

General | Lookup

Display Control	Combo Box
Row Source Type	Value List
Row Source	"Mr";"Mrs";"Miss";"Ms"
Bound Column	1
Column Count	1
Column Heads	No
Column Widths	2.54cm
List Rows	16
List Width	2.54cm
Limit To List	No
Allow Multiple Values	No
Allow Value List Edits	No
List Items Edit Form	
Show Only Row Source V	No

When you wish to enter data into this field a combo box (drop-down box) will give you the choice of Mr, Mrs, Miss or Ms.

Note: Access allows you to store more than one value in a field. It is not appropriate here, but use Help to find out more.

Surname, Forename, Address1 and Address2

1 Select the Field Name: **Surname** and set the **Field Size** to 20. Repeat for **Forename**.
2 Select the Field Name: **Address1** and set the **Field Size** to 30. Repeat for **Address2**.

Address3

The Pass IT Driving School is based in Westford. It is likely that students will live in Westford. It will save time if we set the default value for the **Address3** field to Westford.

1 Click on the **Address3** field.
2 In the **Default Value** box of the Field Properties, enter **Westford**. Access inserts speech marks around the text.
3 Set the **Field Size** to 20. See Figure 1.3.13.

Figure 1.3.13 ▶

General | Lookup

Field Size	20
Format	
Input Mask	
Caption	
Default Value	"Westford"
Validation Rule	
Validation Text	
Required	No
Allow Zero Length	Yes
Indexed	No
Unicode Compression	Yes
IME Mode	No Control
IME Sentence Mode	None
Smart Tags	

Note: More information on Default Values can be found at the end of Unit 4.

Address4

The **Address4** field is the student's postcode.

1. Click on the **Address4** field name.
2. Set the **Field Size** to 10.
3. Click on the **Format** property box and enter **>** as shown in Figure 1.3.14.

This will convert any lower-case letters entered into upper case – for example, **we34 2qy** will become **WE34 2QY**.

Later you will see how to set an Input Mask to make entering postcodes easier.

Figure 1.3.14 ▶

General | Lookup

Field Size	10
Format	>
Input Mask	
Caption	
Default Value	
Validation Rule	
Validation Text	
Required	No
Allow Zero Length	Yes
Indexed	No
Unicode Compression	Yes
IME Mode	No Control
IME Sentence Mode	None
Smart Tags	

TelNo

Select the Field Name: **TelNo** and set the **Field Size** to 15.

Note: Telephone numbers cannot be a number field as they are likely to include a space, brackets or a preceding zero.

DateOfBirth

The student table uses three Date/Time fields. We will use the **Short Date** format for each – for example, 19/06/2007.

1. Select the **DateOfBirth** field.
2. Click in the **Format** box in the **Field Properties**.
3. Choose **Short Date** from the drop-down list. See Figure 1.3.15.

Figure 1.3.15 ▶

General | Lookup

Format	Short Date	
Input Mask	General Date	19/06/2007 17:34:23
Caption	Long Date	19 June 2007
Default Value	Medium Date	19-Jun-07
Validation Rule	Short Date	19/06/2007
Validation Text	Long Time	17:34:23
Required	Medium Time	05:34 PM
Indexed	Short Time	17:34
IME Mode	No Control	
IME Sentence Mode	None	
Smart Tags		
Text Align	General	
Show Date Picker	For dates	

It is also possible to use the Input Mask Wizard to set a placeholder *--/--/----* for each date entered.

4 Click in the **Input Mask** property box and click the three dots icon at the end of the row. Alternatively click the **Builder** button, in the **Tools** group on the Ribbon. You will be asked to save your table first. The Input Mask Wizard window is shown as in Figure 1.3.16.

Figure 1.3.16 ▶

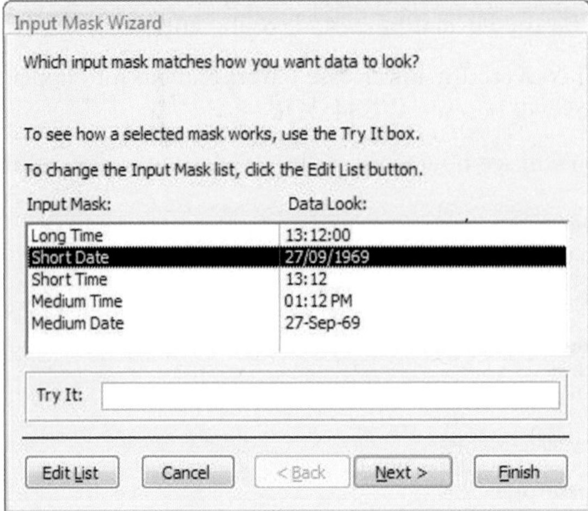

5 Select the **Short Date** option and click on **Next**.

Figure 1.3.17 ▶

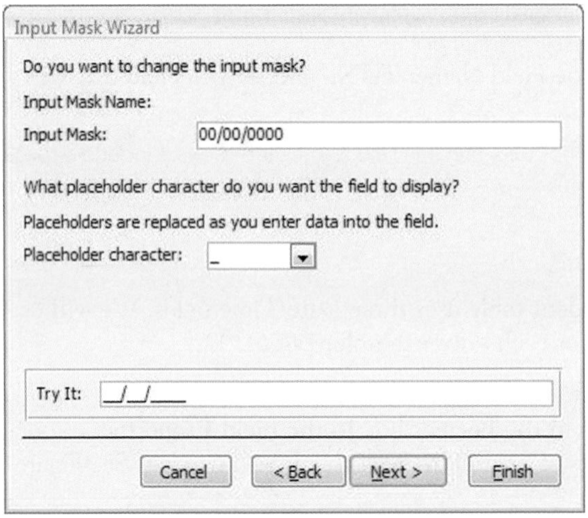

Input Mask Wizard

Do you want to change the input mask?

Input Mask Name:

Input Mask: 00/00/0000

What placeholder character do you want the field to display?

Placeholders are replaced as you enter data into the field.

Placeholder character: _

Try It: __/__/____

Cancel | < Back | Next > | Finish

6 A choice of placeholders is offered. You can click in the **Try It** box to see what it looks like. Click on **Next** and then click on **Finish** (see Figure 1.3.17).

The field properties are set as shown in Figure 1.3.18.

Figure 1.3.18 ▶

General	Lookup
Format	Short Date
Input Mask	00/00/0000;0;_
Caption	
Default Value	
Validation Rule	
Validation Text	
Required	No
Indexed	No
IME Mode	No Control
IME Sentence Mode	None
Smart Tags	
Text Align	General
Show Date Picker	For dates

7 Repeat this for the other two Date/Time fields, **TheoryTestDate** and **PracticalTestDate**.

Note: More information on Input Masks can be found at the end of Unit 4.

Sex

The Sex field can only have the values M and F. We can use the Validation Rule box in the Field Properties only to allow M or F.

1 Select the Field Name: **Sex**.
2 In the **Validation Rule** box enter **M or F**.
3 In the **Validation Text** box enter **Sex must be either M or F**.

This is the error message that will appear if the user tries to enter anything other than M or F into this field. The field properties will appear as shown in Figure 1.3.19.

Figure 1.3.19 ▶

General	Lookup
Field Size	1
Format	
Input Mask	
Caption	
Default Value	
Validation Rule	"M" Or "F"
Validation Text	Sex must be either M or F
Required	No
Allow Zero Length	Yes
Indexed	No
Unicode Compression	Yes
IME Mode	No Control
IME Sentence Mode	None
Smart Tags	

4 Save your table as **tblStudent**.

It is of course equally possible to have used the Lookup Wizard for this field property and limited the choices to M or F.

Note: More information on Validation Rules can be found at the end of Unit 4.

PassedTheoryTest and PassedPracticalTest fields.

The above fields have already been set to **Yes/No** Field types and no further field properties are required.

Unit 4: Entering the Data

In this unit we are going to enter the data into the table tblStudent and set up the remaining tables needed to complete the system.

There are two modes for working with tables. So far we have worked in **Design View**.

Design View is used to set up new tables, to edit the structure and to define validation checks and input masks.

To enter data you have to switch to **Datasheet View**.

In the **Navigation Pane**, double-click **tblStudent** to open the table in **Datasheet View** as shown in Figure 1.4.1.

Figure 1.4.1 ▶

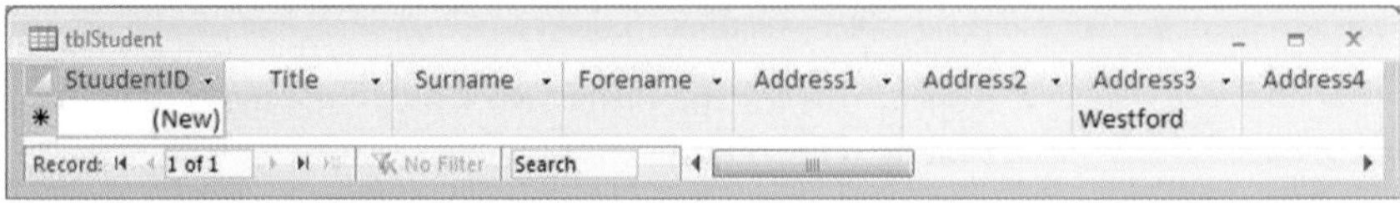

You can switch between modes by clicking the **View** button on the Ribbon.

Entering Data into the Student Table

Enter details of the first student, Robert Brammer, as given below. Use TAB or ENTER to move between fields.

StudentID	Title	Surname	Forename	Address1	Address2	Address3	Address4	TelNo
1	Mr	Brammer	Robert	10 Plymouth Drive	Crickham	Westford	WE28 9LO	01993 885304

DateOfBirth	Sex	TheoryTestDate	PassedTheoryTest	PracticalTestDate	PassedPracticalTest
12/05/1992	M	17/07/2009	Yes	17/08/2009	Yes

You will notice a number of features as you enter the data.

- The StudentID which is an AutoNumber field is entered automatically.
- The Title field has a drop-down box set up by the lookup table wizard (see Figure 1.4.2).

Figure 1.4.2 ▶

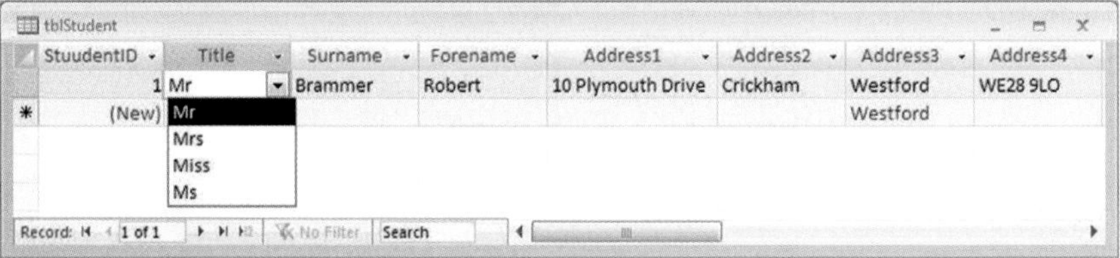

- Data entered into the Sex field is validated and any invalid entries rejected (see Figure 1.4.3).

Figure 1.4.3 ▶

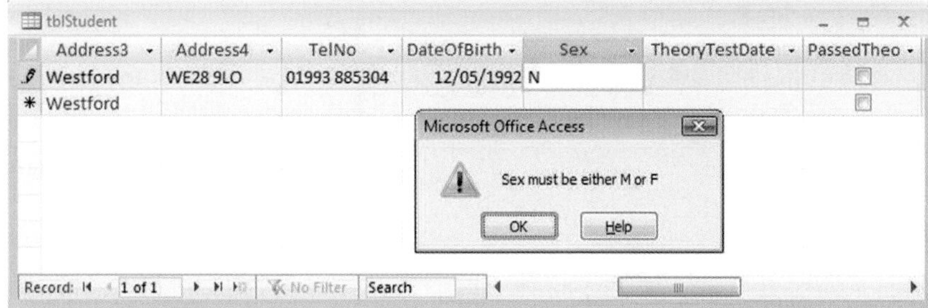

- Placeholders appear in the fields where you have set input masks, to make data entry easier.
- Enter data into Yes/No fields by ticking the check box for Yes and leaving unchecked for No (see Figure 1.4.4).

Figure 1.4.4 ▼

tblStudent

StudentID	Title	Surname	TheoryTestDate	PassedTheoryTest	PracticalTestDate	PassedPracticalTest
1	Mr	Brammer	17/07/2009	☑	17/08/2009	☑
2	Mr	Jenkins	17/07/2009	☑	14/08/2009	☐
3	Miss	Fowler	10/07/2009	☑	13/08/2009	☐

Record: 1 of 3 No Filter Search

- When you have entered the last field in a record, a blank record appears underneath to enter the next record. Don't worry if your table finishes with a blank record. Microsoft Access will ignore it.
- When a new record is created, the Address3 field is set to Westford. This can still be edited.
- Data is saved as soon as it is entered.
- Adjust the column widths by dragging out the column dividers.
- Navigation buttons appear at the bottom of the screen, allowing you to scroll through the records (see Figure 1.4.5).

Figure 1.4.5 ▶

Complete the table **tblStudent** by entering the following data.

StudentID	Title	Surname	Forename	Address1	Address2	Address3	Address4	TelNo
2	Mr	Jenkins	Steven	37 Woodfield Close	Pilton	Westford	WE49 5PQ	01993 539264
3	Miss	Fowler	Sarah	19 Sea View Road	Theale	Westford	WE34 8NT	01993 293751

DateOfBirth	Sex	TheoryTestDate	PassedTheoryTest	PracticalTestDate	PassedPracticalTest
14/05/1992	M	17/07/2009	Yes	14/08/2009	No
05/06/1991	F	10/07/2009	Yes	13/08/2009	No

When you have finished entering the data, close the table by clicking on the **Close** icon (see Figure 1.4.6). You will return to the **Navigation Pane**, with the name of the table highlighted.

Figure 1.4.6 ▶

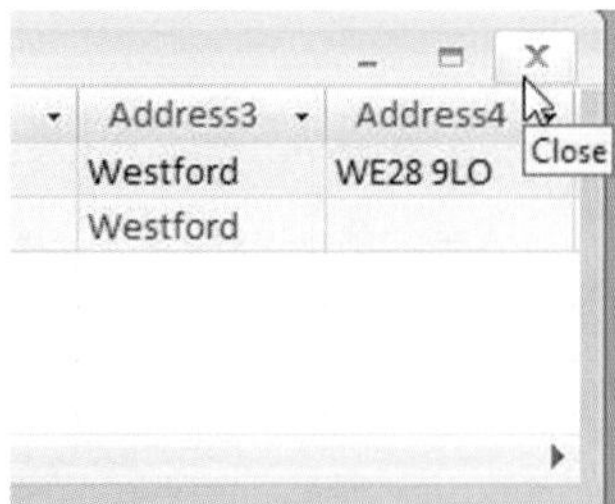

Useful keys for entering data

Key	Action
TAB, ENTER or right arrow	Move to next field
SHIFT + TAB or left arrow	Move to previous field
Down arrow	Move to next record
Up arrow	Move to previous record
HOME	Move to start of field
END	Move to end of field
ESCAPE	Quits editing a record
DELETE	Click on record selector to delete a record

Setting up the Instructor Table

You now need to set up a second table called **tblInstructor** to store the details of the instructors.

On the **Create** tab, in the **Tables** group, click the **Table Design** button. See Figure 1.4.7.

Figure 1.4.7 ▼

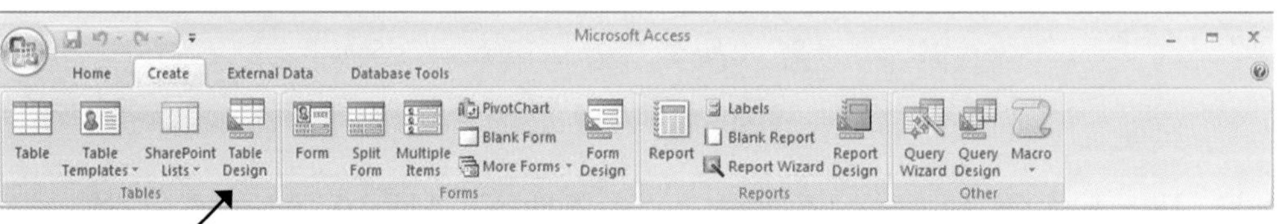

Set up **tblInstructor** with the following structure:

Field name	Data type	Other information
InstructorID	AutoNumber	Set as Primary Key field (click Primary Key button)
Title	Text	Lookup table values: Mr, Mrs, Ms, Miss Field Size 6
Surname	Text	Field Size 20
Forename	Text	Field Size 20
Address1	Text	Field Size 30
Address2	Text	Field Size 30
Address3	Text	Default value = "Westford" Field Size 20
Address4	Text	Field Size 10 and set Format to >
HomeTelNo	Text	Field Size 15
MobileNo	Text	Field Size 15

Your finished table will appear as in Figure 1.4.8

Figure 1.4.8 ▶

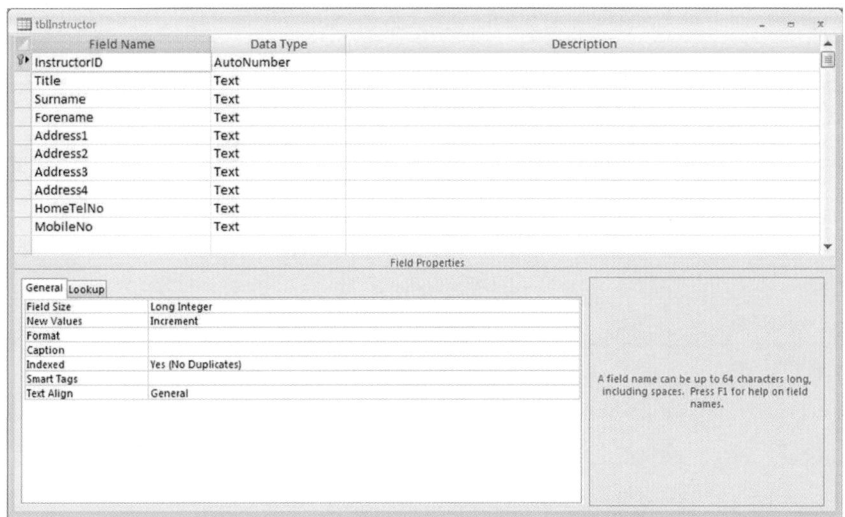

Save the table as **tblInstructor** and switch to **Datasheet View** mode to enter this data.

InstructorID	Title	Surname	Forename	Address1	Address2	Address3	Address4	HomeTelNo	MobileNo
1	Mr	Jones	Derek	45 Grange Road	Pilton	Westford	WE49 5FG	01993 212541	07720 521478
2	Mr	Batchelor	Andrew	13 Abbey Close	Pilton	Westford	WE49 5FH	01993 255247	07980 352145
3	Mr	Smith	Tony	5 Sunhill Road	Blakeway	Westford	WE44 4ED	01993 252452	07980 525214

Setting up the Lesson Type Table

The third table will be the table **tblLessonType**, storing details of the lessons and the cost of each lesson. This is the structure.

Field name	Data type	Other information
LessonType	Text	Set as Primary Key field Field Size 25
Cost	Currency	

Save the table as **tblLessonType** and enter this data.

Lesson Type	Cost
Introductory	£16.00
Pass Plus	£17.00
Standard	£24.00
Test	£22.00

Setting up the Lesson Table

The fourth table will be the **Lesson** table. This is the table that links all the other tables together and stores details of lessons booked with the Driving School. Set up the table with the following structure.

Field name	Data type	Other information
LessonNo	AutoNumber	Set as Primary Key field
StudentID	Number	Long Integer
InstructorID	Number	Long Integer
DateOfLesson	Date/Time	Format: Short Date. **Do not set** an Input Mask. Use the Auto Calendar feature below.
StartTime	Date/Time	Format: Short Time and set an Input Mask
LengthOfLesson	Number	Integer and set validation rule as: Between 1 and 8. Text - Please enter a number between 1 and 8. Set the Default Value = 1
CollectionPoint	Text	Default value = "Home Address" Field Size 30
DropOffPoint	Text	Default value = "Home Address"Field Size 30
LessonType	Text	Lookup Wizard table values (see below): Introductory, Standard, Pass Plus, Test Field Size 25 Note: You could also look up the values from the table Lesson Type.

Note: We do not need to store the name of the student or the name of the instructor in the Lesson table. These are already stored elsewhere.

Auto Calendar

Access 2007 comes with an Auto Calendar feature which pops up when you click in a Date/Time field and allows you to enter dates easily.

We are going to use this feature to enter the DateOfLesson. In the Field Properties for the field **DateOfLesson** set **Show Date Picker** to **For dates**. See Figure 1.4.9.

Figure 1.4.9 ▶

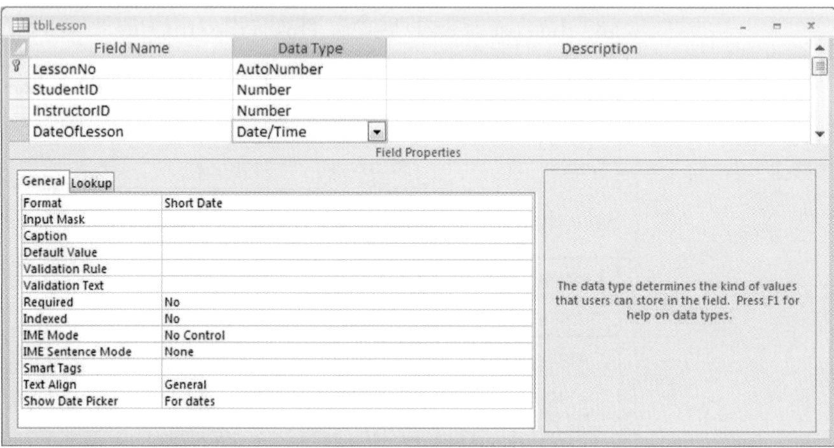

Save the table as **tblLesson** and enter this data.

LessonNo	StudentID	InstructorID	DateOfLesson	StartTime	LengthOfLesson	CollectionPoint	DropOffPoint	LessonType
1	1	1	27/07/2009	09:00	1	Home Address	Home Address	Standard
2	2	1	27/07/2009	11:00	2	Home Address	Home Address	Standard
3	3	1	27/07/2009	14:00	1	Home Address	Home Address	Standard

To enter the date in the **DateOfLesson** field, click the **Date Picker** to pop up the calendar shown in Figure 1.4.10. Select the date required.

Figure 1.4.10 ▶

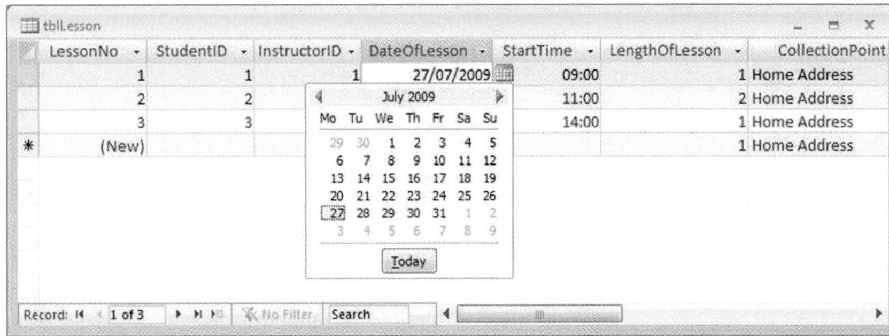

You should now have successfully set up the four tables in your system as shown in Figure 1.4.11 in Tabbed Documents mode. The next unit shows you how to link these tables together.

Figure 1.4.11 ▶

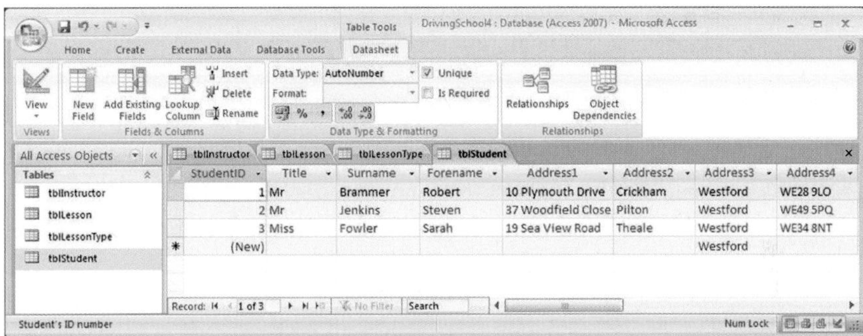

Note: You can move straight to Unit 5 and return if you need further information about setting up tables.

Further Information on Setting up Tables

This section provides a little more detail on a number of the functions you met during setting up the Student table. In particular:

- Data Types
- Field Properties
- Input Masks
- Format field properties
- Default field properties
- Validation Rules.

Data Types

Access has different data types available to store different kinds of data. They are as follows:

Data Type	Meaning
Text	The default setting. Used for shorter text entries. Can be a combination of text, numbers, spaces and symbols. Maximum length 255 characters but can be set to less using the Field Size property.
Memo	Used for longer text entries.
Number	Used to store numeric data.
Date/Time	Stores a date or a time or a date and the time. Several formats for a date/time field.
Currency	Monetary values. Normally in the UK this will be set to pounds and work to 2 decimal places.
AutoNumber	An AutoNumber field numbers records automatically as you enter more data. The field acts as a counter. Duplicates are avoided and so AutoNumber fields are ideal as the primary key field. An AutoNumber cannot be edited and when an AutoNumber record is deleted Access does not allow you to go back and reuse this number.
Yes/No	Only allows logical values such as Yes/No, True/False
OLE Object	An object linked to or embedded in a Microsoft Access table. This might be an image or a sound or a file created in another package such as Microsoft Excel or Microsoft Word.
Hyperlink	A hyperlink address. This can be linked to: ■ an object in your Access file – e.g. another table ■ another locally stored file ■ a web page ■ an e-mail address.
Lookup Wizard	Used to create a lookup table so that you can choose a value from a drop-down box.
Attachment	Used to store files such as images, documents, charts, spreadsheets.

Field Properties

The following table describes the more commonly used field properties:

Property	Description
Field Size	Used to fix the maximum length of a text field. Default value is 50 characters. Maximum length is 255.
Format	Fixes how data can be displayed – e.g. dates can be displayed in many different formats such as 13/01/01 or 13 Jan 01 or 13 January 2001
Input Mask	Sets a pattern for data to be entered into this field.
Caption	The field label in a form or report. You are not likely to need to use this property.
Default Value	The value entered into the field when the record is created. Usually left blank but can be very powerful.
Validation Rule	Defines the data entry rules.
Validation Text	The error message if data is invalid.
Required	Indicates whether an entry must be made or not. If an entry is required, it is best not to set this property until the database is fully working.
Indexed	Allows data to be stored in the order of this field which speeds up searches.
Allow Zero Length	Used with text fields to decide whether records in that field are allowed to contain zero length or empty text strings.

Property	Description
Text Align	You can specify the default alignment of data in fields.
Append Only	Allows you to add data to memo fields.
Text Format	Allows formatting of data in memo fields.
Date Picker	Specifies whether you want Access to display a calendar in a Date/Time field.

Setting Input Masks

Input masks make data entry easier. They display on screen a pattern for the data to be entered into a field.

For example, you may be given the prompt *--/--/--* to enter the date.

They are suitable for data that always has the same pattern, such as dates, times, currency and also for codes like National Insurance numbers, stock numbers or postcodes.

Characters for input masks you are likely to use are as follows:

0 A number (0–9) must be entered.
9 A number (0–9) may be entered.
A number, + or – sign or space may be entered.
L A letter A–Z must be entered.
? A letter A–Z may be entered.
A A letter or digit must be entered.
a A letter or digit may be entered.
C Any character or space may be entered.
& Any character or space must be entered.
< All characters to the right are changed to lower case.
> All characters to the right are changed to upper case.

Examples of Input Masks

A **National Insurance number** in the UK must be of the form **AB123456C**. All letters are in capitals. The input mask would be **>LL000000L**. (It must be two letters followed by six numbers and one letter.)

A **Postcode** consists of one or two letters, then one or two numbers, then a space, a number and two letters. All the letters must be capital letters. Examples are **B1 1BB** or **DE13 0LL**. The input mask would be **>L?09 0LL**.

Car registration numbers such as W125 HGS could have **>L000 LLL** as an input mask.

A **Driving Licence No** of the form BESWO150282 MB9BM could have **>LLLLL#000000#LL0LL** as an input mask.

A **Product Code** of the format A2C-123-4567 might have an input mask of **AAA-000-0000**.

Input masks are very powerful and need a lot of thought. It is possible to use the Input Mask Wizard to set up an input mask for a field. At this stage you may wish to ignore input masks unless you know the exact format of the input data.

The Format Field Property

The formats supplied with Access will suit practically all your needs. However, it is possible to set a custom format of your own. Two commonly used examples follow:

> will change text entered in the field to upper case
< will change text entered in the field to lower case

Note: There is a significant difference between the Format and Input Mask field property. The Format property affects the data in the field **after** it is entered. For example, if you enter 14/07/99 into a Long Date format field, it will appear as 14th July 1999. The Input Mask property controls and restricts data entry. An Input Mask set to --/--/-- will only accept dates in the format 14/07/99.

The Default Field Property

Default values are added automatically when you add a new record. For example, in a table of names and addresses you might set the County field to Derbyshire. Derbyshire then appears automatically each time a new record is added and the user can either leave it or change it to something else.

You can also use expressions in this field property. Typically **=Date()** will return the current date from your PC.

In a library book loaning system, the default value for the **Date of Loan** field could be set to **=Date()** and similarly for the **Date of Return**, the default value could be set to **=Date()+14** (assuming a 14 day loan period).

Setting Validation Rules

Validation rules allow you to control the values that can be entered into a field.

By setting the validation text property, you can choose the message that is displayed if the validation rule is broken. You set up a validation rule by typing an expression into the field properties (see Figure 1.4.12).

Figure 1.4.12 ▶

General | Lookup

Field Size	Long Integer
Format	
Decimal Places	Auto
Input Mask	
Caption	
Default Value	1
Validation Rule	Between 1 And 8
Validation Text	Please enter a number between 1 and 8
Required	No
Indexed	No
Smart Tags	
Text Align	General

In the example in Figure 1.4.12 the user will be forced to only enter numbers between (and including) 1 and 8.

If they do not, the Validation Text message is displayed, as shown in Figure 1.4.13.

Figure 1.4.13 ▶

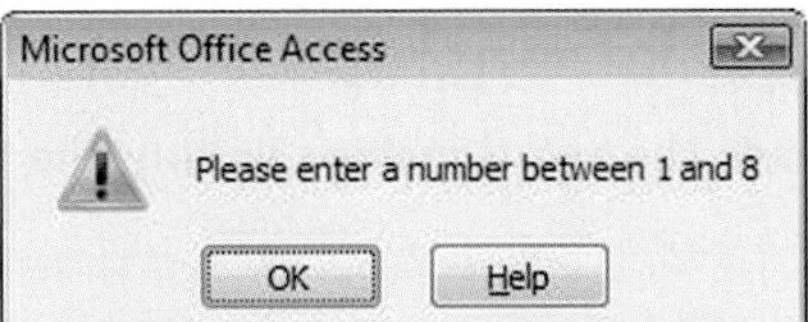

A number of comparison operators are available in Access:

Operator	Meaning
<	Less than
<=	Less than or equal to
>	Greater than
>=	Greater than or equal to
=	Equal to
<>	Not equal to
IN	Test for 'equal to' any item in a list
BETWEEN	Test for a range of values; the two values separated by the AND operator
LIKE	Tests a Text or Memo field to match a pattern string of characters

Examples of Validation Rule settings	Possible Validation Text
>8000	Please enter a salary greater than £8000
<#01/01/01#	You must enter dates before January 1st 2001
>Date()	The date returned must be after today's date!
"S" or "M" or "L"	Sizes can only be S, M or L
Between 0 and 36	Goals scored cannot be greater than 36!
Like "A???? "	Code must be 5 characters beginning with A
<20	Age of student must be less than 20
IN("A","B","C")	Grades must be A, B or C

Unit 5: Defining the Relationships

In this section we will define and create the relationships linking the four tables.

The links that need setting up are shown in Figure 1.5.1.

Figure 1.5.1 ▶

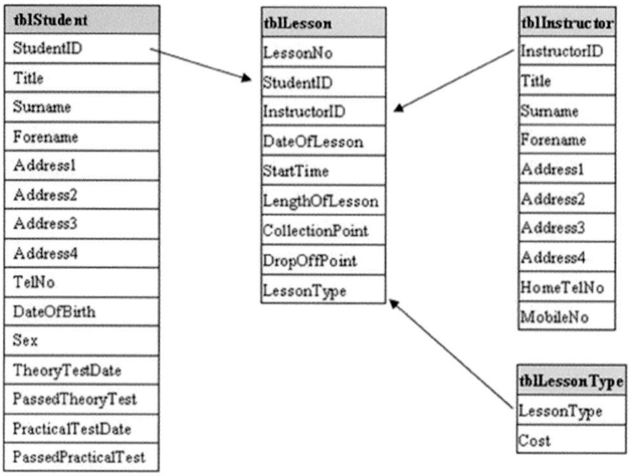

tblStudent
StudentID
Title
Surname
Forename
Address1
Address2
Address3
Address4
TelNo
DateOfBirth
Sex
TheoryTestDate
PassedTheoryTest
PracticalTestDate
PassedPracticalTest
tblLesson
LessonNo
StudentID
InstructorID
DateOfLesson
StartTime
LengthOfLesson
CollectionPoint
DropOffPoint
LessonType
tblInstructor
InstructorID
Title
Surname
Forename
Address1
Address2
Address3
Address4
HomeTelNo
MobileNo
tblLessonType
LessonType
Cost

Adding the Tables

1 On the **Database Tools** tab, click the **Relationships** button. This will open the **Relationships** window (see Figure 1.5.2).

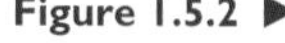

Figure 1.5.2 ▶

Microsoft Access
Relationship Tools
Home
Create
External Data
Database Tools
Design
Clear Layout
Relationship Report
Edit Relationships
Tools
Hide Table
Direct Relationships
All Relationships
Show Table
Close
Relationships
All Access Objects
Tables
tblInstructor
tblLesson
tblLessonType
tblStudent
Relationships
Ready
Num Lock

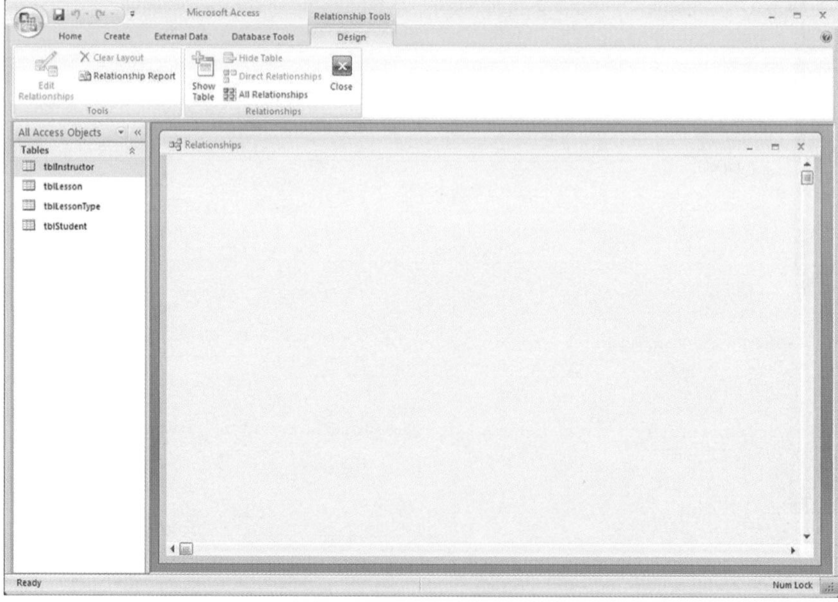

2 Click on the **Show Table** button, in the **Relationships** group. This will open the **Show Table** dialog box (see Figure 1.5.3).

Figure 1.5.3 ▶

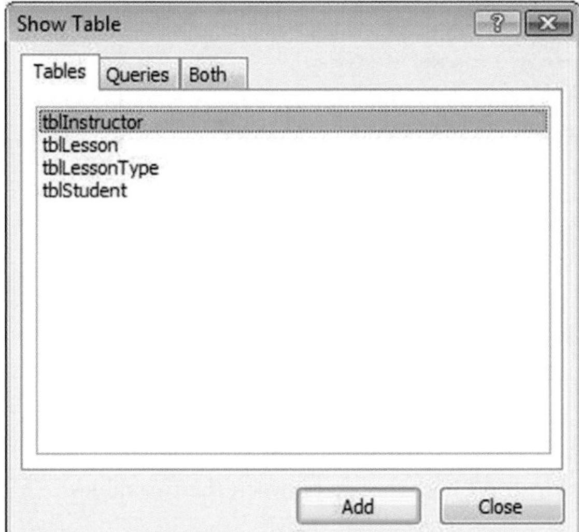

3 Click on **tblInstructor** and click **Add**.
4 Add the other three tables and then **Close** the **Show Table** dialog box.
5 In the **Relationships** window, rearrange the position of the tables by dragging and resizing the table windows (see Figure 1.5.4).

Figure 1.5.4 ▼

Setting the Links

1 Click on **InstructorID** in **tblInstructor**.
2 Drag it on top of **InstructorID** in **tblLesson** and let go. The **Edit Relationships** dialog box appears (see Figure 1.5.5).

Figure 1.5.5 ▶

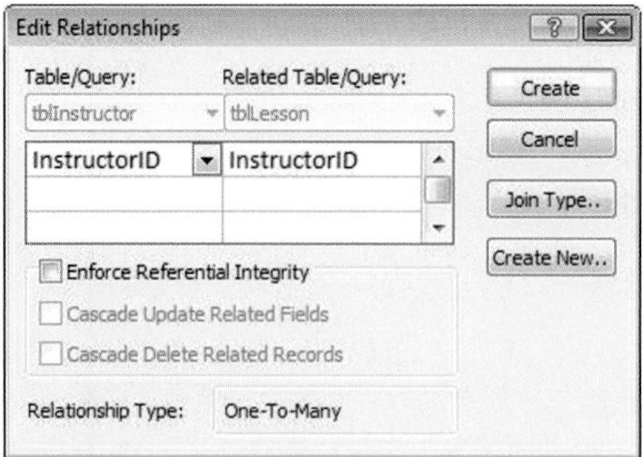

3 Check the **Enforce Referential Integrity** box but DO NOT check the **Cascade Delete Related Records** box. Click on **Create**. A link called the **Relationship Line** is set up between the two tables.

Note: If you had checked **Cascade Delete Related Records** and you chose to delete an instructor from **tblInstructor** then all the lessons for that instructor would be deleted from the **Lesson** table. We will revisit this in later units and explain why this might not be an option just yet in the development of this solution.

4 Click on the **StudentID** field in **tblStudent** and drag it on top of the **StudentID** field in **tblLesson**.
5 Check the **Enforce Referential Integrity** box and click on **Create**.
6 Repeat the process for the **LessonType** field, dragging it from **tblLessonType** to **tblLesson** and check **Enforce Referential Integrity**.

The Relationships window should now look like Figure 1.5.6.

Figure 1.5.6 ▶

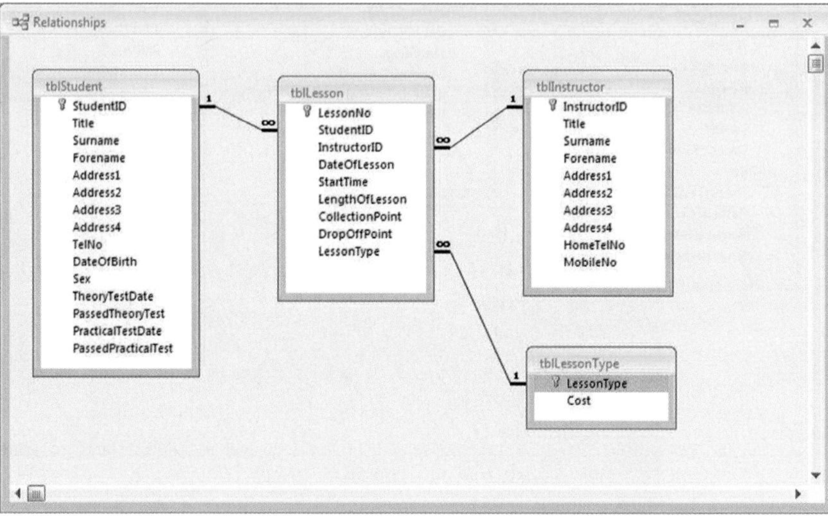

The number 1 and the infinity symbol mean that all three relationships are one-to-many. A **StudentID** can appear only **one** time in **tblStudent** as it is a unique ID. However, a **StudentID** can appear **many** times in **tblLesson**, as the student will need many lessons.

Similarly, the **InstructorID** can only appear once in **tblInstructor** but many times in **tblLesson**. The **LessonType** can appear only once in **tblLessonType** but many times in **tblLesson**.

7 Save your layout by closing the **Relationships** window and confirming, as shown in Figure 1.5.7.

Figure 1.5.7 ▶

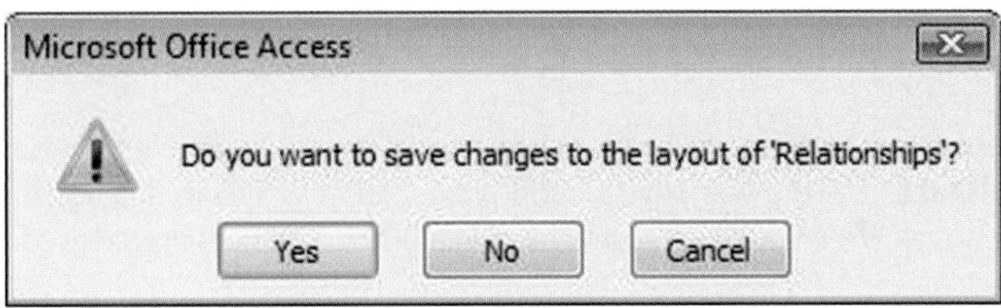

Note: As a rule, the field you use to create a relationship must be of the same type. However, when you create a relationship between tables using an AutoNumber field, the related field must be Numeric and set to Long Integer.

Referential Integrity

Referential integrity is a system of rules that Microsoft Access uses to ensure that relationships between records in related tables are valid and that you don't accidentally delete or change related data.

For example, with Referential Integrity set, you would not be able to book a lesson for a Student ID 46 as no student with ID number 46 appears in the Student table. Similarly, you could not book a lesson for an instructor who was not present in the Instructor table.

Cascading Updates and Deletes

Cascading Updates and Deletes affect what Access does with the data when you update or delete a record in a table that is related to other records in other tables.

If cascade delete is set, then when you delete a record in the Primary table, all related data in other tables is deleted. For example, if a student is deleted from the Student table, then all related records for that student in the Lesson table would also be deleted.

Deleting Relationships

If you wish to delete a relationship:

1 Open the Relationship window as before.
2 Click on the Relationship Line of the relationship you wish to delete and press the DELETE key. Alternatively, you can right-click on it and choose **Delete**.

If you wish to delete a field that contains a relationship, you will have to delete the relationship first.

Editing Relationships

You can edit relationships by going to the Relationships window and double-clicking on the Relationship Line of the relationship you wish to edit.

Tricks and Tips numbers 1 and 5 may help you with some of the problems found when setting up tables and relationships. **Tricks and Tips** numbers 8 and 9 show you how to import data from an Excel file.

Note: The support website www.dynamic-learning-student.co.uk has a downloadable file named **DrivingSchoolData**. It is the working solution produced at Unit 5 in this book. It contains records of over 100 lessons over the period of a fortnight in July 2009. Students are advised to use this file to start Unit 6.

Unit 6: Select queries

In the previous units you set up tables to store information about the students, instructors and lesson bookings in the Pass IT Driving school.

In this unit, and the next two, you will use queries to search and sort the data in your tables according to certain criteria. Queries provide an easy way of asking questions of your database and producing useful information.

For example we might want to:
- find details of lessons booked on a given date
- find contact details for a student whose lesson needs to be cancelled
- view details of instructors' names and addresses.

There are a number of different types of query available in Access:
- Select Query
- Parameter Query
- Multi-Table Query
- Action Query
- Crosstab Query.

We will start by taking you through basic select and parameter queries, progressing to a query involving more than one table. You will meet the other query types as you work through the next two units.

As with many other parts of Microsoft Access, there is a wizard to help you design simple queries. We shall first look at setting up a query without the wizard.

Note: To start Unit 6 students are reminded to use the file named **DrivingSchoolData** downloadable from the internet. It is the working solution produced at Unit 5 with 105 records added.

Query 1 Finding details of lessons booked on a given day

There are usually five steps involved in planning a query:

- choosing which tables to use
- choosing the fields needed in the query
- setting the criteria to produce the output required
- running the query
- saving and/or printing the results.

1 Load the **DrivingSchool** database.

2 On the **Create** tab, in the **Other** group, click the **Query Design** button (see Figure 1.6.1).

Figure 1.6.1 ▶

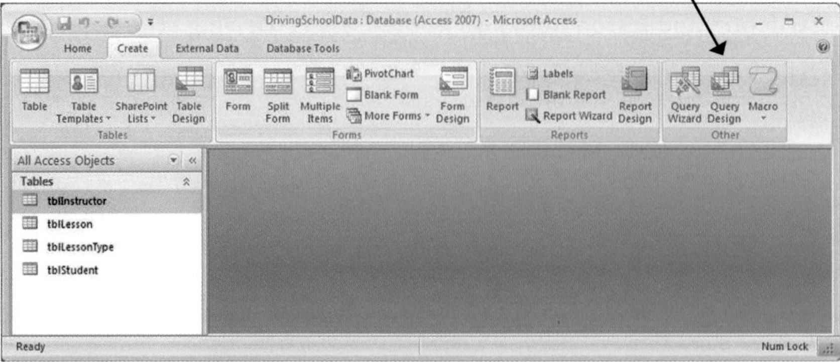

3 In the **Show Table** dialog box, select **tblLesson**, click on **Add** and then **Close** the window (see Figure 1.6.2).

Figure 1.6.2 ▶

The **Query Design View** window is shown in Figure 1.6.3 below the **Query Design** tab.

The window is in two sections. The upper section contains the field list for the tables used in the query, in this case **tblLesson**.

The lower section contains the QBE (Query by Example) grid, where you design the query. Primarily it consists of five blank rows (see Figure 1.6.3).

Figure 1.6.3 ▶

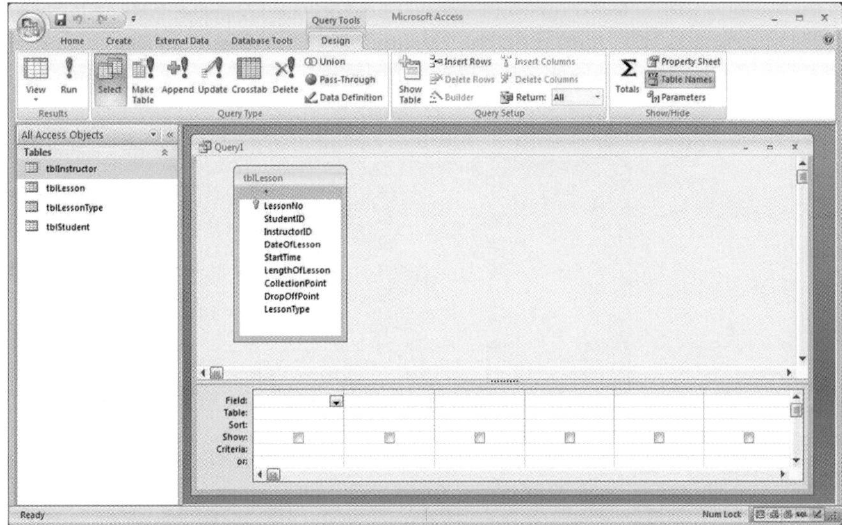

Field	Contains the names of the fields needed for your query.
Table	Holds the name of the table containing the selected field.
Sort	Offers ascending, descending sort options.
Show	Allows you to hide fields from the output.
Criteria	This is where you enter the criteria for your search.

You can maximise the window and use the scroll bars in the usual way. You can resize the upper/lower panes by dragging the dividing line between them up or down.

The next stage is to select the fields needed in our query.

4 Double-click on **LessonNo** in the table **tblLesson** field list. Then double-click on each of the next five fields in turn: **StudentID**, **InstructorID**, **DateOfLesson, StartTime, LengthOfLesson**. The field names will appear in the grid as shown in Figure 1.6.4.
5 Now select the criteria by entering **31/07/09** in the criteria row of the fourth (DateOfLesson) column of the QBE grid. Access surrounds the data with a #.

Figure 1.6.4 ▶

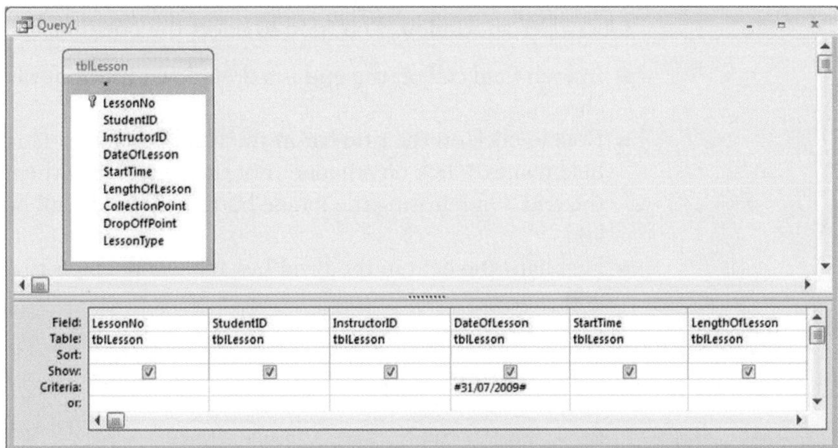

If you have added a field by mistake, click at the top of the column in the QBE grid to select the column and then press DELETE.

6 To run your query, click on the **Datasheet View** button or click the **Run** button on the **Design** tab, in the **Results** group. There should be seven lessons (see Figure 1.6.5).

Figure 1.6.5 ▶

Query1

LessonNo	StudentID	InstructorID	DateOfLesson	StartTime	LengthOfLesson
17	8	1	31/07/2009	09:00	1
18	14	1	31/07/2009	11:00	2
19	11	1	31/07/2009	15:00	1
56	28	2	31/07/2009	10:00	1
57	19	2	31/07/2009	12:00	1
58	27	2	31/07/2009	14:00	1
59	29	2	31/07/2009	16:00	1

Record: 1 of 7 No Filter Search

Hint Double-click the column header dividing line to make the column width fit the contents.

7 Once the query has been run, it can be printed by clicking on the **Office Button** and clicking **Print**.

8 Save the query by clicking the **Save** button on the **Quick Access Toolbar** or by closing the query window. In the **Save As** dialog box, type **qryLessonsOnDate** as in Figure 1.6.6.

Figure 1.6.6 ▶

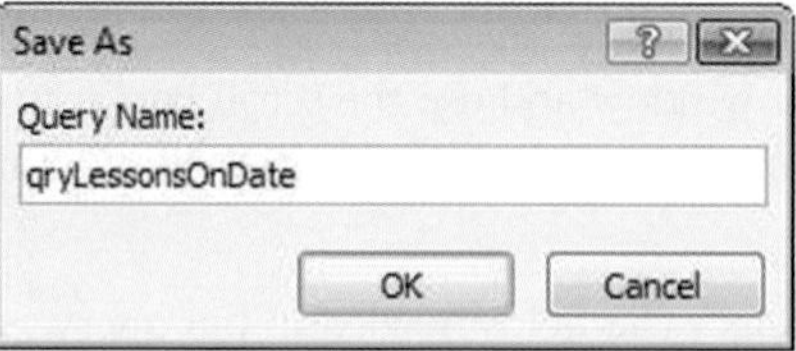

Note: If your query is not listed in the Navigation Pane objects, click the drop-down on the header and click **All Access Objects**.

Selecting fields in Query Design View

There are a number of other ways of selecting a field from the Field list in the Query Design window. You need to select the one that suits you best.

- In each field cell on the grid is a drop-down list from which fields can be chosen.
- Double-click on the title bar in the Field List table. This highlights all the field names. Click on any one (not the *) and drag them to the field cell on the grid. On releasing the mouse button, all fields will be entered into the grid.
- Highlight the field in the Field List table and drag it to the field cell on the grid.

Query 2 Finding the contact details for students who have not passed the theory test

1 On the **Create** tab, in the **Other** group, click the **Query Design** button.
2 In the **Show Table** dialog box, select **tblStudent**, click on **Add** and then **Close** the window.

The next stage is to select the fields needed in our query. We will add them to the QBE grid by dragging and dropping each field.

3 Select **StudentID** in **tblStudent** and drag it to the field cell.
4 Drag and drop the fields **Forename, Surname**, **TelNo** and **PassedTheoryTest** in the same way. The field names will appear in the grid as shown in Figure 1.6.7.
5 Now select the criteria by entering **No** in the criteria row of the **PassedTheoryTest** column. Searching Yes/No fields is just a case of entering **Yes** or **No** in the criteria cell.

Figure 1.6.7 ▶

Field:	StudentID	Forename	Surname	TelNo	PassedTheoryTest
Table:	tblStudent	tblStudent	tblStudent	tblStudent	tblStudent
Sort:					
Show:	☑	☑	☑	☑	☑
Criteria:					No
or:					

6 To run your query, click on the **Datasheet View** button or click the **Run** button on the **Design** tab. The details are shown in Figure 1.6.8. There are seven records.

Figure 1.6.8 ▶

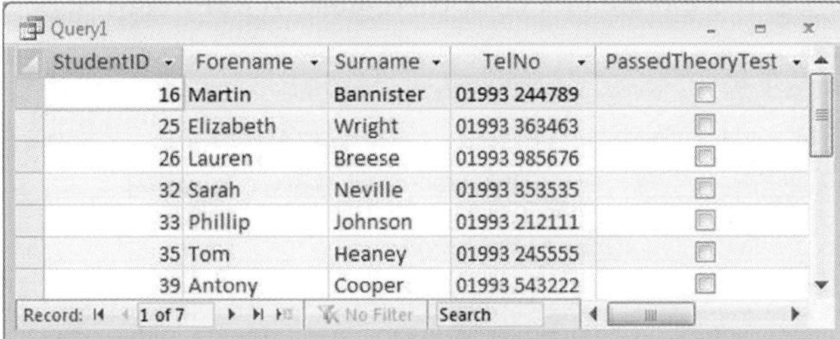

StudentID	Forename	Surname	TelNo	PassedTheoryTest
16	Martin	Bannister	01993 244789	☐
25	Elizabeth	Wright	01993 363463	☐
26	Lauren	Breese	01993 985676	☐
32	Sarah	Neville	01993 353535	☐
33	Phillip	Johnson	01993 212111	☐
35	Tom	Heaney	01993 245555	☐
39	Antony	Cooper	01993 543222	☐

7 Save your query as **qryNotPassTheory**.

Some further hints

Adding and removing tables

- To remove a table from the Query Design grid, double-click the title bar of the field list box and press DELETE.

- To add a table to the Query Design grid, click on the **Show Table** button and add the tables required.
- To clear the Query Design grid, click on the **Home** tab, in the **Sort & Filter** group click on **Advanced** and click **Clear Grid**.

Renaming the field headings

You can give a different name to the column titles in the query grid.

In the field row, click the start of the field name, type in the new name followed by a colon e.g. **Telephone number: TelNo**.

Changing the order of the fields chosen

Click the field selector at the top of the column and drag the field to the new location (see Figure 1.6.9).

Figure 1.6.9 ▶

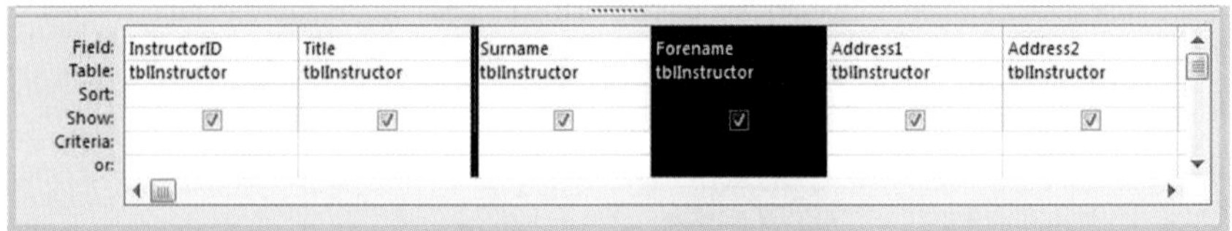

As you drag the field, a solid bar appears, showing where the relocated field will appear.

Deleting a query

Queries that are only used once are not really worth saving. In the Navigation Pane select the query to delete and press DELETE. Alternatively, right-click the query icon and select **Delete** from the menu.

Query 3 Producing a list of instructors' names and addresses

We will use the Query Wizard to design the next query.

1 On the **Create** tab, click the **Query Wizard** button. See Figure 1.6.10.

Figure 1.6.10 ▶

2 In the **New Query** dialog box select **Simple Query Wizard** and click on **OK**.

The Simple Query Wizard dialog box is displayed.

3 Select **tblInstructor** from the Tables/Queries drop-down list.
4 Select the field **InstructorID** in the Available Fields and click the right arrow **>**.
5 Repeat this process for the fields **Surname**, **Forename**, **Address1, Address2**, **Address3** and **Address4** as shown below (see Figure 1.6.11).

Note: Double-clicking an available field will move it to the selected field list. Select all fields by clicking the >> button.

Figure 1.6.11 ▶

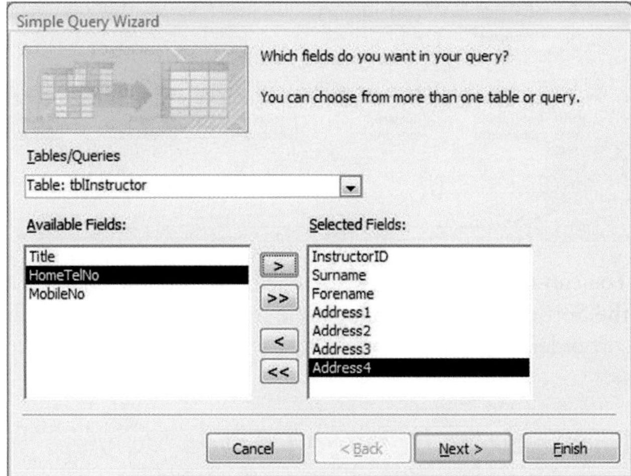

6 Click on **Next**, name the query **qryInstructorAddresses** and click on **Finish** (see Figure 1.6.12).

Figure 1.6.12 ▶

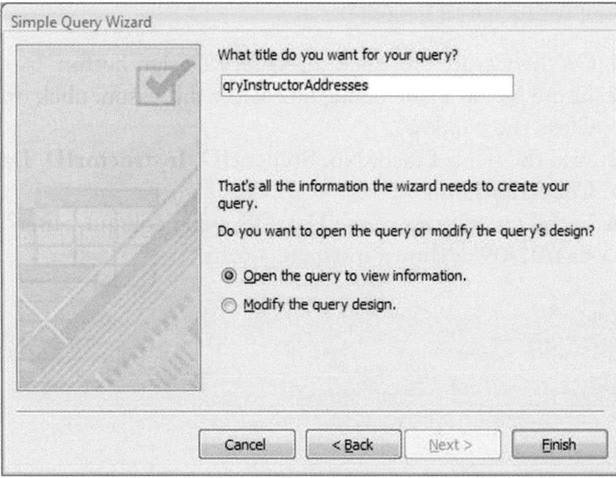

The resulting query opens in Datasheet View, as shown in Figure 1.6.13, giving the details of the instructors' names and addresses.

Figure 1.6.13 ▶

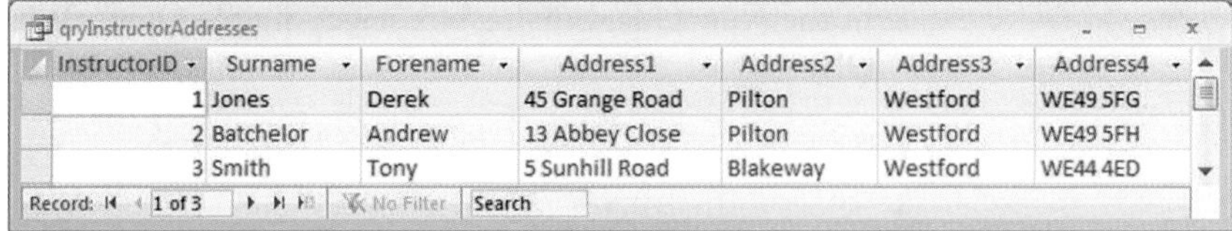

InstructorID	Surname	Forename	Address1	Address2	Address3	Address4
1	Jones	Derek	45 Grange Road	Pilton	Westford	WE49 5FG
2	Batchelor	Andrew	13 Abbey Close	Pilton	Westford	WE49 5FH
3	Smith	Tony	5 Sunhill Road	Blakeway	Westford	WE44 4ED

Close the query window. In the **Navigation Pane** right-click on the **qryInstructorAddresses** icon and open the query in Design View (see Figure 1.6.14).

Figure 1.6.14 ▶

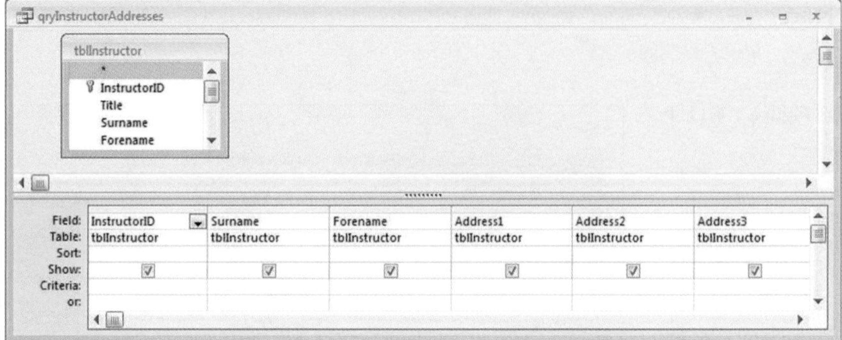

You can refine your query if needed, for example click on the drop-down list in the Sort cell of the Surname field, to choose either ascending or descending sort order.

Query 4 Finding lessons between dates

Suppose we wish to view lessons between certain dates or print a list of lessons for the coming week.

You can select a range of records using the operators < , >, <= , >= , + , - , BETWEEN, AND, NOT.

1 On the **Create** tab, click the **Query Design** button.
2 In the **Show Table** dialog box select **tblLesson**, click on **Add** and then **Close** the window.
3 Add the fields **LessonNo**, **StudentID, InstructorID**, **DateOfLesson** and **CollectionPoint**.
4 In the criteria row of the **DateOfLesson** column, enter **>28/07/09 And <31/07/09** as shown in Figure 1.6.15.

Figure 1.6.15 ▶

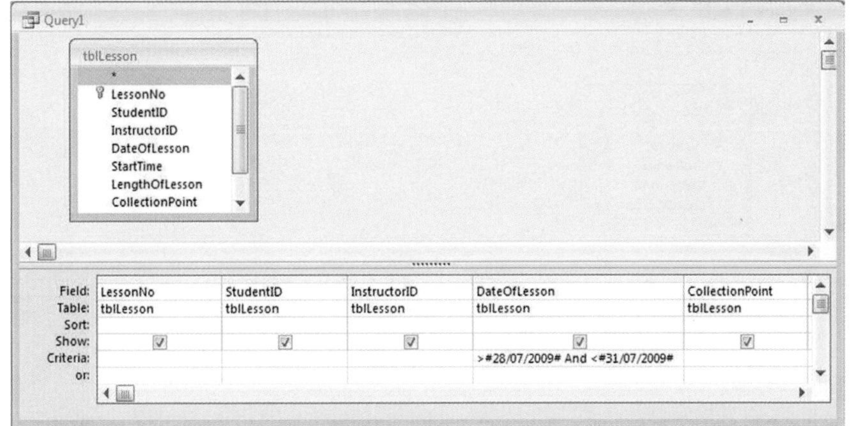

5 Run the query to view the records and then save the query as **qryBetweenDates** (see Figure 1.6.16).

Figure 1.6.16 ▶

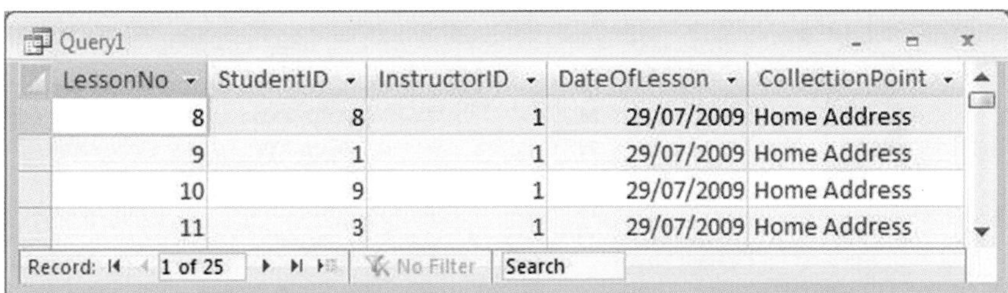

LessonNo	StudentID	InstructorID	DateOfLesson	CollectionPoint
8	8	1	29/07/2009	Home Address
9	1	1	29/07/2009	Home Address
10	9	1	29/07/2009	Home Address
11	3	1	29/07/2009	Home Address

Note: This query could also have been designed by entering the expression **Between 29/07/09 and 30/07/09** in the criteria row of the **DateOfLesson** field cell. The expression includes the stated dates.

Query 5 Finding lessons for an instructor on a given date

It is possible to specify criteria in more than one field. For example, you may want to see details of a specific instructor's lessons on a certain date. This is sometimes known as an AND search because it involves the InstructorID field and the DateOfLesson field.

1 On the **Create** tab, click the **Query Design** button.
2 In the **Show Table** dialog box, select **tblLesson**, click on **Add** and then **Close** the window.
3 Add the fields **StudentID, InstructorID, DateOfLesson, StartTime, CollectionPoint** and **LessonType** (see Figure 1.6.17).

Figure 1.6.17 ▼

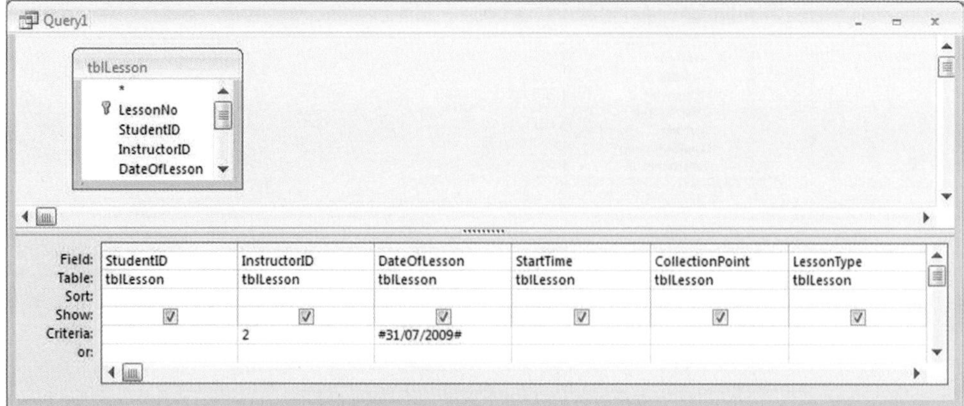

4 In the criteria row of the **InstructorID** column, enter **2** and enter **31/07/2009** in the criteria cell for **DateOfLesson**.

Figure 1.6.18 ►

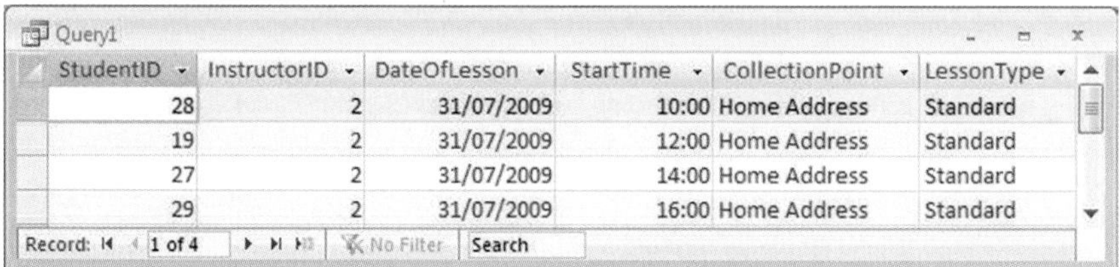
Query1

StudentID	InstructorID	DateOfLesson	StartTime	CollectionPoint	LessonType
28	2	31/07/2009	10:00	Home Address	Standard
19	2	31/07/2009	12:00	Home Address	Standard
27	2	31/07/2009	14:00	Home Address	Standard
29	2	31/07/2009	16:00	Home Address	Standard

Record: 1 of 4 No Filter Search

5 Run the query to view the records shown in Figure 1.6.18. Save your query as **qryInstructorAndDate**.

You may wish to look for records which meet one criterion OR another. For example, you may wish to view lessons on one day or another. This is sometimes known as an OR search.

1 On the **Create** tab, click the **Query Design** button.
2 In the **Show Table** dialog box, select **tblLesson**, click on **Add** and then **Close** the window.
3 Add the fields **StudentID, InstructorID, DateOfLesson, StartTime, CollectionPoint** and **LessonType** as shown in Figure 1.6.19.
4 In the criteria row of the **DateOfLesson** column enter **30/07/09** and enter **31/07/09** in the row below.

Figure 1.6.19 ▼

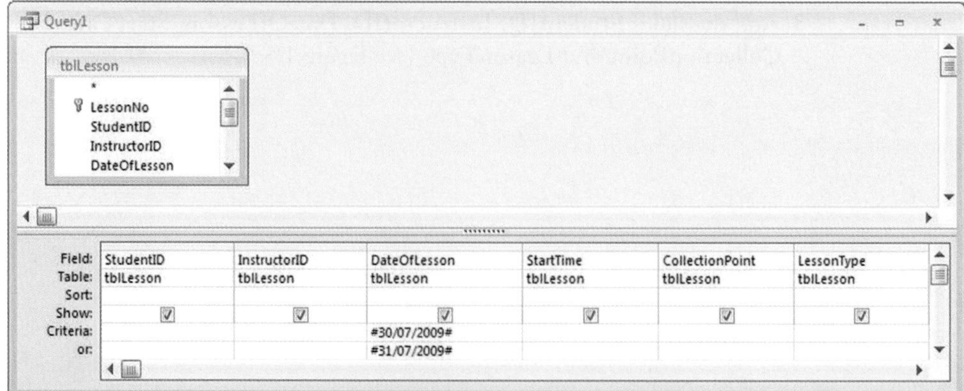

5 Run the query to view the records (there are 17) and then save as **qryOrDates** (see Figure 1.6.20).

Figure 1.6.20 ▶

StudentID	InstructorID	DateOfLesson	StartTime	CollectionPoint	LessonType
10	1	30/07/2009	10:00	Barton School	Standard
12	1	30/07/2009	12:00	Home Address	Standard
2	1	30/07/2009	14:00	Home Address	Standard
13	1	30/07/2009	16:00	Home Address	Standard
8	1	31/07/2009	09:00	Home Address	Standard
14	1	31/07/2009	11:00	Home Address	Standard

Note: All the queries set up in Unit 6 (see Figure 1.6.21) were only for demonstration purposes. They are not needed as part of the Pass IT Driving School System. It is a good idea to go to the **Navigation Pane** and delete them now by right-clicking the icon and selecting **Delete**.

Figure 1.6.21 ▼

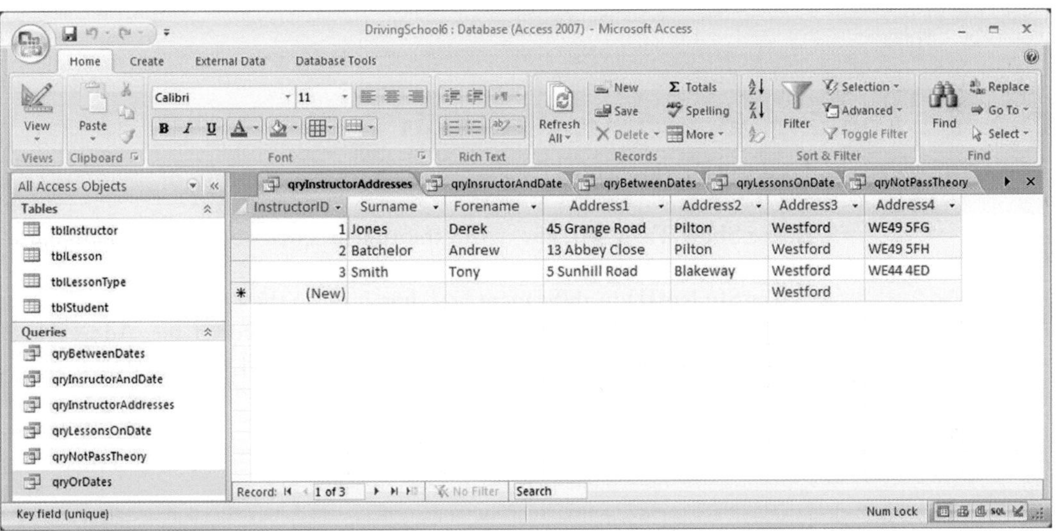

InstructorID	Surname	Forename	Address1	Address2	Address3	Address4
1	Jones	Derek	45 Grange Road	Pilton	Westford	WE49 5FG
2	Batchelor	Andrew	13 Abbey Close	Pilton	Westford	WE49 5FH
3	Smith	Tony	5 Sunhill Road	Blakeway	Westford	WE44 4ED
(New)					Westford	

Unit 7: Further queries

All the queries so far have been select queries. Select queries are not very useful if you have to run the query frequently and use different criteria each time.

In this unit you will be shown how to use the **Date()** function and will be introduced to **Parameter queries**.

Parameter queries overcome the problem by allowing you to enter the criteria each time the query is run. On running the query, a dialog box will appear asking you to enter the details (see Figure 1.7.1).

Figure 1.7.1 ▶

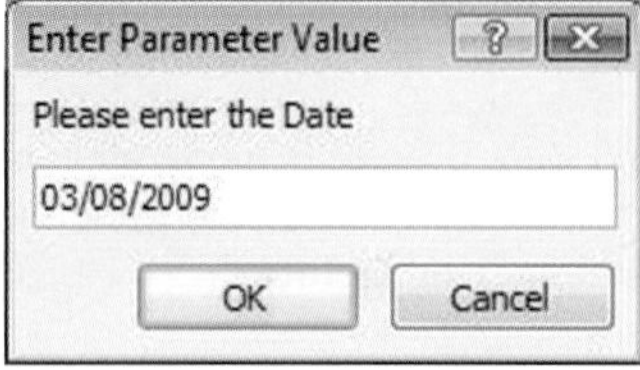

In the example shown in Figure 1.7.1, you would enter the date and the records matching that date would be displayed.

Query 1 Looking up a student's details

1 Load the **DrivingSchool** database.
2 On the **Create** tab, click the **Query Design** button.
3 In the **Show Table** window, select **tblStudent**, click on **Add** and then **Close** the window.
4 Select **StudentID** in **tblStudent** and drag it on to the QBE grid.
5 Drag and drop the fields (or double-click) **Surname**, **Forename**, **Address1**, **Address2**, **Address3**, **Address4**, **TelNo**, **DateOfBirth** and **Sex** in the same way. The field names will appear as in Figure 1.7.2.

Figure 1.7.2 ▼

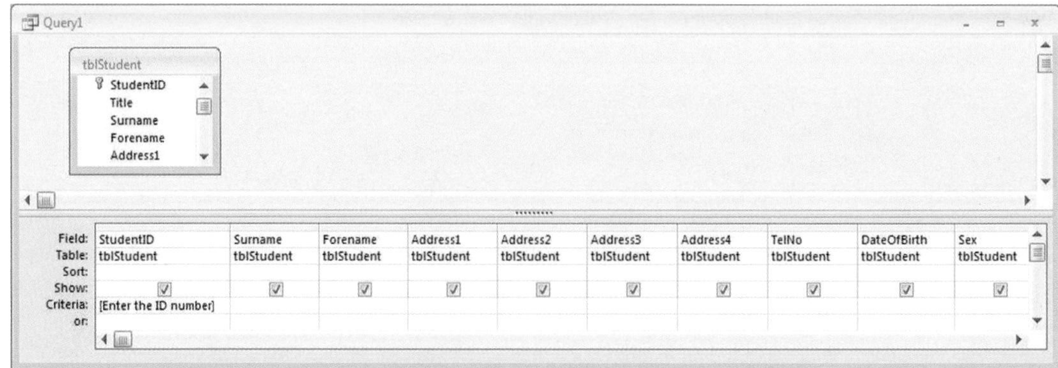

6 In the criteria cell for the **StudentID** field, type in **[Enter the ID number]**. The square brackets are required.

7 Run the query and enter **2** in the dialog box, as shown in Figure 1.7.3.

Figure 1.7.3 ▶

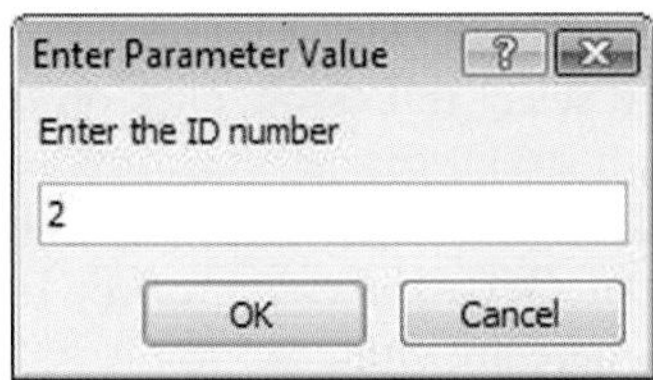

8 The query will display the details of Student number 2, Steven Jenkins. Save your query as **qrySearchStudentID**.

Query 2 Looking up a student's lessons

1 On the **Create** tab, click the **Query Design** button.
2 In the **Show Table** window, select **tblLesson**, click on **Add** and then **Close** the window.
3 From **tblLesson**, double-click the fields **StudentID, DateOfLesson**, **StartTime** and **LengthOfLesson**. The field names should appear in the query grid, as shown in Figure 1.7.4.

Figure 1.7.4 ▶

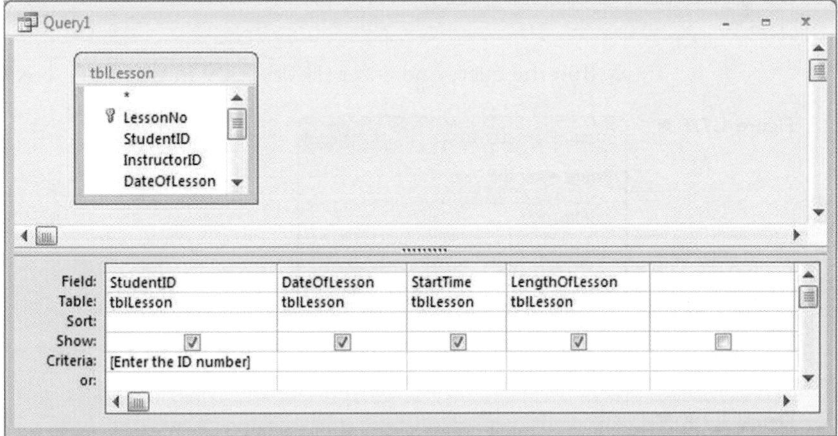

4 In the criteria cell for the **StudentID** field, type in **[Enter the ID number]** The square brackets are required.
5 Run the query and enter **2** in the dialog box. The query will display the two lessons for Student number 2, as shown in Figure 1.7.5. Save your query as **qryStudentLesson**.

Figure 1.7.5 ▶

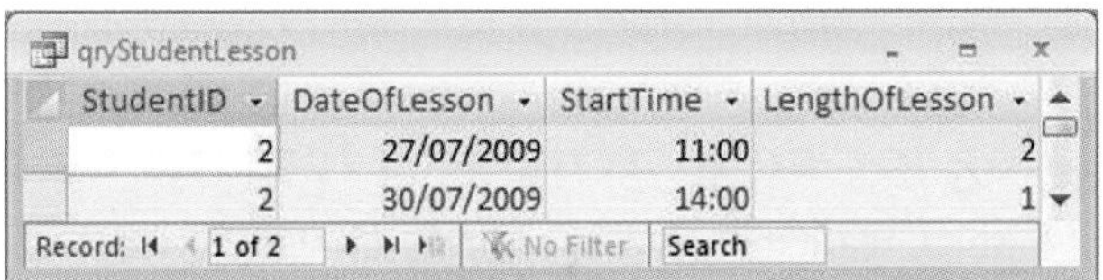

StudentID	DateOfLesson	StartTime	LengthOfLesson
2	27/07/2009	11:00	2
2	30/07/2009	14:00	1

Query 3 Searching for lessons on any date

1 On the **Create** tab, click the **Query Design** button.
2 In the **Show Table** window, select **tblLesson**, click on **Add** and then **Close** the window.
3 Add all the fields to the query grid, as shown in Figure 1.7.6.
4 In the criteria row of the **DateOfLesson** column, type in **[Please enter the Date]**. The square brackets here are vital.

Figure 1.7.6 ▼

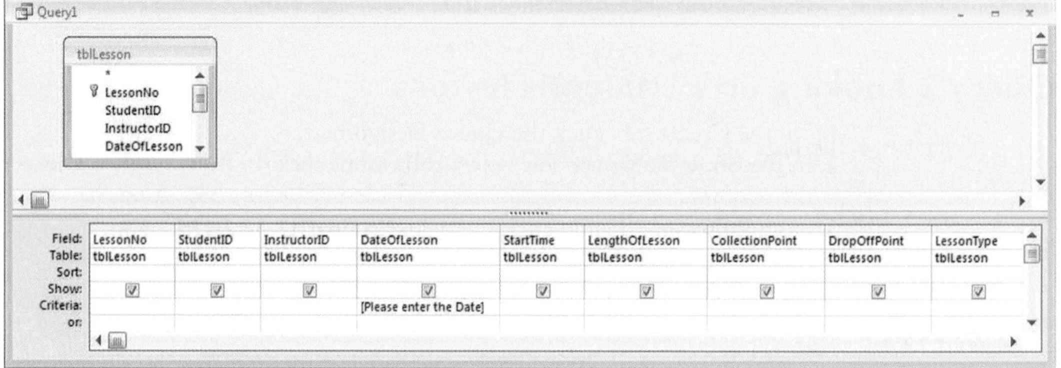

5 Run the query and enter **03/08/2009** in the dialog box (see Figure 1.7.7).

Figure 1.7.7 ▶

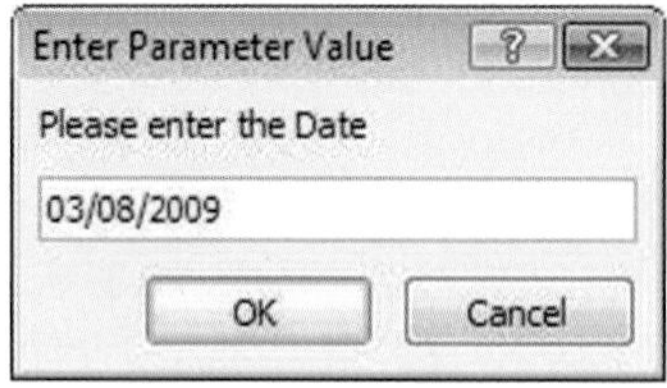

6 The result of the query is shown in Figure 1.7.8. Save your query as **qrySearchLessonDate**.

Figure 1.7.8 ▼

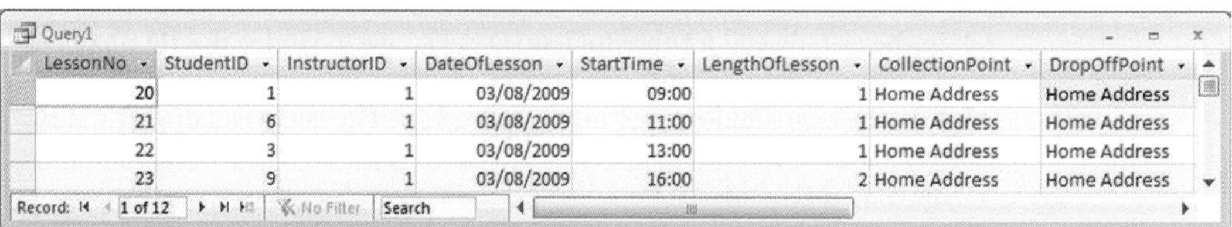

LessonNo	StudentID	InstructorID	DateOfLesson	StartTime	LengthOfLesson	CollectionPoint	DropOffPoint
20	1	1	03/08/2009	09:00	1	Home Address	Home Address
21	6	1	03/08/2009	11:00	1	Home Address	Home Address
22	3	1	03/08/2009	13:00	1	Home Address	Home Address
23	9	1	03/08/2009	16:00	2	Home Address	Home Address

Record: 1 of 12 No Filter Search

Query 4 Searching for an instructor's lessons by date

1 On the **Create** tab, click the **Query Design** button.
2 In the **Show Table** window, select **tblLesson**, click on **Add** and then **Close** the window.
3 Add all the fields to the grid by double-clicking the title bar of the **Field List** table and dragging the highlighted fields to the field cell (see Figure 1.7.9).

Figure 1.7.9 ▶

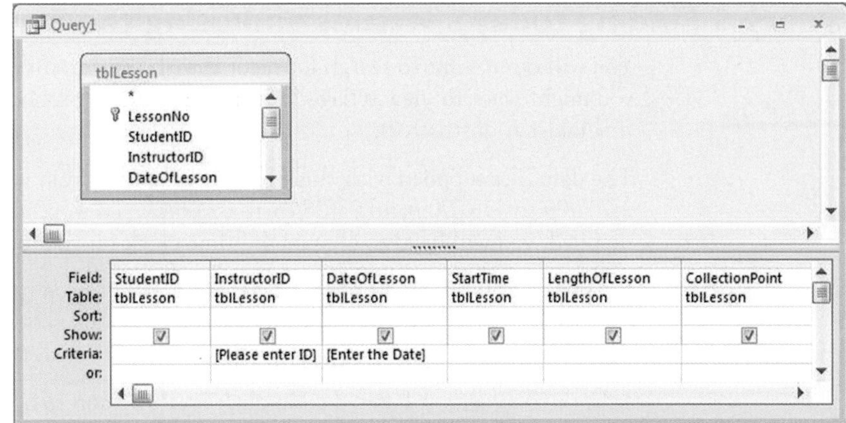

4 Remove fields **LessonNo**, **DropOffPoint** and **LessonType** by highlighting the column selector and clicking the **Delete Columns** button on the **Design** tab.

5 In the criteria cell for the field **InstructorID,** type in **[Please enter ID]**.

6 In the criteria cell for the field **DateOfLesson**, type in **[Enter the Date]**.

7 Run the query and enter **1** for the **InstructorID** (see Figure 1.7.10).

Figure 1.7.10 ▶

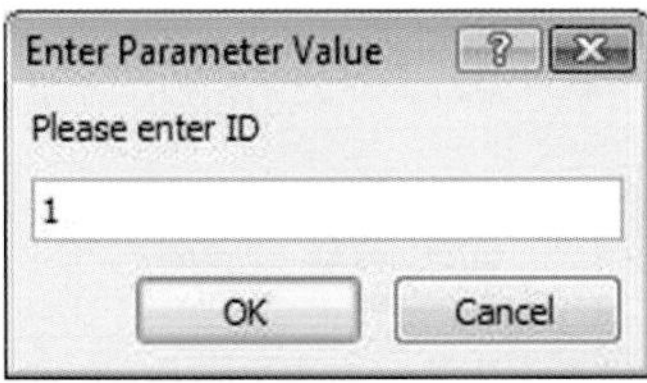

8 Enter **31/07/09** for the date (see Figure 1.7.11).

Figure 1.7.11 ▶

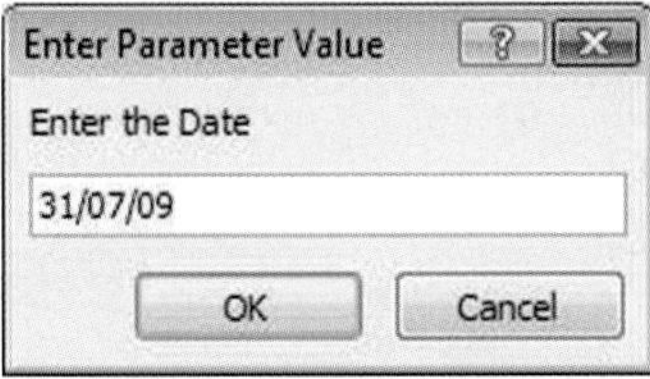

9 The result of the query is shown in Figure 1.7.12.

Figure 1.7.12 ▶

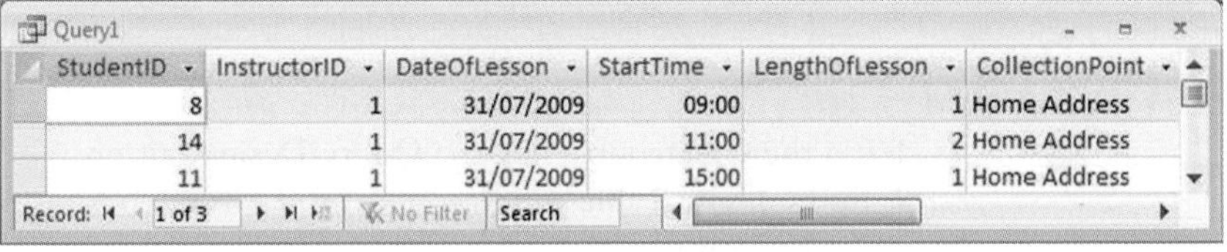

StudentID	InstructorID	DateOfLesson	StartTime	LengthOfLesson	CollectionPoint
8	1	31/07/2009	09:00	1	Home Address
14	1	31/07/2009	11:00	2	Home Address
11	1	31/07/2009	15:00	1	Home Address

10 Save your query as **qryInstructorLessonsDate**.

Query 5 Finding today's lessons and using the Date() function

You will often want to search for records with the current date. For example, you might want to view today's lessons at the driving school or issue weekly timetables to instructors.

The data files supplied with this book cover lessons from week beginning 27/07/09 to 31/07/09 and 03/08/09 to 07/08/09. To work with the data supplied, you will need to change the time clock on your computer to 27/07/09.

If you do not have access rights to do this, you will need to use Find and Replace to replace 27/07/09 with today's date, as shown here. It might be advisable to make a copy of your database and work with the copy.

1 In the Navigation Pane, double-click on **tblLesson** to open it in **Datasheet View**. Place the cursor at the start of the **DateOfLesson** column.
2 On the **Home** tab, in the **Find** group, click the **Replace** button. In the **Find and Replace** dialog box, enter 27/07/2009 in **Find What** and today's date in **Replace With**, for example 23/09/2009
3 Select **DateOfLesson** from the **Look In** drop-down and **Whole Field** in the **Match** drop-down.
4 Click **Find Next** to find the date that needs replacing and **Replace** to carry out the change as shown below in Figure 1.7.13. Click **Replace All** to make all changes. You can now set up the query.

Figure 1.7.13 ▶

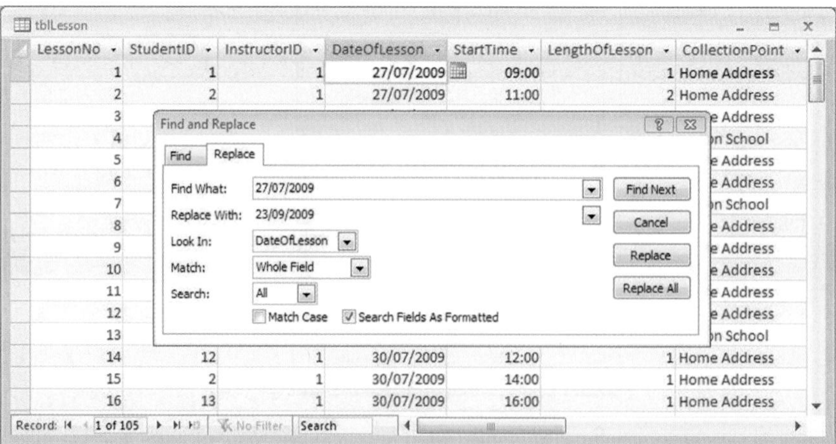

Setting up the query

1 On the **Create** tab, click the **Query Design** button.
2 In the **Show Table** window, select **tblLesson**, click on **Add** and then **Close** the window.
3 Add the fields **LessonNo**, **StudentID**, **InstructorID**, **DateOfLesson** and **StartTime**, as shown in Figure 1.7.14.

4 In the criteria row of the **DateOfLesson**, column enter **Date()**.

Figure 1.7.14 ▶

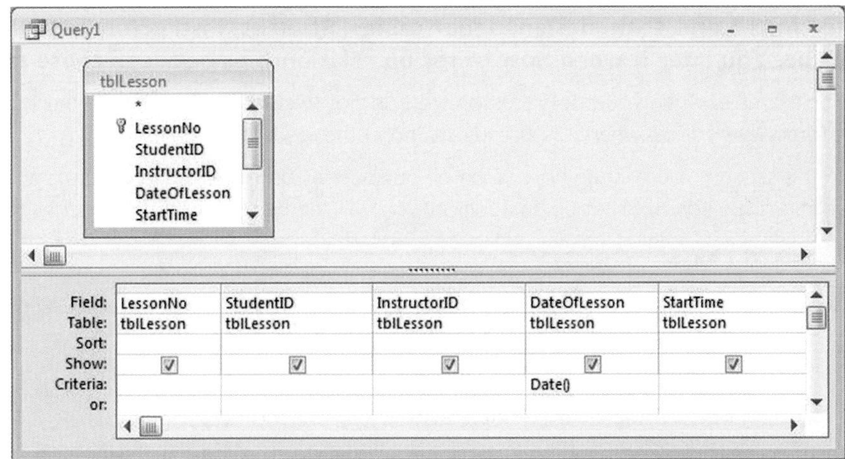

5 Run the query to view the records and save it as **qryTodaysLessons**.

Note: Remember to use Find and Replace option to restore your dates to their original state.

The date function is a powerful tool in query work and will form the basis of a number of queries later in the units.

Use **Tricks and Tips** numbers 10 and 11 to explore queries further.

Unit 8: Setting up multi-table queries

In Units 3 and 4 you designed four tables: Student, Instructor, Lesson and Lesson Type. You later learned how to set up relationships between those tables.

For example, when you book a lesson, you do not want to have to key in the student's name and address every time, when it is already stored in the student table.

In this section, you will see how to base your queries on more than one table and start to use the relationships you have set up. In addition, you will see how you can use queries to do calculations.

Figure 1.8.1 ▶

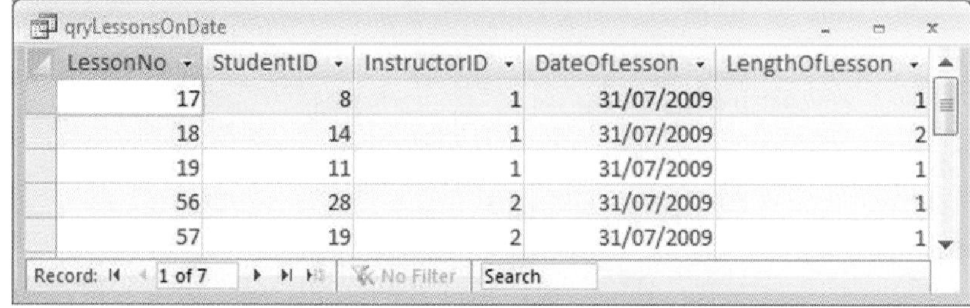

qryLessonsOnDate

LessonNo	StudentID	InstructorID	DateOfLesson	LengthOfLesson
17	8	1	31/07/2009	1
18	14	1	31/07/2009	2
19	11	1	31/07/2009	1
56	28	2	31/07/2009	1
57	19	2	31/07/2009	1

Record: 1 of 7 No Filter Search

At the start of Unit 6, you set up a query called **qryLessonsOnDate** to output the lessons booked on a given date.

The output is shown in Figure 1.8.1, based on the table **tblLesson**. If we wanted the output to include the students' names we would have to base the query on the table **tblLesson** (which stores the details of the lessons, dates and ID numbers) and the **tblStudent** (where the students' names are stored).

Query 1 Producing a list of lessons, together with student names

1 Load the **DrivingSchool** database.
2 On the **Create** tab, click the **Query Design** button.
3 In the **Show Table** window, select **tblLesson** and click on **Add** (see Figure 1.8.2).

Figure 1.8.2 ▶

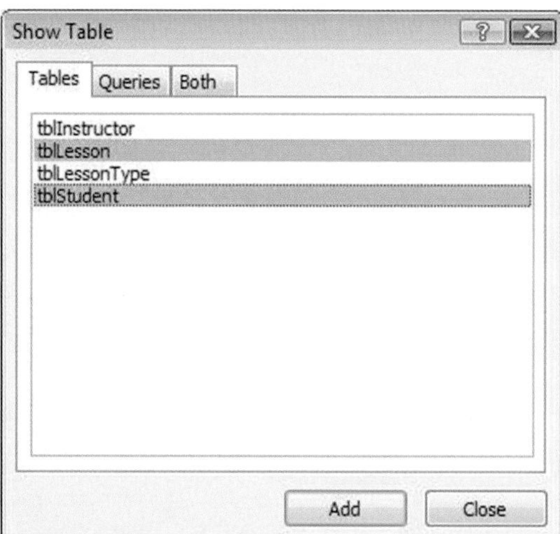

4 Select **tblStudent**, click on **Add** and then **Close** the window. You can use CTRL in the usual way to select both tables and then click **Add**.

5 The **Query Design View** window is shown in Figure 1.8.3 with the two tables and their relationships.

Figure 1.8.3 ▼

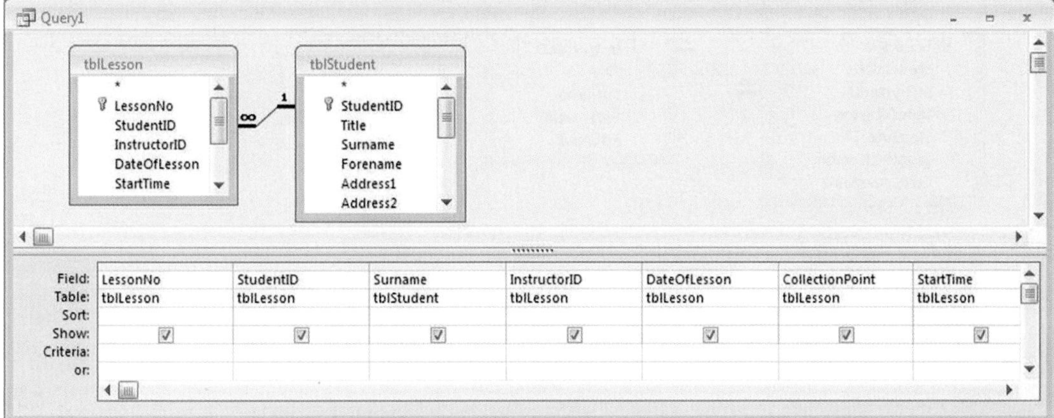

6 From **tblLesson**, drag and drop (or simply double-click) the fields **LessonNo**, **StudentID**, **InstructorID**, **DateOfLesson**, **CollectionPoint** and **StartTime** into the field cells.

7 From **tblStudent**, drag and drop the **Surname** field.

8 Move its position by clicking on the column header and dragging to a position after the **StudentID** column. Alternatively, you could enter the fields in the order shown.

9 On the **Design** tab, click the **Run** button to run the query and save it as **qryLessonAndNames**.

10 The results of your query are shown in Figure 1.8.4.

Figure 1.8.4 ▶

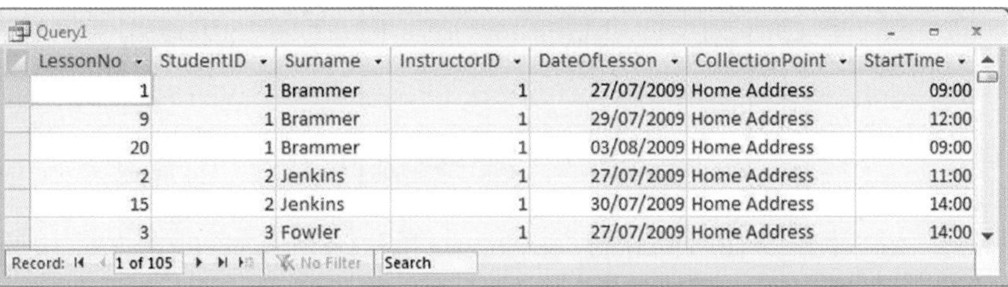

Query1

LessonNo	StudentID	Surname	InstructorID	DateOfLesson	CollectionPoint	StartTime
1	1	Brammer	1	27/07/2009	Home Address	09:00
9	1	Brammer	1	29/07/2009	Home Address	12:00
20	1	Brammer	1	03/08/2009	Home Address	09:00
2	2	Jenkins	1	27/07/2009	Home Address	11:00
15	2	Jenkins	1	30/07/2009	Home Address	14:00
3	3	Fowler	1	27/07/2009	Home Address	14:00

Record: 1 of 105 No Filter Search

Query 2 Searching for an instructor's lessons

This query will enable us to key in an Instructor's ID and find all their lessons.

1 On the **Create** tab, click the **Query Design** button.

2 In the **Show Table** dialog box, select **tblLesson** and click on **Add**.

3 Select **tblInstructor**, click on **Add** and then **Close** the window.

4 The Query Design grid is now shown in Figure 1.8.5 with the two tables and their relationships.

Figure 1.8.5 ▼

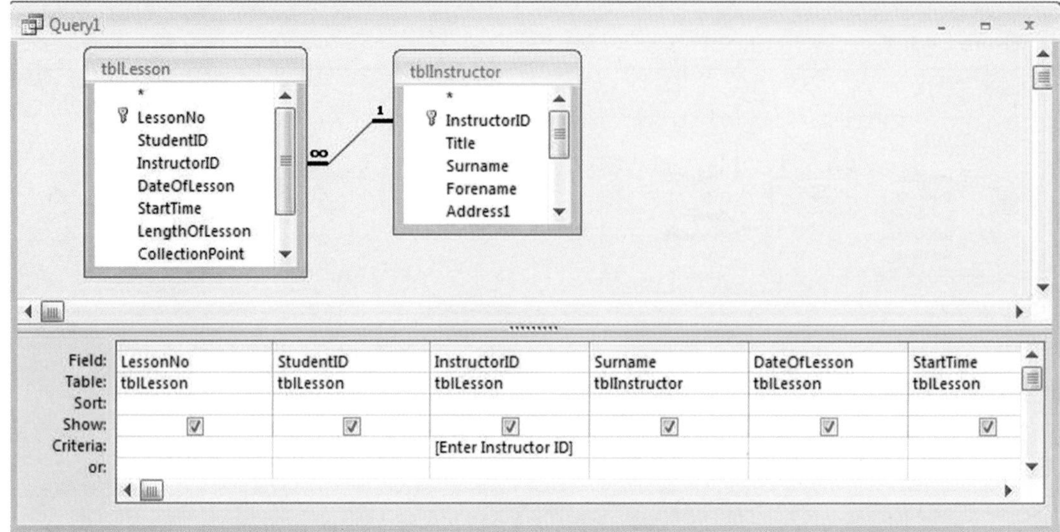

5 From **tblLesson**, drag and drop the fields **LessonNo, StudentID, InstructorID**, **DateOfLesson** and **StartTime**.

6 From **tblInstructor**, drag and drop the **Surname** field.

7 Move its position by clicking on the column header and dragging to a position after the **InstructorID** column. See Figure 1.8.5.

8 In the criteria cell of the **InstructorID**, type **[Enter Instructor ID]**.

9 On the **Design** tab, click the **Run** button to run the query and enter **2** in the dialog box (see Figure 1.8.6).

Figure 1.8.6 ▶

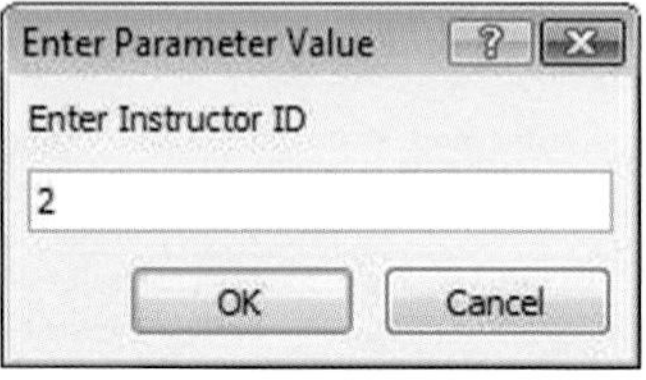

10 The query produces a list of 43 lessons for Instructor ID 2, as shown in Figure 1.8.7.

Figure 1.8.7 ▶

LessonNo	StudentID	InstructorID	Surname	DateOfLesson	StartTime
37	14	2	Batchelor	27/07/2009	10:00
38	15	2	Batchelor	27/07/2009	11:00
39	16	2	Batchelor	27/07/2009	14:00
40	29	2	Batchelor	27/07/2009	17:00

Record: 1 of 43 No Filter Search

11 Save the query as **qryInstructorLessons** by closing the query window.

Query 3 Viewing all lessons with full details of instructor and student names

We will use the Query Wizard to design the next query.

1 On the **Create** tab, click the **Query Wizard** button.
2 In the **New Query** window, select **Simple Query Wizard** and click on **OK**.

The Simple Query Wizard dialog box is displayed.

3 Select **tblLesson** from the Tables/Queries drop-down.
4 Click the double right arrow **>>** to put all the fields in the Selected Fields area (see Figure 1.8.8).

Figure 1.8.8 ▶

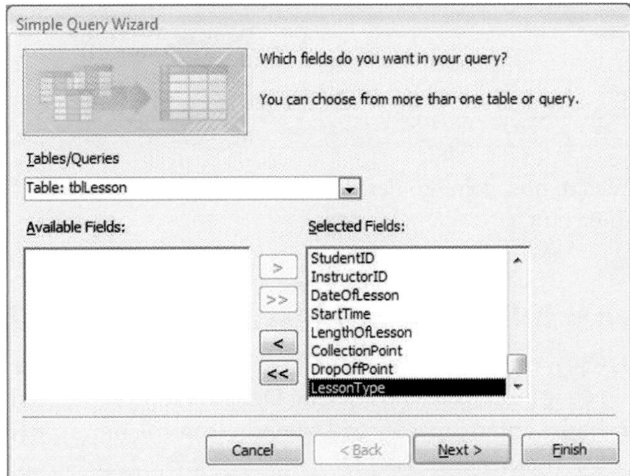

5 Select **tblInstructor** from the Tables/Queries drop-down.
6 Select fields **Surname** and **Forename** and add to the selected fields by clicking the right arrow **>**.

Figure 1.8.9 ▶

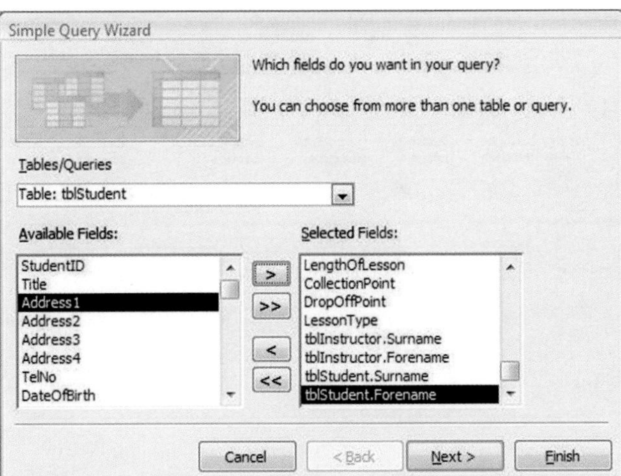

7 Select **tblStudent** from the **Tables/Queries** drop-down and add the fields **Surname** and **Forename** to the selected fields (see Figure 1.8.9).

8 Click on **Next**, choose **Detail**, click on **Next** again, call the query **qryFullDetails** and click on **Finish**.

The resulting query opens in Datasheet View (see Figure 1.8.10), giving full details of the lessons, the students and instructors, along with their names. (You will need to drop into Design View to position names alongside IDs).

Figure 1.8.10 ▶

LessonNo	StudentID	InstructorID	DateOfLesson	StartTime	LengthOfLesson	CollectionPoint
1	1	1	27/07/2009	09:00	1	Home Address
2	2	1	27/07/2009	11:00	2	Home Address
3	3	1	27/07/2009	14:00	1	Home Address
4	4	1	27/07/2009	16:00	1	Barton School
5	5	1	28/07/2009	10:00	1	Home Address
6	6	1	28/07/2009	12:00	1	Home Address
7	7	1	28/07/2009	14:00	2	Barton School
8	8	1	29/07/2009	09:00	1	Home Address

We are now going to develop two more queries which will be used later in these units.

Query 4 Viewing full details of lessons on a certain date

1 Open the **qryFullDetails** in Design View by right-clicking its icon in the Navigation Pane and clicking **Design View** on the menu**.**

2 In the criteria row of the **DateOfLesson** column, type **[Please enter the Date]** (see Figure 1.8.11).

Figure 1.8.11 ▶

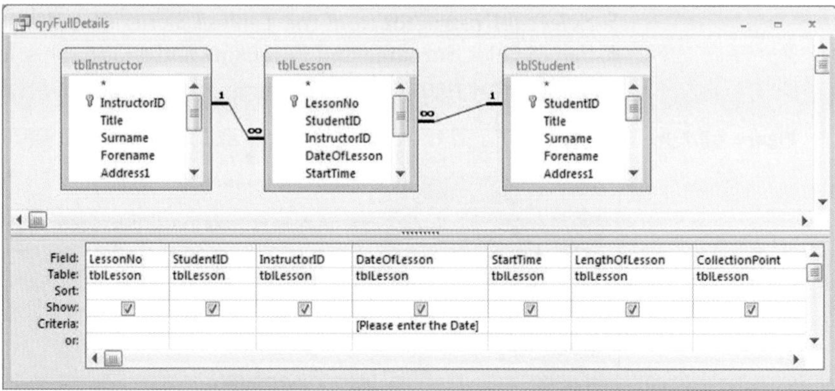

3 Click the **Office Button** and click **Save Object As** to save the query as **qryFullDetailsByDate**.

Figure 1.8.12 ▶

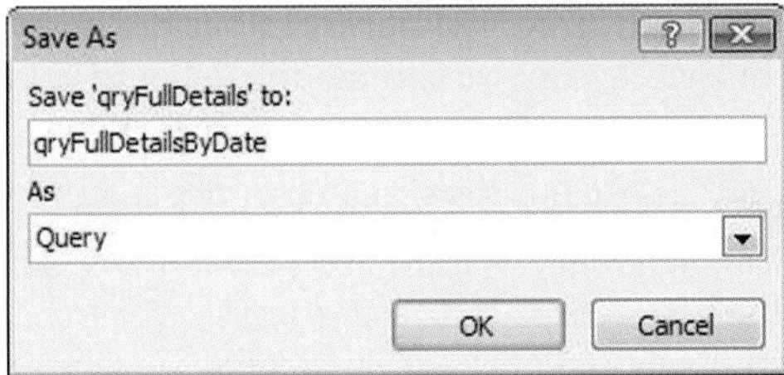

When you run this query, you will be prompted for a date. Access will display full details of the lessons on that date, along with the names of the students and instructors.

Query 5 Viewing full details of lessons this week

This query uses the **Date()** function again. The data files supplied with this book cover lessons from week beginning 27/07/09 to 31/07/09 and 03/08/09 to 07/08/09. To work with the data supplied, you will need to change the time clock on your computer to 27/07/09.

If you do not have access rights to do this, you will need to use Find and Replace to switch the data to a two-week period, starting with today's date. See Unit 7.

1 Open the **qryFullDetails** in Design View again.
2 In the criteria row of the **DateOfLesson** column, enter **Between Date() and Date()+7**. This will return all lessons booked in the next 7 days, starting from the current date (see Figure 1.8.13).

Figure 1.8.13 ▶

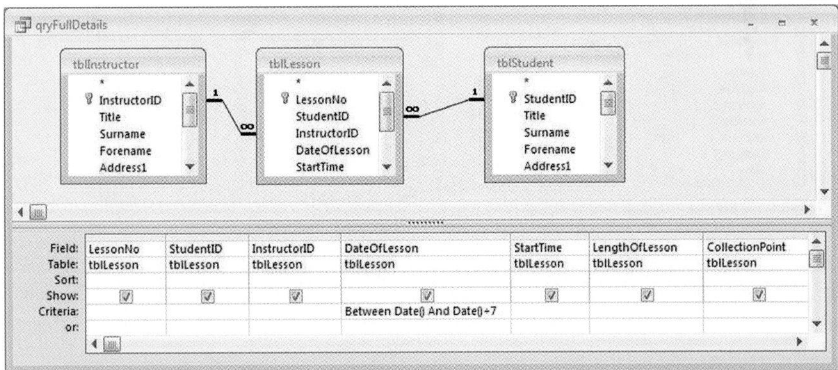

3 Click the **Office Button**, click **Save Object As** and save the query as **qryNextWeeksLessons**.
4 Open the query in Design View again and edit the criteria to **Date().** Save again as **qryTodayLessons**.
5 Remember to return your data to its original state.

Query 6 Adding a calculated field to a query

A calculated field is an added field in a query that displays the results of a calculation. For example, if we multiply together the hourly rate for each lesson and the length of each lesson, we can use the query to work out the cost of each lesson.

1. On the **Create** tab, click the **Query Wizard** button.
2. Select the **Simple Query Wizard** and click on **OK**. The Simple Query Wizard dialog box is displayed.
3. Click on **tblLesson** and click on the double arrow **>>** to select every field.
4. Select **tblLessonType** table and click on the field **Cost**. Click on the single arrow **>** to select just this field.
5. Select **tblInstructor** and click on the field **Forename**. Click on the single arrow to select just this field. Add the **Surname** field also.
6. Select **tblStudent** and click on the field **Forename**. Click on the single arrow to select just this field. Then add the **Surname, Address1** and **Address2** fields as well.
7. Click on **Next**. Click on **Next** again and call the query **qryLessonCost**. Click on **Finish**.
8. Close the Query window and switch to **Design View**. You will need to rearrange the tables by dragging to more suitable positions (see Figure 1.8.14).
9. Using drag-and-drop, rearrange the order of fields in the QBE grid so that InstructorID comes after LessonNo, followed by Instructor Forename and Surname, then StudentID, followed by Student Forename, Surname, Address1 and Address2 (see Figure 1.8.14).

Figure 1.8.14 ▼

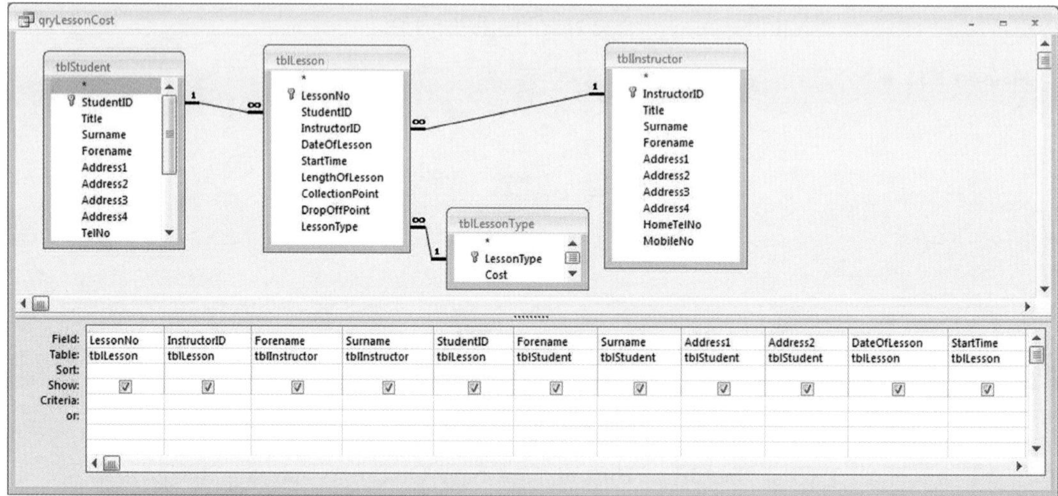

10. Scroll to the right and find the first blank column of the QBE grid. If there is no blank column, select the last field and, in the **Query Setup** group, click on the **Insert Columns** button.

11 In the field row of the blank column enter **TotalCost: [LengthOfLesson]*[Cost]** (see Figure 1.8.15).

Figure 1.8.15 ▼

LengthOfLesson	CollectionPoint	DropOffPoint	LessonType	Cost	TotalCost: [LengthOfLesson]*[Cost]
tblLesson	tblLesson	tblLesson	tblLesson	tblLessonType	
☑	☑	☑	☑	☑	☑

12 Save the query again (by closing the window) as **qryLessonCost**.

13 Run the query, to test the calculations are correct (see Figure 1.8.16) (some columns have been hidden).

Figure 1.8.16 ►

qryLessonCost

LessonNo	InstructorID	DateOfLesson	StartTime	LengthOfLesson	LessonType	Cost	TotalCost
1	1	27/07/2009	09:00	1	Standard	£24.00	£24.00
2	1	27/07/2009	11:00	2	Standard	£24.00	£48.00
3	1	27/07/2009	14:00	1	Standard	£24.00	£24.00
4	1	27/07/2009	16:00	1	Introductory	£16.00	£16.00
5	1	28/07/2009	10:00	1	Introductory	£16.00	£16.00
6	1	28/07/2009	12:00	1	Standard	£24.00	£24.00
7	1	28/07/2009	14:00	2	Test	£22.00	£44.00

Record: 1 of 105 No Filter Search

Use **Tricks and Tips** numbers 13, 14, 15 and 16 to explore queries further.

Unit 9: Setting up forms

In this section, you will learn how to start setting up the forms to enter, edit and view data in the Pass IT Driving School database.

So far, you have entered data directly into a table using Datasheet View, as shown in Figure 1.9.1.

Figure 1.9.1 ▶

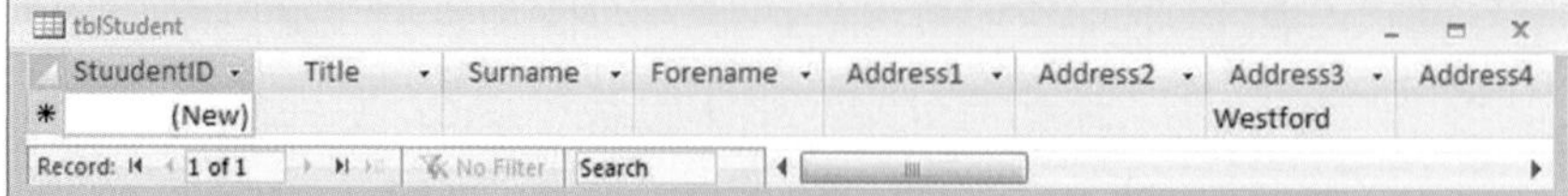

Access has a number of Form tools, including Form Wizards, to help you set up forms quickly and easily. These can be found on the Ribbon, in the Forms group, on the Create tab. See Figure 1.9.2.

Figure 1.9.2 ▶

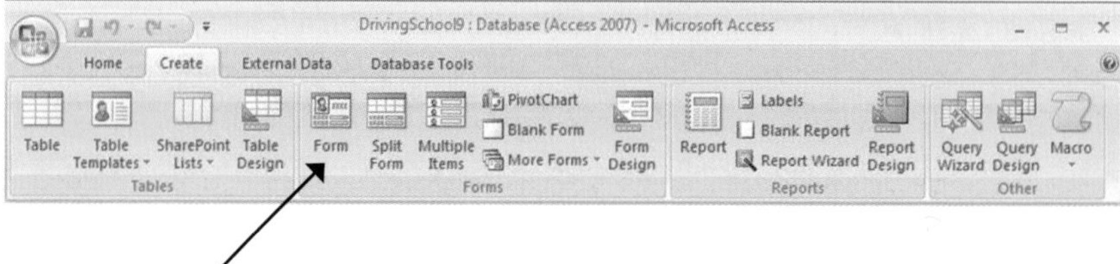

Setting up the Student form using the Form Wizard

Before setting up a form, you need to decide on the table or query that will supply the fields and data for your form. In this case, it will be the Student table.

1 Load the **DrivingSchool** database. On the **Create** tab, click the **More Forms** button.
2 Click on the **Form Wizard** button to display the Form Wizard dialog box.

Figure 1.9.3 ▶

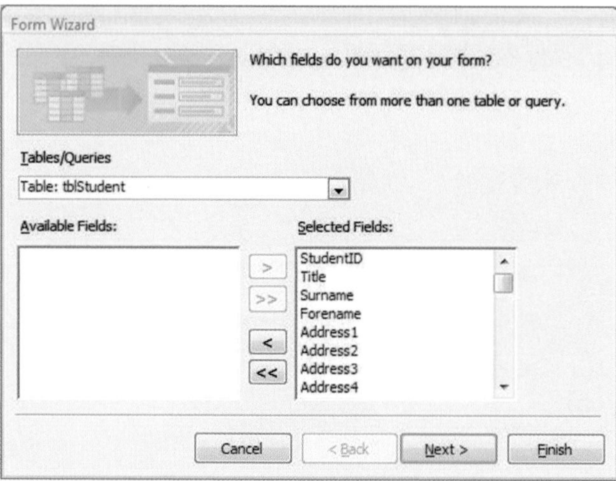

3 Select **tblStudent** from the Tables/Queries drop-down. Click the double arrow **>>** to move all **Available Fields** across to the **Selected Fields** area and click on **Next**. See Figure 1.9.3.

Note: The single arrow allows you to select one field at a time and the left arrows allow you to deselect fields. Use the single arrow to choose selected fields in a different order from that shown.

4 Select **Columnar** from the range of layouts shown and click on **Next** (see Figure 1.9.4).

Figure 1.9.4 ▶

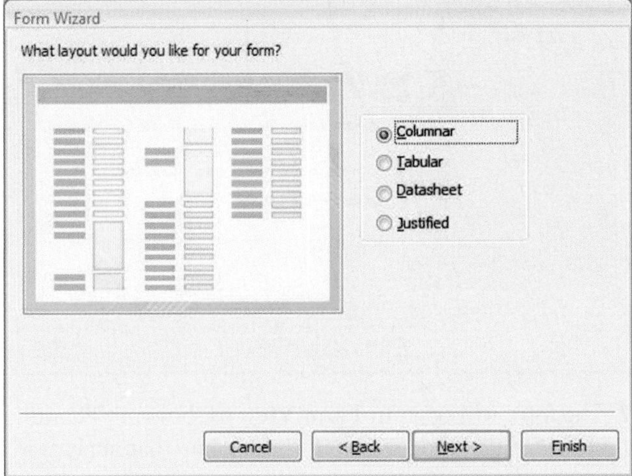

5 Select **Access 2007** from the choice of styles and click on **Next** (see Figure 1.9.5).

Figure 1.9.5 ▶

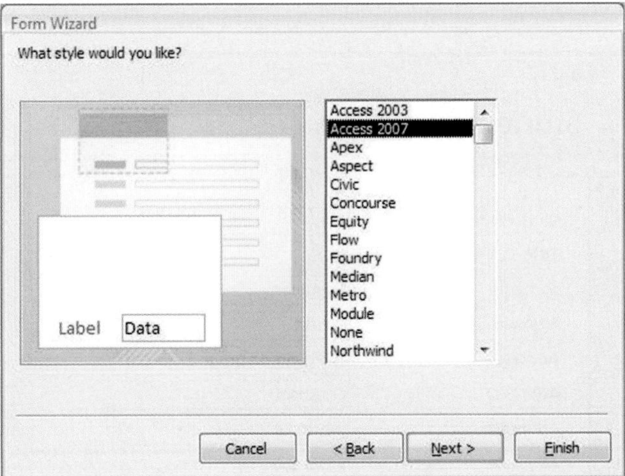

6 The next window asks you for a title for your form. Type in **Students** and click on **Finish**. See Figure 1.9.6.

Figure 1.9.6 ▶

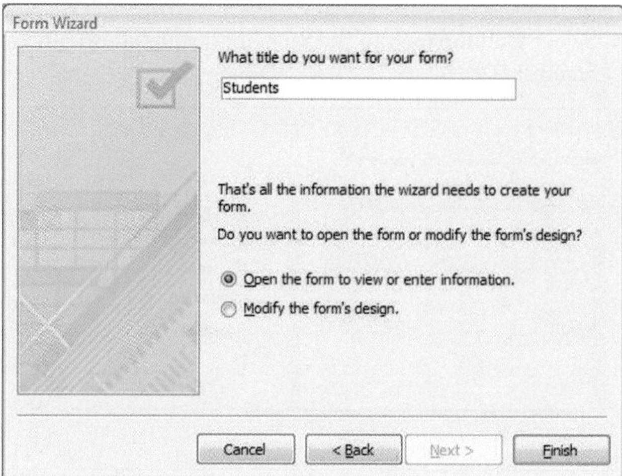

7 The form will open in **Form View** as shown in Figure 1.9.7. The name you chose for the Title in step 6 is the name that appears in the Form Header.

You can use the **Record** navigation buttons at the foot of the form to scroll through the records. Click on the last icon to add a **New (blank) record**. To search for a particular record, you can key a word or phrase into the **Search** box.

Figure 1.9.7 ▶

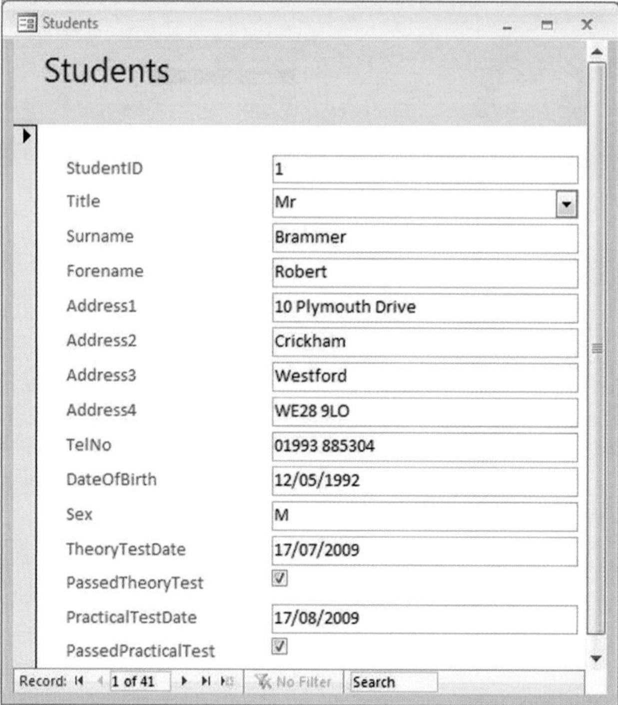

You will notice in the Navigation Pane that your form is saved automatically as **Students**. For good practice, rename it **frmStudent** by right-clicking the icon and selecting the **Rename** option. See details of Access naming standards in Unit 3. Click **Delete** if you wish to remove the form from the Navigation Pane.

Setting up the Lesson Type form using the Form Wizard

1 On the **Create** tab, click the **More Forms** button.
2 Click on the **Form Wizard** button to display the **Form Wizard** window.
3 Select the **tblLessonType** table from the drop-down list and click the **>>** to select both fields. Click on **Next**.
4 Choose a **Tabular** layout and click on **Next**. Choose the **Access 2007** style and click on **Next** again.
5 Give your form the title **Lesson Types** and click **Finish**.

The form opens in **Form View** as shown in Figure 1.9.8. The form is saved automatically as **Lesson Types**. Rename it to **frmLessonType** if you want to use standard naming conventions again.

Figure 1.9.8 ►

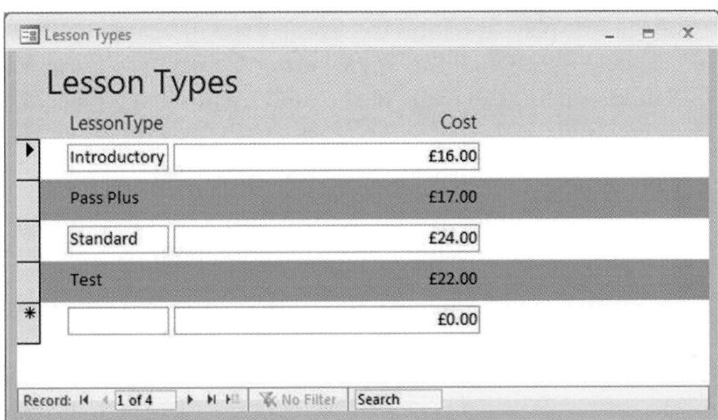

Hint To remove the alternate colours. Go into **Design View**, right-click in the **Detail** area and set the **Alternate Fill/Back Color** option to **None**.

Access 2007 offers a number of other ways of setting up forms at the click of a button, including the **Form** tool and Split Forms. You might like to experiment with the different tools to help decide which method is best for you.

Setting up the Instructor form using Split Forms

Split Forms give you two views of your data at the same time, Form View and Datasheet View. The views are synchronised, allowing you to locate a record easily in Datasheet View and then edit it in Form View.

1 In the **Navigation Pane,** click **tblInstructor** to highlight the Instructor table.
2 On the **Create** tab, click the **Split Form** button.

Figure 1.9.9 ▶

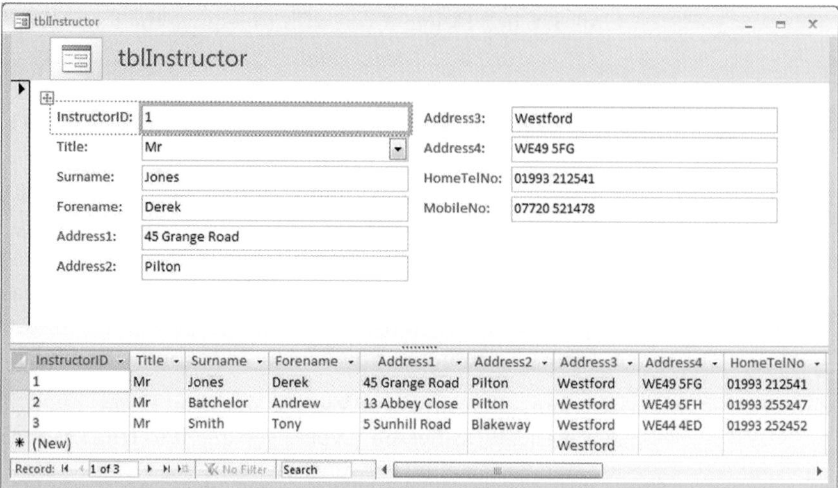

Access displays the form in Layout View indicated by the orange grid (see Figure 1.9.9). Click the **View** button to switch to **Form View**. A title is added (tblInstructor, the name of the table), as well as a placeholder ready for a logo if required.

The upper part of the form displays a single Instructor record, while the lower part displays all the records for the Instructor table in Datasheet View. Scroll through the records using the navigation buttons.

3 To save your form, click the **Close** button and type **frmInstructorDetails** in the **Save As** dialog box.

Hint Tidy up the columns by moving the cursor over the border between column headings and double-clicking to give a best fit.

Setting up the Instructor form using the Form tool

1 In the **Navigation Pane**, click **tblInstructor** to highlight the Instructor table.
2 On the **Create** tab, click the **Form** button. Access displays the form in Layout View as shown in Figure 1.9.10.

Figure 1.9.10 ▶

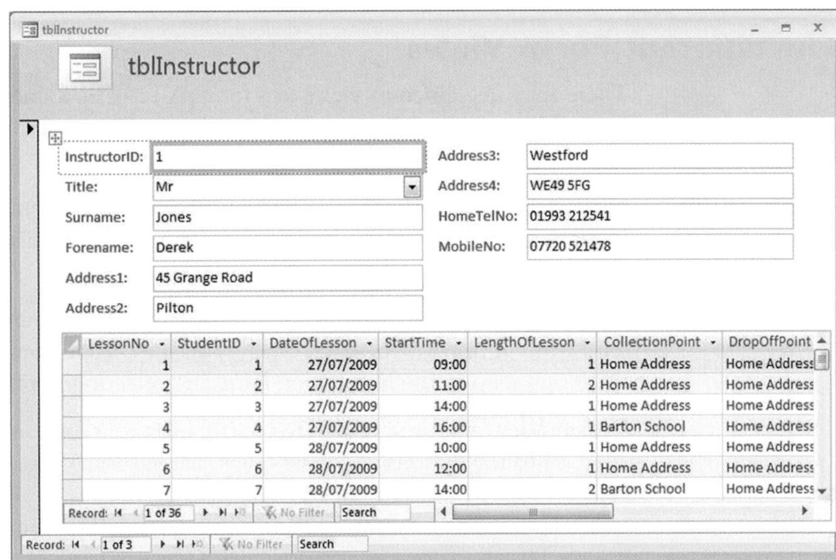

A subform appears in the lower half of the table showing data in a related table, if one exists. In this case, the lessons for each instructor are shown in the subform. Scroll the navigation buttons to view.

3 To save the form, click the **Close** button and type **frmInstructorLessons** in the **Save As** dialog box.

Figure 1.9.11 ▼

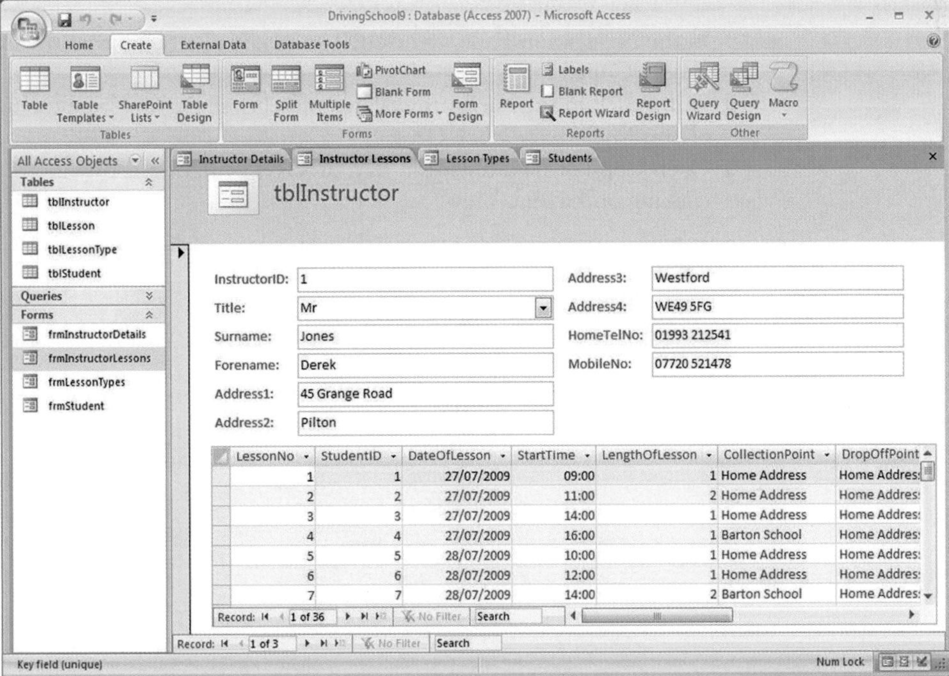

If you have been working in Tabbed Documents mode, your Access window will look similar to Figure 1.9.11. All the forms need a little tidying which we will cover in later units; we have just renamed the tabs. For more on Tabbed Documents and Overlapping Windows see Unit 2.

The different Form Views

There are three different views to a form. All can be found on the **Home** tab, in the **Views** group. Clicking the **View** button always displays the alternate view to the current view.

Form View allows you to view and edit records. You cannot modify the form in Form View. Open forms in Form View by double-clicking the form's icon in the Navigation Pane.

In **Layout View**, you can make simple layout and appearance changes to the form while it displays the data. Open forms in Layout View by right-clicking the form's icon in the Navigation Pane and selecting from the menu.

Design View gives you complete control over your form and its properties. In addition to the options in Layout View, Design View allows you to add a greater range of controls. Open forms in Design View by right-clicking the form's icon in the Navigation Pane and selecting from the menu.

Working in Layout View

You will grasp the concepts more easily by practising and experimenting with the tasks in this section. If you are confident with working in Layout View you can move on to Unit 10.

We will start by working on a copy of a form, so that if you make a mistake it will not affect the final system.

1 In the **Navigation Pane**, right-click on **frmStudent** and from the menu choose **Copy**.
2 Right-click in the **Navigation Pane** and choose **Paste**. Name the form **Copy of frmStudent** and click **OK**.
3 Open **Copy of frmStudent** in Layout View by right-clicking its icon and clicking on **Layout View**.

Figure 1.9.12 ▶

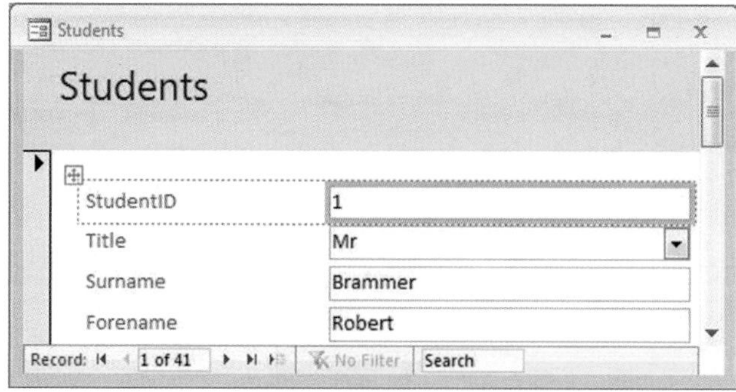

4 The Student form appears in **Layout View** as shown in Figure 1.9.12. Access also displays the **Format** tab which displays the **Form Layout Tools** available. See Figure 1.9.13

Figure 1.9.13 ▼

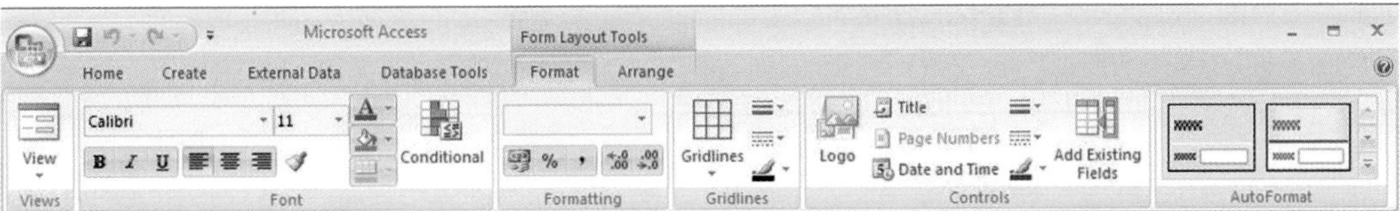

When you open a form which has been created with one of the Form tools in Layout View, Access puts the labels and text boxes into guides called control layouts.

The control layout is indicated by an orange grid as shown in Figure 1.9.12. You can select the layout by clicking the layout selector at the upper-left corner to the left of the Student ID control as shown in Figure 1.9.14.

Changing the order of the controls

5 Click the **Forename** label or text box and drag to a position above the **Surname** control. The I-bar indicates the correct position. Access snaps the control to the layout. See Figure 1.9.14.

Figure 1.9.14 ▶

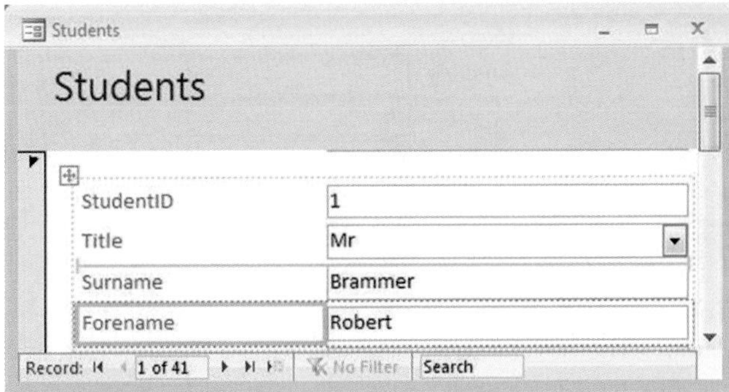

Formatting the controls

6 Click in the **StudentID** label. Move the mouse pointer over the top edge of the **StudentID** label until it turns to a black arrow. Click to select the column. See Figure 1.9.15.

Figure 1.9.15 ▶

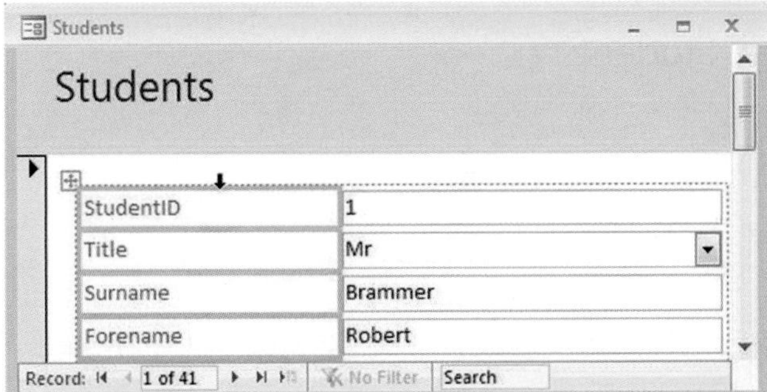

7 On the **Home** tab, in the **Font** group, click the **Bold** and **Align Text Right** buttons. See Figure 1.9.16.

Figure 1.9.16 ▶

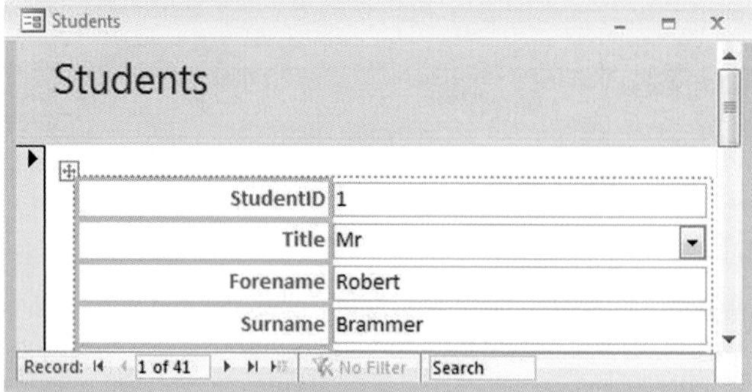

Resizing the text boxes

8 Click in the **StudentID** text box. Move the mouse pointer to the end of the text box until it turns to a double-headed arrow and resize the box by dragging to the left. All the text boxes will resize. See Figure 1.9.17.

Figure 1.9.17 ▶

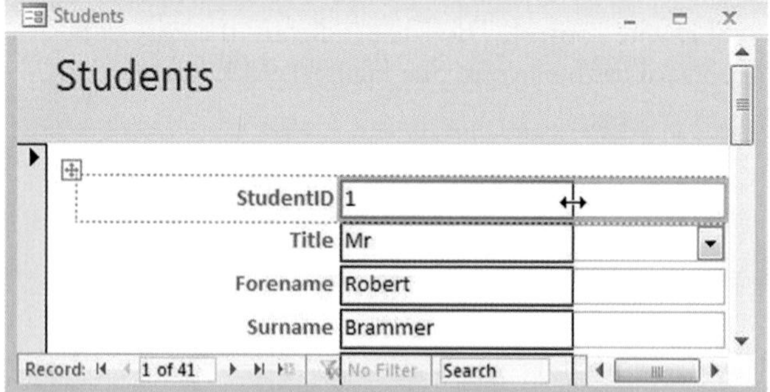

You can scroll through the records using the navigation buttons to see if the data fits the boxes. This is one advantage of using Layout View.

Resizing and moving controls independently

9 Select the layout by clicking in any control and selecting the small box to the left of the first control, see Figure 1.9.18. On the **Arrange** tab, in the **Control Layout** group, click the **Remove** button.

Figure 1.9.18 ▶

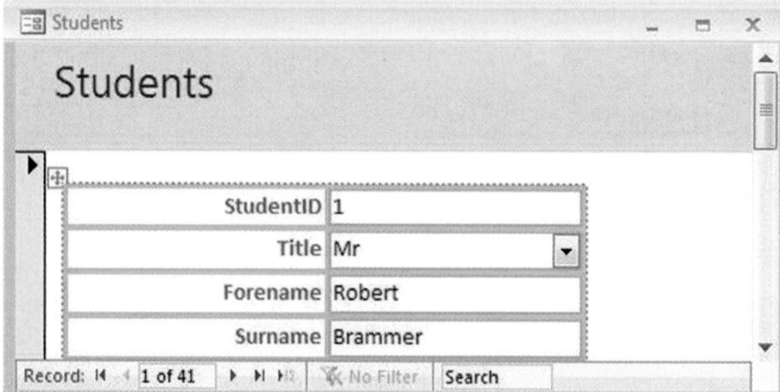

You can now move each control individually. See Figure 1.9.19.

Figure 1.9.19 ▶

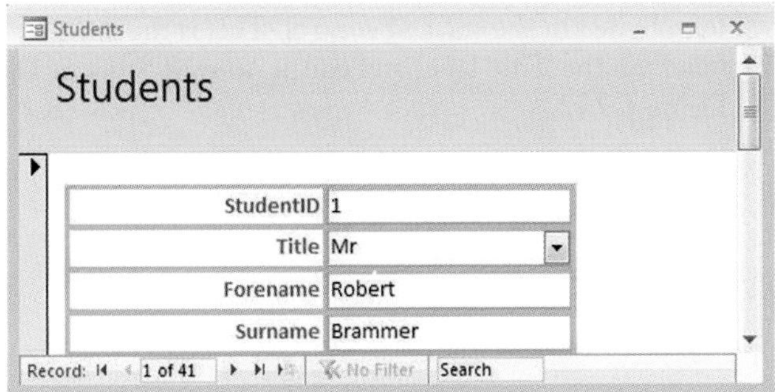

10 Highlight all the controls, from field **Address1** to the **Sex** field and drag the controls over to the right-hand side. Hold down SHIFT to select more than one control. On the **Arrange** tab, in the **Control Layout** group, click the **Stacked** button, to apply a control layout. See Figure 1.9.20.

Figure 1.9.20 ▶

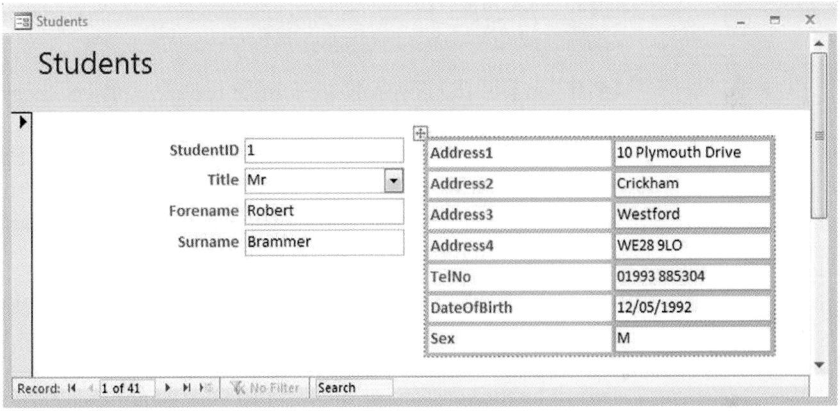

11 Select the remaining labels and text boxes in the left-hand column. On the **Arrange** tab, in the **Control Layout** group, click the **Stacked** button. You may need to select the controls at the top of each column and click the **Top** button, in the **Control Alignment** group, on the **Arrange** tab.

Figure 1.9.21 ▶

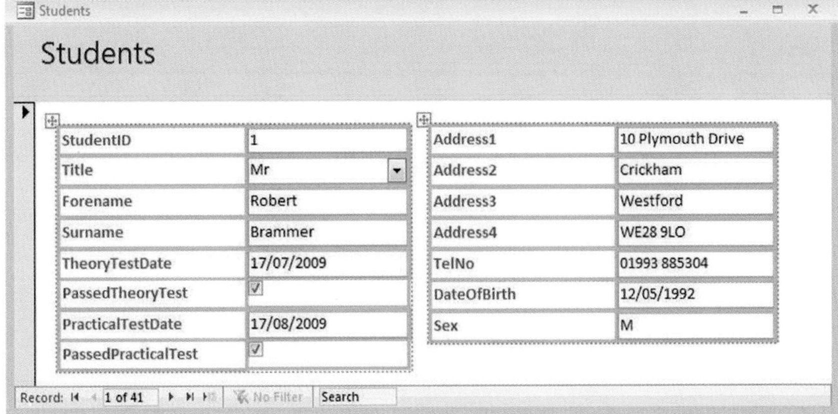

12 Double-click in each label to edit the text by inserting spaces, as shown in Figure 1.9.22. You may notice that Access puts the labels back to left-aligned in the stacked control. This is the default.

13 Click on the **Title** label and edit it, to read **Student Details.** See Figure 1.9.22

Figure 1.9.22 ▶

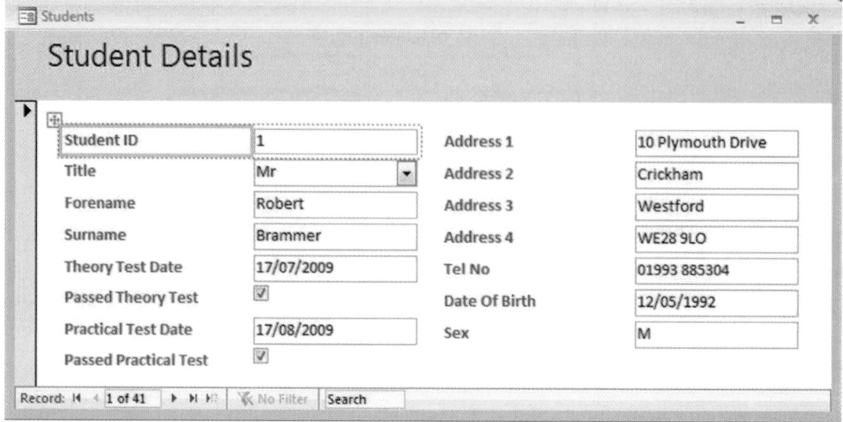

14 If you feel the controls are a little too close, then select both layouts by clicking the layout selectors while holding down SHIFT. On the **Arrange** tab, in the **Control Layout** group, click the **Control Padding** button. The default setting is **Narrow**, but you can experiment with each option.

15 If you wish, save your form although it won't be needed later in the system. Delete the form **Copy of frmStudent**.

Layout View allows you to arrange and edit your form while viewing the data. It is often common practice to use the Form Wizard to set up a form and then use Layout View to quickly arrange and edit the controls. Design View is then used to further customise the form to your requirements. This approach will be developed in Unit 10.

Note: Use **Tricks and Tips** number 40 to find out how to build a form from scratch.

Unit 10: Working in Form Design View

Most of the forms you have produced so far are all standard in layout. Form Design View allows you to customise a form to suit your requirements.

In this section you will learn how to:

- find your way around a form in Design View
- move, align and edit controls
- edit the appearance of your form.

Form Design View

You will grasp the concepts more easily by practising and experimenting with the tasks in this section.

We will start by working on a copy of a form as we did in Unit 9, so that if you make a mistake it will not affect the final system. You can use the copy from Unit 9 or quickly set one up again.

1 In the **Navigation Pane**, right-click on **frmStudent** and from the menu choose **Copy**.
2 Right-click in the **Navigation Pane** and choose **Paste**. Name the form **Copy of frmStudent** and click **OK**.
3 Open **Copy of frmStudent** in Design View by right-clicking its icon and clicking on **Design View**, as shown in Figure 1.10.1

Figure 1.10.1 ▶

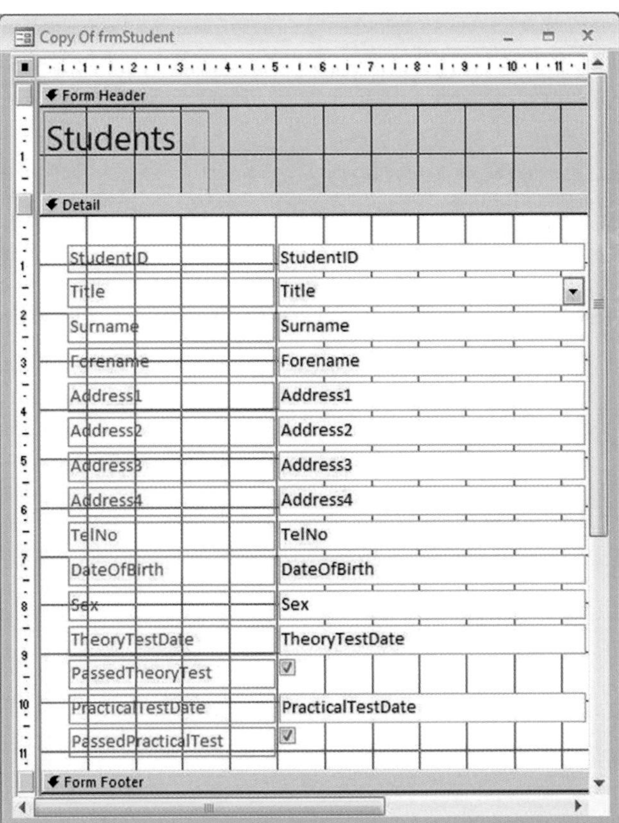

The form opens with the following features showing:

- A **Form Header** section – this area can contain text, headings, titles and graphics. Toggle the **Form Header** off and on by right-clicking in the Header and selecting **Form/Header Footer**.

Note: If the Header contains controls, you will not be able to turn it off.

- A **Detail** section – this contains the **controls** that display the data in your tables.
- A number of **Controls** each made up of a **Label** containing the field name and a **Text Box** which will contain the data in **Form View**.
- A **Form Footer** section which can be used in the same way as the Header.
- A **Right Margin** which can be dragged wider using the mouse.
- A **Ruler** and **Grid** to help you with the layout of your form. Toggle these features on and off by right-clicking in the **Detail** area and clicking on **Ruler** or **Grid** from the menu.
- The **Ribbon** shows the **Design** tab, from which you can add text, lines, shapes, controls, buttons and many other features which will be covered in the following units, see Figure 1.10.2.

Figure 1.10.2 ▼

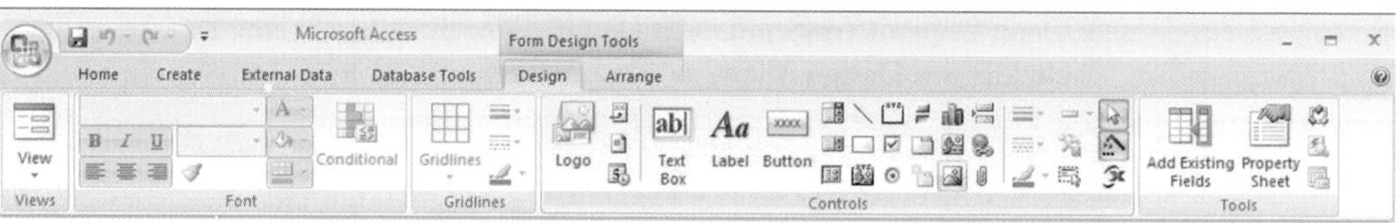

Getting a feel for your working area

When working with forms in Design View, you might need to create more room on screen. Simply click the **Open/Close Shutter Bar** to close the Navigation Pane and/or you can minimise the Ribbon by clicking the drop-down next to the **Quick Access Toolbar** and clicking **Minimize the Ribbon.**

1 With **Copy of frmStudent** open in **Design View** and maximised as shown in Figure 1.10.3, move the mouse over the right margin until it turns into a cross and drag the margin wider by about 12 cm. You can use the ruler as a guide.

2 Select the **StudentID** label and click the **Layout Selector** at the upper-left corner as shown. Remove the Layout by clicking the **Remove** button, on the **Arrange** tab. You will now be able to move the controls independently.

Figure 1.10.3 ▼

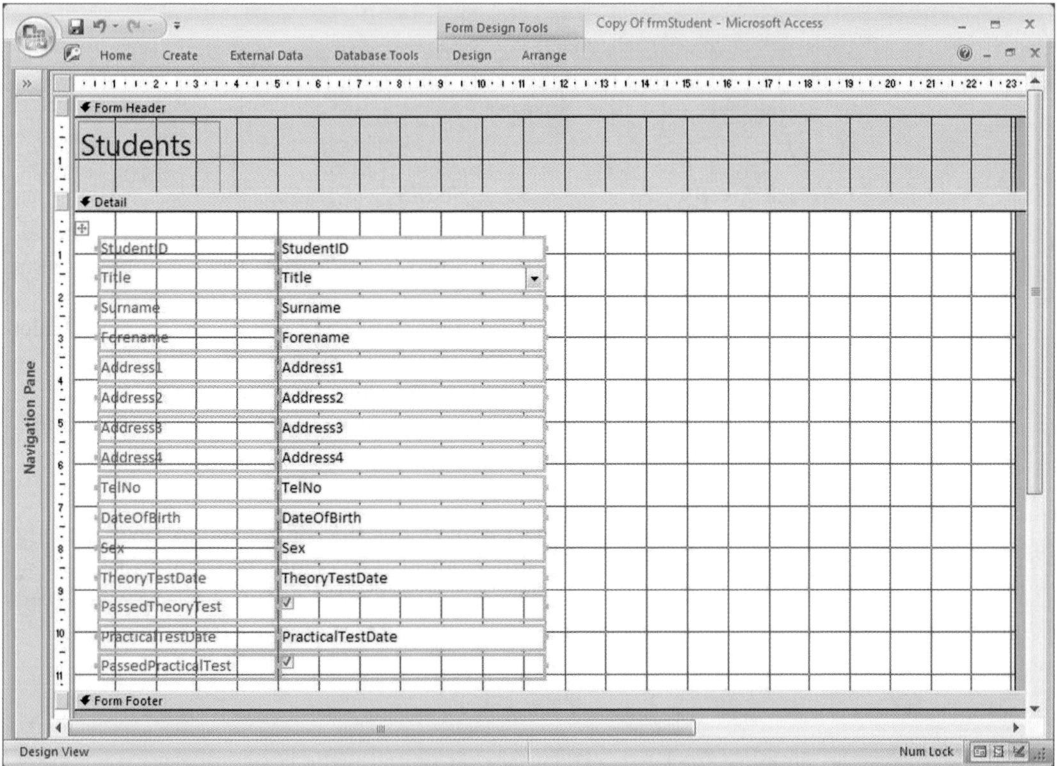

Working with controls

It is worth practising all the following steps on the currently opened **Copy of frmStudent** until you feel confident and competent with handling the controls.

Selecting controls

- To resize, move, delete, copy or change the properties of a control, first you must select it.
- Simply click anywhere in the control and it will be highlighted with 8 *sizing handles* as shown in Figure 1.10.4.

Figure 1.10.4 ►

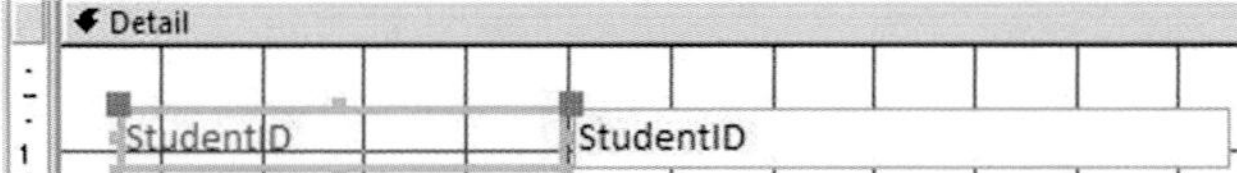

- To select more than one control, simply drag out a rectangle across the controls you want to select or select the first control and hold down SHIFT while selecting further controls. See Figure 1.10.5.

Figure 1.10.5 ▶

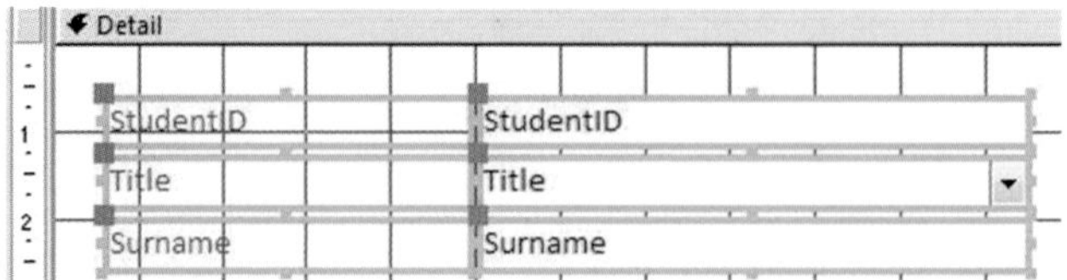

Resizing controls

- Click on the control to select it and move the mouse pointer over a selection handle until it turns to a two-headed arrow. Drag in or out to resize it. See Figure 1.10.6.

Figure 1.10.6 ▶

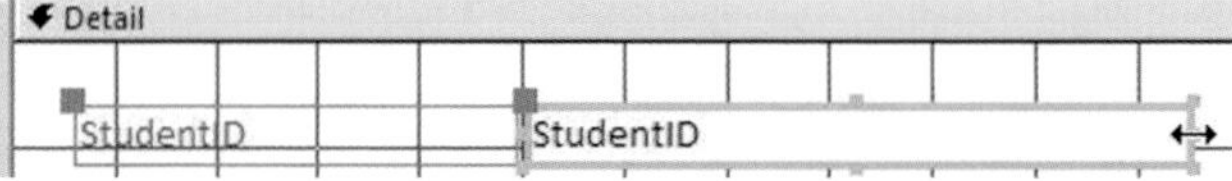

Moving controls

- Click on the control to select it. To move the control and its label, move the pointer to the border of the control. The pointer turns into a four-headed arrow as shown in Figure 1.10.7. Drag the control to a new position.

Figure 1.10.7 ▶

- To move the label without its control, select the label and place the pointer over the *larger handle* in the top left corner of the control. The pointer changes to a four-headed arrow as shown in Figure 1.10.8. Drag the control to a new position.

Figure 1.10.8 ▶

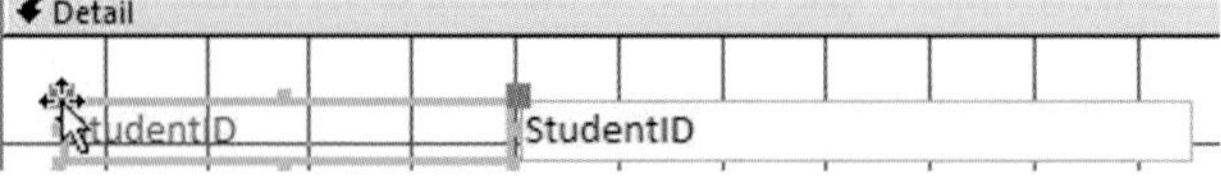

You can select more than one control, as outlined earlier, and move them at the same time.

Deleting and adding controls

- To delete a control, simply select the control and press the DELETE key.
- If you want to add a control for a field, for example, because you have deleted it, click on the **Design** tab and click the **Add Existing Fields** button.

Figure 1.10.9 ▶

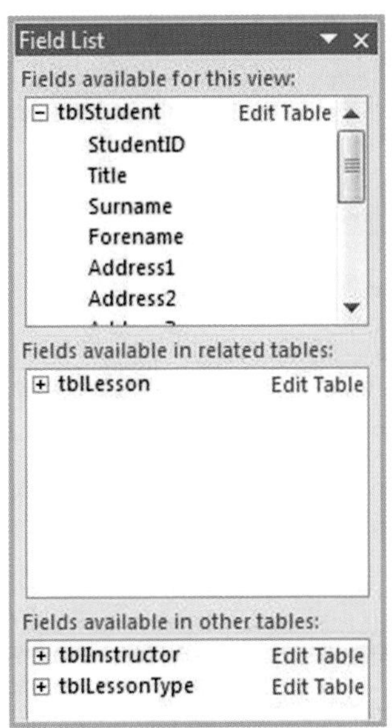

- The **Field list** will appear on the screen, Figure 1.10.9. Highlight the field and drag and drop it to the required position.

Developing a form

1. With **Copy of frmStudent** open in Design View, drag the **Form Footer** down a little.
2. Drag around the controls in the left-hand column to select the labels. Resize by dragging in a little.
3. Drag around the controls in the right-hand column to select the text boxes. Resize again by dragging in a little. See Figure 1.10.10.

Figure 1.10.10 ▶

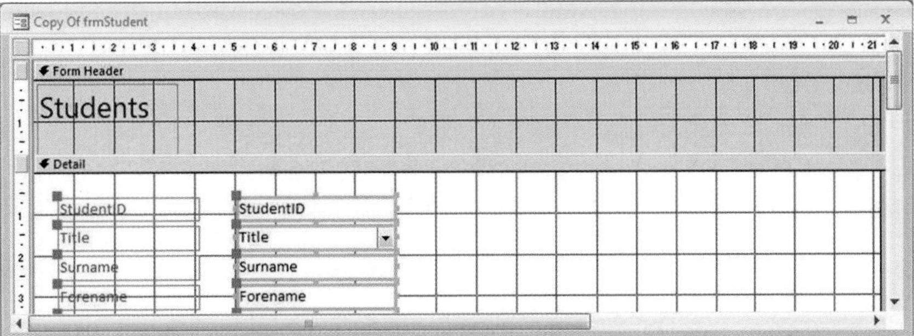

4 Select the **TelNo** control and move the control to the right-hand side, roughly in line with the **StudentID** field. See Figure 1.10.11.

Figure 1.10.11 ▶

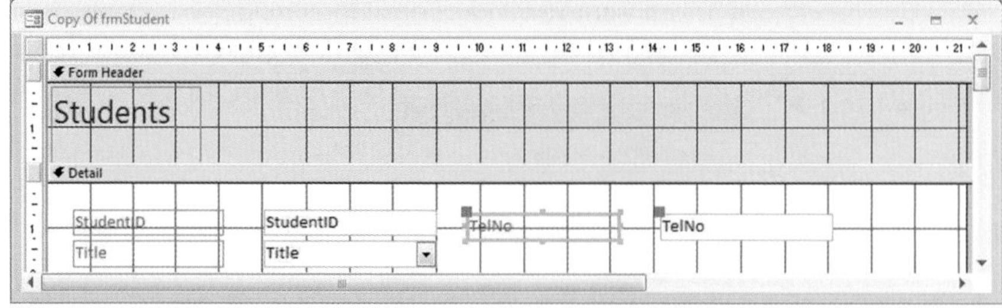

5 Drag-and-drop the remaining controls over to the right-hand side as shown in Figure 1.10.12.

Do not worry about accuracy. Access provides a number of formatting tools to help you. The untidier the better!

6 Drag down each of the controls in the left-hand column to give yourself some room on the screen. See Figure 1.10.12.

Figure 1.10.12 ▶

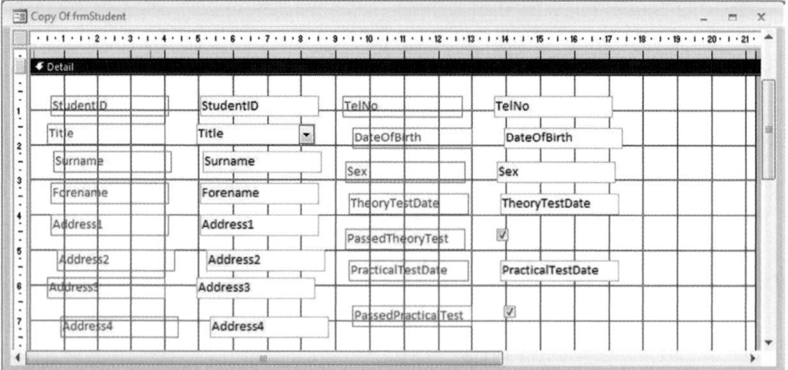

Using the Arrange tab

The **Arrange** tab shown in Figure 1.10.13 offers a number of tools to align and arrange your controls. There is no set way but the following steps should ensure accuracy. Remember you can use the **Undo** option!

Figure 1.10.13 ▼

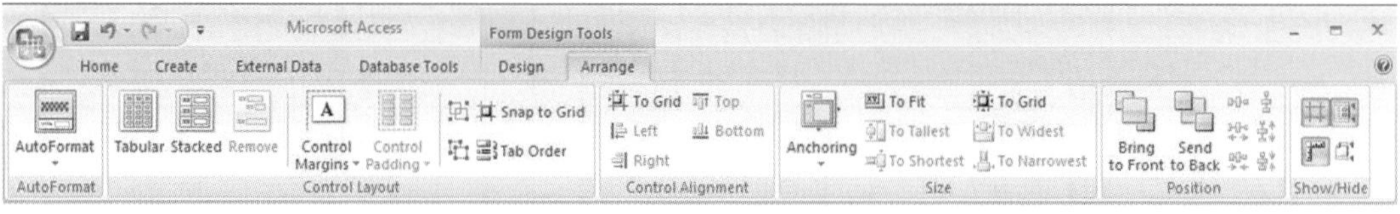

The **Arrange** tab is particularly useful for fine-tuning forms and reports.

The **Control Alignment** group of buttons allows you to select a group of controls, such as labels and command buttons, and align them to the **Top**, **Left**, **Right** or **Bottom**.

The **Size** group allows you to select a group of controls, such as labels and command buttons, and make them equal in size by sizing to the **Tallest**, **Smallest**, **Widest** or **Narrowest**.

In the **Position** group are buttons that allow you to **Increase**, **Decrease** or **Make Equal** the distance between controls.

From the **Show/Hide** group, you can control **Gridlines**, **Ruler**, **Headers** and **Footers**.

1 Highlight the labels in the first column of controls by dragging over them. On the **Arrange** tab, in the **Control Alignment** group, click on the **Left** button.
2 Highlight the text boxes in the first column of controls by dragging over them. On the **Arrange** tab, in the **Control Alignment** group, click on the **Left** button again.
3 Repeat the same steps for the controls in the right-hand column.
4 Align the control **StudentID** with **TelNo** to establish the uppermost position for each column. Select both controls, and on the **Arrange** tab, in the **Control Alignment** group, click on the **Top** button. See Figure 1.10.14.

Figure 1.10.14 ▶

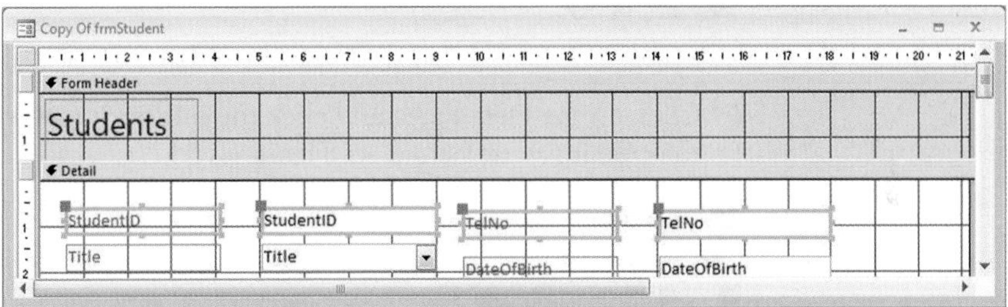

5 Highlight the first column of controls (labels and text boxes). On the **Arrange** tab, in the **Position** group, click on the **Make Vertical Spacing Equal (Equal Vertical)** button**.** There are **Increase** and **Decrease** options to help further.
6 Highlight the second column of controls. On the **Arrange** tab, in the **Position** group, click on the **Make Vertical Spacing Equal** button. You might consider aligning the lowermost controls and repeating the process.
7 Drag the **Form Footer** up and **Right Margin** in to make better use of the screen. If you are happy with your design, switch to **Form View**, minimise the window and, on the **Home** tab, click the **Size to Fit Form** button in the **Window** group.
8 Save your form. It should appear as shown in Figure 1.10.15.

Figure 1.10.15 ▶

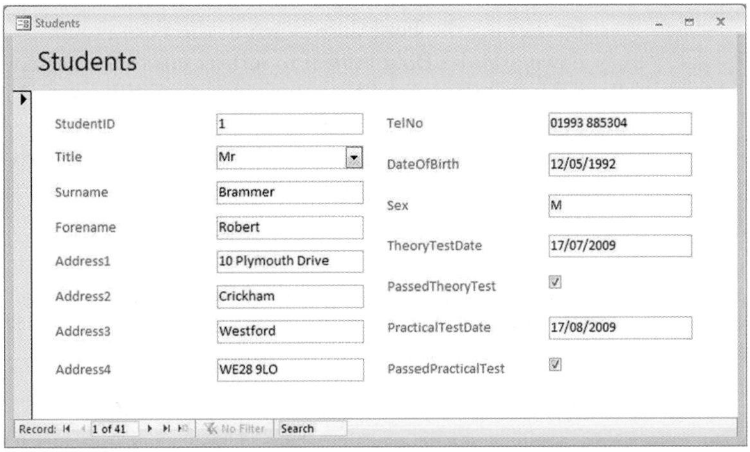

During the course of the next exercises you will be introduced to a number of ways of improving the appearance of your form. Throughout this section, do not be afraid to practise and experiment. Remember, you can always delete it and start again or, as a last resort, get the wizards to do it again!

Fonts, colours, special effects, rectangles and lines

1 Open the **Copy of frmStudentCopy** in Design View.

On the **Design** tab, in the **Font** group, is a range of formatting options which will be familiar to students who have a working knowledge of Windows software, see Figure 1.10.16.

Figure 1.10.16 ▶

2 Click on the **Detail** area and click the **Fill/Back Color** drop-down to show the colour palette below, see Figure 1.10.17.

Figure 1.10.17 ▶

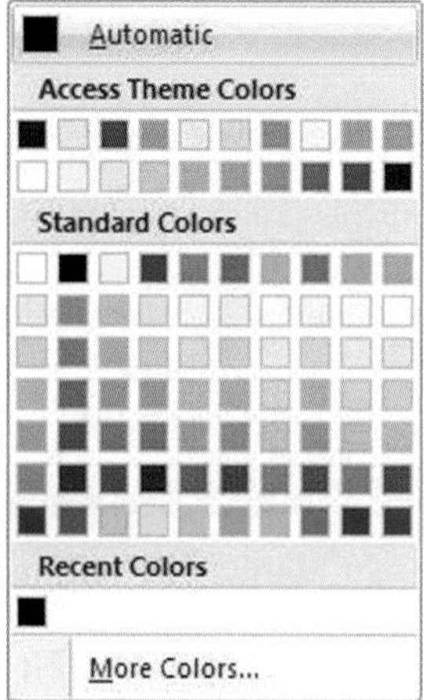

3 Select a suitable colour for the background to your form.

4 Select the labels of all the controls and set the font to one of your choice by clicking the **Font** drop-down in the **Font** group. Use the **Font Size** drop-down and the **Bold** button to further customise the controls.

5 Select all the labels again and click the **Fill/Back Color** drop-down in the **Font** group.

6 Choose a colour to make your labels stand out from the background colour of the form. Remember, switching to Form View will show you how your changes will look.

On the **Design** tab, in the **Controls** group, is a range of further options as shown in Figure 1.10.18, some of which are worth experimenting with here.

Figure 1.10.18 ▶

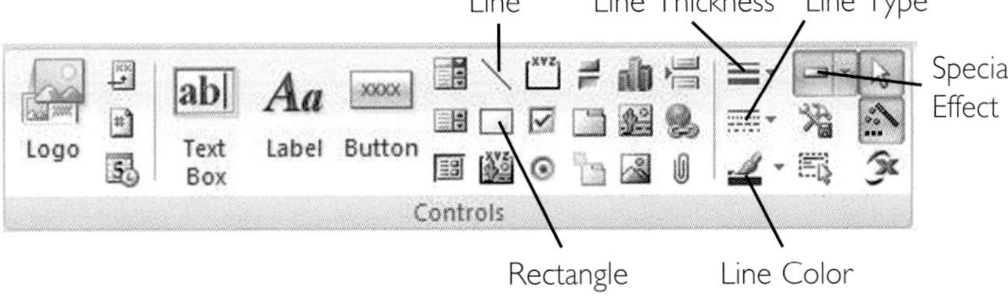

7 With the labels still selected, click the **Special Effect** drop-down in the **Controls** group and choose **Raised** from the **Special Effect** window shown in Figure 1.10.19.

Figure 1.10.19 ▶

8 Delete the Title label in the Form Header. On the **Design** tab, click the **Label** button and drag out a rectangle in the **Form Header**. Type in a suitable heading and press ENTER.
9 Set the font, background colour and special effect as required.
10 Click on the **Rectangle** button and drag out a box around the control. Select the box and use the **Line Type**, **Line Thickness** and **Line Color** drop-downs to customise the rectangle.
11 There is no need to save your form. The next section starts on the Student form which will go through to become part of our final solution.

Note: If you right-click in the **Detail** area or on any control, you will get a menu from which a number of options are offered for quicker access.

Making a start on the Student form

We now need to go back to our original Student form and develop it for later use.

1 Open the **frmStudent** in **Layout View**. Highlight the **Text Box** column and drag the controls in a little, to fit the data. You might consider reducing the sizes of the labels in the same way.
2 Click on the **Layout** selector. On the **Arrange** tab, click the **Remove** button. You can now move the controls independently.

3 Switch to **Design View** and move the controls from **TelNo** to **PassedPracticalTest** to the top of the right-hand column. Align the **TelNo** field to the **Title** field, as shown in Figure 1.10.20.

Figure 1.10.20 ▶

4 Delete the **Label** in the **Form Header** section by selecting it and pressing DELETE. Click on the **Label** button and drag out a rectangle in the **Form Header**. Type in the text **Pass IT Driving School** and press ENTER (see Figure 1.10.21).

Figure 1.10.21 ▶

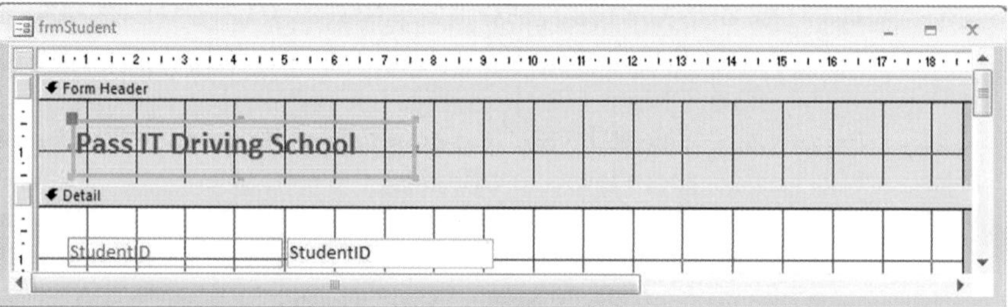

5 With the new control selected, set the **Font Colour** to **Dark Blue (Text Dark)** and the **Font Size** to **18-pt**, **Bold Calibri**. Remember to switch to Form View to see your changes.

Setting control properties

You can customise any control on a form by opening its **Property Sheet**. With the control selected as shown in Figure 1.10.21, click on the **Property Sheet** button, in the **Tools** group on the **Design** tab.

Note: You can also right-click on the control and select **Properties** from the menu, or simply press **F4**.

Figure 1.10.22 shows the Property Sheet for the control in the Form Header with the **Font Name**, **Font Size**, **Font Weight** and **Font (fore) Color** set to **Calibri, 18 pt, Bold, Text Dark**. You might wish to explore some of the other options.

Figure 1.10.22 ▶

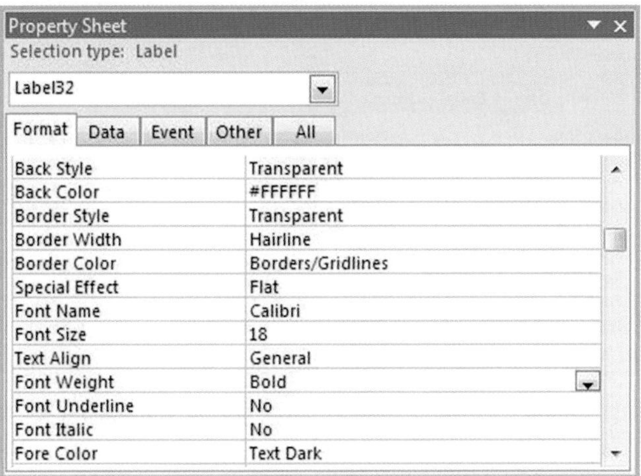

You will now put a simple frame around the controls.

6 Click on the **Rectangle** button in the **Controls** group and drag a rectangle around all the controls in the **Detail** section. You will need to create a little room to do this by repositioning all the controls. See Figure 1.10.23.
7 Click on the **Property Sheet** button for the control and ensure the **Special Effect** property is set to **Flat**.
8 Repeat the process by placing a rectangle around the title in the **Form Header** section.

Figure 1.10.23 ▶

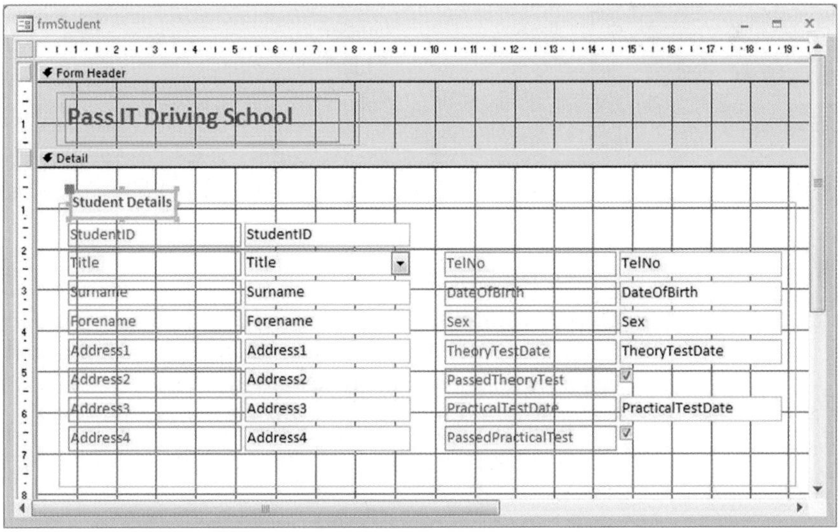

9 Add a **Label** with the text **Student Details**. Click the **Property Sheet** button and set the **Back Style** to **Normal** with the **Font Name**, **Font Size** and **Font Weight** set to **Calibri, 11 pt** and **Bold**. See Figure 1.10.24.

10 Maximise the form and drag the **Right Margin** in and **Form Footer** up to best fit the size of your form. Switch to **Form View**, minimise the form and in the Window group, click on the **Size to Fit Form** button.

Figure 1.10.24 ▶

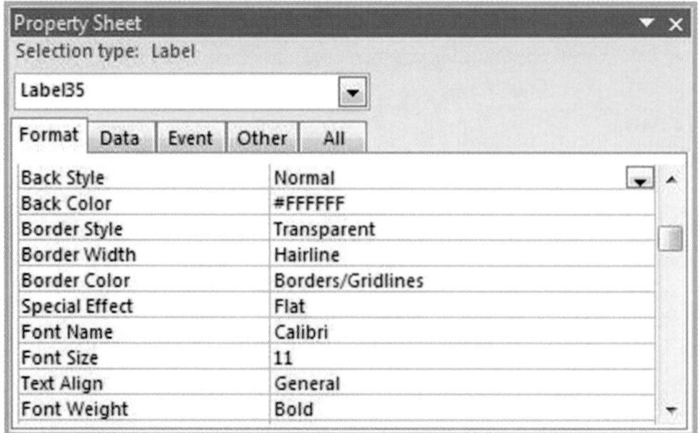

11 Save your form as **frmStudent**. It should appear as in Figure 1.10.25. The form contains a Dividing Line, Record Selector and Navigation Buttons. The next step will explain how to customise those features.

Figure 1.10.25 ▶

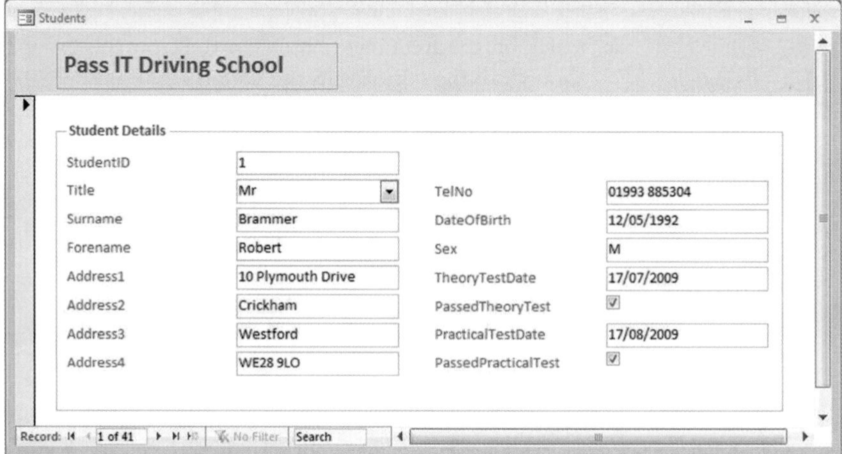

Setting Form Properties

You can control the behaviour and appearance of your form by setting the form's properties. In the Student form you have just completed it may look better without a number of features.

It still has the Record Selector, the Record Navigation Controls, Maximise, Minimise and Close buttons. These can be removed using the Form Property Sheet.

Note: The record selector is a column on the left-hand side of a form used to select a whole record in a form. For example, you might use this to delete a record rather than just delete one field.

1 In **Design View**, double-click on the **Form Selector** (see Figure 1.10.26) at the top left of the form.

Figure 1.10.26 ▶

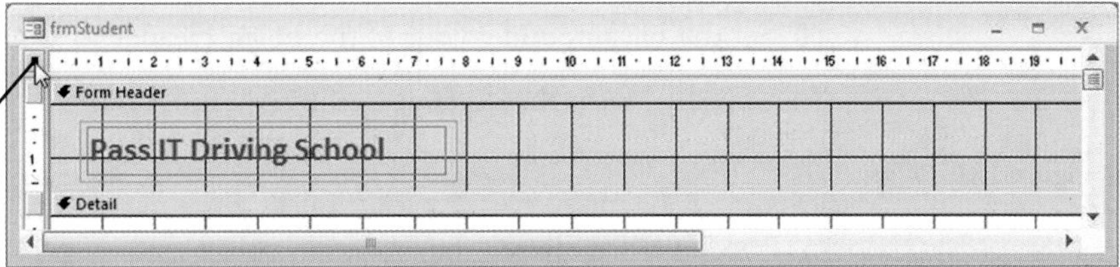

2 The Property Sheet for the form is displayed (see Figure 1.10.27).

There are far too many properties to cover all the available options here.

The properties are grouped for easier access. Clicking on the **Format** tab will give a range of options covering the appearance of your form.

3 Change the form caption using the **Caption** property to **Student Details**.

Figure 1.10.27 ▶

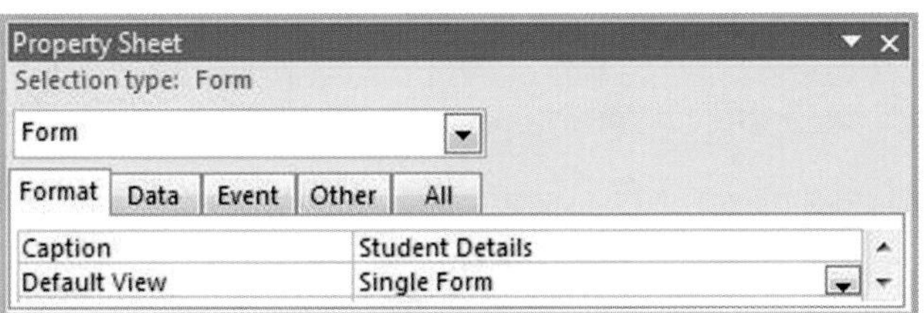

4 Remove the Scroll Bars at the bottom and right-hand side of the form by setting the **Scroll Bars** property to **Neither**.

Figure 1.10.28 ▶

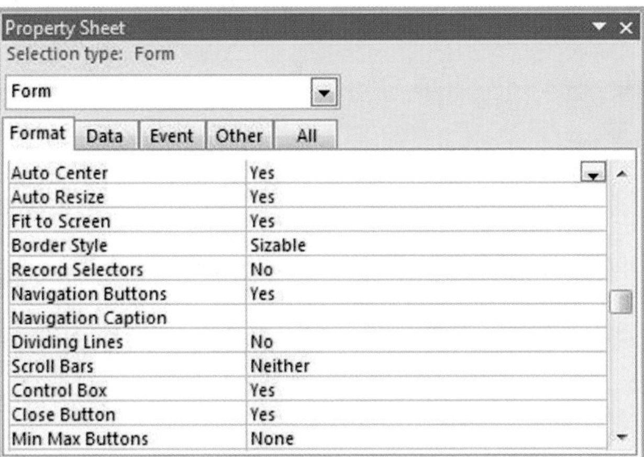

5 Remove the Record Selector on the form by setting the **Record Selectors** property to **No**.

6 We will leave the Navigation Buttons at the bottom of the form, but they can be removed by setting the **Navigation Buttons** property to **No**.

7 Make the form appear in the middle of the screen by setting the **Auto Center** property to **Yes.**

8 Remove the Maximise and Minimise buttons from a form by setting the **Min Max Buttons** property to **None**.

9 While in **Design View**, edit the Labels to be more user-friendly, for example, change DateOfBirth to Date of Birth. Edit the Label directly or double-click the **Label** and edit the **Caption** property.
10 Set the background colour of the **Form Header** to **White**.

Your finished form should appear as in Figure 1.10.29.

Figure 1.10.29 ▶

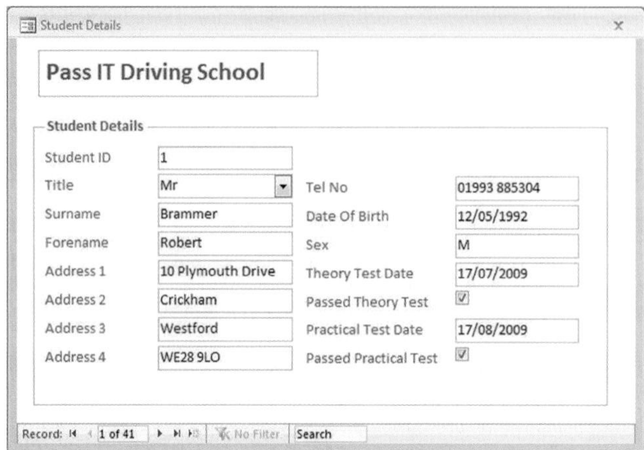

Unit 11: Taking form design further

This section describes some of the additional features that you can add to your forms to create a professional feel to your system.

You will learn how to:

- add graphics
- add the date and time
- add command buttons
- add combo boxes
- create forms to display data from more than one table.

Adding graphics to the form

Graphics can easily be added to your form using copy and paste. The graphic appears in an unbound object frame enabling you to move or size the frame as needed. Alternatively, follow these steps.

1 Ensure the image is already saved in a format that Access can recognise, such as **jpg**, **gif** or **bmp**. Our image is the PASS IT logo (see Figure 1.11.1). The image is available on the support website.

Figure 1.11.1 ▶

PA55 IT

2 Open **frmStudent** in **Design View**.

3 Click the **Image** button in the **Controls** group (see Figure 1.11.2) and drag out a rectangle in the Form Header.

Figure 1.11.2 ▼

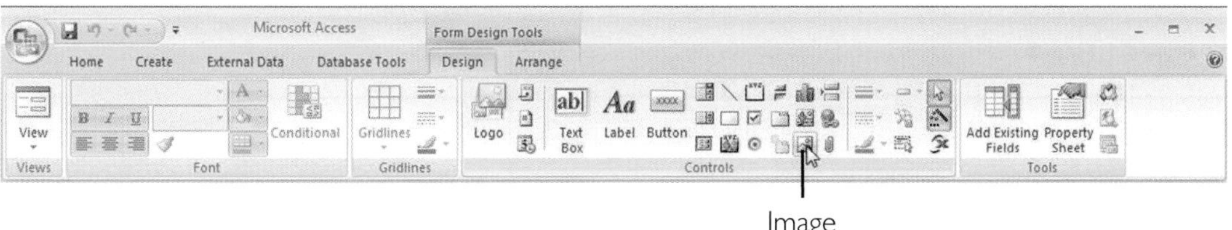

4 Select the image you want to add to the form from the **Insert Picture** dialog box. If the image does not fit the frame, then right-click on the image, select **Properties** and set the **Size Mode** property to **Zoom** or **Clip**. Alternatively, resize it by dragging the resize handles in/out. See Figure 1.11.3.

Figure 1.11.3 ▶

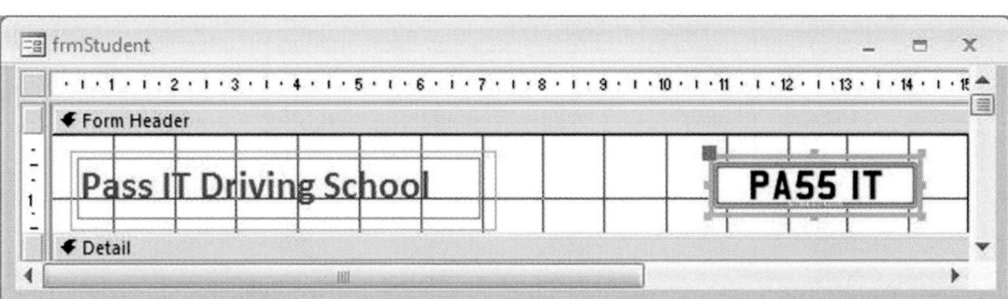

5 Set the **Special Effect** property of the image to **Flat** and its **Border Style** property to **Transparent**. Place a rectangle around it in the same way as you did for the header in Unit 10. See Figure 1.11.4.

Figure 1.11.4 ▶

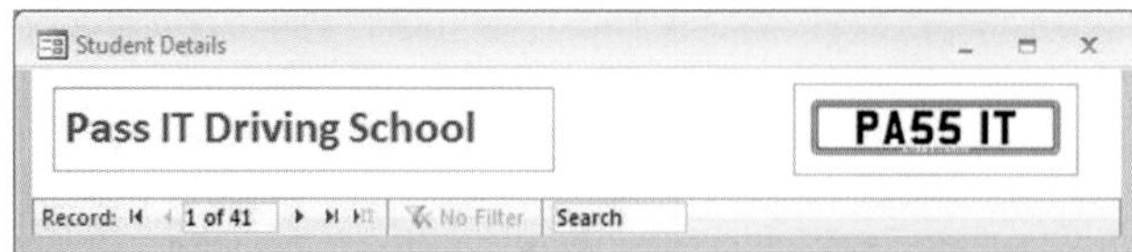

6 Save your form as **frmStudent**. The header should appear as in Figure 1.11.4.

Note: On the **Design** tab there is a **Logo** button which operates in much the same way as the above method, by default placing the logo in the form header.

Adding the Date and Time to a form

1 With **frmStudent** open in Design View, click on the **Date & Time** button (see Figure 1.11.5).

Figure 1.11.5 ▶

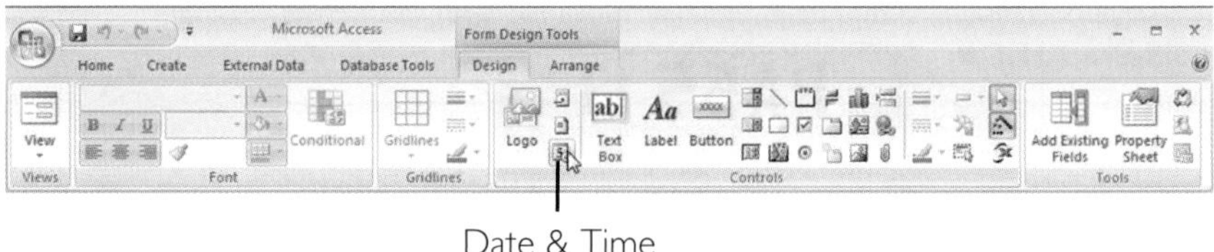

2 The **Date and Time** window is shown, Figure 1.11.6. Select the **Date/Time** options and click on **OK**.

Figure 1.11 6 ▶

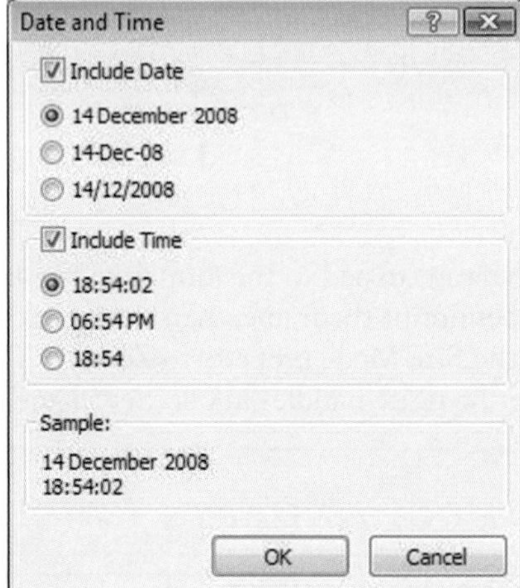

3 Position and resize the controls between the **Logo** and **Title**. Set the **Font** to **Calibri**, **9pt**, **bold**, **dark blue** and **Centre Align** the text (see Figure 1.11.7).

Figure 1.11.7 ▶

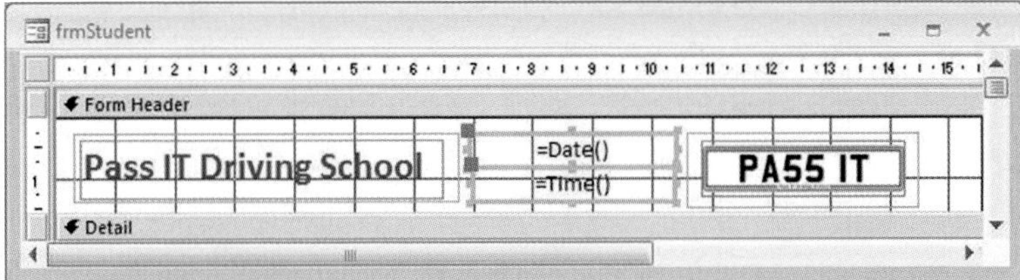

4 Add a frame around the controls and save your form as **frmStudent** (see Figure 1.11.8).

Figure 1.11.8 ▶

Student Details

Pass IT Driving School | 14 December 2008 18:55:38 | PA55 IT

Student Details

Student ID	1		
Title	Mr	Tel No	01993 885304
Surname	Brammer	Date Of Birth	12/05/1992
Forename	Robert	Sex	M
Address 1	10 Plymouth Drive	Theory Test Date	17/07/2009
Address 2	Crickham	Passed Theory Test	☑
Address 3	Westford	Practical Test Date	17/08/2009
Address 4	WE28 9LO	Passed Practical Test	☑

Record: 1 of 41 No Filter Search

The Instructor form

In exactly the same way as you developed the Student form, you now need to develop the Instructor form to look as shown in Figure 1.11.9.

You will notice Pass IT has been removed from the header and replaced with the logo. The Special Effect property of the logo has been set to Raised. You may experiment and come up with a better design but make sure that all the forms have the same layout. We will show you how to add the command buttons in the next section.

Figure 1.11.9 ▶

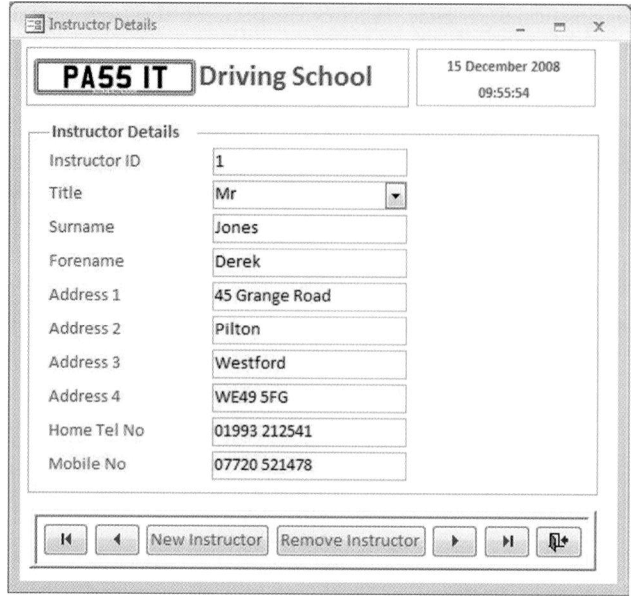

Adding command buttons

Access allows you to automate tasks by creating command buttons and placing them on your form.

Command buttons can be added to deal with a number of operations including:

- Record navigation
- Opening forms and reports
- Printing
- Other commonly used operations.

You can set up a command button in one of two ways:

- Use the Command Button Wizard to set up the button and attach the operation.
- Create the button without the Wizard and attach it to a macro or code.

We will be dealing with macros later. We will start by using the Wizards to set up buttons to move between the records, add/delete records and quit the application from our Student form (see Figure 1.11.8).

1. Open **frmStudent** in Design View.
2. We are going to add the buttons to the lower section of the form. You will have to drag down the Form Footer area to create a little room. See Figure 1.11.10.

Figure 1.11.10 ▶

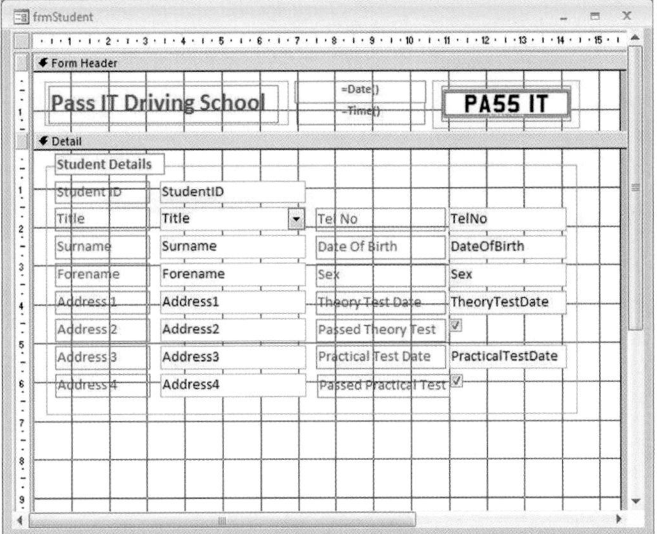

3 In the **Controls** group, click on **Button** (see Figure 1.11.11) and click on the form where you want to place the button. This displays the Command Button Wizard dialog box (see Figure 1.11.12).

Figure 1.11.11 ▼

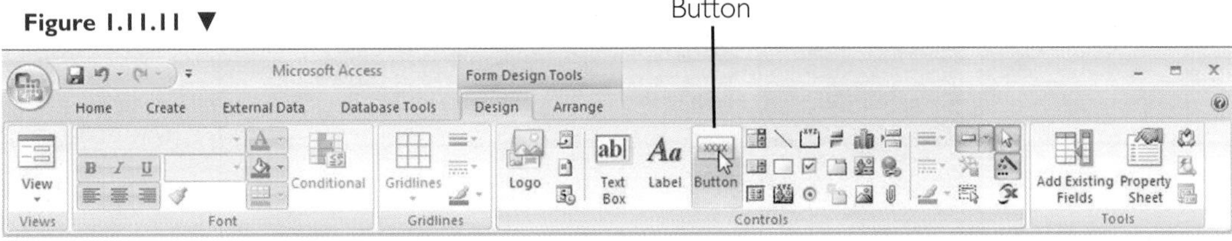

Figure 1.11.12 ▶

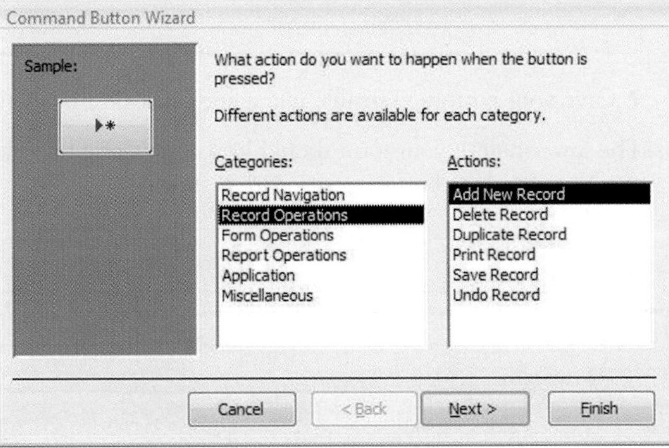

4 In the Categories list, select **Record Operations**.
5 In the Actions list, select **Add New Record** and click on **Next**.

The next window offers you a choice of putting pictures or text on the button. If you choose text, you can type in the text you want to go on the button.

If you choose picture you can select from a list or browse the file area to find one of your own (see Figure 1.11.13).

Figure 1.11.13 ▶

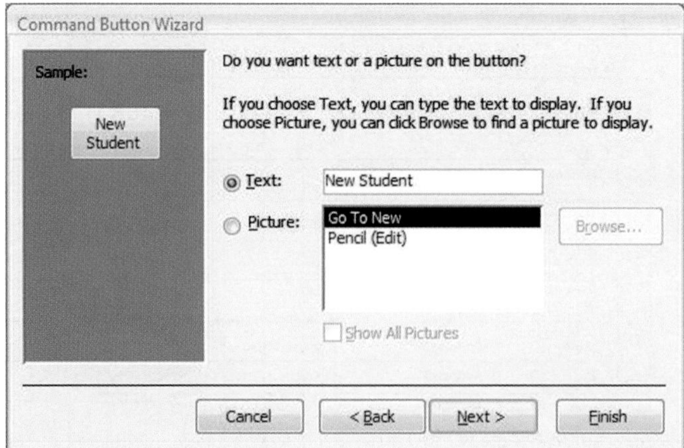

6 We are going to use text, so choose the **Text** option, enter **New Student** and click on **Next**.

Figure 1.11.14 ▶

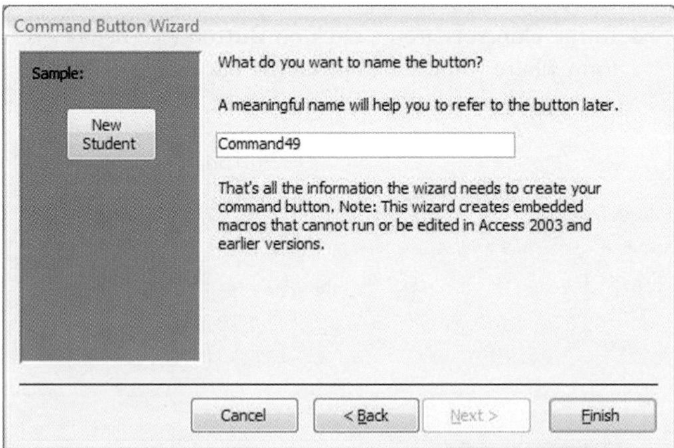

7 Give your button a sensible name and click on **Finish** (see Figure 1.11.14).

The lower half of your form should look something like Figure 1.11.15, with the **New Student** button positioned as shown.

Figure 1.11.15 ▶

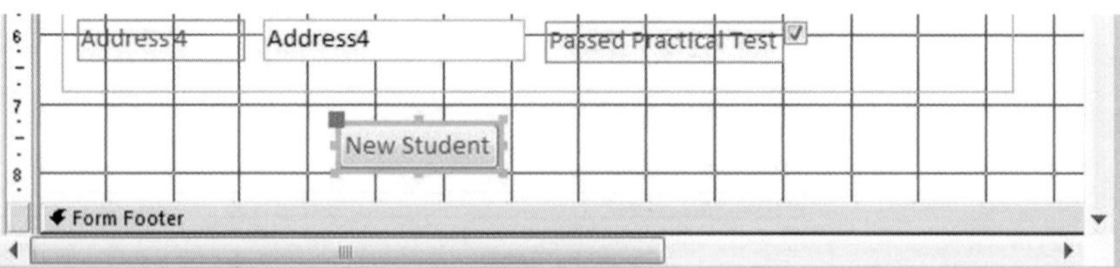

Hint You may want to change the Font on the button. Open the **Property Sheet** for the button and set the **Fore Color** property to **Text Dark** (our choice). On the **Design** tab, in the **Controls** group, click the **Set Control Defaults** button. Text Dark will become the default for all your buttons.

8 Add another button from the **Record Operations** to **Delete a Record**, label it **Remove Student**.

9 Add extra buttons from the **Record Navigation** category using the actions **Go To First Record**, **Go To Previous Record**, **Go To Next Record** and **Go To Last Record**. Don't worry about aligning the buttons yet.

10 Add the **Close Form** button from the **Form Operations** category.

You need to arrange the buttons in the order shown in Figure 1.11.16.

Figure 1.11.16 ▶

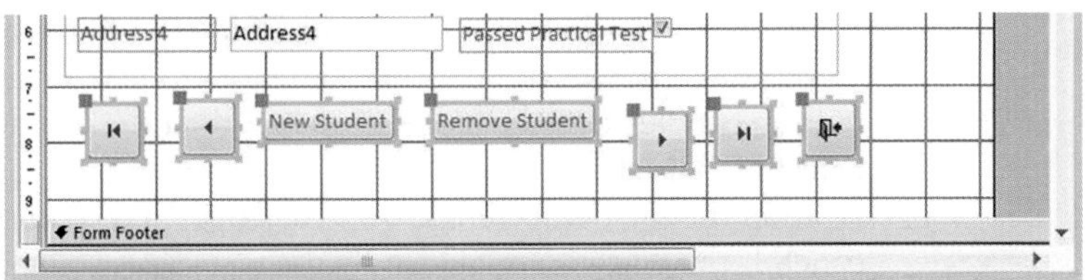

11 Select all the controls and align them by clicking on the **Top** button, in the **Control Alignment** group on the **Arrange** tab.

Hint Move the mouse pointer over the vertical ruler until it changes to a pointing arrow. Drag down the ruler to select a range of controls.

12 Distribute the buttons evenly by again selecting all and clicking on the **Make Horizontal Spacing Equal (Equal Horizontal)** button, in the **Position** group on the **Arrange** tab.

13 You may want to make the buttons smaller and the same size, as shown in Figure 1.11.17. Select all the buttons and click on the **Size to Shortest** button in the **Size** group on the **Arrange** tab.

14 We will remove the Navigation Buttons later now that we no longer need them. Save your form.

Note: Remember you will not be able to use the option Remove Student because of referential integrity and the Cascade Delete option has not been checked. Removing records at this point would remove related records in the Lesson table. We will discuss this later in the units.

Figure 1.11.17 ▶

Student Details

Pass IT Driving School

14 December 2008
19:51:50

PA55 IT

Student Details

Student ID	1		
Title	Mr	Tel No	01993 885304
Surname	Brammer	Date Of Birth	12/05/1992
Forename	Robert	Sex	M
Address 1	10 Plymouth Drive	Theory Test Date	17/07/2009
Address 2	Crickham	Passed Theory Test	☑
Address 3	Westford	Practical Test Date	17/08/2009
Address 4	WE28 9LO	Passed Practical Test	☑

New Student Remove Student

Record: 1 of 41 No Filter Search

Adding a control panel

It is common practice to keep user buttons away from data entry areas. We are going to add a background to give a control-panel effect.

1 On the **Design** tab, click on the **Rectangle** button and drag out a rectangle big enough to cover the buttons.
2 Select the rectangle and set its **Special Effect** to **Sunken**.
3 Select the rectangle and use copy and paste to make a copy of it. Use the resizing handles to make it slightly larger than the first and set its **Special Effect** to **Raised.**
4 Position the smaller rectangle over the larger and centre the buttons on the panel. If the buttons are hidden by the rectangles you may need to go to the **Arrange** tab and click on the **Bring to Front** button (see Figure 1.11.18).

Figure 1.11.18 ▶

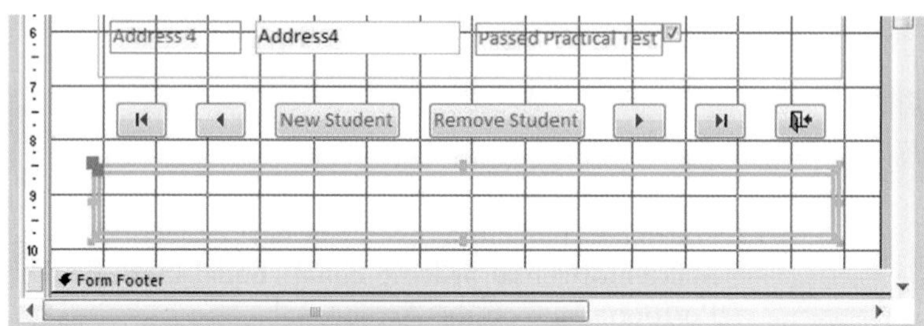

5 You may wish to set the **Fill Color** property of the rectangle to make it stand out. Save your form as **frmStudent**. Your form should now appear as in Figure 1.11.19.

Figure 1.11.19 ▶

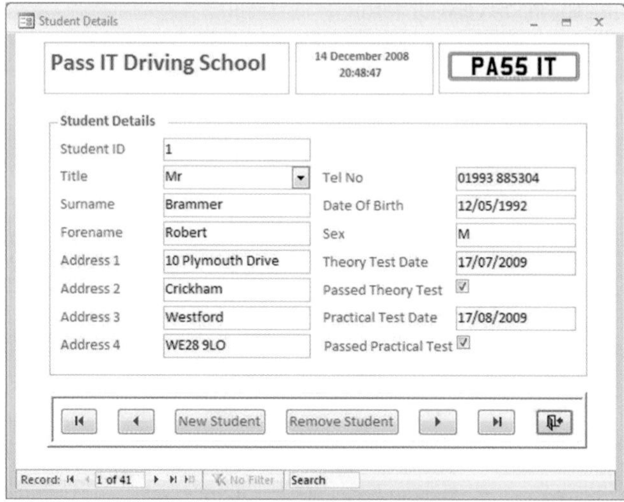

You could now go into the **Form Properties** and set the **Navigation Buttons** property to **No**. The next stage is to set up a control panel and buttons in exactly the same way on the **frmInstructor**.

Combo boxes

Combo boxes are drop-down boxes that allow the user to select data from a list of choices or type in data of their own. We will set up a combo box on the Student form so that user can simply enter M or F in the Sex field by selecting from a drop-down box.

Adding a combo box to enter student details

1 Open the form **frmStudent** in Design View.
2 Select the **Sex** control and press the DELETE key.
3 On the **Design** tab, in the **Controls** group, click on the **Combo Box** button (see Figure 1.11.20).

Figure 1.11.20 ▼

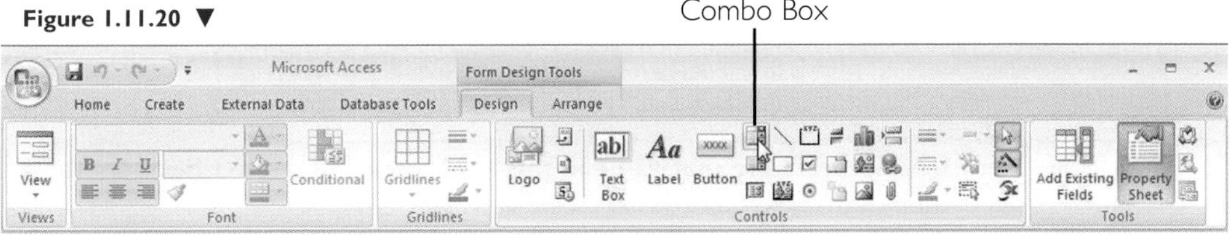

4 Drag out a small rectangle where the **Sex** control was.
5 The **Combo Box Wizard** dialog box is displayed. Check "**I will type in the values that I want**" and click on **Next** (see Figure 1.11.21).

Figure 1.11.21 ►

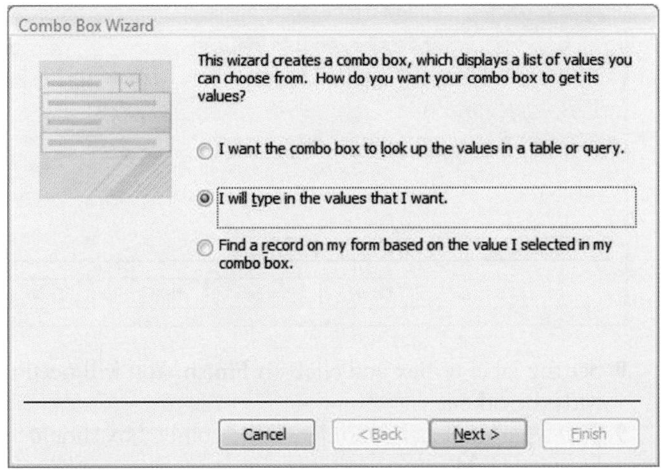

6 Enter **M** and the **F** pressing the TAB key in between entries and click on **Next** (see Figure 1.11.22).

Figure 1.11.22 ▶

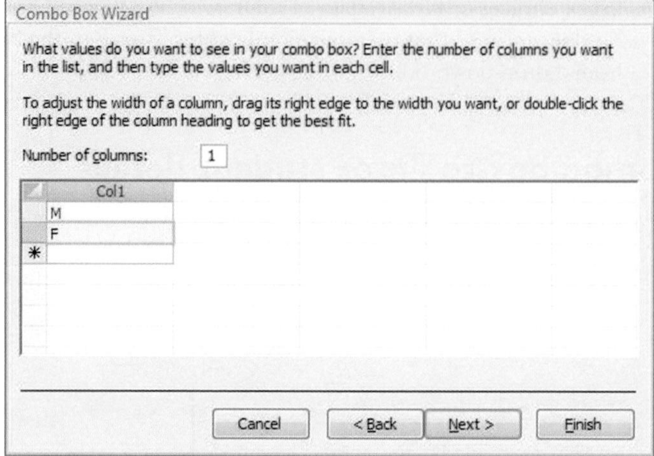

7 Check the "**Store that value in this field**" option and select **Sex** from the drop-down box. Click **Next** (see Figure 1.11.23).

Figure 1.11.23 ▶

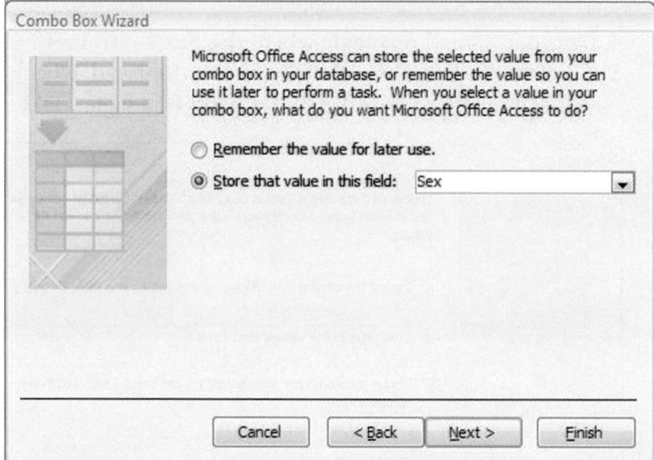

8 Set the label to **Sex** and click on **Finish**. You will need to align the control with the others.

9 Save your form as **frmStudent**. The combo box should appear as in Figure 1.11.24.

Figure 1.11.24 ▶

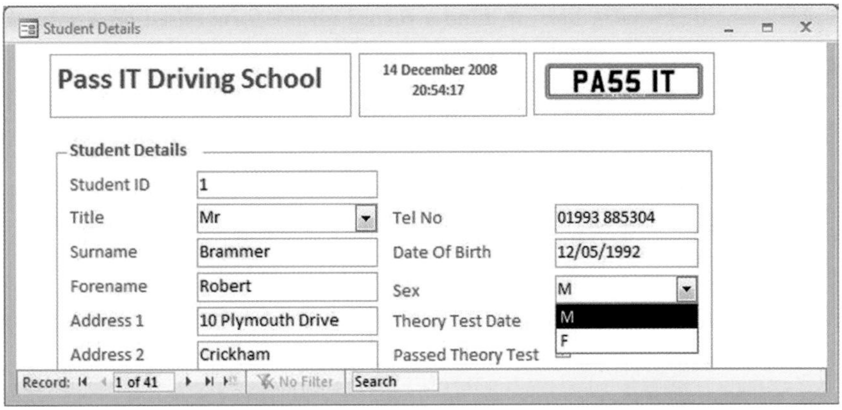

Student Details
Pass IT Driving School
14 December 2008
20:54:17
PA55 IT
Student Details
Student ID
1
Title
Mr
Tel No
01993 885304
Surname
Brammer
Date Of Birth
12/05/1992
Forename
Robert
Sex
M
Address 1
10 Plymouth Drive
Theory Test Date
M
Address 2
Crickham
Passed Theory Test
F
Record: 1 of 41
No Filter
Search

List boxes

List boxes can also be used on forms when a user can only select from a set of predefined choices. They can be added to the form using the List Box button in the same way as combo boxes.

Using Option Buttons and Option Groups are other methods Access offers for entering data on a form. Further information on this can be found in the **Tricks and Tips** sections **Using option buttons** and **Using option groups**.

Adding a combo box to look up student details

We are going to set up a combo box to display the names of all our students.

When a student is selected in the combo box, their details will appear on the form.

1 Open **frmStudent** in Design View.
2 Click on the **Combo Box** button on the **Design** tab.
3 Drag out a rectangle above the second column of controls to start the **Combo Box Wizard**. You may have to group the controls and move them a little to create room (see Figure 1.11.25).

Figure 1.11.25 ▶

frmStudent
Form Header
Pass IT Driving School
=Date()
=Time()
PA55 IT
Detail
Student Details
Student ID
StudentID
Combo57:
Unbound
Title
Title
Tel No
TelNo

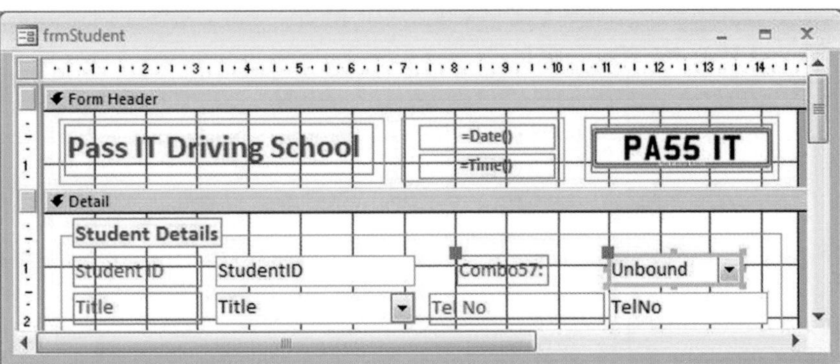

4 Click on "**Find a record on my form based on a value I selected in my combo box**". Click on **Next** (see Figure 1.11.26).

Figure 1.11.26 ▶

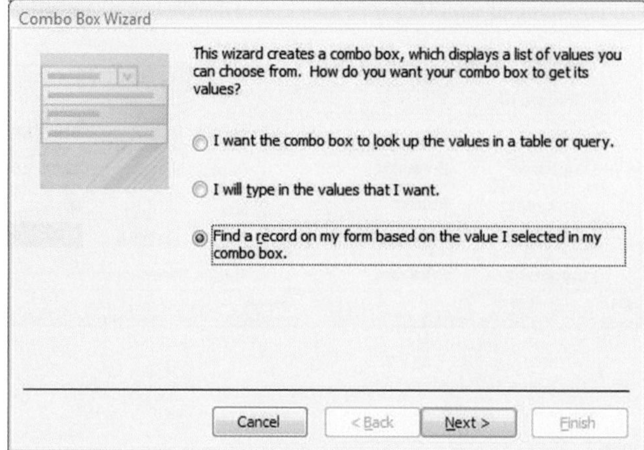

5 Click on the **Surname** field and select it with the **>** icon. Click on **Next** (see Figure 1.11.27).

Figure 1.11.27 ▶

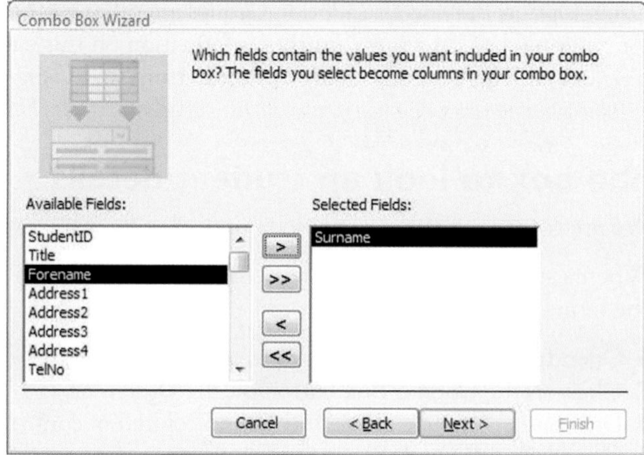

6 The **Combo Box Wizard** dialog box then displays the names. Click on **Next** again (see Figure 1.11.28).

Figure 1.11.28 ▶

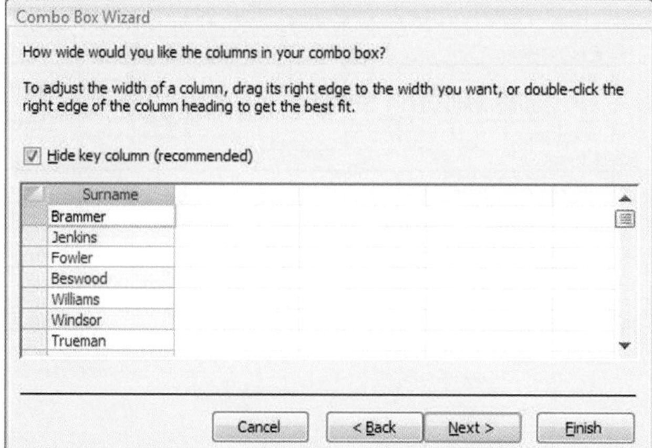

7 Give the combo box the name **Find Record** and click on **Finish**.
8 Switch to **Form View** and **frmStudent** should appear as in Figure 1.11.29. You will need to align and size the control with its label set to bold.

Figure 1.11.29 ▶

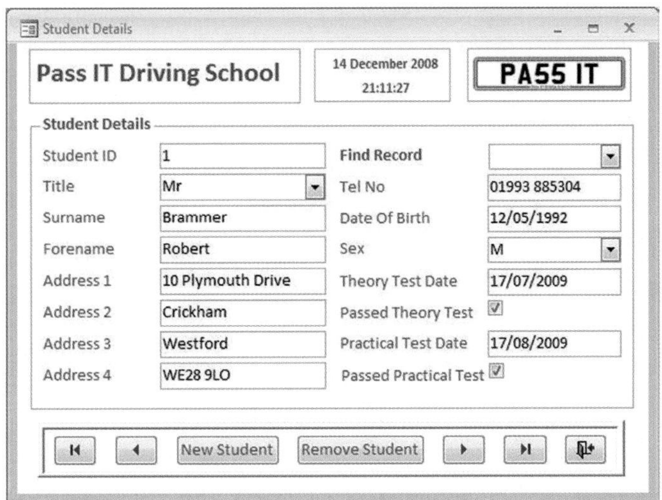

Displaying the names in the combo box in alphabetical order

The names in the drop-down list from the combo box on the Student form are in Student ID order and not alphabetical order. To sort these names into alphabetical order:

1 Open **frmStudent** in Design View and select the **Find Record** combo box.
2 Click on the **Property Sheet** button or right-click the combo box and click on **Properties**. Click on the **Data** tab.
3 Click on **Row Source** and click on the three dots icon (see Figure 1.11.30).

Figure 1.11.30 ▶

Property Sheet
Selection type: Combo Box
Combo55
Format | Data | Event | Other | All

Control Source	
Row Source	SELECT [tblStudent].[StudentID],
Row Source Type	Table/Query
Bound Column	1
Limit To List	Yes
Allow Value List Edits	Yes
List Items Edit Form	
Inherit Value List	Yes
Show Only Row Source Values	No

4 The Query Builder window opens (see Figure 1.11.31). It looks similar to Query Design View. In the **Surname** column of the QBE grid, select **Ascending** in the Sort row.

Figure 1.11.31 ▶

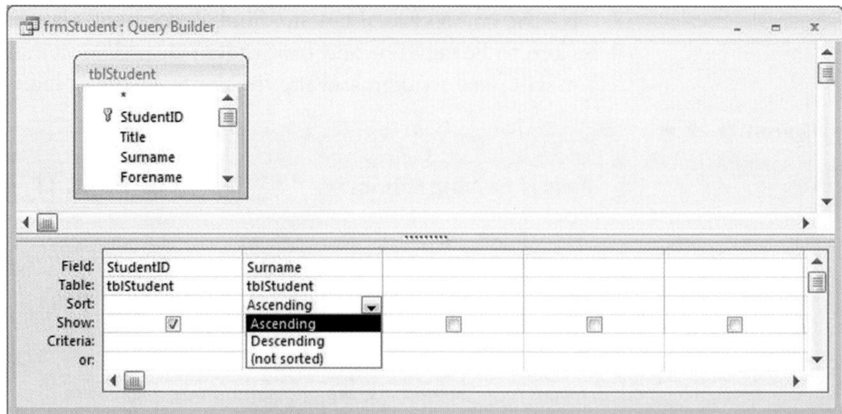

5 Close the **Query Builder** window and save the changes.
6 Go into **Form View** and test that the names are in alphabetical order.

It just remains to add one or two touches to finalise the appearance of the Student form.

We have set a **Fill/Back Color** to a shade of blue (**Light Blue 1**) and set the **Font Color** of the **Form Button** controls to **Text Dark**. See Figure 1.11.32.

Figure 1.11.32 ▶

Student Details

Pass IT Driving School

14 December 2008
21:12:09

PA55 IT

Student Details

Student ID	1	Find Record	
Title	Mr	Tel No	01993 885304
Surname	Brammer	Date Of Birth	12/05/1992
Forename	Robert	Sex	M
Address 1	10 Plymouth Drive	Theory Test Date	17/07/2009
Address 2	Crickham	Passed Theory Test	☑
Address 3	Westford	Practical Test Date	17/08/2009
Address 4	WE28 9LO	Passed Practical Test	☑

New Student | Remove Student

Creating a form to display data from more than one table

In Unit 9 we used the wizards to design simple Student and Instructor forms. We could also have designed a form to book lessons, as shown in Figure 1.11.33. The form is based on the table **tblLesson**.

Figure 1.11.33 ▶

In the real system it is probable the student would not know their ID number or the operator booking their lesson would want to confirm an ID by seeing the student name on screen.

In this section we will set up the Lesson Booking form. You will find out how to base a form on a query. This will enable us to key in the Student ID on the Booking form and Access will find the student's name in the student table.

Creating the Lesson Booking form

1 In the Navigation Pane double-click on **qryLessonCost** to run the Query.

The output in Figure 1.11.34 shows the query bringing in the information from all the tables (some of the columns have been hidden to fit the screen). This is the information that will be displayed in your form.

Figure 1.11.34 ▶

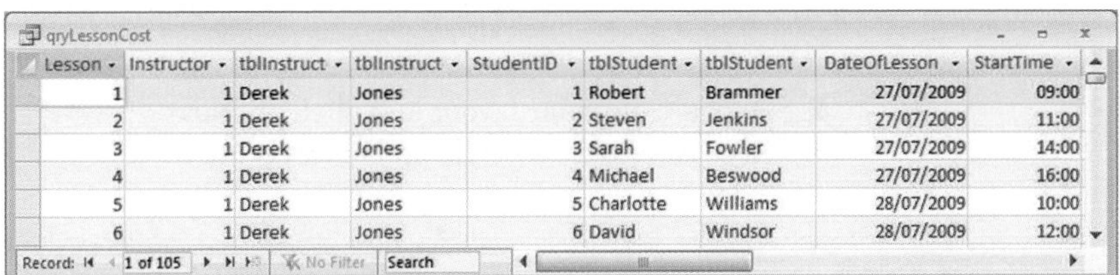

qryLessonCost

Lesson	Instructor	tblInstruct	tblInstruct	StudentID	tblStudent	tblStudent	DateOfLesson	StartTime
1	1	Derek	Jones	1	Robert	Brammer	27/07/2009	09:00
2	1	Derek	Jones	2	Steven	Jenkins	27/07/2009	11:00
3	1	Derek	Jones	3	Sarah	Fowler	27/07/2009	14:00
4	1	Derek	Jones	4	Michael	Beswood	27/07/2009	16:00
5	1	Derek	Jones	5	Charlotte	Williams	28/07/2009	10:00
6	1	Derek	Jones	6	David	Windsor	28/07/2009	12:00

Record: 1 of 105 No Filter Search

2 **Close** the Query. In the Navigation Pane, highlight the query **qryLessonCost.**

3 On the **Create** tab, click **More Forms** and click the **Form Wizard** button. Select **qryLessonCost** from the drop-down. See Figure 1.11.35.

Figure 1.11.35 ▶

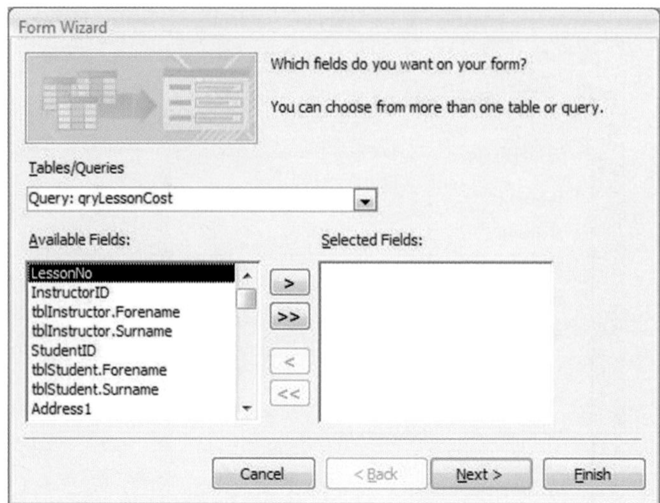

4 Click the double arrow >> to select all fields as shown in Figure 1.11.36 and click on **Next**.

Figure 1.11.36 ▶

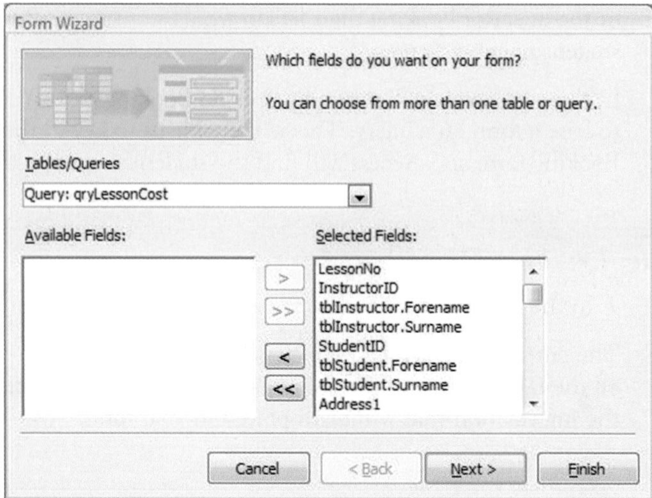

5 Select a **Columnar** layout and click on **Next**.

6 Select **Access 2007** style and click on **Next**.

7 Name the form **frmLessonBooking** and click on **Finish**. It should appear as in Figure 1.11.37.

Figure 1.11.37 ▶

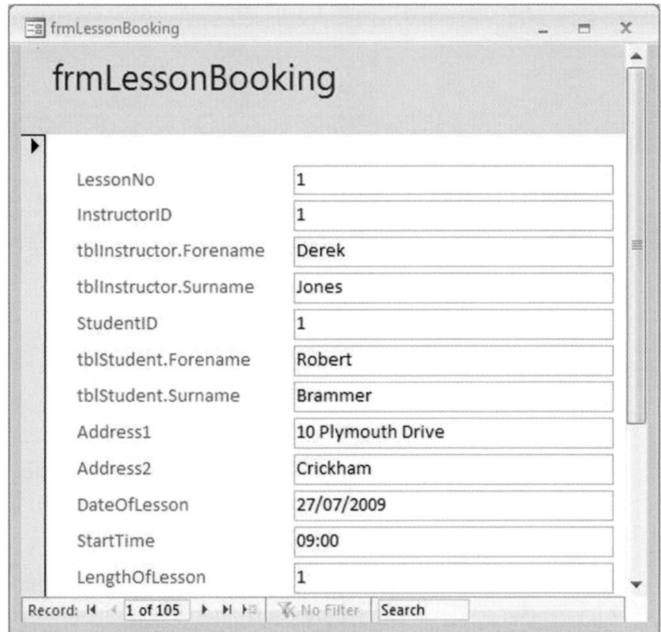

We now need to customise the form to give it the same look and feel as the Student and Instructor forms.

In Form Design View, make the following changes:

- Add a header to the Form Header section in the same font, font size and colour and add the PASS IT logo. You can use copy and paste.
- Edit the labels for the Instructor and Student name control by removing the tbl. Tidy all the other labels.
- Add the control panel.
- Add the buttons using the Wizards as before.
- Set the form properties to the same as the Student and Instructor forms.

Your finished Lesson Booking form should appear as in Figure 1.11.38.

Figure 1.11.38 ▶

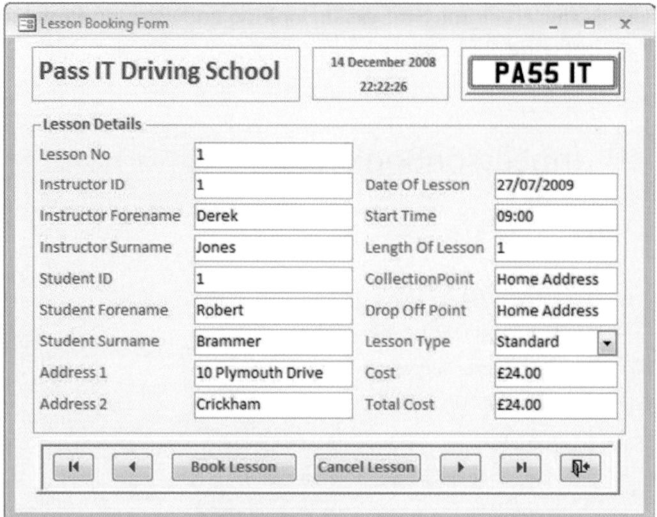
Lesson Booking Form

Pass IT Driving School

14 December 2008
22:22:26

PA55 IT

Lesson Details

Lesson No	1		
Instructor ID	1	Date Of Lesson	27/07/2009
Instructor Forename	Derek	Start Time	09:00
Instructor Surname	Jones	Length Of Lesson	1
Student ID	1	CollectionPoint	Home Address
Student Forename	Robert	Drop Off Point	Home Address
Student Surname	Brammer	Lesson Type	Standard
Address 1	10 Plymouth Drive	Cost	£24.00
Address 2	Crickham	Total Cost	£24.00

Book Lesson | Cancel Lesson

When you book a lesson and enter an Instructor ID number, click on another control or press the TAB key, the instructor's forename and surname will appear.

Similarly, after you enter the Student ID, click on another control or press the TAB key, the student's forename, surname and address will appear.

One of the problems is that you need to know the Student and/or Instructor ID. You might like to read the section called **Adding a combo box to enter a student's details** in Unit 17. This shows you how to drop down student details from a combo box and automatically enter the data.

Note: To save time, we have not developed a **Lesson Type** form but one has been included in the files available for download.

Use **Tricks and Tips** numbers 27, 34, 35 and 37 to further customise your forms. Use **Tricks and Tips** number 63 to add a Spinner control.

Unit 12: Setting up reports

In this section you will learn how to set up reports to output information from the Pass IT Driving School database.

A report is a way of presenting data on screen or in printed format. Reports can be based on either a table or a query.

Like a form, a report can be fully customised to suit the user's requirements. Output from a report can include images. Text can be positioned where required and the font, size and colour of text can be formatted, as shown in Figure 1.12.1.

Figure 1.12.1 ▶

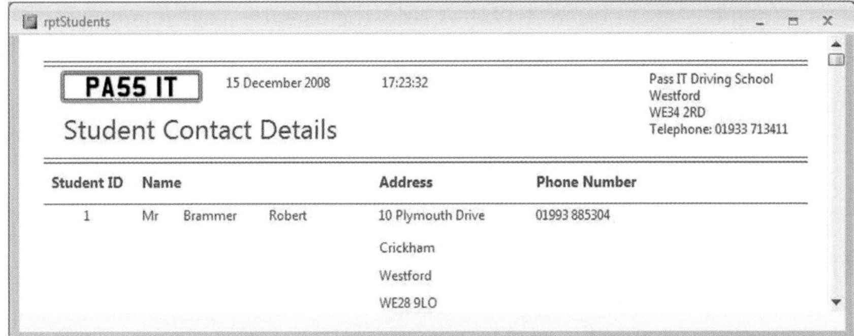

Access has a number of **Report** tools including a **Report Wizard** to help you set up reports quickly and easily. These can be found on the **Ribbon** – in the **Reports** group on the **Create** tab. See Figure 1.12.2.

Figure 1.12.2 ▼

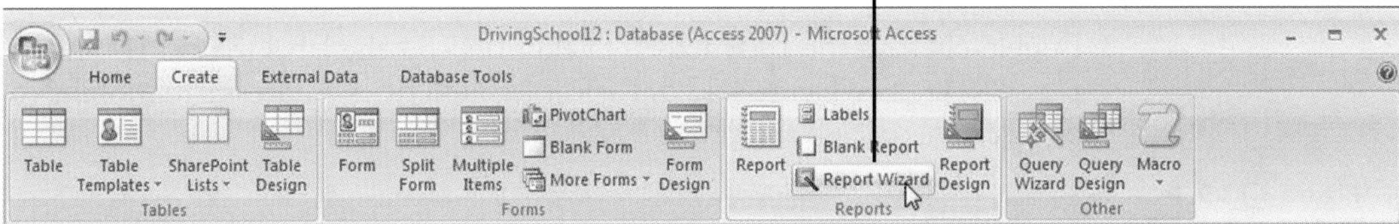

The **Report** tool is a quick and easy way of getting an instant report. The **Report Wizard** gives you greater control over what fields appear on the report.

It is normal practice to use the Report Wizard or Report tool to set up a report and then to use Design View and Layout View to customise it to your requirements.

In this unit we will set up three reports:

- a report to show all instructor contact details
- a report to show all student contact details
- a report to show details of student lessons.

Report 1: Setting up a report to display instructor contact details

We want to set up a report to show a list of all instructors and their contact details. This report will be based on the Instructor table.

1 In the **Navigation Pane**, click **tblInstructor** to highlight the Instructor table.
2 On the **Create** tab, click the **Report** button.

Figure 1.12.3 ▶

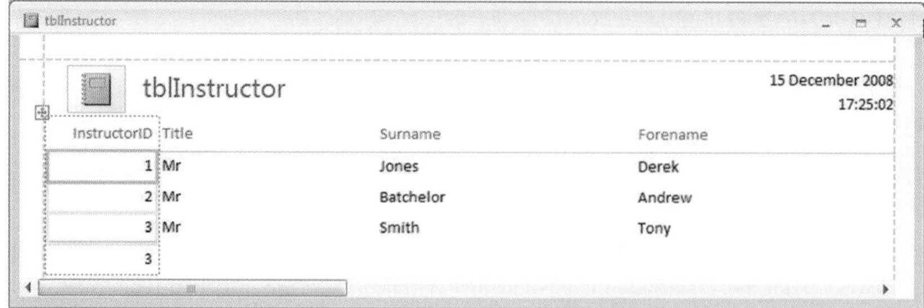

The **Report** tool generates the report and displays it in **Layout View**, as shown in Figure 1.12.3. A title, the date, the page number and a placeholder for a logo are automatically inserted.

Access adds a **Record Count** to the InstructorID column. You can remove this by clicking the **Totals** button, in the **Grouping & Totals** group and uncheck **Count Records**.

Access also displays the **Format** tab, which displays the **Report Layout Tools** available in Layout View. See Figure 1.12.4.

Figure 1.12.4 ▶

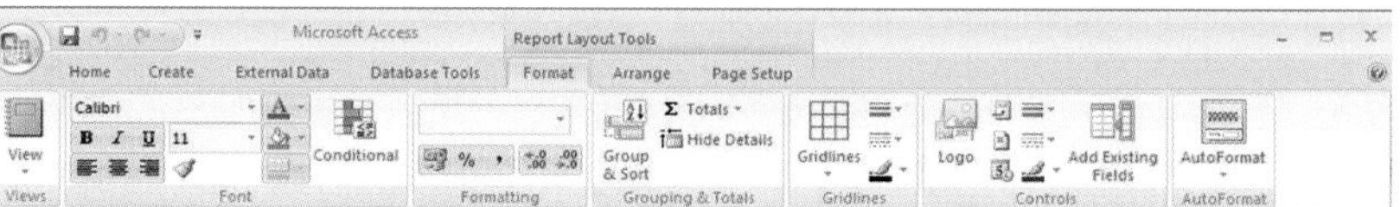

Layout View allows you to fine-tune the report by adjusting the column widths, rearranging columns and most other tasks that affect the appearance and layout of the report.

3 Double-click on the **InstructorID** field title, edit the label to read **ID** and press ENTER. See Figure 1.12.5. Repeat for field titles **Address1** to **MobileNo** by inserting spaces to improve readability.

Figure 1.12.5 ▶

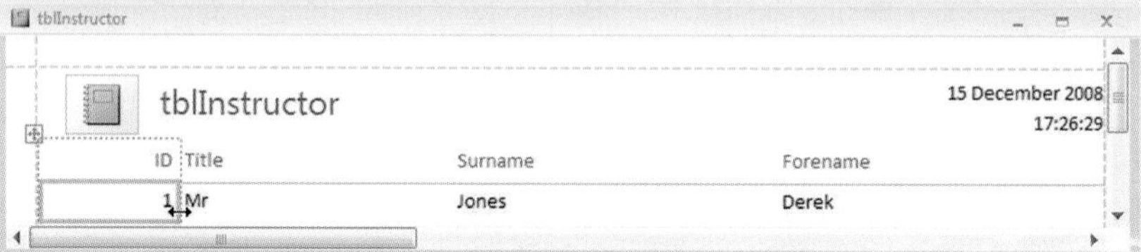

4 The columns are clearly too wide. Click in each field title box and move the mouse pointer to the end of the label until it turns to a double-headed arrow (see Figure 1.12.5). Resize the box by dragging to the left. You should be able to fit all the fields just inside the right-hand margin. See Figure 1.12.6.

Figure 1.12.6 ▶

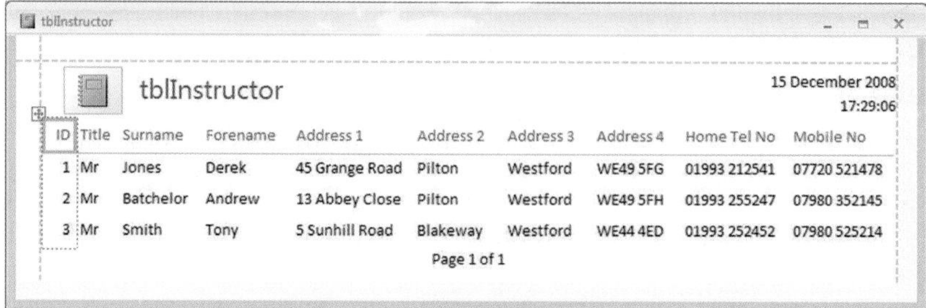

Click on the **View** drop-down and click the **Print Preview** button to help you adjust the layout. You may prefer to switch to **Landscape**.

Hint While in Print Preview mode use the Zoom Slider at the bottom right of your screen, to quickly zoom in and out of your report by dragging the slider control.

5 Double-click on the **Title** label and edit it to read **Instructor Contact Details.** Set the **Font** to **Calibri, Bold, 18pt**.

6 Click on the **Date** and **Time** fields and set the **Font** to a **Dark Blue (Text Dark), Bold**. Click on each field title to set the **Font**. (Hold down SHIFT to select more than one field.) We have used the default.

Figure 1.12.7 ▶

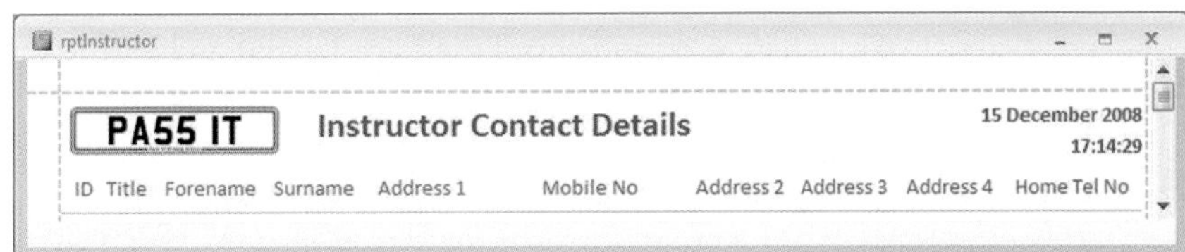

7 Add a logo by clicking on the **Logo** button and selecting the image you want to add from the **Insert Picture** dialog box. If the image does not fit the frame, then right-click on the image, select **Properties** and set the **Size Mode** property to **Clip**. Alternatively, resize by dragging the resize handles in/out.

8 Switch to **Print Preview** to view the report. It should appear as in Figure 1.12.8. As the cursor moves over the report it turns into a magnifying glass. Click once to zoom out to see the whole page. Click again to zoom in to actual size.

9 Save your report as **rptInstructor**.

Figure 1.12.8 ▶

rptInstructor

PA55 IT — Instructor Contact Details — 15 December 2008 17:36:29

ID	Title	Forename	Surname	Address 1	Mobile No	Address 2	Address 3	Address 4	Home Tel No
1	Mr	Derek	Jones	45 Grange Road	07720 521478	Pilton	Westford	WE49 5FG	01993 212541
2	Mr	Andrew	Batchelor	13 Abbey Close	07980 352145	Pilton	Westford	WE49 5FH	01993 255247
3	Mr	Tony	Smith	5 Sunhill Road	07980 525214	Blakeway	Westford	WE44 4ED	01993 252452

Page 1 of 1

The different report views

There are four different views to a report:

- **Report View** allows you to view your report roughly as it will be printed. You cannot modify the report in **Report View**. In **Report View** you can copy text to the clipboard.
- In **Layout View** you can make simple layout and appearance changes to the report while it displays the data.

- **Design View** gives you complete control over your report and its properties. In addition to the options in Layout View, Design View allows you to add a greater range of controls and is described later.
- **Print Preview** allows you to see what the report will look like when you print it out. Figure 1.12.9 shows the Print Preview tab.

Figure 1.12.9 ▼

From here you can control the **Page Layout** and set the **Print** options. Click the **Close Print Preview** button to return to the previous view.

Access offers a number of ways of switching between views:

- Click the **View** button to toggle between views or click the **View** drop-down.
- Right-click the report in the **Navigation Pane** and choose the view required.
- Right-click the Report's tab or title bar and choose the view required.

Working in Layout View

It is worth practising and experimenting with the following operations to familiarise yourself with working in Layout View. If you feel confident, move straight on to Report 2.

Formatting a field label

Click in the label and select from the **Font** and **Formatting** options on the **Format** tab. Hold down SHIFT to select multiple labels. See Figure 1.12.10.

Figure 1.12.10 ▶

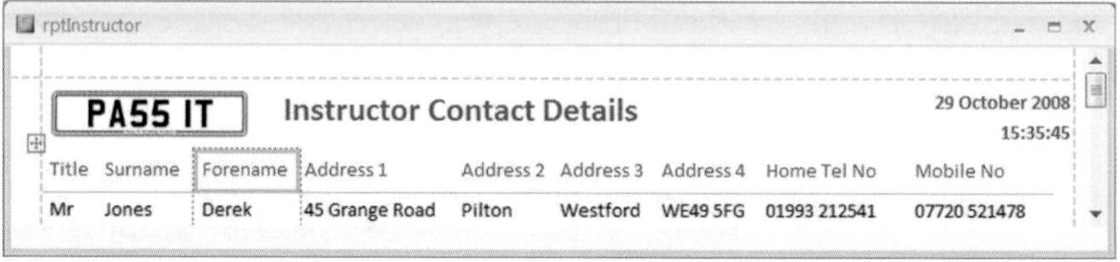

Changing the format of a field

Click the field and use the options on the **Format** tab. See Figure 1.12.11.

Figure 1.12.11 ▶

Selecting all field labels

Click in a field label. Move the pointer to the left border until it changes to an arrow and click to select all labels. See Figure 1.12.12.

Figure 1.12.12 ▶

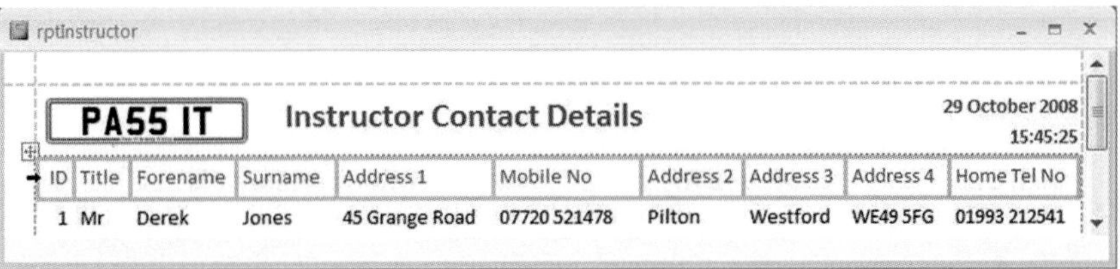

Selecting all fields

Click in a field. Move the pointer to the left border until it changes to an arrow and click to select all fields. See Figure 1.12.13.

Figure 1.12.13 ▶

Deleting a field in Layout View

Click the field title and press DELETE. See Figure 1.12.14.

Figure 1.12.14 ▶

Adding a field

Click the **Add Existing Fields** button and drag and drop the field from the **Field List** to the required position. See Figure 1.12.15.

Figure 1.12.15 ▶

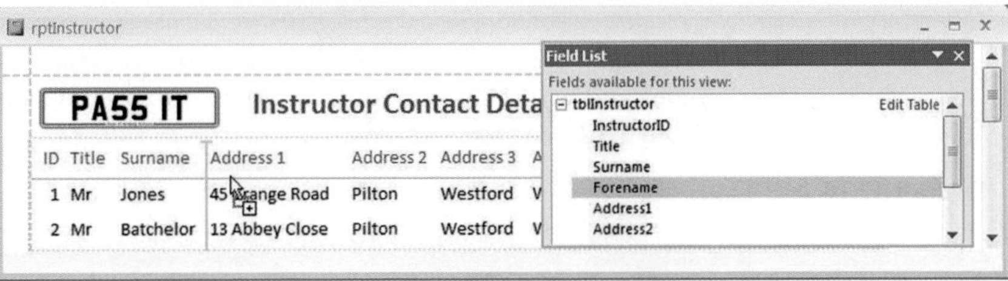

Rearranging the position of fields

Drag the control to its new position. As you drag the field, a vertical bar indicates where it will be placed when you release the mouse. See Figure 1.12.16.

Figure 1.12.16 ▶

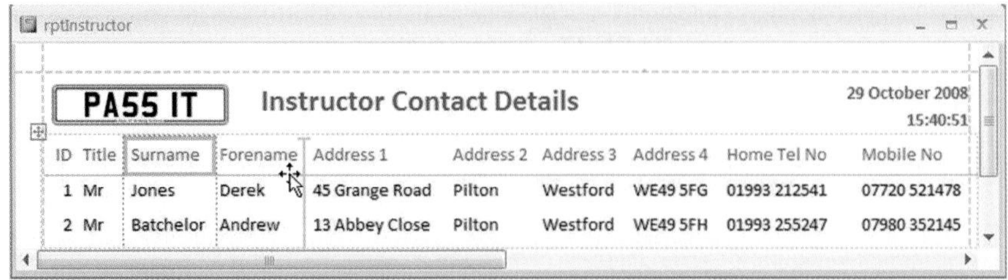

Report 2: Setting up a report to display Student Contact Details

We are going to set up a report to show a list of all students and their contact details. This report will be based on the Student table.

We will develop this report using Design View. It is worth practising and experimenting with the techniques. Eventually you will be able to develop reports using a mix of working in Layout View and Design View. There is no set way, so choose whatever suits the situation!

Design View allows you to customise and develop your reports in much the same way as working with forms.

1 In the **Navigation Pane**, click the **tblStudent** to highlight it. On the **Create** tab, click the **Report** button.
2 The report opens in Layout View. Click the **Layout Selector** as shown in Figure 1.12.17.

Figure 1.12.17 ▶

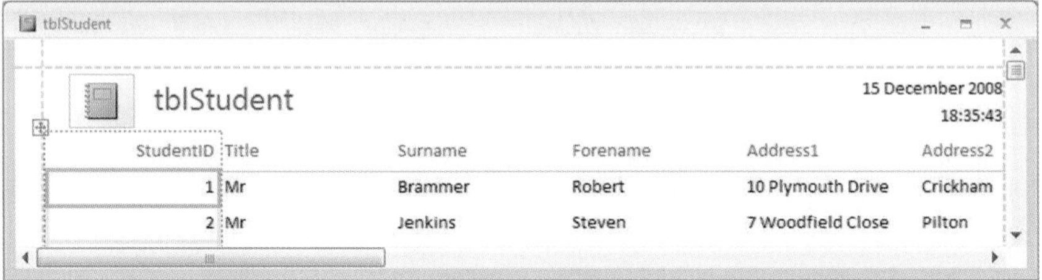

3 On the **Arrange** tab, click the **Remove** button. This removes the layout guides and will allow you to move your controls independently. See Figure 1.12.18.

Figure 1.12.18 ▶

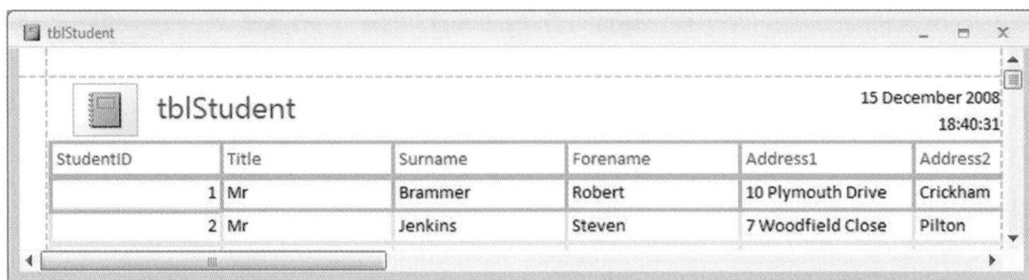

4 On the **Home** tab, click the **View** drop-down and select **Design View**. See Figure 1.12.19.

Figure 1.12.19 ▶

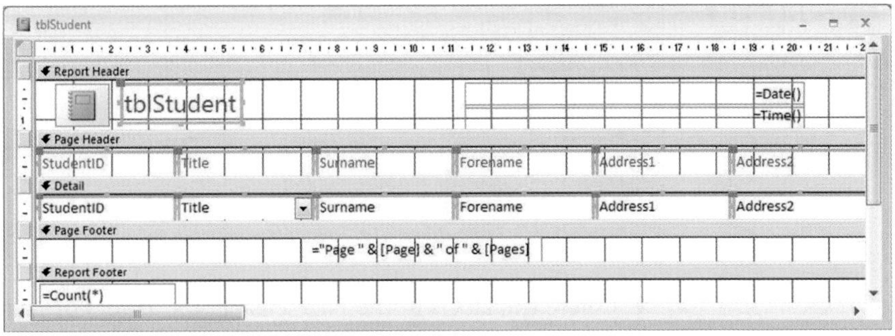

The top part of the report is the **Report Header**. Controls in the Report Header appear only once at the beginning of the report. It is suitable for titles and other information needed at the start of a report.

The second part of the report is the **Page Header**. Controls in the Page Header appear at the top of every page. It is suitable for column headings.

The third part of the report is the **Detail**. This is used for the data in the report.

The fourth part of the report is the **Page Footer**. Controls in the Page Footer appear at the bottom of every page. It is here the Report tool has inserted the page number.

The final part of the report is the **Report Footer**. Controls in the Report Footer appear only once at the end of the report. Access adds a **Record Count**. You can remove this by clicking on the control and pressing DELETE.

5 It is worth scrolling across to get a feel for the working area. Some of the columns (e.g. Title) are too wide and many of the controls are off the paper limits. The first stage will be to rearrange the controls to fit the page.

6 Select the **Title** control in the **Detail** section and, holding the SHIFT key down, select the **Title** control in the **Page Header** section. Drag the resizing handles in to make one of the controls smaller. The other control will also be resized (see Figure 1.12.20).

Figure 1.12.20 ▶

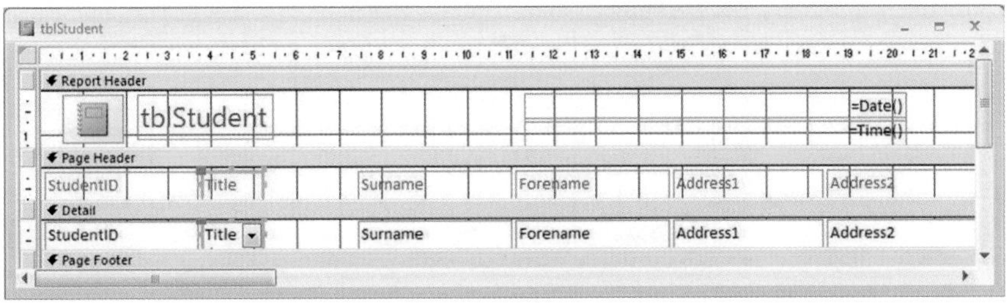

7 Scroll across and select all the controls to the right of **TelNo** in the **Page Header** and the **Detail** sections. (Use the SHIFT key to select multiple controls.) With care you may find it easier to drag out a rectangle across the controls. Press DELETE to remove the controls.

8 Select all the other controls to the right of **Title** in the **Page Header** and the **Detail** sections. Slide all these controls to the left (see Figure 1.12.21).

Figure 1.12. 21 ▶

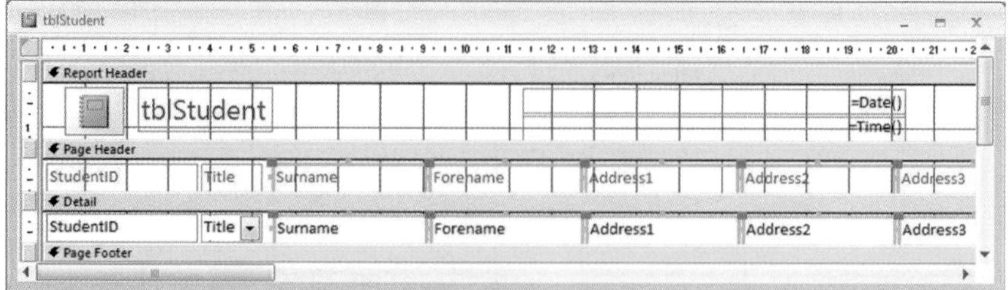

9 Delete the labels in the Page Header for **Title, Forename, Address 2, Address 3** and **Address 4**. (Select each label in turn and press DELETE.)

Note: If you accidentally delete a control, click on the **Add Existing Fields** button and drag across the control from the **Field List**.

10 Edit the remaining labels to read **Student ID, Name, Address** and **Phone Number**. Drag the **Name, Address** and **Phone Number** labels across as shown in Figure 1.12.22.

Figure 1.12.22 ▶

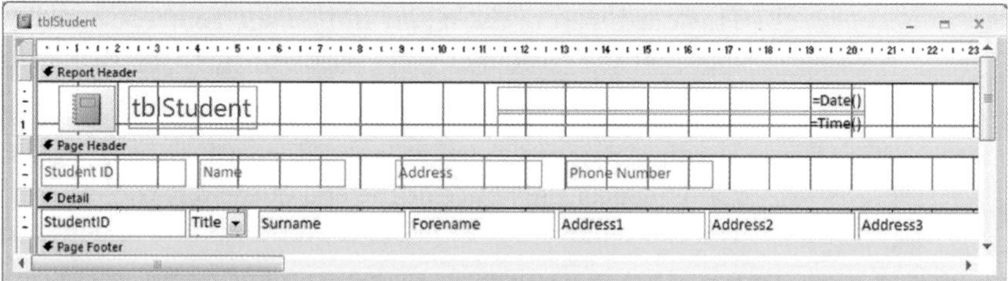

11 Drag down the detail area. Move the **Address** and **TelNo** fields in the **Detail** section to look roughly as in Figure 1.12.23.

Figure 1.12.23 ▶

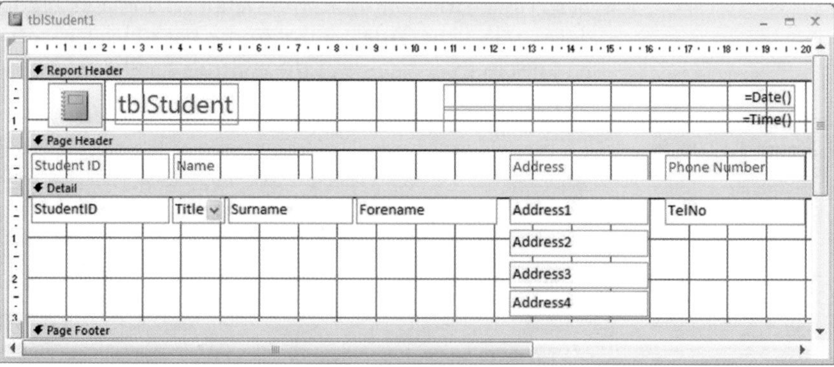

12 Select all the **Address** controls and use the **Control Alignment** tools on the **Arrange** tab to align them. Use the **Vertical Spacing** tools on the **Arrange** tab to position the controls exactly.

13 Switch to **Print Preview** to see the finished report, which will look something like Figure 1.12.24. There is still some tidying to do. You will need to drag in the right margin if **Print Preview** puts in a blank page.

Figure 1.12.24 ▶

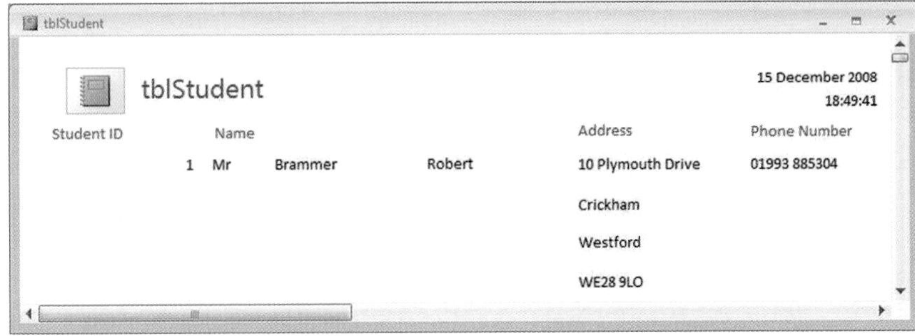

14 Click the **Close Print Preview** button. In **Design View**, reduce the size of the **StudentID**, **Title**, **Surname** and **Forename** fields. Move the **Address** and **Phone Number** controls to suit. Use the **Control Alignment** and **Spacing** tools to help you. See Figure 1.12.25.

Figure 1.12.25 ▶

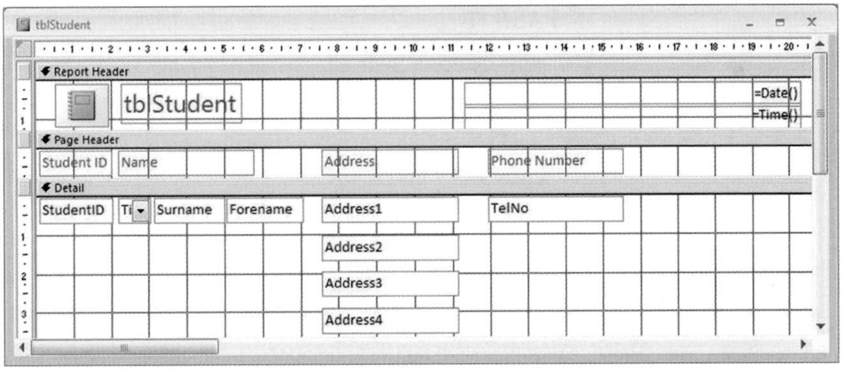

15 Save your report as **rptStudents**. It should appear as in Figure 1.12.26. The next stage is to further customise the report with an in-house style which will be used across all the reports.

Figure 1.12.26 ▶

In the Report Header

1 Click on the title in the **Report Header**. Drag the resizing handles out to increase the size of the control and change the text in the control to **Student Contact Details** (see Figure 1.12.27).

Figure 1.12.27 ▶

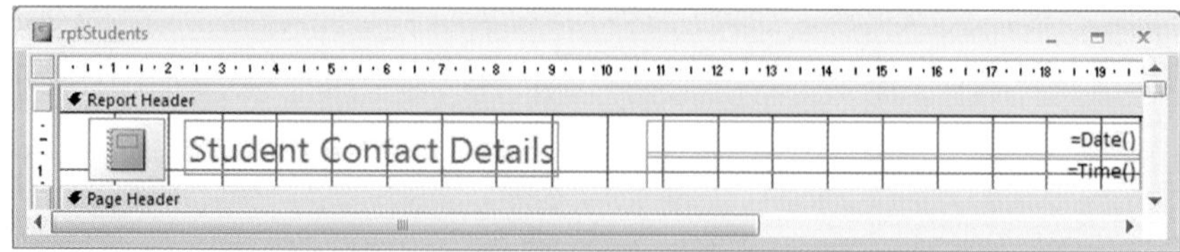

2 On the **Design** tab, click on the **Logo** button. Find the image you want to insert and resize it as necessary. Move the **Student Contact Details** title as shown in Figure 1.12.28. You will have to drag the **Page Header** down a little.

Figure 1.12.28 ▶

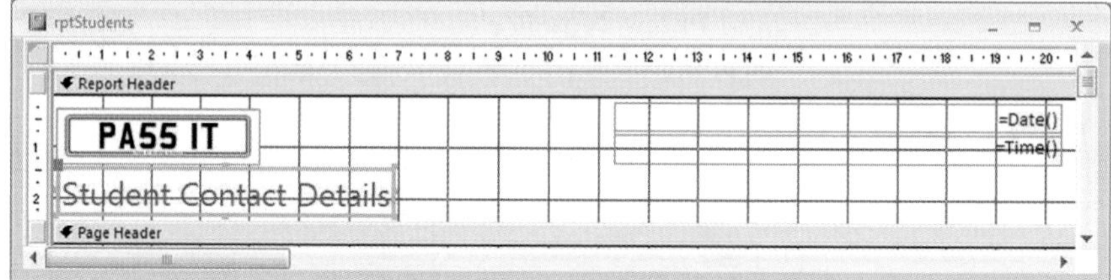

3 Resize the **Date** and **Time** controls and drag them across to align with the logo, as shown in Figure 1.12.29. Select both controls and click the **Property Sheet** button. Set the **Font Name** to **Segoe UI**, **Font Size** to **9**, **Fore Color** to **Text Dark** and **Text Align** to **Left.**

Figure 1.12.29 ▶

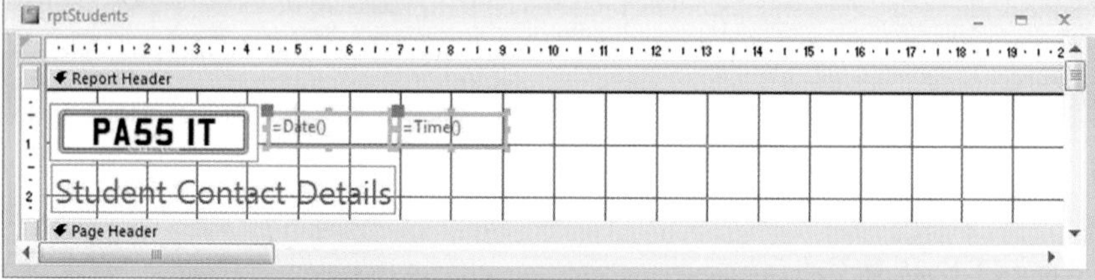

Note: There are many ways to view an object's properties on a report, for example, use the menus, right-click the object or press F4. It is worth exploring some of the other options available in the Property Sheet.

4 Click on the **Label** tool and drag out a label to enter the details: Pass IT Driving School, Westford, WE34 2RD, Telephone: 01933 713411. Use CTRL + ENTER to force a carriage return.

5 Right-click on the label to view its properties. Set the **Font Name** to **Segoe UI**, **Font Size** to **9** and **Fore Colour** to **Text Dark**, as shown in Figure 1.12.30.

Figure 1.12.30 ▶

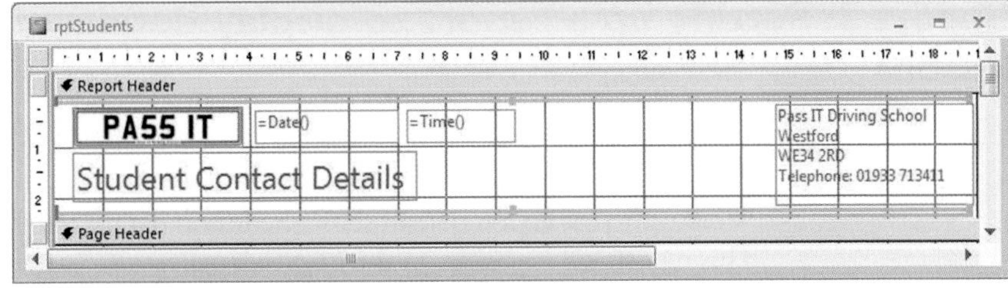

6 Click on the **Line** tool and drag out a line the width of the Report Header. This will be about 18cm. View its properties and set its **Border Width** to **Hairline** and **Border Color** to **Text Dark**. Use copy and paste to position two lines at the top of the header and two at the bottom.

Note: It is worth spending some time getting the Report Header area as you want it. It is then easy to copy and paste to all reports.

In the Page Header

7 Select all the Heading controls and click the **Property Sheet** button. Set the **Font Name** to **Segoe UI**, **Font Size** to **10** and **Fore Color** to **Text Dark**.

8 Click on the **Line** tool and drag out a line the width of the Page Header. View its properties and set its **Border Width** to **1 pt** and **Border Color** to **Text Dark**. It may be easier to simply copy one of the lines used in the Report Header.

Hint When drawing the line, hold down SHIFT as you click and draw to make it exactly straight.

In the Detail Section

9 Select all the field controls and click the **Property Sheet** button. Set the **Font Name** to **Segoe UI**, **Fore Color** to **Black** and **Font Size** to **9**.

In the Page Footer

10 Select the Page Numbering control and set its **Font** properties to **Segoe UI**, **Text Dark**, **Bold**, **9pt**. Copy the line from the Page Header and position it in the Page Footer above the numbering control. Your finished report should appear as in Figure 1.12.31.

Figure 1.12.31 ▶

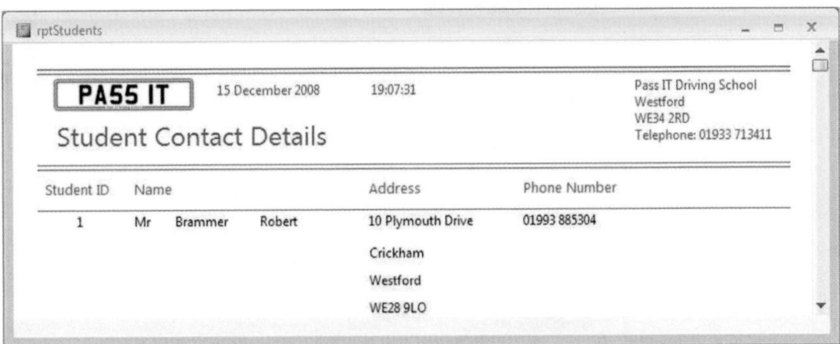

Report 3: Setting up a report to display details of student lessons

In Units 6–8 you set up a number of queries to display information. All these queries can be used as a basis for a report.

We want to set up a report to show the lesson details for a particular student. This report will be based on the **qryStudentLesson**. You are asked to enter a Student ID and the query returns the lesson details for that student. You might like to run the query to remind yourself.

1 In the **Navigation Pane**, click on **qryStudentLesson** to highlight the query.
2 On the **Create** tab, click on the **Report Wizard** button. In the drop-down list click on **qryStudentLesson**.
3 Click on the double arrow to choose all the fields **StudentID**, **DateOfLesson**, **StartTime** and **LengthOfLesson** and click on **Next**. (See Figure 1.12.32.)

Figure 1.12.32 ▶

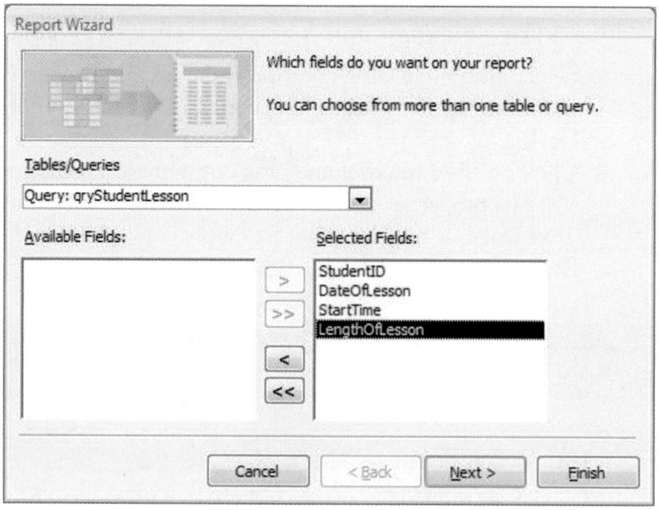

Report Wizard

Which fields do you want on your report?

You can choose from more than one table or query.

Tables/Queries

Query: qryStudentLesson

Available Fields:

Selected Fields:

StudentID
DateOfLesson
StartTime
LengthOfLesson

Cancel | < Back | Next > | Finish

4 From the next dialog box, click on **Next** to ignore any grouping levels. Access will automatically set to group by **StudentID**. (See Figure 1.12.33.)

Figure 1.12.33 ▶

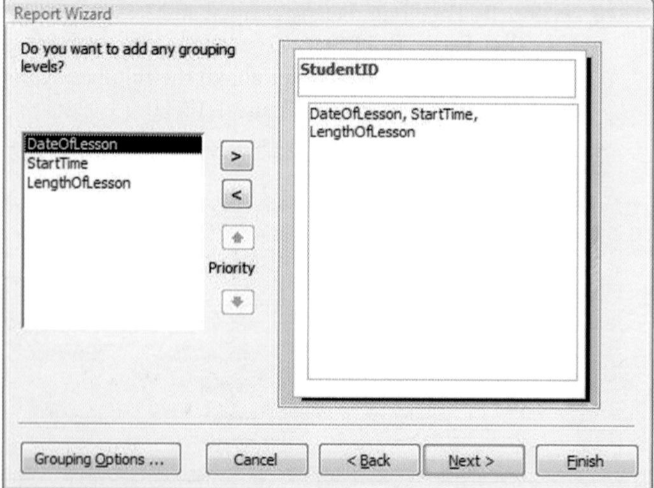

5 From the next dialog box, choose to **Sort** by **DateOfLesson**. Click on **Next**. (See Figure 1.12.34.)

Figure 1.12.34 ▶

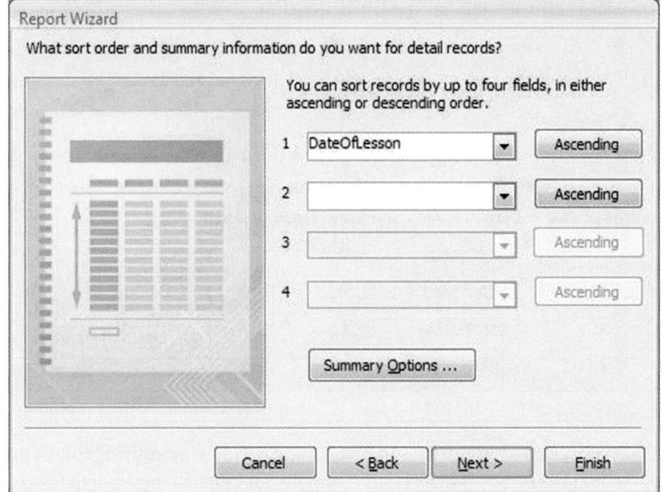

6 Select **Outline** and **Portrait.** Click on **Next**. (See Figure 1.12.35.)

Figure 1.12.35 ▶

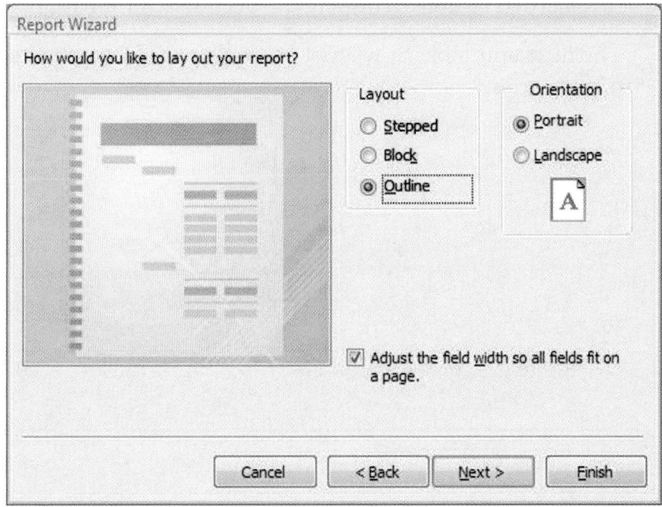

7 Select **Access 2007** and click on **Next**. Call the report **rptStudentLesson** and click on **Finish**.

8 You will be prompted to enter a **StudentID**. Enter Student ID **1**.

The report will open in Print Preview, as shown in Figure 1.12.36.

Figure 1.12.36 ▶

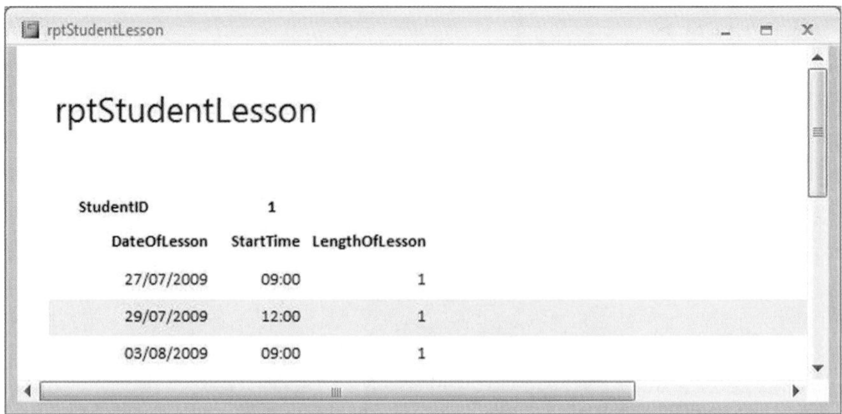

Note: When designing reports, it is important that the information is **meaningful**. In the **rptStudentLesson** in Figure 1.12.36 it clearly lacks details of the student's name, their instructor and their collection point.

These details exist in other tables, which means you would have to redesign the query to be able to display the necessary information.

The next unit looks at ways of producing more complex reports based on multi-table queries.

Unit 13: Further reports

In this section we are going to design three more reports, all based on multi-table queries:

- a report to produce all the instructors' timetables for a particular date
- a report to produce details of all students' lessons
- a weekly timetable report.

Report 1: Instructors' Timetable report

We are going to set up a report showing all the instructors' timetables for a particular date. We will base this report on the query called **qryFullDetailsByDate** set up in Unit 8.

This report introduces you to grouping data in reports and forcing page breaks.

1 On the **Create** tab, in the **Reports** group, click the **Report Wizard** button.
2 Select **qryFullDetailsByDate** from theTables/Queries drop-down (see Figure 1.13.1).

Figure 1.13.1 ▶

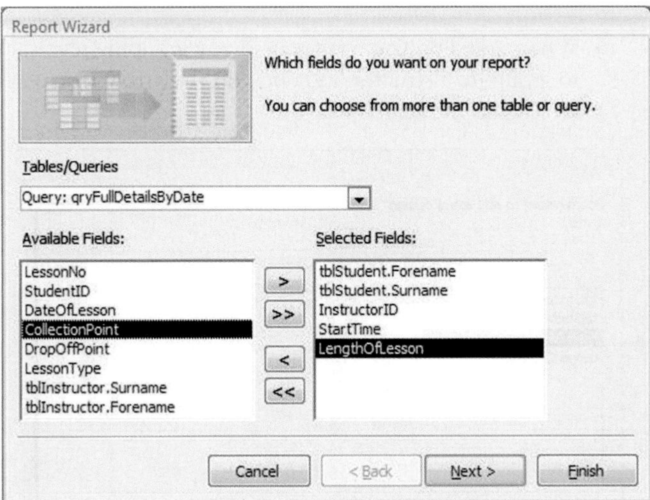

3 Click on the field **tblStudent.Forename**, then click on the single arrow > to add to the Selected Fields. In the same way add **tblStudent.Surname**, **InstructorID**, **StartTime**, **LengthOfLesson** and click on **Next**.

4 The next dialog box asks how you want to view your data. Click on **tblLesson**. Click on **Next** (see Figure 1.13.2).

Figure 1.13.2 ▶

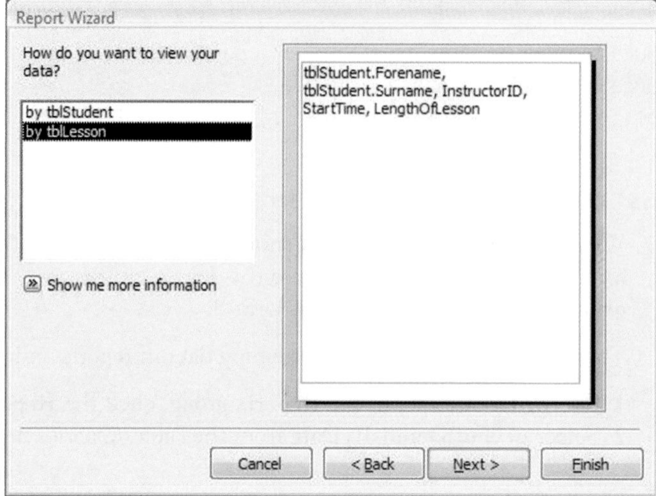

5 When asked do you want to add any grouping levels, click on **InstructorID** to group by instructor and click on the arrow icon **>**. Click on **Next** (see Figure 1.13.3).

Figure 1.13.3 ▶

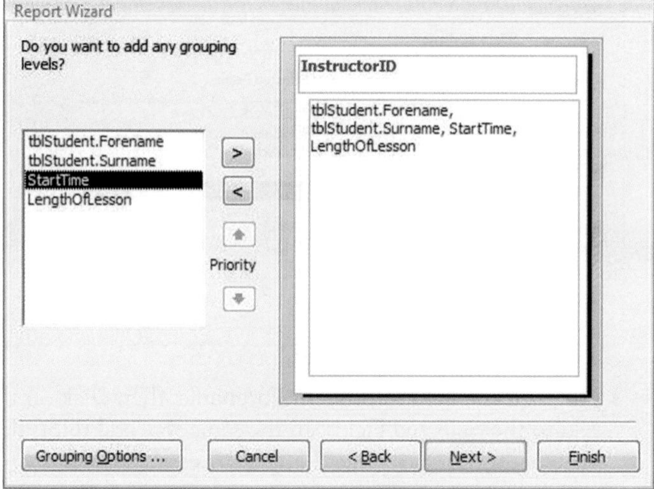

6 Sort by **StartTime**. Click on **Next**.
7 Click on **Outline** and **Portrait**. Click on **Next**.
8 Click on **Access 2007** and click on **Next**.
9 Call it **rptInstructorTimetable** and click on **Finish**.
10 Enter the date **31/07/09** when prompted.

The report should look like the one in Figure 1.13.4. The output is grouped by instructor. It might be worthwhile exploring the Block and Stepped options offered by the Report Wizard during setup.

Figure 1.13.4 ▶

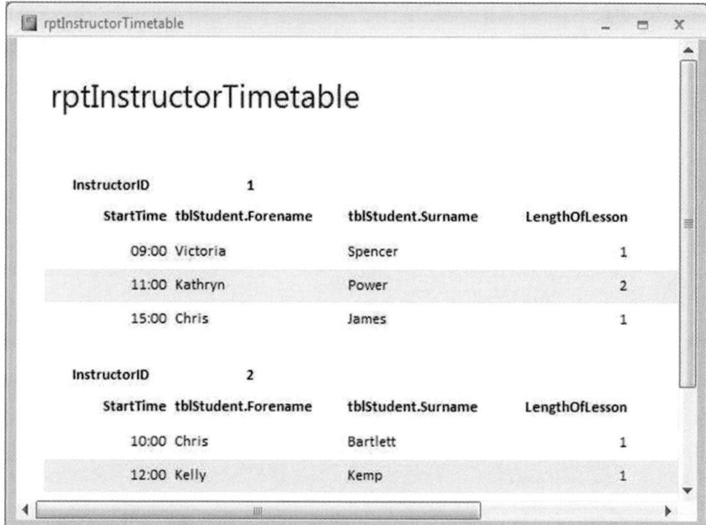

The report is rather unsatisfactory because:

- the instructors' names are not on the report
- the date is not on the report
- the column headings are tblStudent.Forename and tblStudent.Surname.

Close Print Preview and switch to **Design View**. You will see that Access has inserted an InstructorID Header. This is because you chose to group by InstructorID. Controls placed here will head each section about each instructor.

Figure 1.13.5 ▶

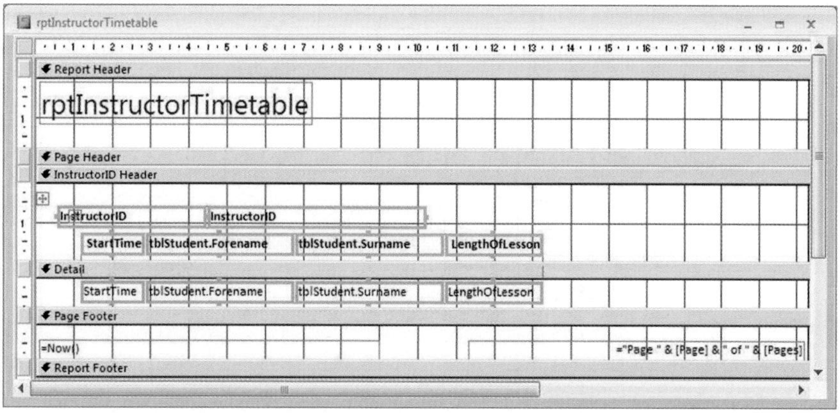

1 Figure 1.13.5 shows the report in Design View. Highlight the two Layout Selectors as shown and on the **Arrange** tab, click **Remove**. Click on a blank area to remove the selection.
2 In the **InstructorID Header**, edit the **tblStudent.Forename** column heading to **Name** (see Figure 1.13.6).
3 Delete the **tblStudent.Surname** column heading by selecting it and pressing DELETE.

Figure 1.13.6 ▶

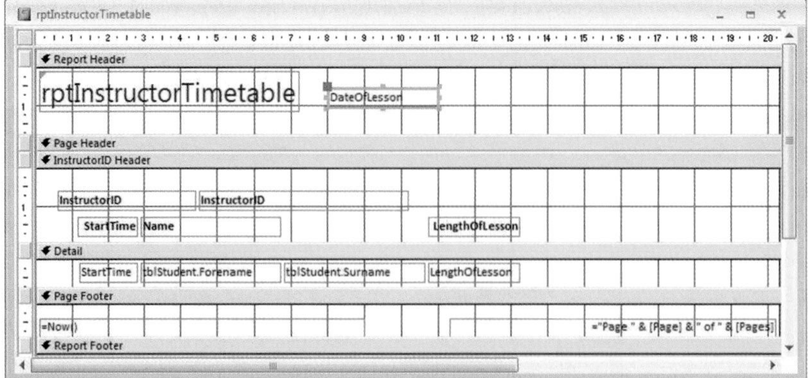

4 On the **Design** tab, click on the **Add Existing Fields** button to display the **Field List** window (see Figure 1.13.7). Scroll down and drag the **DateOfLesson** field on to the Report Header. Select the label for the **DateOfLesson** field and delete it by pressing DELETE (see Figure 1.13.6).

Figure 1.13.7 ▶

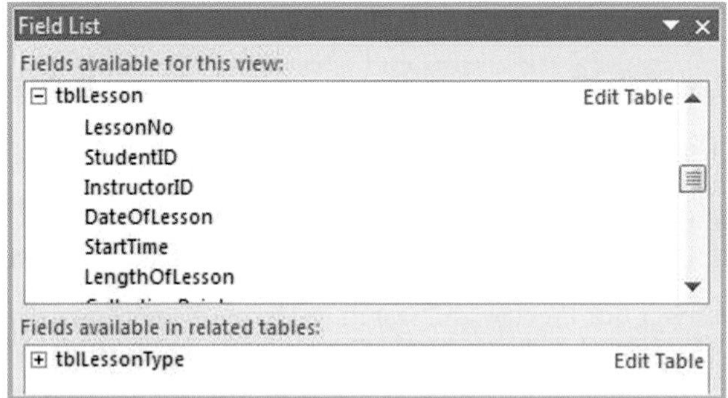

5 Select the **DateOfLesson** control. Click on the **Property Sheet** button and set the **Format** property to **Long Date**.

Figure 1.13.8 ▶

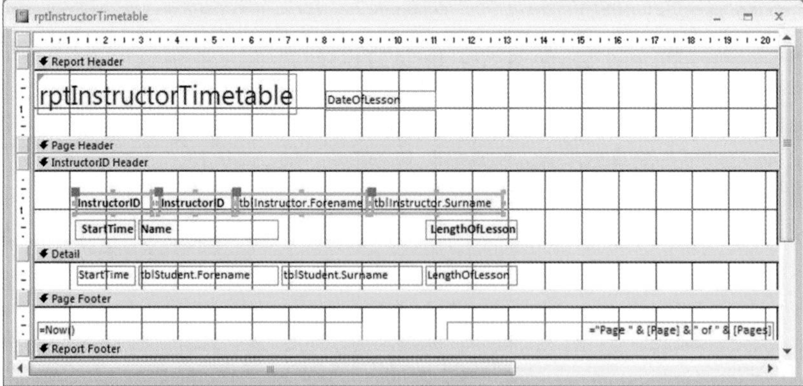

6 Drag both the **tblInstructor.Forename** and **tblInstructor.Surname** from the **Field List** on to the **InstructorID Header**. Select the labels for these fields and delete them (see Figure 1.13.8).

7 Switch to **Print Preview** mode. Enter the date **31/07/09**. The report should look similar to Figure 1.13.9. Save your report as **rptInstructorTimetable.** We can align and format the controls later.

Figure 1.13.9 ▶

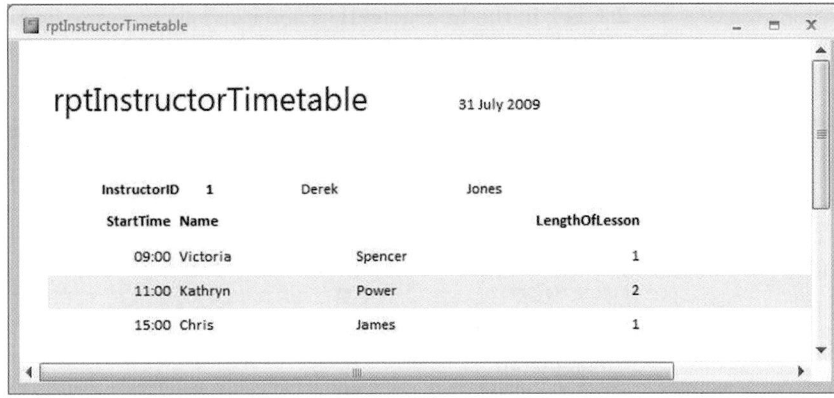

Putting each instructor on a new page

Sometimes you might want each section of a report on a new page. For example, in the above report, you might want the timetable for each instructor printed on a separate page, one to give to each instructor.

To force a new page in a report

1 Load the report in Design View. We need to set up an **InstructorID Footer**. Click on the **Group & Sort** button to display the **Group, Sort and Total** options. Click on **More** and select **with a footer section** from the **without footer section** drop-down, as shown in Figure 1.13.10.

Figure 1.13.10 ▼

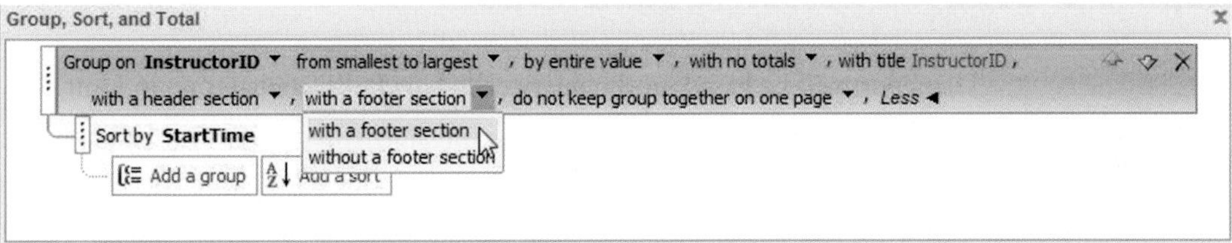

A blank **InstructorID Footer** has now appeared below the **Detail** section (see Figure 1.13.11). Close the **Group, Sort and Total** dialog box.

Figure 1.13.11 ▶

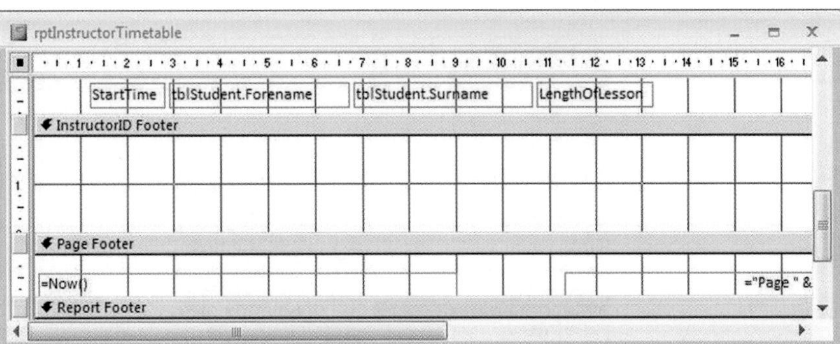

2 Click in the **InstructorID Footer** and click on the **Property Sheet** button. Click on the **Format** tab and set the **Force New Page** property to **After Section** (see Figure 1.13.12).

Figure 1.13.12 ▶

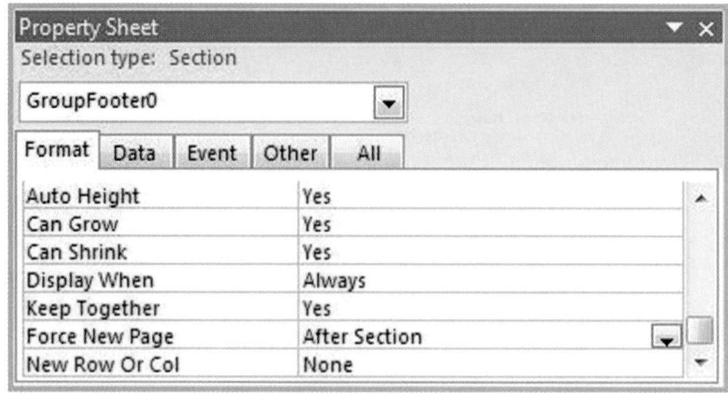

3 Switch to **Print Preview** mode to check that each instructor is on a new page. Save your report as **rptInstructorTimetable.**

Note: You will notice that the title Instructor Timetable and date appear at the top of the report on page 1. These details should be in the Page Header and not the Report Header so that they appear on every page. Enlarge the Page Header, then select the contents of the Report Header and drag them into the Page Header.

You may want to customise with the same report header style used in Unit 12.

Report 2: Student Lesson Details report

We are now going to set up a report to display details of all student lessons. The report will be based on the query called **qryFullDetails** set up in Unit 8.

1 On the **Create** tab, in the **Reports** group, click the **Report Wizard** button.
2 Select **qryFullDetails** from the list. Add the fields **tblStudent.Forename**, **tblStudent.Surname**, **tblInstructor.Forename**, **tblInstructor.Surname**, **DateOfLesson**, **StartTime**, **LengthOfLesson** and **CollectionPoint** and click on **Next** (see Figure 1.13.13).

Figure 1.13.13 ▶

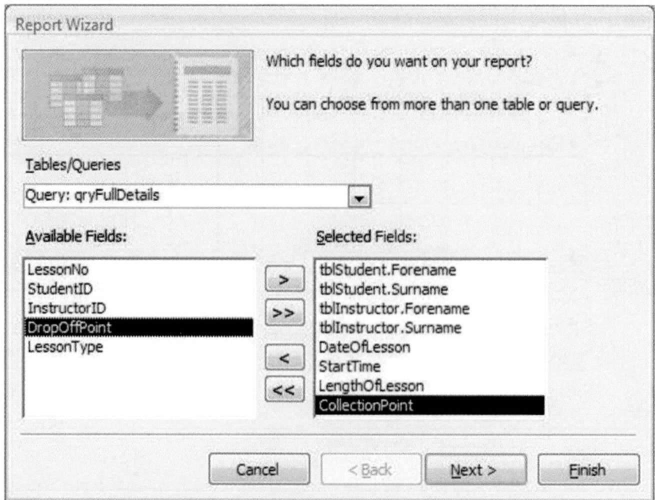

3 The next dialog box will ask you how to view the data. Click on **tblStudent** and then **Next** (see Figure 1.13.14).

Figure 1.13.14 ▶

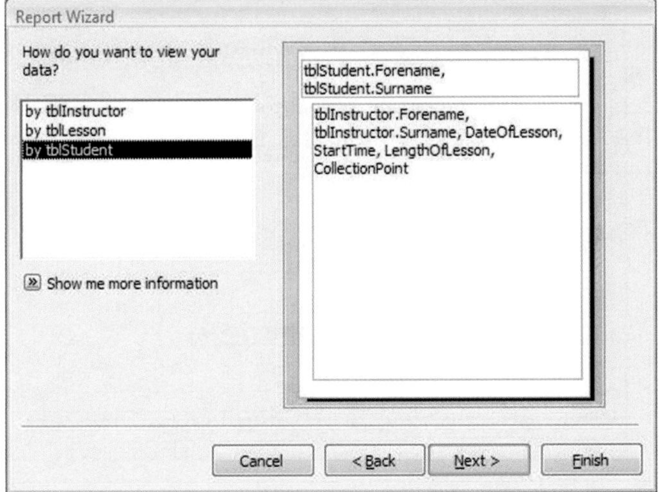

4 When asked do you want to add any grouping levels, Access will automatically select **tblStudent.Forename** and **tblStudent.Surname**, click on **Next** to accept (see Figure 1.13.15).

Figure 1.13.15 ▶

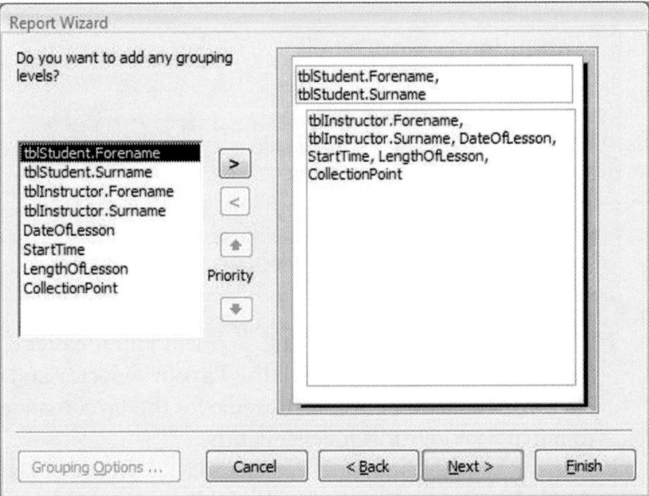

5 Sort by **DateOfLesson** and **StartTime** and click on **Next** (see Figure 1.13.16).

Figure 1.13.16 ▶

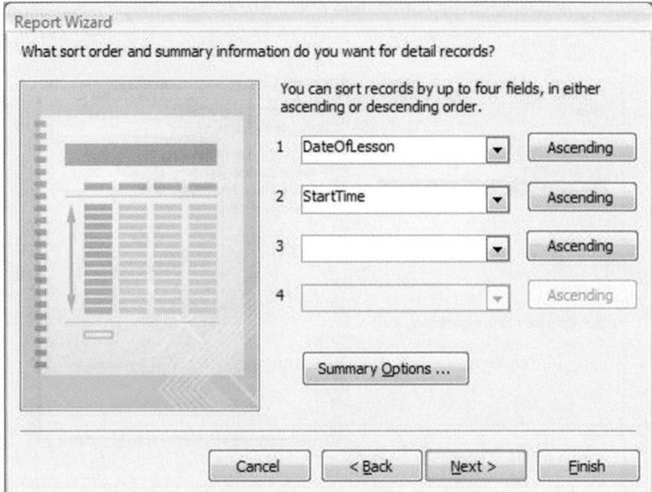

6 Select **Stepped** for layout and **Access 2007** style. Save your report as **rptStudentLessonDetails** and click on **Finish**. The report will open in Print Preview mode as shown below in Figure 1.13.17.

Figure 1.13.17 ▶

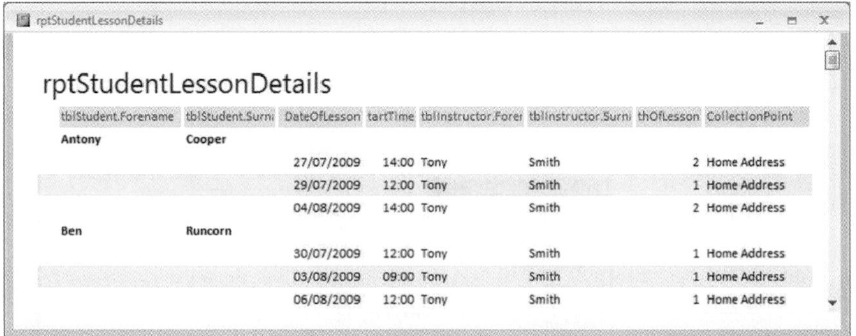

7 The report will need improving. You will find it easier to remove the Layout Selector. In Design View click the **Layout Selector** and on the **Arrange** tab, click the **Remove** button. This removes the layout guides and will allow you to move your controls independently.

8 Edit the label **tblStudent.Forename** to read **Student Name**. Delete the label **tblStudent.Surname**. Edit the label **tblInstructor.Forename** to read **Instructor Name**. Delete the label **tblInstructor.Surname**. See Figure 1.13.18.

Figure 1.13.18 ▶

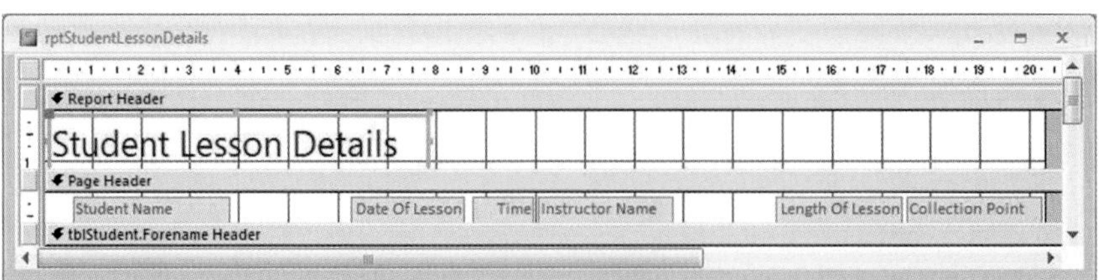

9 Edit the other Page Header labels to read **Date Of Lesson, Time, Length Of Lesson** and **Collection Point**, as shown in Figure 1.13.18.

10 Edit the **Title** label to **Student Lesson Details**, as shown in Figure 1.13.18.

11 The report needs tidying up further by aligning controls and columns. There is no set way. Use the **Align Left** and **Align Top** buttons on the **Arrange** tab and the **Align Text** buttons on the **Design** tab.

Hint To quickly highlight a row of controls, move the cursor to the side (vertical) ruler. When it changes to a pointing arrow, click to highlight the controls. Drag down to highlight a range of controls. See Figure 1.13.19.

Figure 1.13.19 ▶

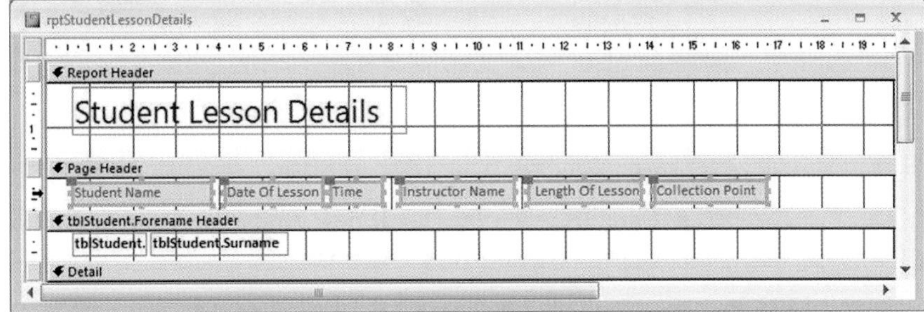

Your finished report should look similar to Figure 1.13.20. You may want to continue to change fonts, background colours and layout.

Figure 1.13.20 ▼

rptStudentLessonDetails

Student Lesson Details

Student Name		Date Of Lesson	Time	Instructor Name		Length Of Lesson	Collection Point
Antony	**Cooper**						
		27/07/2009	14:00	Tony	Smith	2	Home Address
		29/07/2009	12:00	Tony	Smith	1	Home Address
		04/08/2009	14:00	Tony	Smith	2	Home Address
Ben	**Runcorn**						
		30/07/2009	12:00	Tony	Smith	1	Home Address
		03/08/2009	09:00	Tony	Smith	1	Home Address

12 Use the techniques shown in the Instructor Timetable Report previously to force each student to a new page and save your report as **rptStudentLessonDetails**.

Report 3: Producing a Weekly Timetable

The final report in this unit will produce a weekly timetable of lessons. The report will be based on the query called **qryNextWeeksLessons** set up in Unit 8.

1. On the **Create** tab, in the **Reports** group, click the **Report Wizard** button.
2. Select **qryNextWeeksLessons** from the drop-down list. Add the fields **DateOfLesson, StartTime, tblStudent.Forename, tblStudent.Surname, tblInstructor.Surname, LengthOfLesson** and **CollectionPoint.** Click on **Next**.
3. The next dialog box will ask you how to view the data. Click on **tblLesson** and click on **Next**.

4 When asked do you want to add any grouping levels, click on **DateOfLesson** and click on the arrow icon **>**. Do not click **Next** just yet.

5 **DateOfLesson by Month** is displayed in the dialog box. Click on **Grouping Options** and select **Day** from the **Grouping intervals** drop-down, as shown in Figure 1.13.21. Click on **OK**.

Figure 1.13.21 ▶

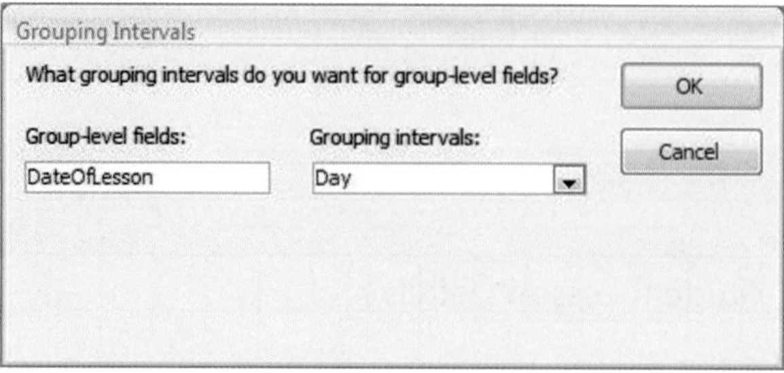

6 **DateOfLesson by Day** is now displayed in the dialog box, as shown in Figure 1.13.22. Click on **Next**.

Figure 1.13.22 ▶

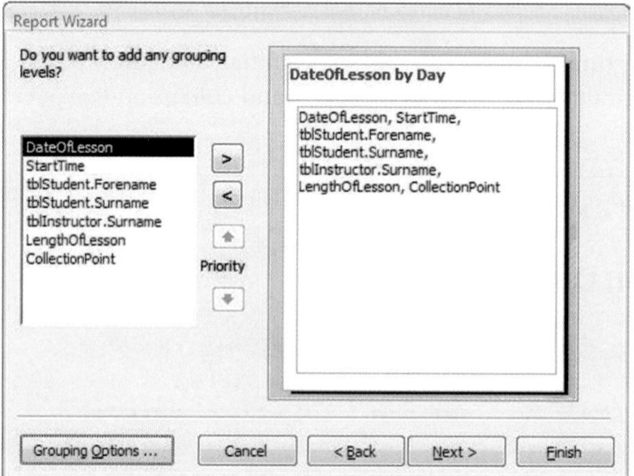

7 Sort by **DateOfLesson**. Select **Stepped** for layout and **Access 2007** style. Save your report as **rptWeeklyTimetable** and click on **Finish**. Your report should appear as in Figure 1.13.23.

Note: You will need to adjust the dates or change the time/date on your PC. In the example here the date has been set to 27/07/2009.

Figure 1.13.23 ▼

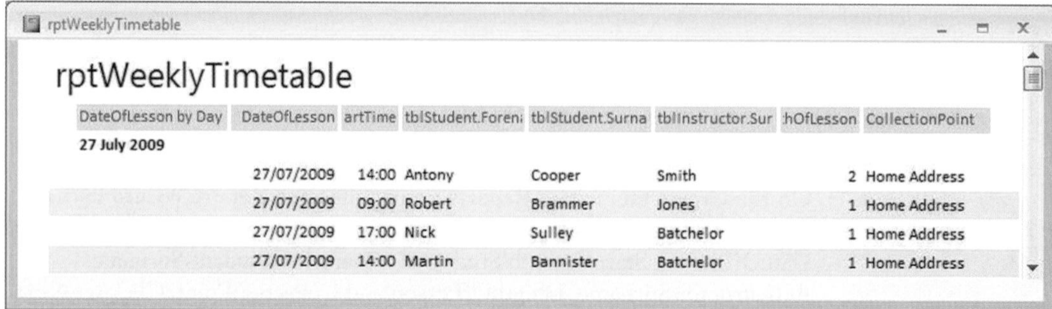

rptWeeklyTimetable

DateOfLesson by Day	DateOfLesson	artTime	tblStudent.Foren	tblStudent.Surna	tblInstructor.Sur	hOfLesson	CollectionPoint
27 July 2009							
	27/07/2009	14:00	Antony	Cooper	Smith	2	Home Address
	27/07/2009	09:00	Robert	Brammer	Jones	1	Home Address
	27/07/2009	17:00	Nick	Sulley	Batchelor	1	Home Address
	27/07/2009	14:00	Martin	Bannister	Batchelor	1	Home Address

We are now going to develop the report using the in-house style shown in Unit 12. Switch to **Design View** and take the following steps, as shown in Figure 1.13.24.

8 Delete the controls in the Report Header and copy and paste the Report Header from the **rptInstructor** set up in Unit 12. Edit the title to **Weekly Timetable**.

9 Remove the Layout Selector in the usual way.

Figure 1.13.24 ▶

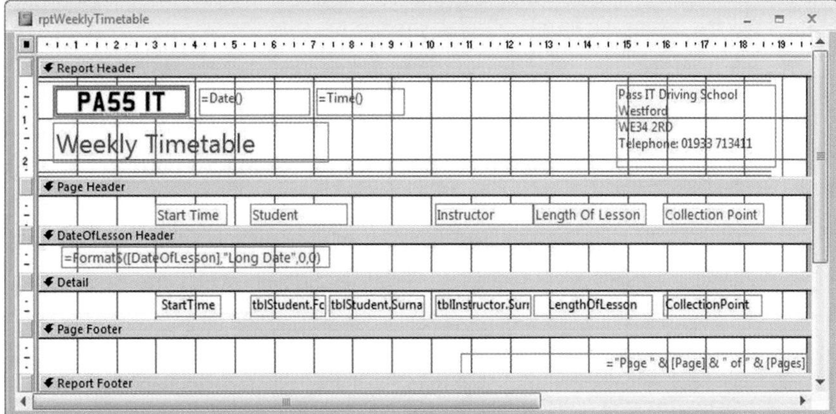

10 In the Page Header, remove the **DateOfLesson by Day** label. Edit, position and align the other labels in the Page Header as shown in Figure 1.13.24. Set the **Font** of all controls in this section to **Segoe UI, Text Dark, 10pt**.

11 In the **DateOfLesson Header**, set the font of the **DateOfLesson** control as above.

12 In the Detail section, change the font of the data controls to **Segoe UI, 9pt**.

13 In the Page Footer, remove the **Date** control. Select the Page Numbering control and set its **Font** properties to **Segoe, Text Dark, 9pt**. Your report should appear as in Figure 1.13.25. Save your report.

Figure 1.13.25 ▼

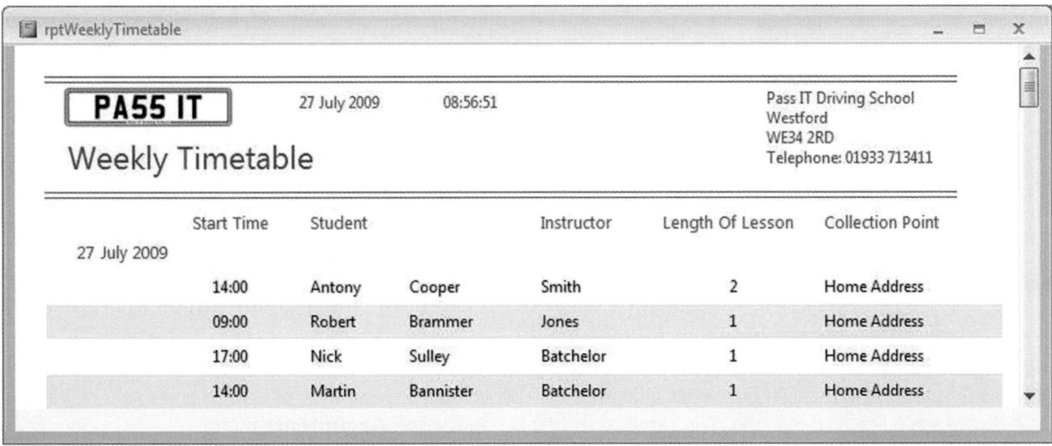

Hint Use **Tricks and Tips** number 46 to set up Mailing Labels and/or Membership Cards.

Unit 14: Macros

A macro combines a series of Access instructions into a single command. Macros can be run by clicking a button, such as on a form or switchboard, or can be triggered by an event, such as closing a form.

The Pass IT system consists so far of the three forms to manage information about the students, instructors and lesson bookings, together with a number of reports.

In this section you will learn how to use a few simple macros to begin to automate the system. Macros will be dealt with in more detail later.

Macro 1: A macro to open the Student form

1 On the **Create** tab, click on the **Macro** button.

Figure 1.14.1 ▶

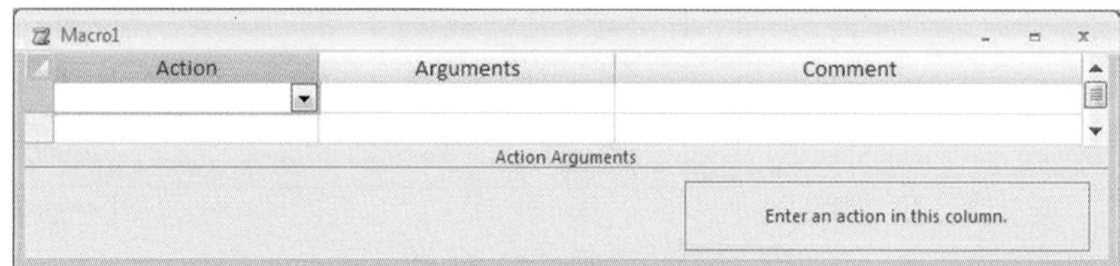

The **Macro** window opens, as shown in Figure 1.14.1. It consists of an **Action** column from which you choose the actions and a **Comment** column where you can add comments to remind you of each function.

2 Click on the drop-down arrow in the **Action** column and click on **OpenForm** (see Figure 1.14.2).

Figure 1.14.2 ▶

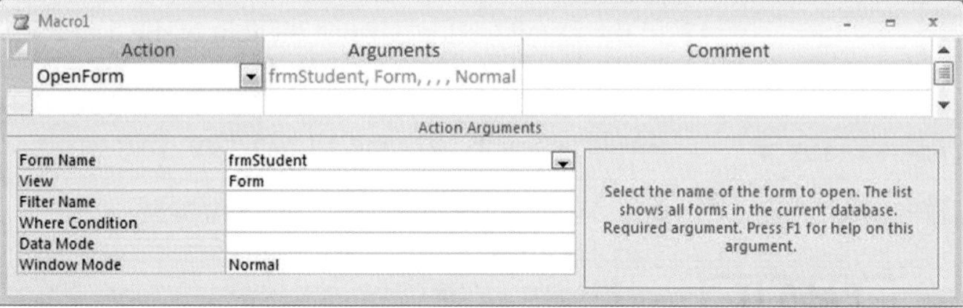

You now need to choose which form to open in the Action Arguments section in the lower pane of the window.

3 Click on the **Form Name** box in the Action Arguments and click on **frmStudent** from the drop-down list, as shown in Figure 1.14.2.

The **View** box will be set by default to **Form** and **Window Mode** to **Normal**, as shown in Figure 1.14.2.

Note: Access 2007 has an **Arguments** column, which allows you to view (not edit) an action's arguments on the same line as the action. You can turn this off by clicking the **Arguments** button.

4 Close the **Macro** window and save as **mcrStudentForm**.
5 In the Navigation Pane, test the macro by double-clicking on the **mcrStudentForm** icon.

Macros can have more than one action. When you open a form, you may want to add a new student by default. We can edit the macro to open the form with a new blank record.

6 Open the **mcrStudentForm** in Design View by right-clicking its icon and selecting **Design View** from the menu. In the second row of the Action column select **GoToRecord** from the drop-down list (see Figure 1.14.3).

Figure 1.14.3 ▶

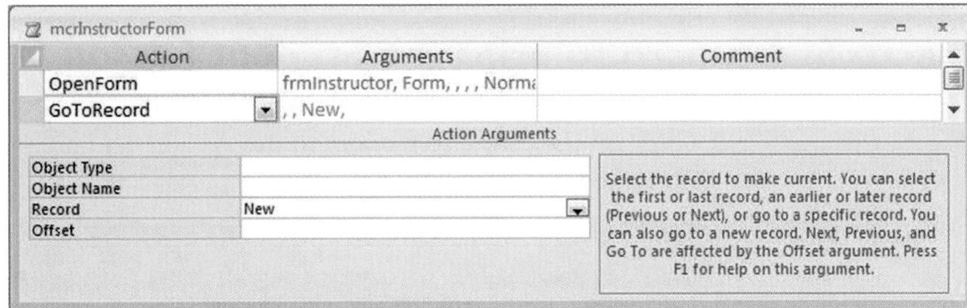

7 In the **Action Arguments** section, set **Record** to **New** (see Figure 1.14.3).
8 Save the macro. Go back to the Navigation Pane and test it works.

Macro 2: Set up another macro called **mcrInstructorForm** to open **frmInstructor** in the same way.

Macro 3: Set up another macro called **mcrLessonBookingForm** to open **frmLessonBooking** in the same way.

Macro 4: Setting up a Message Box

Most software packages have an About message box, giving details of the company or developer. This can be set up using a macro.

1 On the **Create** tab, click on the **Macro** button.
2 Select **MsgBox** in the Action column.
3 In the Action Arguments, click on the **Message** box and type **System by Ian Rendell © 2009**.
4 In the **Beep** box, select **Yes**.
5 In the **Type** box, select **Information**.
6 In the **Title** box, type **Pass IT Driving School** (see Figure 1.14.4).

Figure 1.14.4 ▶

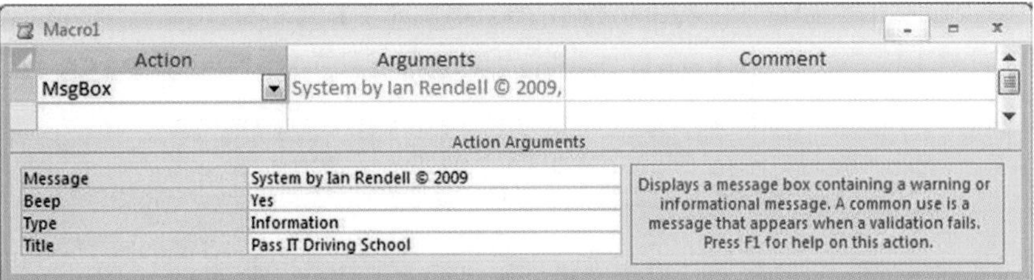

7 Save the macro as **mcrAbout** and test it (see Figure 1.14.5).

Figure 1.14.5 ▶

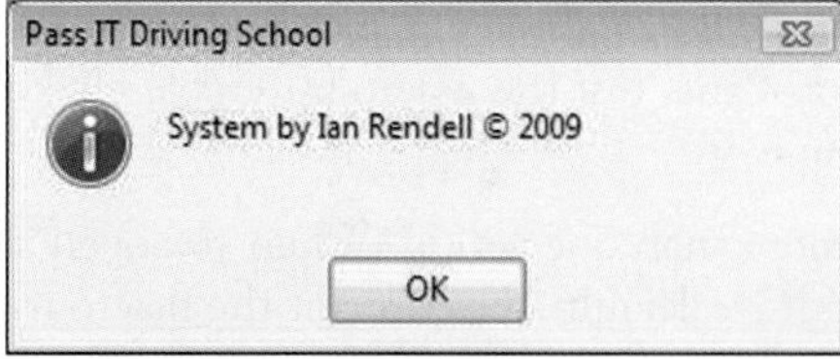

Hint To get the copyright symbol, type (c) in Microsoft Word. AutoCorrect changes it into © and you can use copy and paste to take it into Access.

Macro 5: A macro to print the Student Lesson Details report

1 On the **Create** tab, click on the **Macro** button.
2 Click on the drop-down arrow in the **Action** column and click on **OpenReport** (see Figure 1.14.6).

Figure 1.14.6 ▶

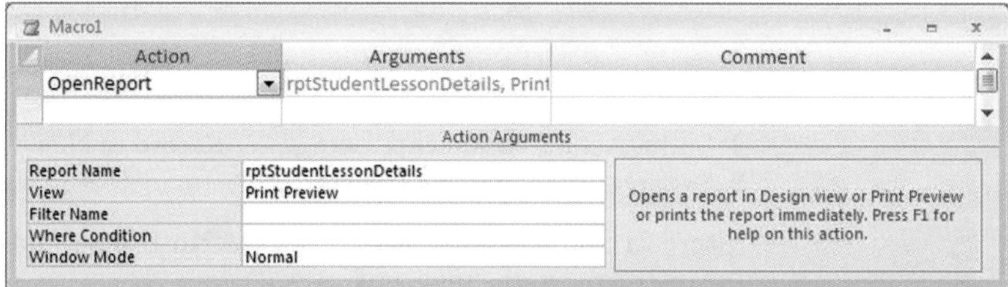

3 Click on the **Report Name** box in the Action Arguments and click on **rptStudentLessonDetails** from the drop-down list, as shown in Figure 1.14.6.
4 In the **View** box select **Print Preview**.
5 Close the Macro window and save as **mcrStudentLessonDetailsReport**.
6 Using the **OpenReport** macro command, set up three further macros to run the following reports: **rptInstructor**, **rptInstructorTimetable**, and **rptWeeklyTimetable**. Save your macros as **mcrInstructorReport**, **mcrInstructorTimetableReport** and **mcrWeeklyTimetableReport**.

Using macros to customise a front end menu

You can use macros to link your system together and produce an automated front end (see Figure 1.14.7).You may use this as an alternative to the switchboard shown in Unit 15.

Figure 1.14.7 ▶

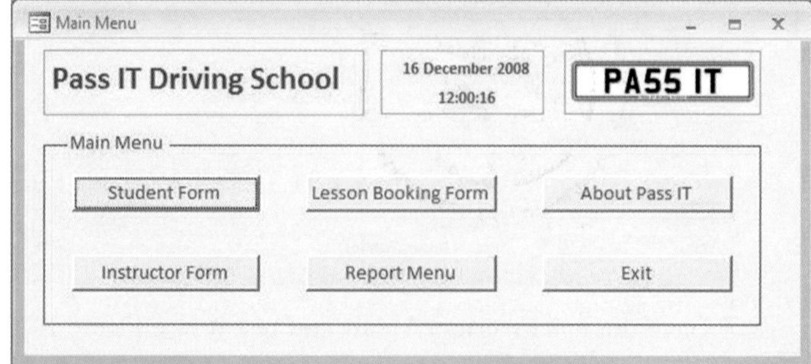

1 On the **Create** tab, click on the **Blank Form** button. Click on **Design View**. This produces a blank form. You will need to resize it to about 15cm by 7cm.
2 Open **frmStudent** in Design View and copy and paste the Form Header controls on to the blank form, as shown in Figure 1.14.8.

Figure 1.14.8 ▶

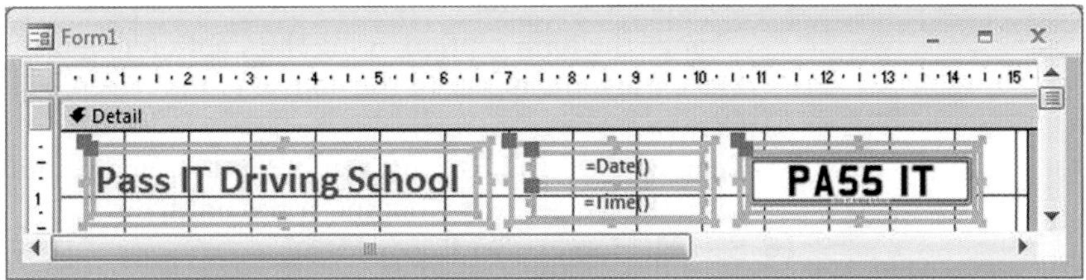

3 We are going to add a button to run the macro that opens the Student form. On the **Design** tab, in the **Controls** group, click on the **Button** button. Click on the form where you want to place your button. This will trigger the Command Button Wizard which you used in Unit 11.
4 Click on **Miscellaneous** and select **Run Macro**. Select **mcrStudentForm** and set the text on the button to **Student Form**.
5 Add further command buttons to run the macros to open the **Instructor** and **Lesson Booking** forms. Set the text for the buttons as shown in Figure 1.14.7.
6 Add another button to run the **About** macro. Set the text to **About Pass IT**. Position and align the buttons as shown in Figure 1.14.7.
7 Set up another command button. Click on **Application.** Click on **Quit Application** and set the text to **Exit**. Position and align the button as shown in Figure 1.14.7. You will need to add the Report Menu option later.
8 Double-click on the **Form Selector** to display the Form Property Sheet. Change the form caption, using the **Caption** property, to **Main Menu**. Make the form appear in the middle of the screen by setting the **Auto Center** property to **Yes**.
9 Remove the scroll bars, navigation buttons and record selector.
10 Save the form as **frmMainMenu**.

The next stage is to create the Report Menu (see Figure 1.14.9) and link to the Main Menu.

Figure 1.14.9 ▶

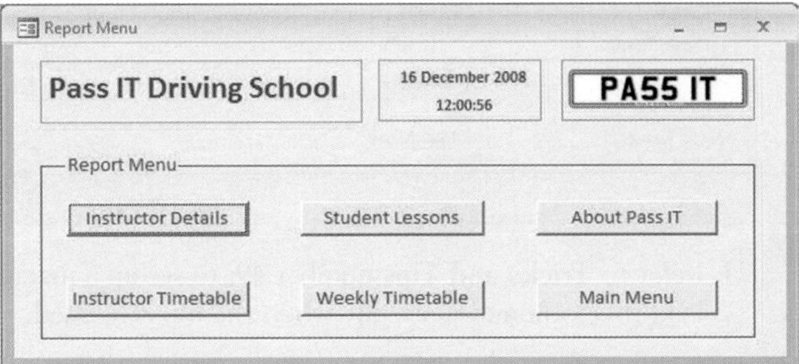

11 On the **Create** tab, click on the **Blank Form** button. Click on **Design View**. This produces a blank form. You will need to resize it to about 15cm by 7cm.

12 Add command buttons to run the macros to open reports **rptInstructor**, **rptWeeklyTimetable**, **rptInstructorTimetable** and **rptStudentLessonDetails**. You will have to click on **Miscellaneous** and select **Run Macro**. Set the text for the buttons as shown in Figure 1.14.9.

13 Add another button to run the **About** macro and set the text as previously.

14 Double-click on the **Form Selector** to display the **Form Property Sheet**. Change the form caption, using the **Caption** property, to **Report Menu**. Make the form appear in the middle of the screen by setting the **Auto Center** property to **Yes**.

15 Remove the scroll bars, navigation buttons and record selector. Copy and paste the header over from the **frmMainMenu.**

16 Save the form as **frmReportMenu**.

17 The next step is to link the two menus. Set up a new macro with two actions. In the **Action** column, click on **Close** and set the **Action Arguments** to **Close** the **Form** called **frmReportMenu**, as shown in Figure 1.14.10.

18 Select the **OpenForm** action and click on **frmMainMenu** in the Action Arguments. When run, this macro will close the Report Menu and open the Main Menu. Save your macro as **mcrOpenMainMenu**.

Figure 1.14.10 ▶

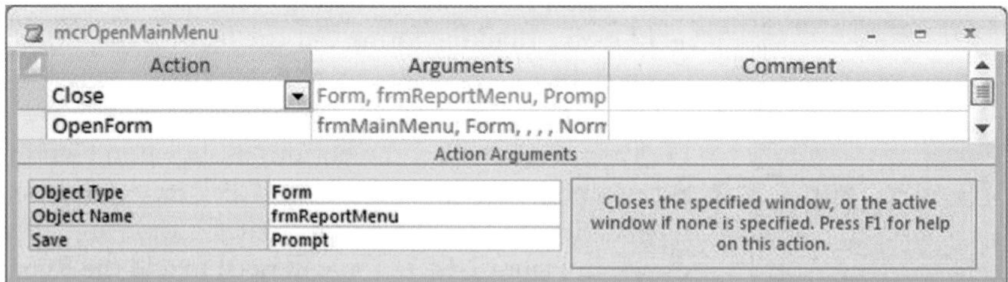

19 Open **frmReportMenu** in Design View and add a command button to run the macro **mcrOpenMainMenu**, as shown in Figure 1.14.9.

20 In the same way, set up a macro to close the Main Menu (see Figure 1.14.11) and open the Report Menu. Save your macro as **mcrOpenReportMenu** and add a command button to run the macro from the **frmMainMenu**, as shown in Figure 1.14.7.

Figure 1.14.11 ▶

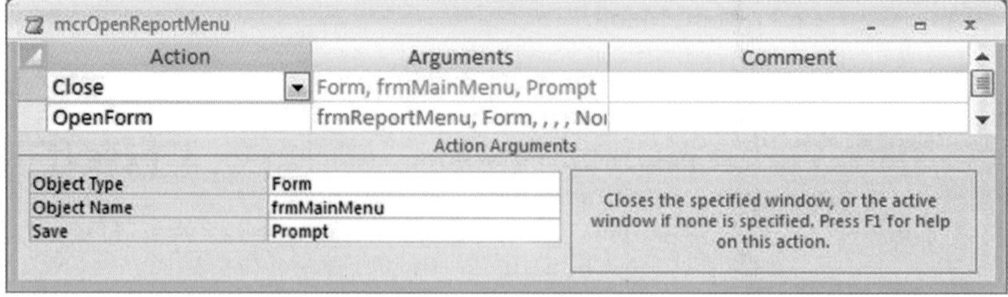

21 Refer to **Tricks and Tips** number 49, to set up a macro called **Autoexec** to load this form automatically when the file is opened.

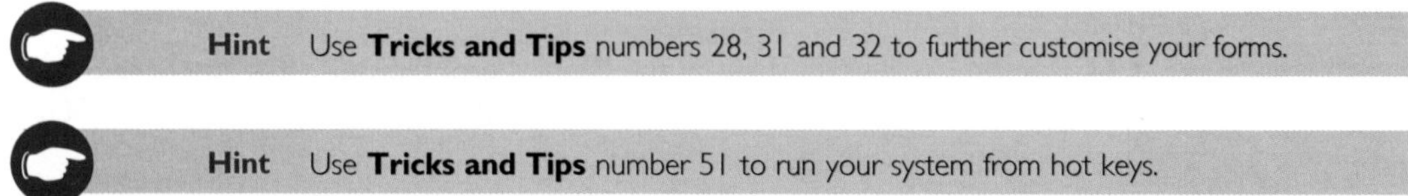

Hint Use **Tricks and Tips** numbers 28, 31 and 32 to further customise your forms.

Hint Use **Tricks and Tips** number 51 to run your system from hot keys.

Unit 15: Adding a switchboard

In the previous units you have designed the tables, queries, forms and reports that go to make up the Pass IT system.

All these options need to be available from a menu that loads when you start up your system. This is sometimes known as the front end or, in Access, as the switchboard. (See Figure 1.15.1.)

Figure 1.15.1 ▶

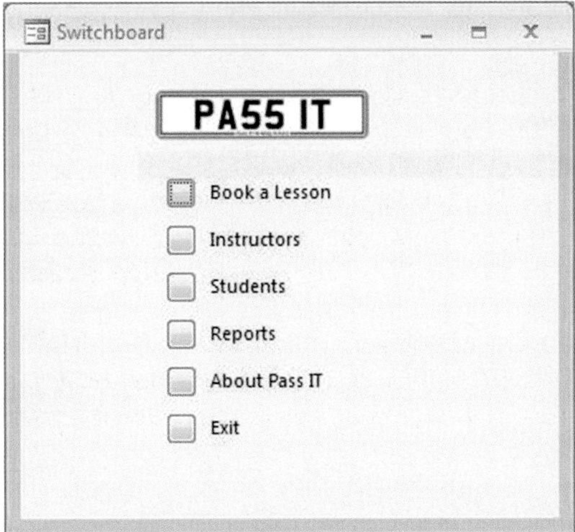

In this section we look at creating the switchboard shown above. The switchboard will need to be able to:

- open the Lesson Booking form (frmLessonBooking) to find out lesson details or book a lesson
- open the Student form (frmStudent) to find out student details
- open the Instructor form (frmInstructor) to find out instructor details
- produce a list of contact details for instructors (rptInstructor)
- produce details of all student lessons (rptStudentLessonDetails)
- produce a timetable for an instructor (rptInstructorTimetable)
- produce a weekly timetable of lessons (rptWeeklyTimetable)
- run the About (message box) macro
- exit from the system.

To fit on all these options, it is best to use two switchboards. One switchboard will link to the reports and the main switchboard will link to all the other options.

Creating a switchboard with the Switchboard Manager

To set up a new switchboard, first load the **DrivingSchool** database.

1 Click on the **Database Tools** tab and, in the **Database Tools** group, click the **Switchboard Manager** button. It will ask if you want to create a switchboard (see Figure 1.15.2). Click on **Yes**.

Figure 1.15.2 ▶

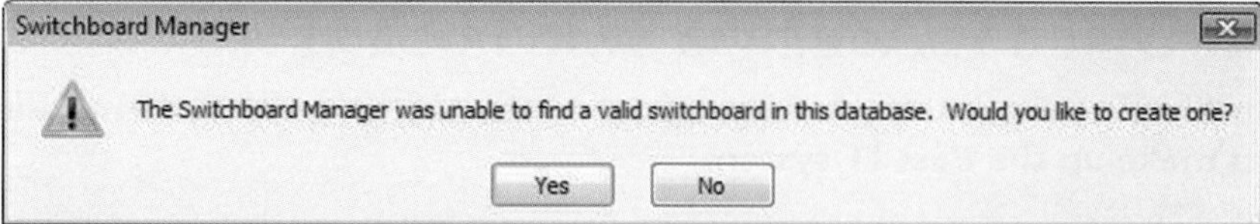

This sets up a default switchboard called the Main Switchboard (see Figure 1.15.3). From here we need to set up another switchboard for the reports.

Figure 1.15.3 ▶

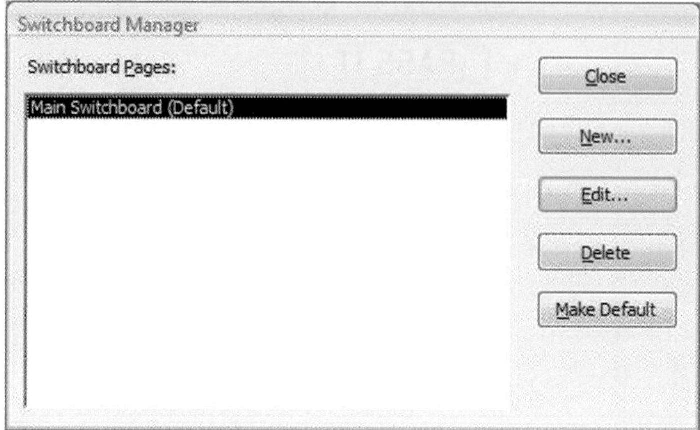

2 On the **Switchboard Manager** dialog box, click on **New** (see Figure 1.15.3). Enter the name of the second switchboard, **Report Switchboard**, and click on **OK** (see Figure 1.15.4).

Figure 1.15.4 ▶

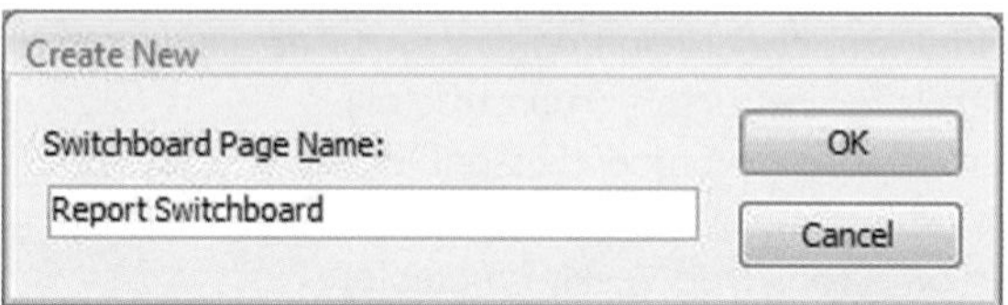

3 Select the **Main Switchboard** and click on **Edit** (see Figure 1.15.5).

Figure 1.15.5 ▶

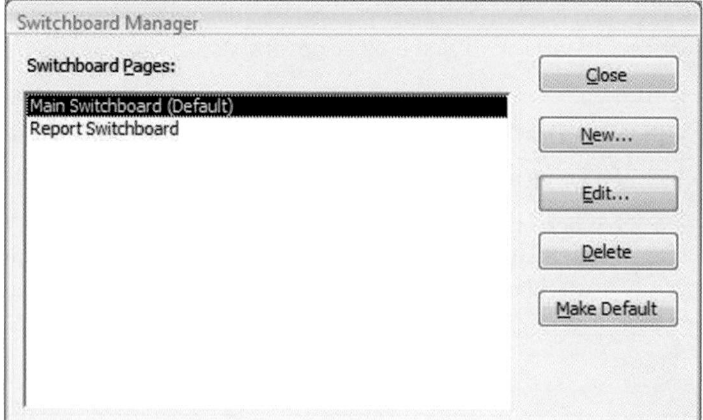

4 On the **Edit Switchboard Page** dialog box, click on **New** (see Figure 1.15.6).

Figure 1.15.6 ▶

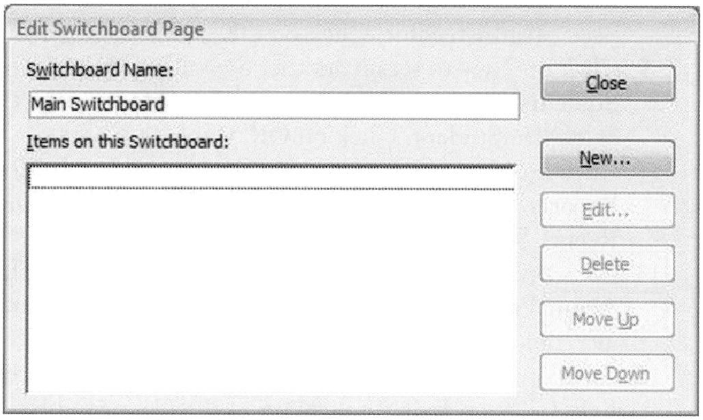

5 Edit the **Text** in the **Edit Switchboard Item** dialog box so that it reads **Book a Lesson** (see Figure 1.15.7).
6 Click on **Open Form in Edit Mode** from the drop-down in the **Command** box.
7 Click on **frmLessonBooking** in the **Form** box. Click on **OK**.

Figure 1.15.7 ▶

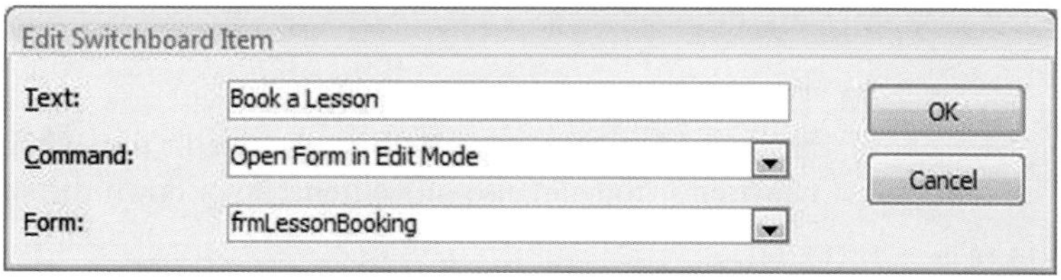

These steps set up the first button on our switchboard with the text **Book a Lesson**. When you click the button it will open the **frmLessonBooking**.

There are many options at this stage (see Figure 1.15.8). It is worth exploring the different options.

Figure 1.15.8 ▶

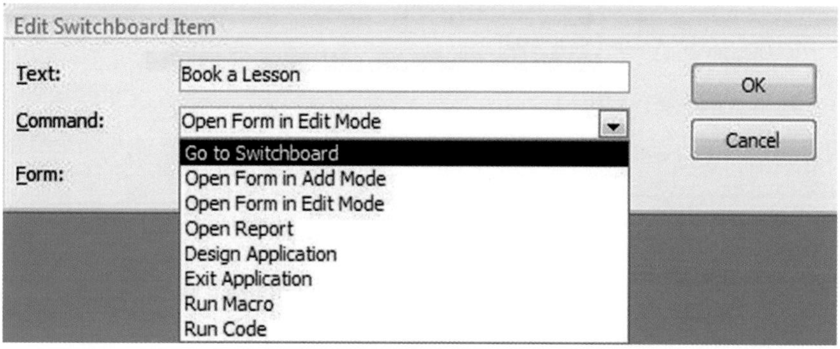

We will now continue to set up the other buttons on the switchboard.

8 Click on **New** to set up another Switchboard item. The text should be **Instructors**. Click on **Open Form in Edit Mode** in the **Command** box. Select **frmInstructor**. Click on **OK**.

9 Click on **New** to set up another Switchboard item. The text should be **Students**. Click on **Open Form in Edit Mode** in the **Command** box. Select **frmStudent**. Click on **OK**.

10 Click on **New** to set up another Switchboard item. The text should be **Reports**. Click on **Go to Switchboard** in the **Command** box. Select **Report Switchboard**. Click on **OK**.

11 Click on **New** to set up another Switchboard item. The text should be **About Pass IT**. Click on **Run Macro** in the **Command** box. Select **mcrAbout**. Click on **OK**.

12 Click on **New** to set up another Switchboard item. The text should be **Exit.** Click on **Exit Application** in the **Command** box (see Figure 1.15.9). Click on **OK**.

Figure 1.15.9 ▶

13 The **Edit Switchboard Page** dialog box will now appear as in Figure 1.15.10. You can use this page to edit the switchboard, delete or add new items. You can also move items up or down the switchboard list.

Figure 1.15.10 ▶

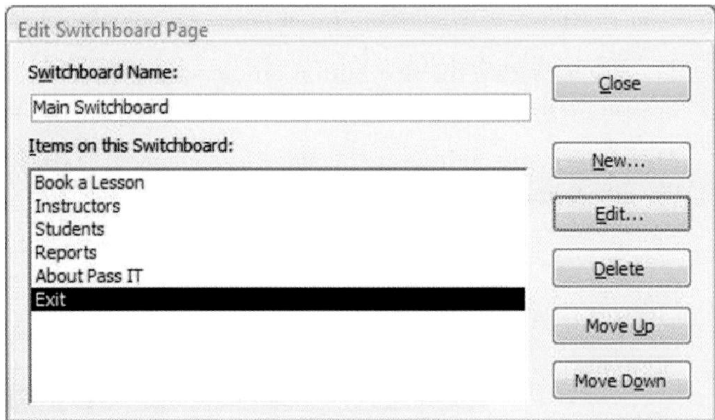

14 You have now set up a switchboard with six options. Click on **Close** twice to go back to the Access window and the Navigation Pane. There will now be a new form listed called **Switchboard** (see Figure 1.15.11).

Figure 1.15.11 ▶

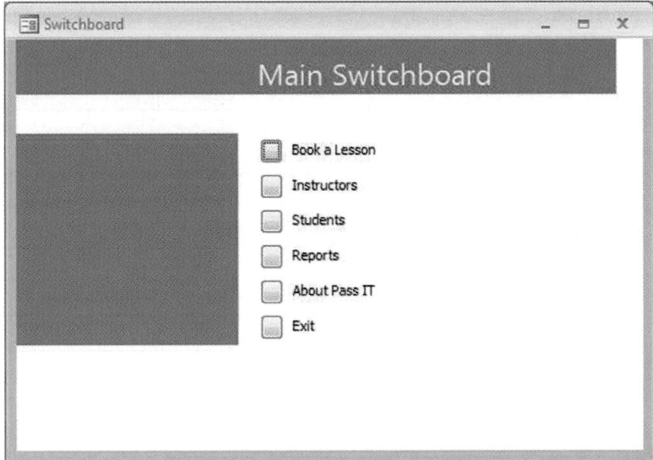

15 Open the **Switchboard** form. Test that each of the buttons works. The Report Switchboard will not yet be available.

Customising the switchboard

1 Open the switchboard in Design View so that it can be edited. See Figure 1.15.12. You will notice a button in the Detail area and a Label in the Form Header. Do not delete them.

Figure 1.15.12 ▶

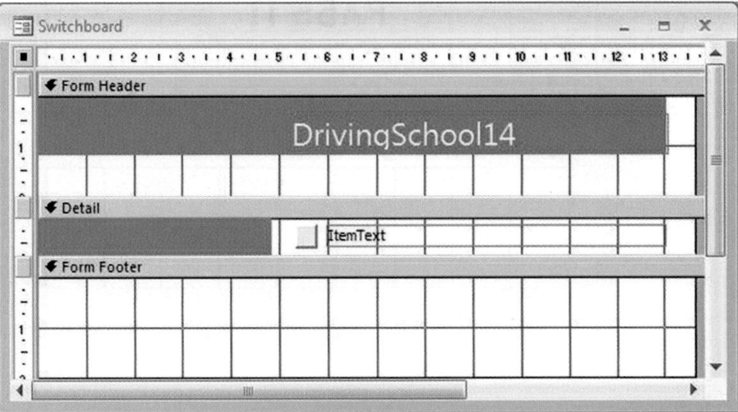

2 There are two green rectangles and one dark grey rectangle. Select them and press DELETE. Select the Label control and surrounding border. Click the **Property Sheet** and set the **Visible** property to **No**. See Figure 1.15.13.

Figure 1.15.13 ▶

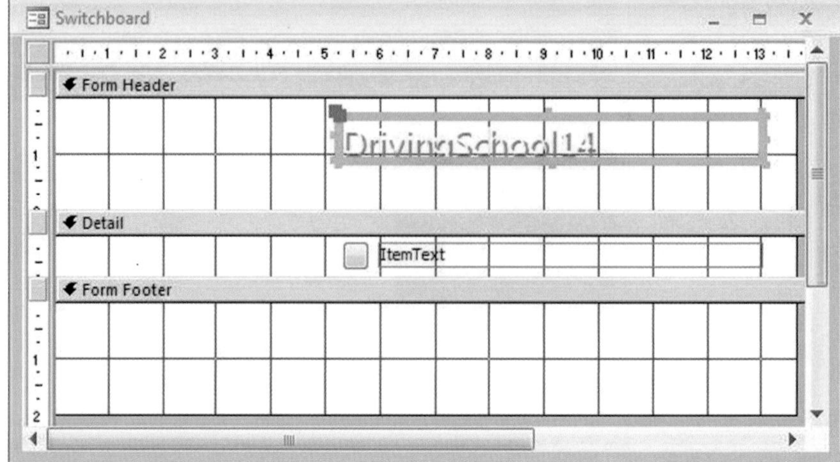

3 You will need to move the controls to the left of the form and then make the form narrower, as shown in Figure 1.15.14. It will help to reduce the size of the Item Text field and Label controls.

Figure 1.15.14 ▶

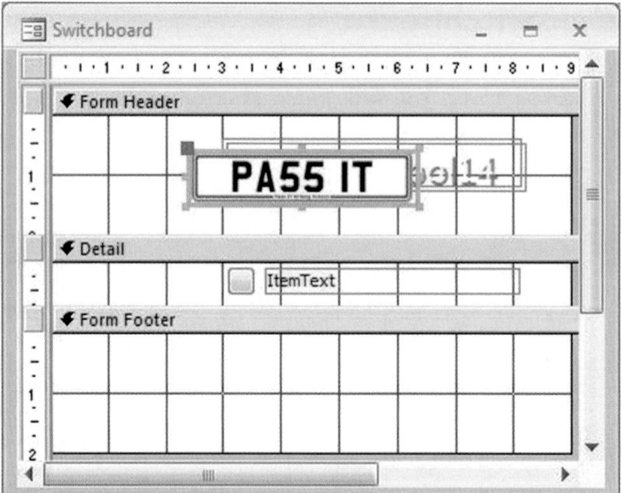

4 Insert the **Pass IT logo**, set the **Item Text** field to **Segoe UI** and the **Background Color** to **Light Blue 1**. The completed switchboard is shown in Figure 1.15.15.

Figure 1.15.15 ▶

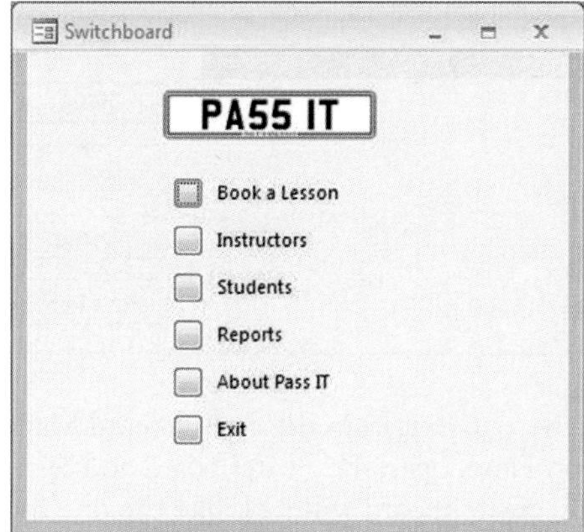

Adding the Report Switchboard

1 On the **Database Tools** tab, click the **Switchboard Manager** button to load the Switchboard Manager again. Click on **Report Switchboard** and click on **Edit**.

2 Click on **New** to set up another Switchboard item. The text should be **Instructor Contact Details.** Select **Open Report** in the **Command** box. Select **rptInstructor.** Click on **OK** (see Figure 1.15.16).

Figure 1.15.16 ▶

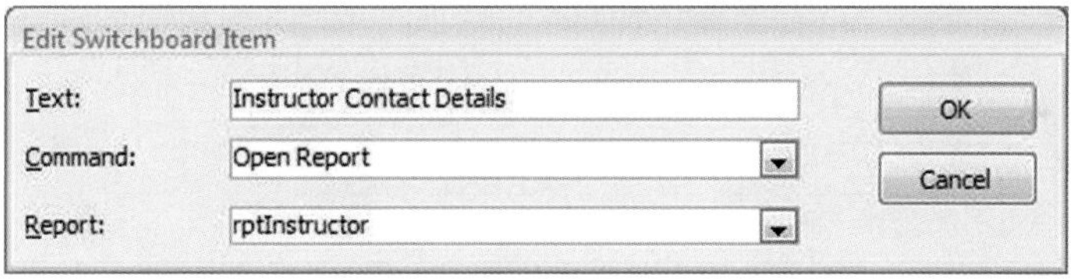

Edit Switchboard Item

Text: Instructor Contact Details

Command: Open Report

Report: rptInstructor

OK

Cancel

3 Click on **New** to set up another Switchboard item. The text should be **Instructor Timetable**. Select **Open Report** in the **Command** box. Select **rptInstructorTimetable**. Click on **OK**.

4 Click on **New** to set up another Switchboard item. The text should be **Weekly Timetable**. Select **Open Report** in the **Command** box. Select **rptWeeklyTimetable**. Click on **OK**.

5 Click on **New** to set up another Switchboard item. The text should be **Student Lesson Details**. Select **Open Report** in the **Command** box. Select **rptStudentLessonDetails**. Click on **OK**.

6 Click on **New** to set up the final Switchboard item. The text should be **Main Menu**. Click on **Go to Switchboard** in the **Command** box. Select **Main Switchboard**.

The Edit Switchboard Page dialog box is now shown, as in Figure 1.15.17.

Figure 1.15.17 ▶

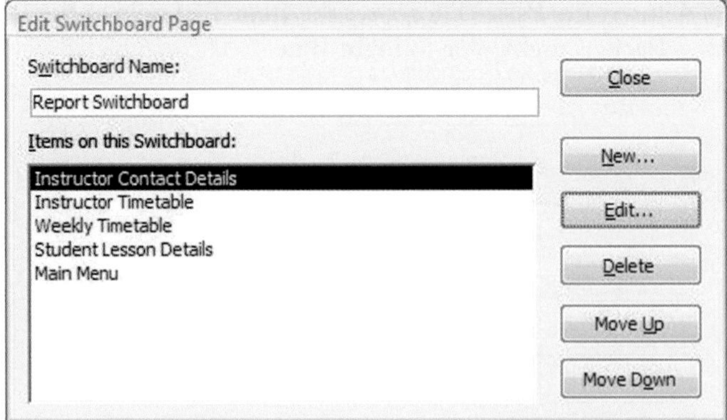

7 Click on **Close** twice to exit from the Switchboard Manager.
8 In the Navigation Pane, open the Switchboard and test that all the buttons work. The Report Switchboard will look like the one shown in Figure 1.15.18.

Figure 1.15.18 ▶

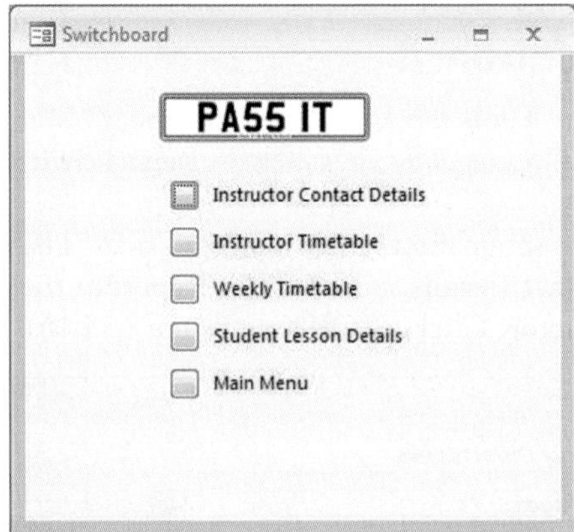

If you go back to the Navigation Pane, you will see that an additional table called **Switchboard Items** has been set up. If you open the table (see Figure 1.15.19), you can see that it controls the switchboard.

Figure 1.15.19 ▶

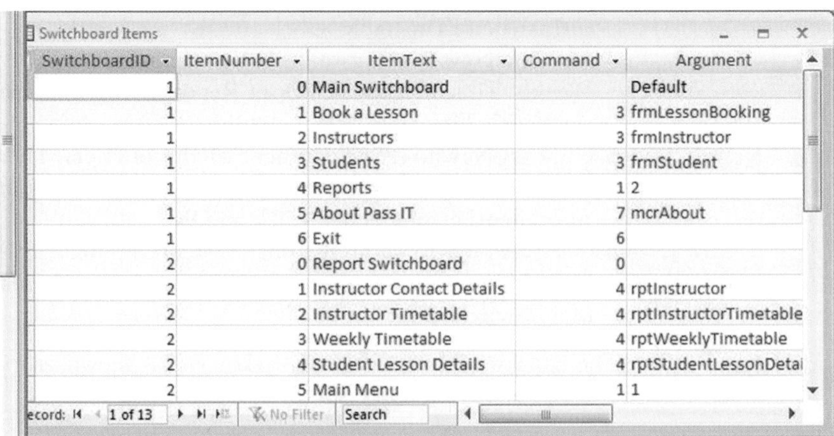

Switchboard Items

SwitchboardID	ItemNumber	ItemText	Command	Argument
1	0	Main Switchboard		Default
1	1	Book a Lesson	3	frmLessonBooking
1	2	Instructors	3	frmInstructor
1	3	Students	3	frmStudent
1	4	Reports	1	2
1	5	About Pass IT	7	mcrAbout
1	6	Exit	6	
2	0	Report Switchboard	0	
2	1	Instructor Contact Details	4	rptInstructor
2	2	Instructor Timetable	4	rptInstructorTimetable
2	3	Weekly Timetable	4	rptWeeklyTimetable
2	4	Student Lesson Details	4	rptStudentLessonDetai
2	5	Main Menu	1	1

ecord: 1 of 13 No Filter Search

This table can be used to edit the switchboard text.

Setting the startup options

We want the switchboard to load automatically when the file is opened. One way of doing this is to use **Access Options**.

Set it up as follows:

1 Load the **DrivingSchool** database. Click on the **Office Button** and select **Access Options**. The **Access Options** window will be displayed (see Figure 1.15.20). Click on **Current Database**.

Figure 1.15.20 ▶

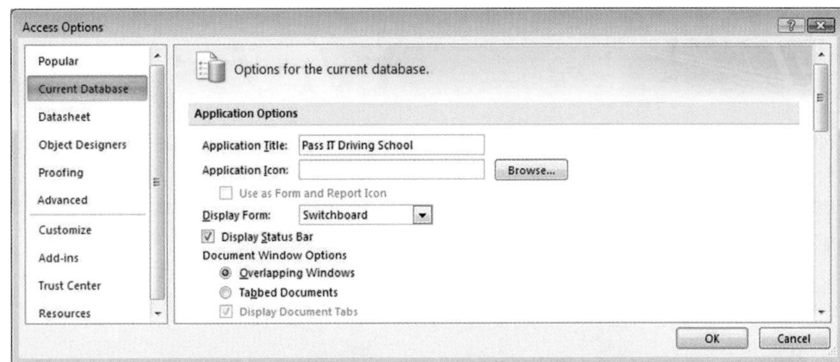

2 Click on the **Display Form** drop-down arrow and select **Switchboard.** This is the name of the form you want to load on start-up.
3 In the **Application Title** box, enter **Pass IT Driving School.** This is the text that appears at the top of the Access screen.
4 Close your system and reload it. Test that the switchboard opens when the system loads and that the application title is displayed.

Unit 16: Giving forms a new look with Access 2007

Access 2007 has many new features which allow you to give your forms a modern fresh look.

The forms developed so far have used the traditional **Overlapping Windows** approach, which allows you to place forms and objects side by side. This will be preferred by some people and applications.

Access 2007 offers an option to use a **Tabbed** interface so objects such as forms and reports can be opened at once. See Figure 1.16.1

Figure 1.16.1 ▼

Access 2007 allows you to resize and reposition controls as the user resizes or maximises the form. This is useful if you are working with **Tabbed Documents**. Controls can be individually set to resize and reposition by using the **Anchoring** controls found in the **Size** group, on the **Arrange** tab. See Figure 1.16.2.

Figure 1.16.2 ▶

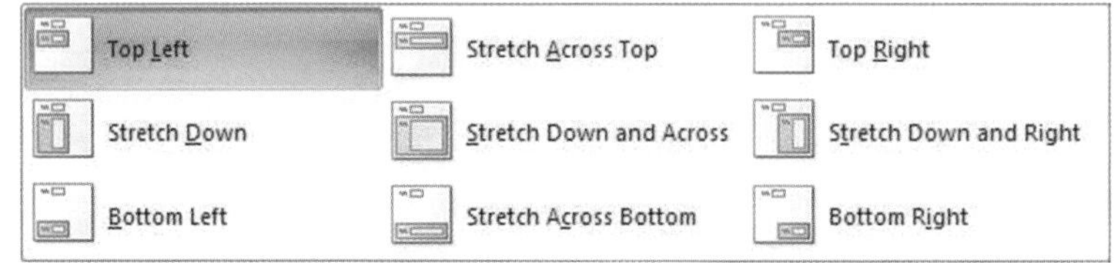

Access 2007 allows you to easily create a web-styled interface with **Transparent** buttons including text and graphics, along with a **Hyperlink Hand** rather than traditional pointer. See Figure 1.16.3.

Figure 1.16.3 ▶

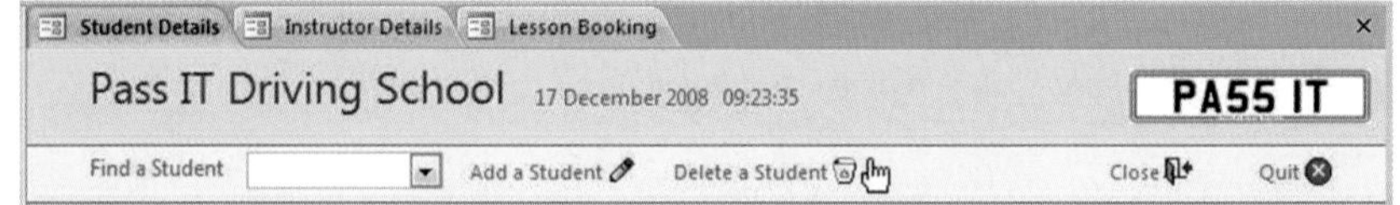

Access 2007 encourages users to use the newer fonts, such as **Calibri** and **Segoe UI**. Forms can also have colour themes, such as **Background Form** for the detail section and **Dark Text** for labels.

Access 2007 introduces 25 **Autoformat** themes that can be used across your solution and enable you to keep forms consistent in style. These are found on the **Arrange** tab in Design View or the **Format** tab in Layout View. They are shown in Figure 1.16.4.

Figure 1.16.4 ▶

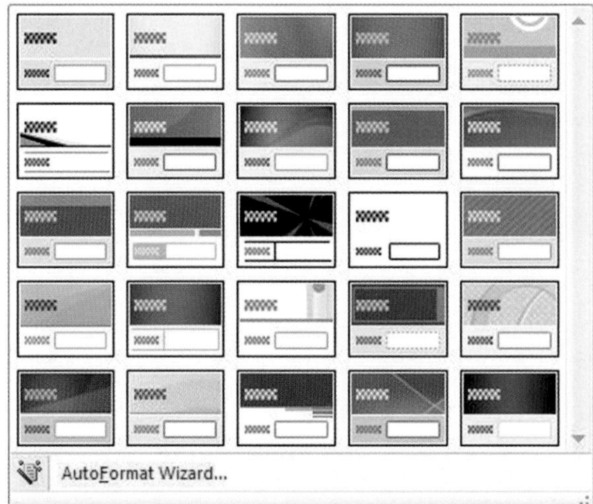

The following steps take you through giving the Student form in our Pass IT system a new look and demonstrate these features. You may prefer to work with a copy of your **frmStudent**.

1 Load **frmStudent** in Design View. Remove the control panel by dragging around the controls and pressing DELETE. Also remove the rectangle placed around the controls in the Header and the Detail sections. Set **Navigation Buttons** property to **Yes**, if they are not showing. See Figure 1.16.5.

Figure 1.16.5 ▶

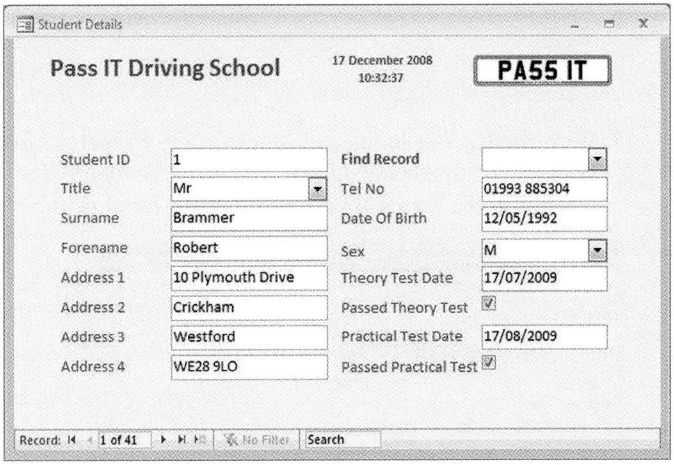

2 In the Form Header, change the **Font** of the **Title** control to **Segoe UI, 18pt**. Change the **Font** of the **Date and Time** controls to **Segoe UI, 9pt**. The **Font Color** should be set to **Text Dark** already. You will need to remove the **Bold** setting, if used.
3 Click the **Form Selector** to select the form. On the **Arrange** tab, click the **AutoFormat** drop-down and select the **Access 2007** style (second option). This will give your form the style used in Unit 9. See Figure 1.16.6.
4 In the Detail section, highlight all the **Label** controls and change the font to **Segoe UI, 10pt**.
5 Re-arrange the **Date and Time** controls horizontally. It is best to do this in Layout View so you can see if the data fits the control.

Figure 1.16.6 ▶

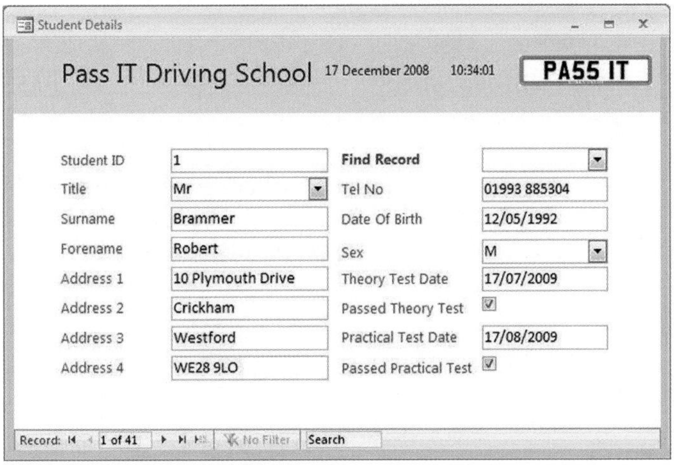

6 In the Form Header, drag out the right margin a little and drag down the Detail section. On the **Design** tab, click on the **Rectangle** tool and drag out a rectangle, as shown in Figure 1.16.7.

Figure 1.16.7 ▶

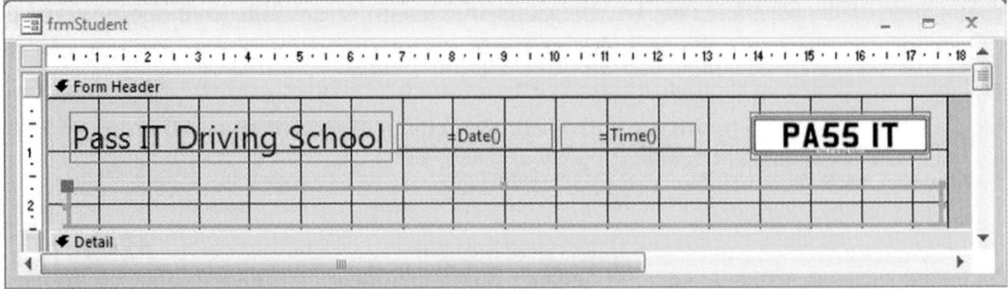

7 With the **Rectangle** selected, click on the **Property Sheet** button and set the **Back Color** to **Access Theme 2** and the **Border Color** to **Text Dark**. See Figure 1.16.8. This will become a banner for our controls.

Figure 1.16.8 ▶

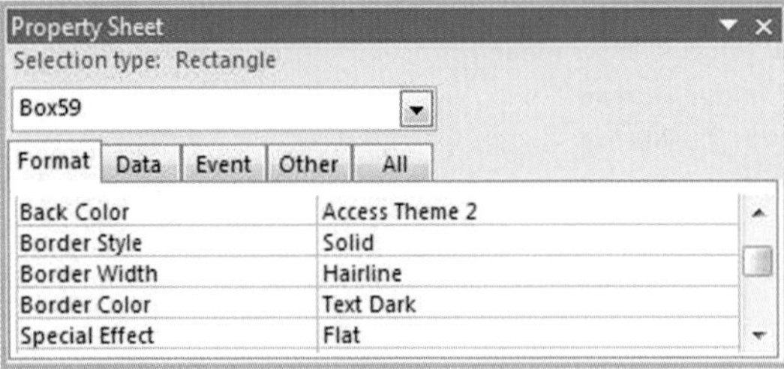

8 Switch to **Form View** to view your form. See Figure 1.16.9.

Figure 1.16.9 ▶

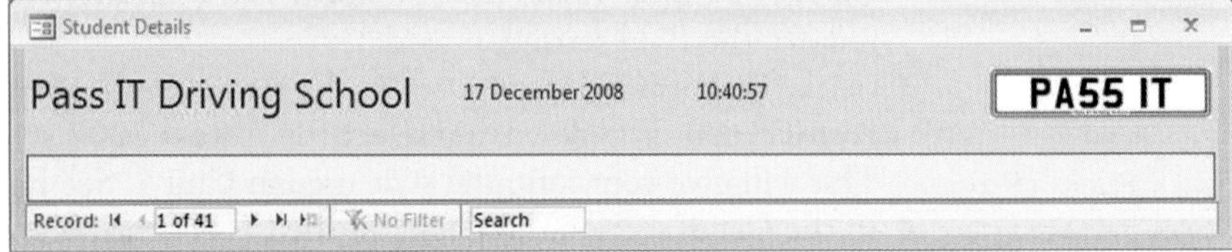

9 Click the **Office Button** and use the **Access Options** to switch to **Tabbed Documents** mode. See Figure 1.16.10. You will notice that, as the form expands, the logo and rectangle stay fixed.

Figure 1.16.10 ▶

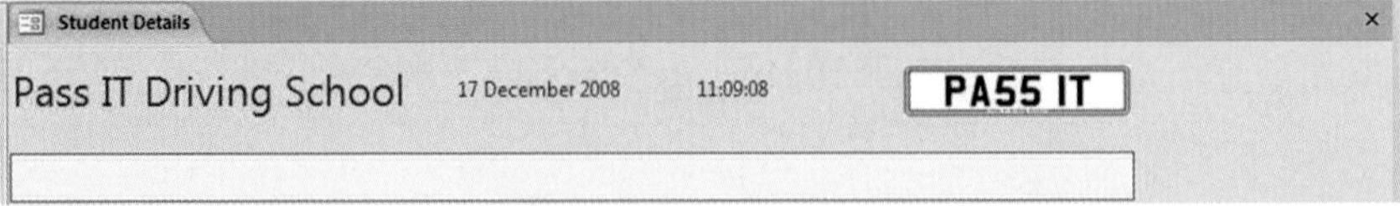

Access comes with a range of anchoring options that enable you to anchor a control to a position on the form. We want the banner and logo to anchor to the right of the screen/form, as the form expands.

10 Switch to **Design View** and click on the **Title** label. Click the **Property Sheet** button and scroll down to view its **Horizontal Anchor** and **Vertical Anchor** properties. They are set to **Left** and **Top**, as shown in Figure 1.16.11.

Figure 1.16.11 ▶

Property Sheet
Selection type: Label
Label31
Format
Data
Event
Other
All
Horizontal Anchor
Left
Vertical Anchor
Top
Display When
Always

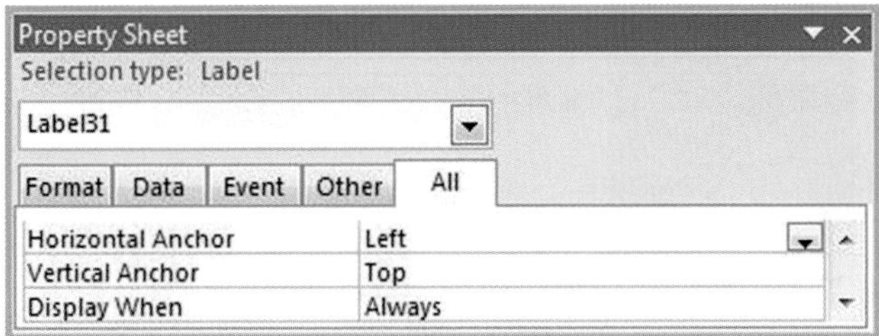

If you click on all the controls, you will see this is the default setting. We want to pin the logo to the right and the rectangle to both the left and right.

11 Click on the **Pass IT logo** and set the **Horizontal Anchor** and **Vertical Anchor** properties to **Right** and **Top**, as shown in Figure 1.16.12.

Figure 1.16.12 ▶

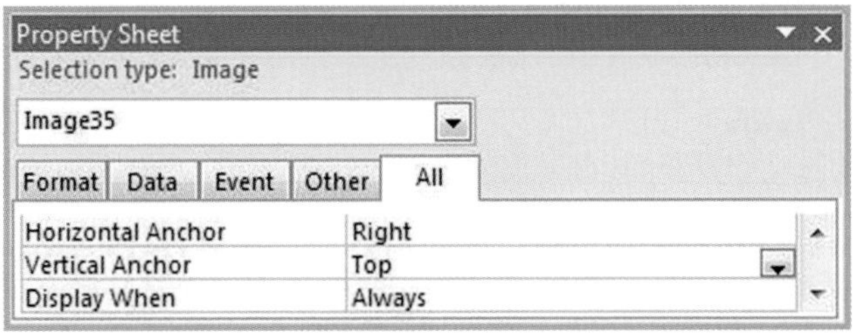

Property Sheet
Selection type: Image
Image35
Format
Data
Event
Other
All
Horizontal Anchor
Right
Vertical Anchor
Top
Display When
Always

12 Select the banner control and set the **Horizontal Anchor** and **Vertical Anchor** properties to **Both** and **Top**. Switch to **Form View**. Your form should appear as in Figure 1.16.13.

Figure 1.16.13 ▼

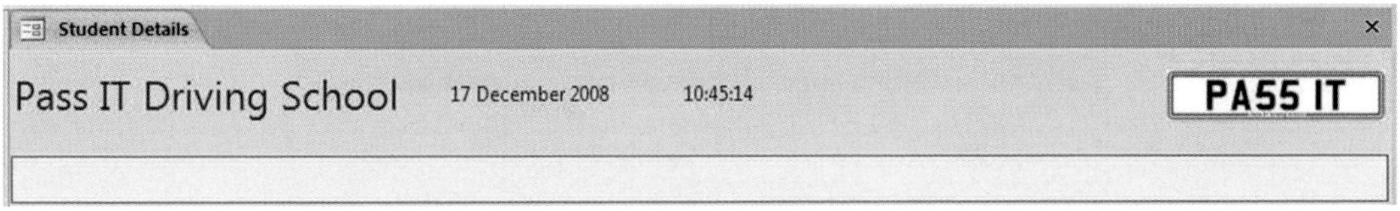

Student Details
Pass IT Driving School
17 December 2008
10:45:14
PA55 IT

13 The next stage is to add the command buttons to the banner. In Design View, click on **Button** in the **Controls** group and click on the form where you want to place the button. In the Categories list, select **Record Operations**. In the Actions list, select **Add New Record** and click on **Next**.

14 The next window offers you a choice of putting pictures or text on the button. We are going to use a picture, so choose the **Picture** option and select **Pencil (Edit)**, as in Figure 1.16.14. Click on **Next**, then on **Finish**. Your button will appear as in Figure 1.16.15.

Figure 1.16.14 ▶

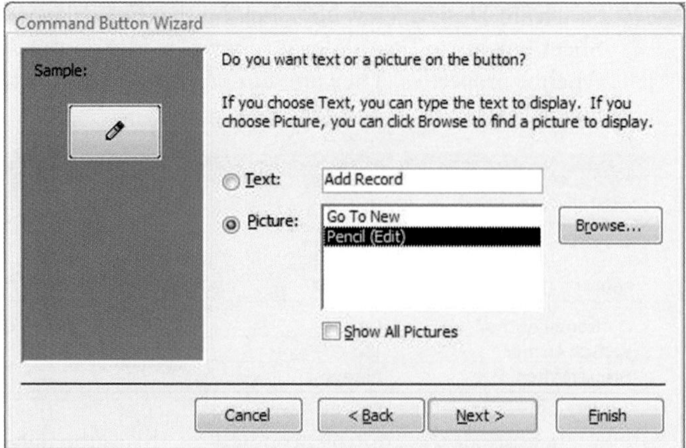

Figure 1.16.15 ▶

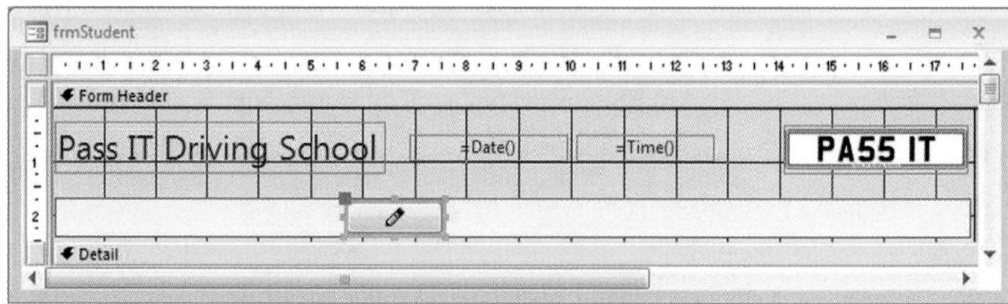

15 With the button selected, click the **Property Sheet** button and set the **Caption** to **Add a Student**, **Picture Caption Arrangement** to **Left**, **Cursor on Hover** to **Hyperlink hand** and **Back Style** to **Transparent**. Set the **Font** on the button to **Segoe UI**, **9pt**, **Text Dark**. See Figure 1.16.16.

Hint Select the button in Design View and click on the **Set Control Defaults** button in the **Controls** group to apply your settings to future buttons.

Figure 1.16.16 ▶

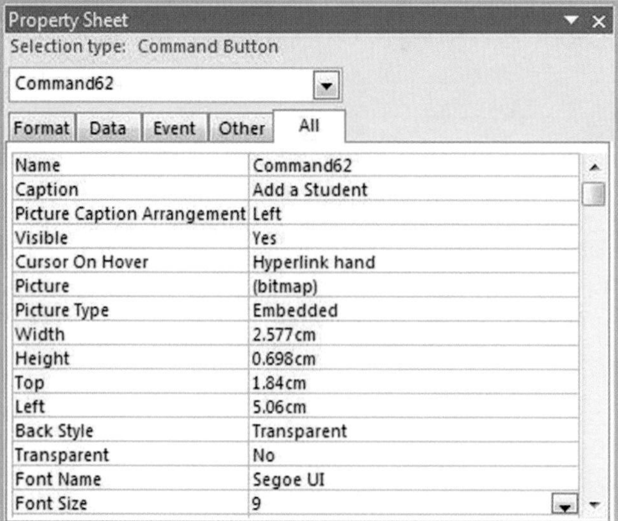

16 Switch to **Form View**. Your button should appear as in Figure 1.16.17.

Figure 1.16.17 ▶

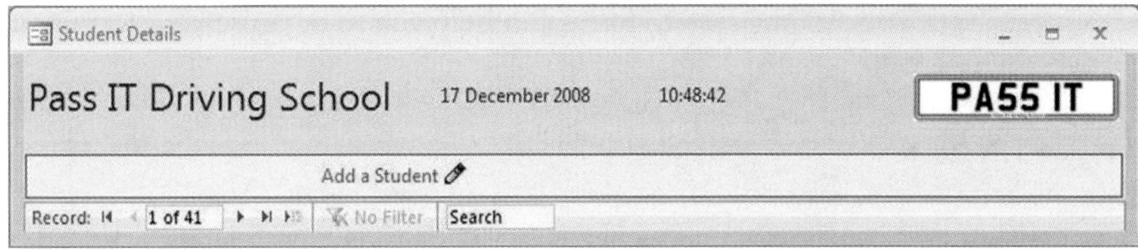

17 If you are familiar with setting up buttons from earlier in the unit, it should be easy to complete the form by adding **Close Form**, **Quit** and **Delete Record** buttons. See Figure 1.16.18. We have dragged the **Find Record Combo Box** on to the banner and edited the label to **Find a Student** with the font set to **Segoe UI, 9pt**.

Figure 1.16.18 ▶

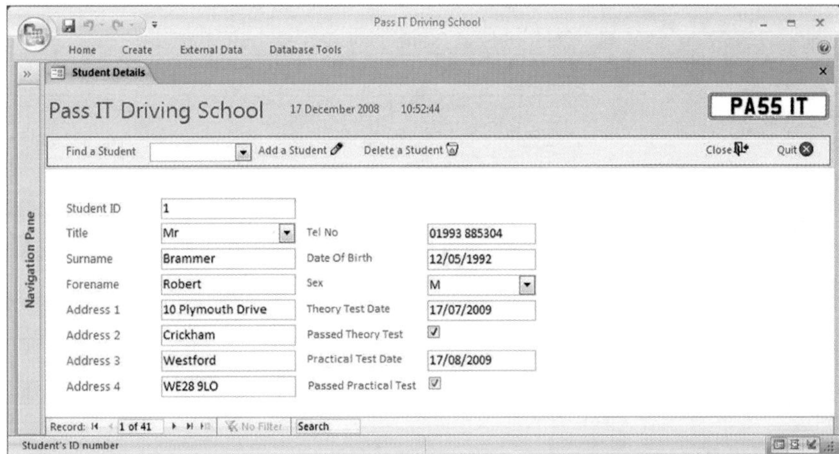

18 Figure 1.16.18 shows the finished Student form in Tabbed Documents mode. Figure 1.16.19 shows the finished Student form in Overlapping Windows mode.

Figure 1.16.19 ▶

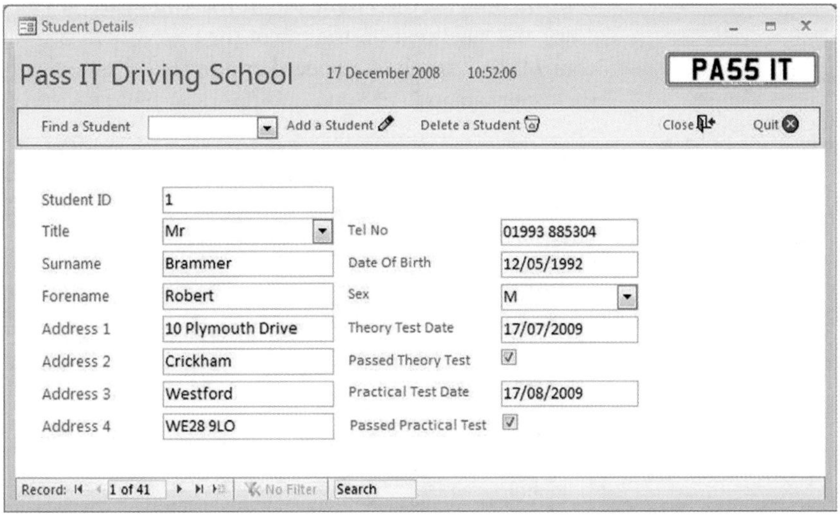

Creating a Tabbed Form

Adding tabs to forms can help you to organise your form and make it easier to use.

Figure 1.16.20 ▶

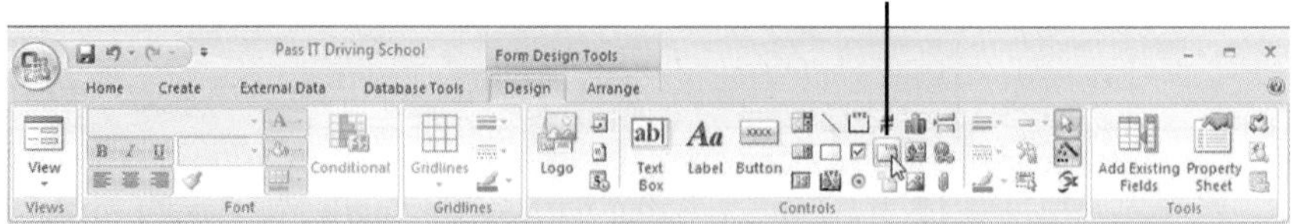

1 In Design View, drag your controls to the right of the screen to create some room for the tab control. In the **Controls** group, click on the **Tab Control** and click on the form where you want to place the control. You may need to drag the control out a little. See Figure 1.16.21.

Figure 1.16.21 ▶

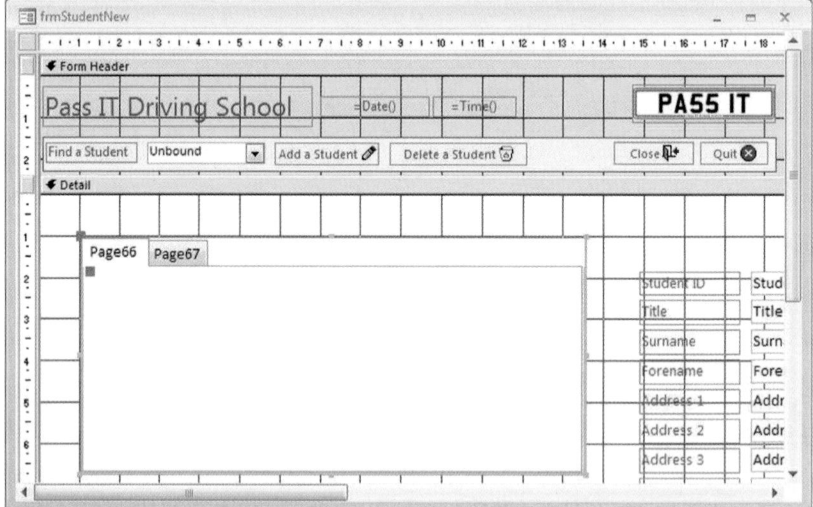

2 By default, Access sets up two tab pages. Select the left-hand column of controls and, on the **Home** tab in the **Clipboard** group, click **Cut**.

3 Click the label text on the tab of the page where you want to place the controls and, on the **Clipboard** group, click **Paste**. See Figure 1.16.22. Select the other tab and cut and paste the right-hand controls to it.

Figure 1.16.22 ▶

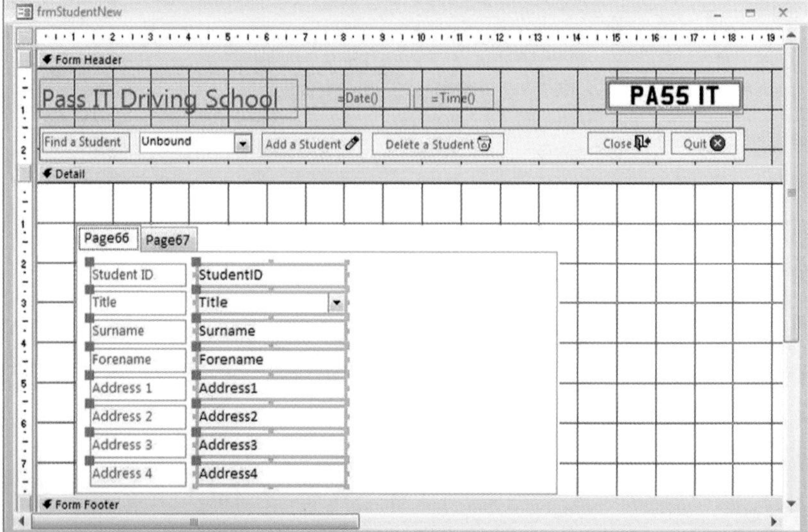

4 Double-click on the first **Tab Control** and, in the **Property Sheet**, set the **Name** property to **Student Details**. **Name** the second **Tab Control, Test Details**. See Figure 1.16.23. You would probably want to choose the controls differently, but for the purpose of this exercise we will leave it.

5 Click in the **Detail** section and click on the **Property Sheet**. Set the **Back Color** to **Background Form**.

6 As you resize the form, it would be useful to resize the tabbed page. In Design View, select the tabbed form and set the **Horizontal Anchor** and **Vertical Anchor** properties to **Both** and **Both**, or **Both** and **Top** if you want the control to only resize horizontally. Save your form as **frmStudentNew**.

Figure 1.16.23 ▶

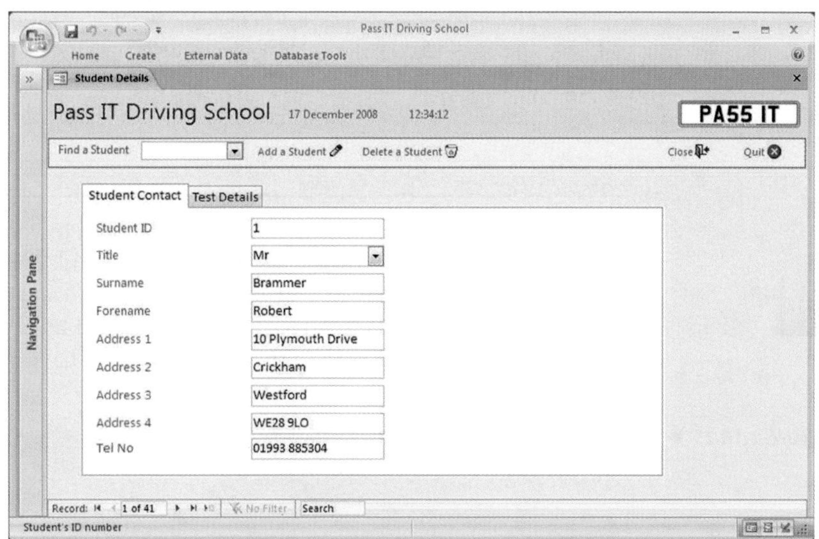

Your finished form should appear as in Figure 1.16.23. It is a relatively easy job now to set up the Lesson Booking and Instructor forms in this style using Tabbed Documents. Using copy, paste and simple editing should produce the Lesson Booking form shown in Figure 1.16.24.

In Unit 14 we set up some simple macros to open the Instructor and Student forms called **mcrInstructorForm** and **mcrStudentForm**. We have added two command buttons to the banner to run these macros. You could also run the macros to print reports from here.

Save your forms as **frmInstructorNew** and **frmLessonBookingNew**.

Figure 1.16.24 ▶

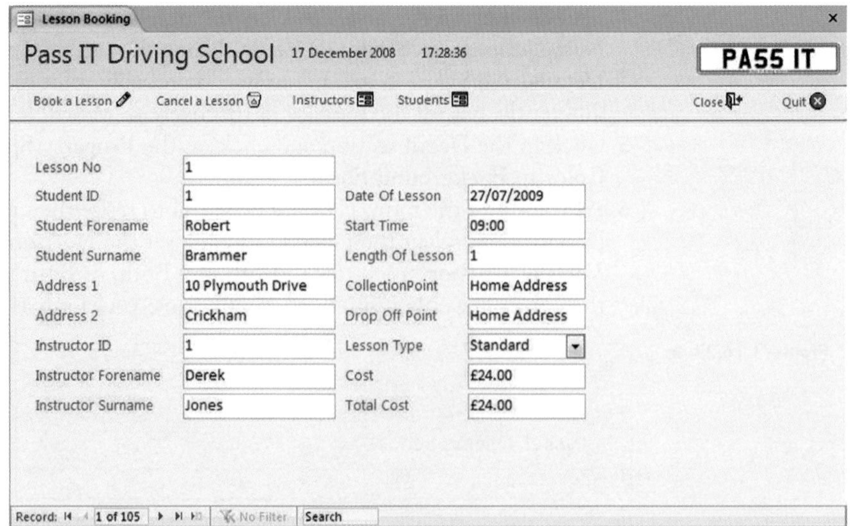

You may at this point go on and develop a front end to your solution or use those developed in earlier units. We have used a Blank Form and added some details about the company Pass IT and could go on to add opening hours and lesson prices, etc, see Figure 1.16.25. We have added links to the key forms and reports in the same style as the other interfaces. We have called it **frmHome** for the purpose of the next stage.

Figure 1.16.25 ▶

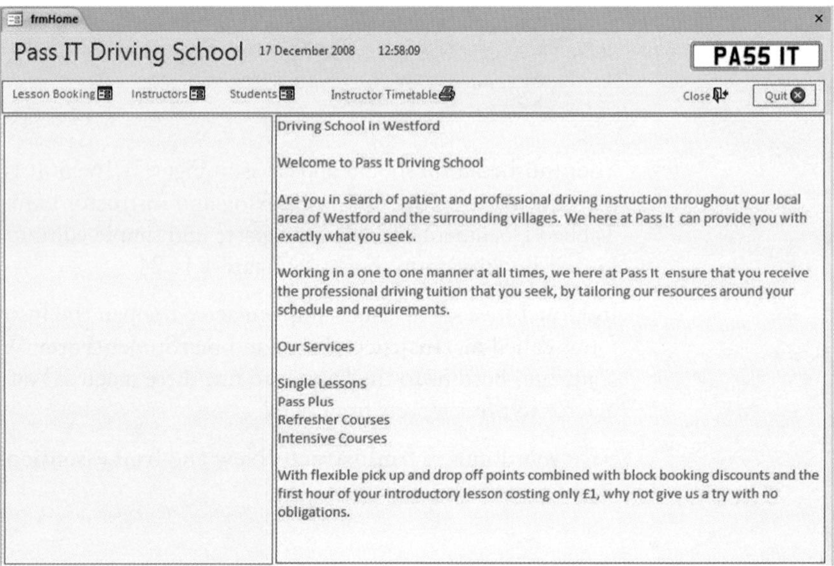

Using the Navigation Pane to control your solution

As you have worked through these units, you have used the Navigation Pane to manage the objects in your solution.

Figure 1.16.26 ▶

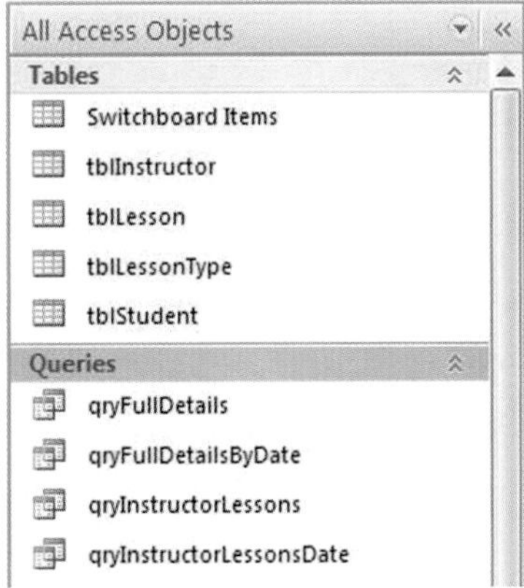

The list of objects can become long and unfriendly. You can limit the objects a user sees by creating a custom category. The custom category will display the most commonly used objects and make it easier to use your database.

1 Right-click the menu at the top of the Navigation Pane and click **Navigation Options**.
2 In the **Navigation Options** dialog box, click on **Custom** and click **Rename Item**. Enter **Pass IT Driving School** and press ENTER.
3 In the right-hand pane, select **Custom Group 1** and click on **Rename Group**. Enter **Forms** and press ENTER.
4 Click on **Add Group** and set up two further groups called **Reports** and **Procedures**. Click **OK**. See Figure 1.16.27.

Figure 1.16.27 ▶

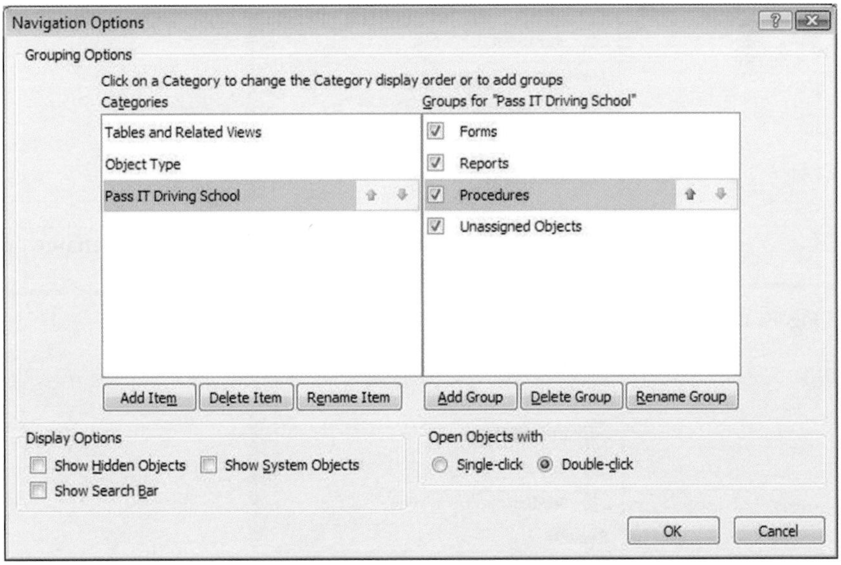

Navigation Options
Grouping Options
Click on a Category to change the Category display order or to add groups
Categories
Groups for "Pass IT Driving School"
Tables and Related Views
Object Type
Pass IT Driving School
Forms
Reports
Procedures
Unassigned Objects
Add Item
Delete Item
Rename Item
Add Group
Delete Group
Rename Group
Display Options
Show Hidden Objects
Show System Objects
Show Search Bar
Open Objects with
Single-click
Double-click
OK
Cancel

5 Click the menu at the top of the Navigation Pane and select **Pass IT Driving School**. You can see the groups you have set up with all the objects allocated to the **Unassigned Objects** group, as shown in Figure 1.16.28.

Figure 1.16.28 ▶

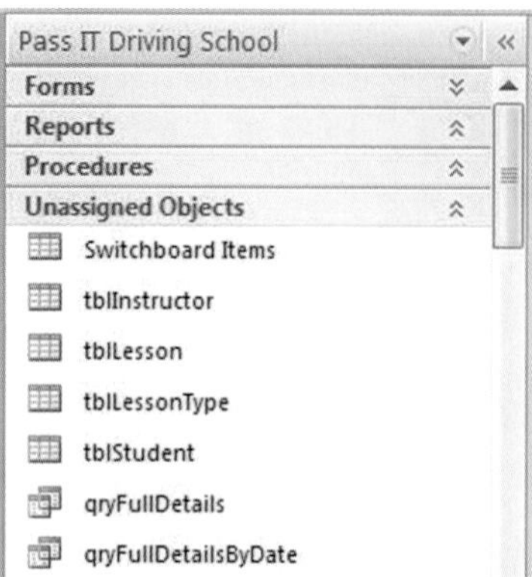

6 Drag and drop **frmHome** (if developed) on to the **Forms** title bar. Repeat this process for the new **Instructor**, **Student** and **Lesson Booking** forms. You can multi-select by holding SHIFT in the usual way.

7 Drag and drop the key reports you want the user to use on to the **Reports** title bar. Drag the **mcrAbout** in to the **Procedures** group. See Figure 1.16.29.

Figure 1.16.29 ▶

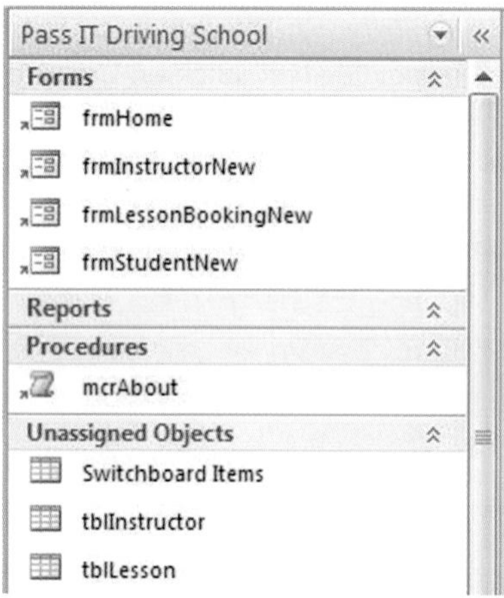

8 Right-click in turn on each icon and use the **Rename** option to give your objects friendlier names. See Figure 1.16.30.

Figure 1.16.30 ▶

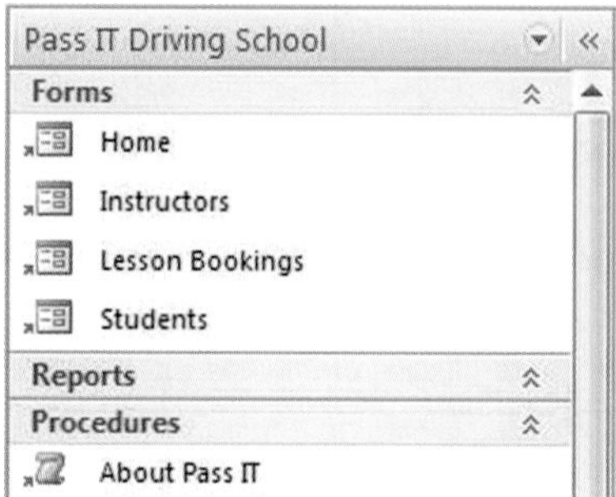

9 Right-click the menu at the top of the Navigation Pane and click on **Navigation Options**. Click on **Pass IT Driving School** and in the right pane clear the **Unassigned Objects** checkbox to hide the group in the Navigation Pane. See Figure 1.16.31.

Figure 1.18.7 ▼

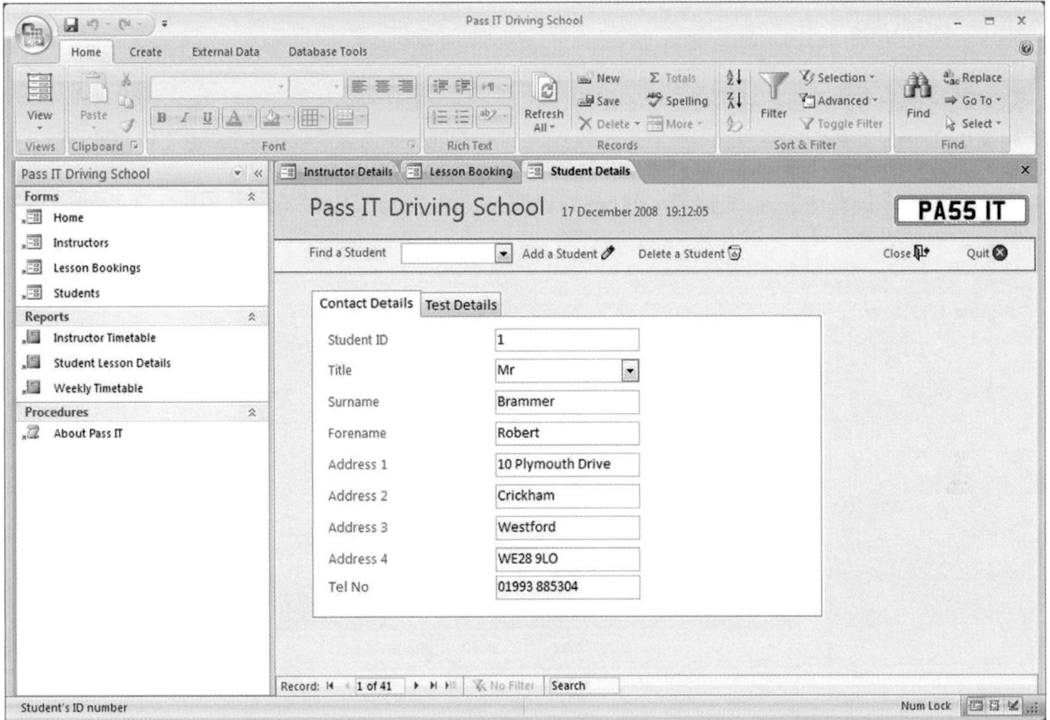

Unit 17: Using SubForms

In this section you will learn how to use SubForms.

In Access 2007 systems there will be many instances when it is necessary to see data from related tables on one screen. Using a SubForm is one of a number of ways of doing this.

Some examples

- In a video loans system you might want to have membership details on screen alongside details of videos loaned by that member.
- In a customer ordering system when a customer phones up with an order enquiry it would be useful to have the customer details and details of their orders on screen.
- In the Pass IT Driving School you might want to view instructor details alongside their lessons, as shown in Figure 1.17.1. The Instructor form is set to just show details of name and ID. A SubForm is added showing details of the lessons for that instructor.

Figure 1.17.1 ▶

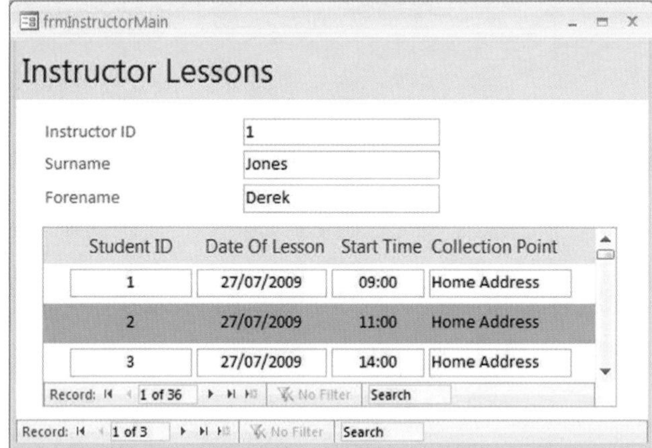

Typically in this sort of scenario a main form is set up based on the primary table Instructor, with a SubForm based on the Lesson table. This is the simplest way forward, but you will see later how to have greater control over the SubForm by basing it on a query.

The following two examples take you through setting up similar uses of SubForms but in slightly different ways. It is worthwhile practising the different methods to grasp the concepts involved here.

Example 1

The following steps show you how to set up the SubForm as shown above. We will use the wizard to make a start.

1 On the **Create** tab, click **More Forms** and then click on the **Form Wizard** button to bring up the **Form Wizard** dialog box.

2 Select **tblInstructor** from the drop-down and choose the fields **InstructorID**, **Surname** and **Forename** from the available fields. Remember you can select the fields one by one by clicking the single arrow. Do not click **Next** yet. See Figure 1.17.2.

Figure 1.17.2 ▶

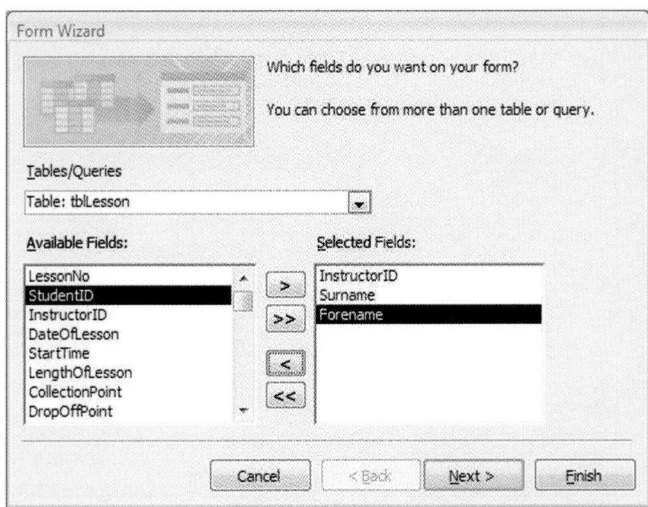

3 We now want to select the fields for the SubForm. Select **tblLesson** from the drop-down and add **StudentID**, **DateOfLesson**, **StartTime** and **CollectionPoint** from the available fields. Click on **Next** (see Figure 1.17.3).

Figure 1.17.3 ▶

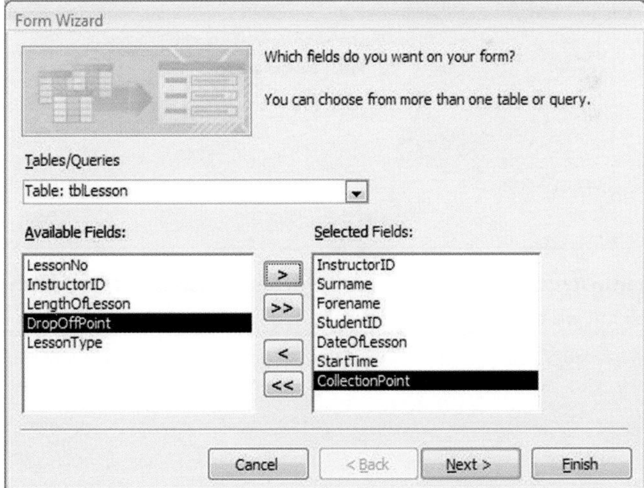

4 The **Form Wizard** then asks you **How do you want to view your data?** Make sure **by tblInstructor** is selected and **Form with SubForms(s)** is checked. Click on **Next** (see Figure 1.17.4).

Figure 1.17.4 ▶

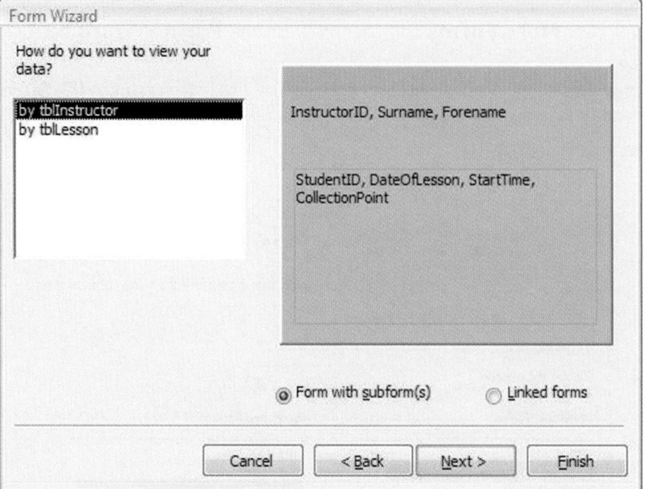

5 Select a **Tabular** layout and click on **Next**. Select **Access 2007** style and click on **Next**.

Figure 1.17.5 ▶

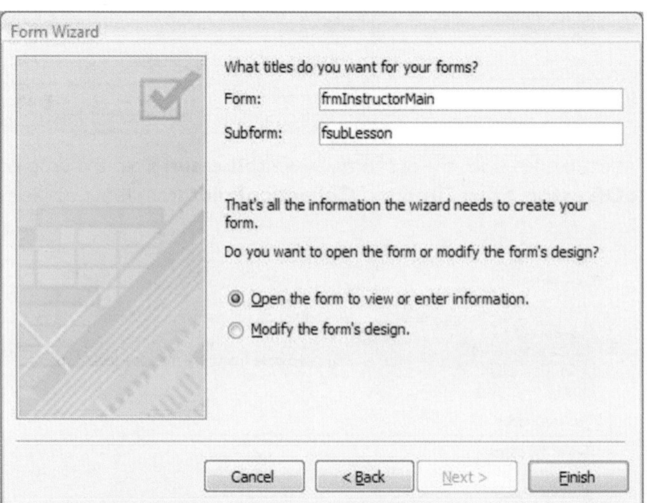

6 Name the form **frmInstructorMain** and the SubForm **fsubLesson**. Click on **Finish** (see Figure 1.17.5).

Your Main form/SubForm will open in **Form View** and should appear a little like Figure 1.17.1, at the start of the unit.

Its appearance will need a little fine-tuning using **Layout View** and **Design View**. You can quickly use **Layout View** to resize and align controls to better fit the data as shown in Figure 1.17.6 and use **Design View** to fine-tune.

Figure 1.17.6 ▶

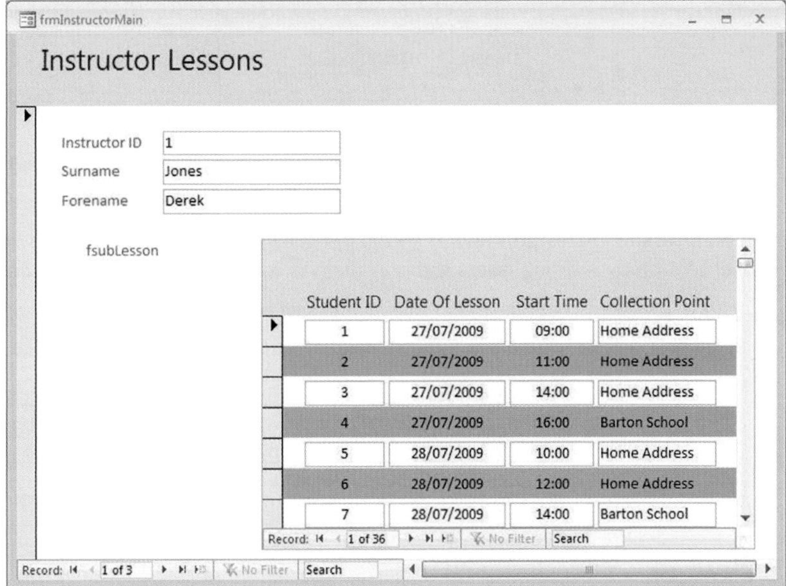

7 Switch to **Design View** and highlight the layout selectors. Remove them by clicking the **Remove** button on the **Arrange** tab. Delete the **fsubLesson** label and drag the SubForm across as shown in Figure 1.17.7.

Figure 1.17.7 ▶

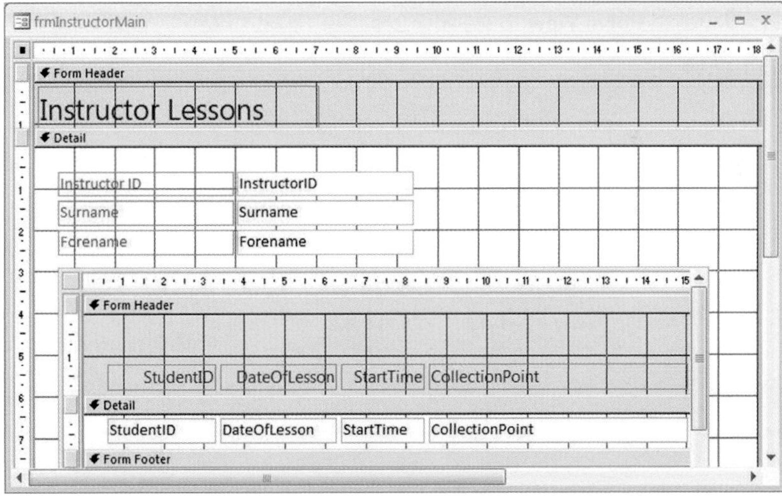

8 Edit the **Header** label to read **Instructor Lessons** and close the **Form Header** up a little. Align and edit the controls on the main form, if not done already, as shown in Figure 1.17.7

9 In **Design View** double-click on the Form Selector on **frmInstructorMain** to bring up the **Property Sheet**. Remove the scroll bars and record selectors. Save your work.

Figure 1.17.8 ▶

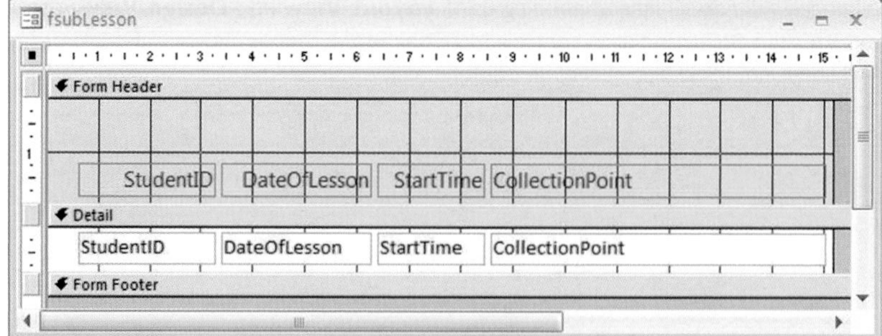

10 Open **fsubLesson** in **Design View**, as shown in Figure 1.17.8. From here you can edit the SubForm. Edit the label controls by inserting spaces and drag them to the top of the **Form Header**. See Figure 1.17.9.

Figure 1.17.9 ▶

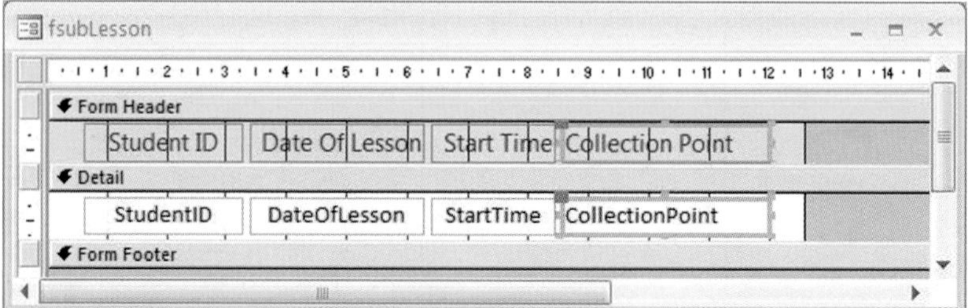

11 Align the controls in the **Detail** area (we have centre-aligned all but **Collection Point**) and reduce the size of the **Collection Point** controls by dragging in the handles. You can now drag in the right margin as well. See Figure 1.17.9. Again you may have done this in **Layout View**; there is no set way.

12 Double-click on the **Form Selector** and remove the horizontal scroll bars and record selectors. Save your work. Switch to **Form View** to see your form. See Figure 1.17.10.

Figure 1.17.10 ▶

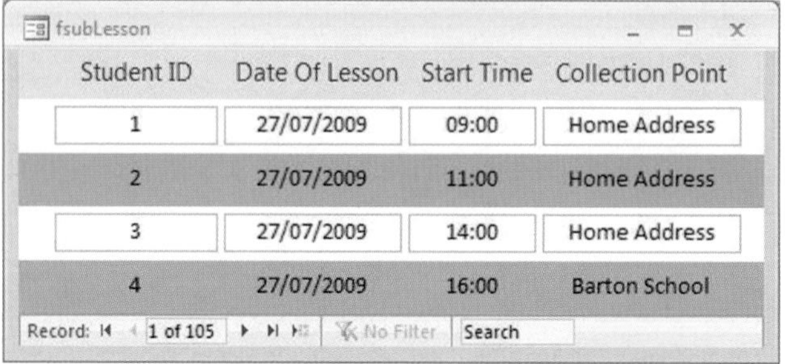

13 Open **frmInstructorMain** and scroll through the instructor details to view the details of their lessons in the SubForm (see Figure 1.17.11). You will probably have to go into **Design View** and drag the right margin in and the **Form Footer** up, to tidy the form to suit.

Figure 1.17.11 ▶

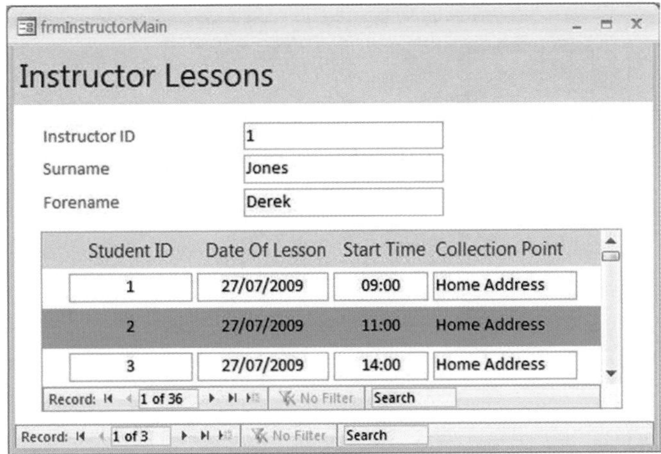

There are a number of ways of setting up SubForms in Access. As ever, you choose the method that suits you best. The next example will take you through setting up a SubForm in a slightly different way.

Example 2

We are going to set up a SubForm on the Student form giving details of each student's lessons.

1 On the **Create** tab, click **More Forms** and then click on the **Form Wizard** button to bring up the **Form Wizard** dialog box.

2 Select **tblStudent** from the drop-down and choose all the fields from **StudentID** down to **Address4**. Choose a **Columnar** layout, **Access 2007** style and name your form **frmStudentLessonMain**.

3 Open your form in **Design View**. Remove the label in the **Form Header** and close up the **Form Header** section. Re-arrange and resize the controls as shown in Figure 1.17.12.

Figure 1.17.12 ▶

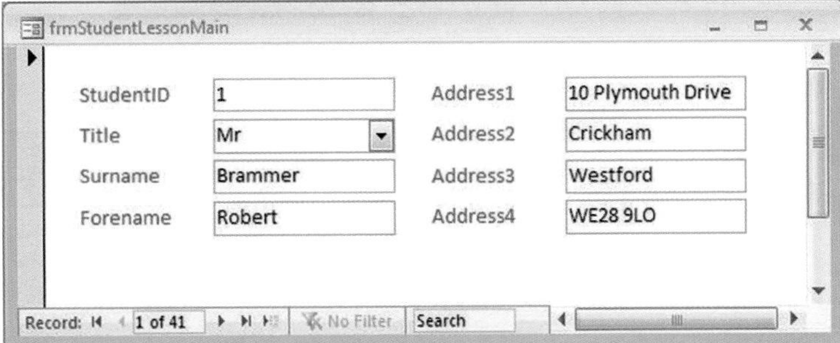

4 Switch to **Design View** (if not already in it) and, on the **Design** tab, in the **Controls** group, click the **SubForm/SubReport** button. Drag out a rectangle about 13cm by 2cm across the foot of the form, in the Detail area.

5 The **SubForm Wizard** is displayed. Check **Use existing Tables and Queries**. Click on **Next** (see Figure 1.17.13).

Figure 1.17.13 ▶

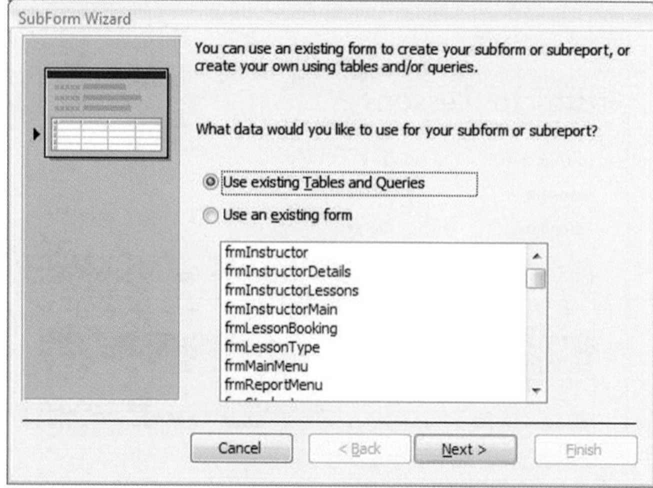

6 From the next **SubForm Wizard** dialog box, select **tblLesson** from the drop-down and select the fields as shown in Figure 1.17.14. Click on **Next**.

Figure 1.17.14 ▶

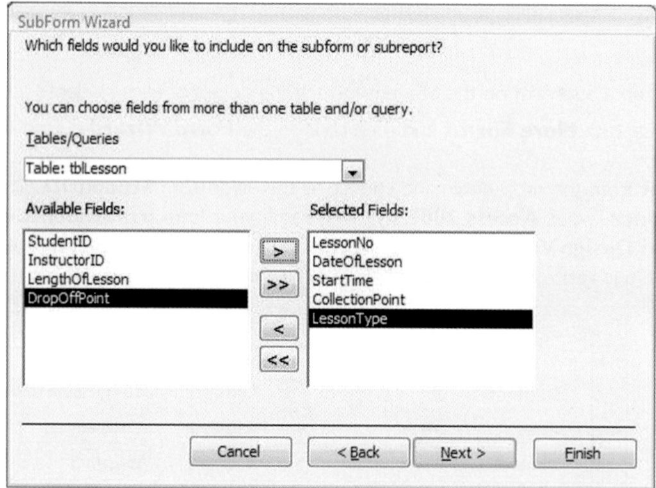

7 In the next **SubForm Wizard** dialog box, the wizard detects the linking fields for you so just click on **Next** (see Figure 1.17.15).

Figure 1.17.15 ▶

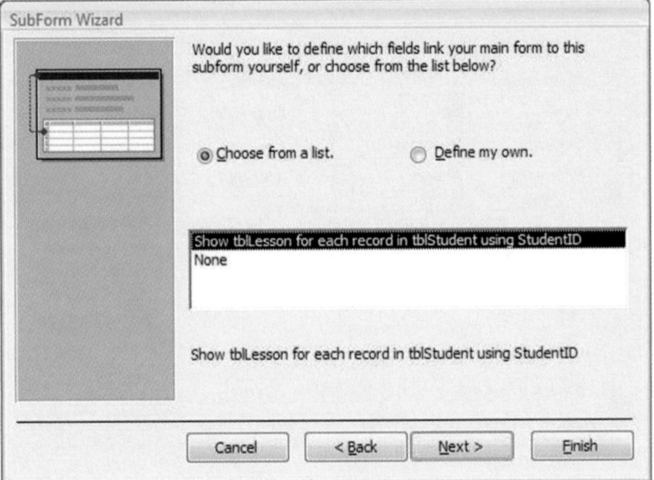

8 Call your SubForm **fsubLessonDetails** and click on **Finish**.
9 Save your form as **frmStudentLessonMain**.
10 Open **frmStudentLessonMain** in **Form View**. You will see that it needs some editing to improve its appearance.
11 Switch to **Design View** (see Figure 1.17.16). Double-click on the Form Selector of the Main form to display the **Property Sheet** and remove the record selector and scroll bars. Insert spaces in the label controls and remove the SubForm label **fsubLessonDetails**.

Figure 1.17.16 ▶

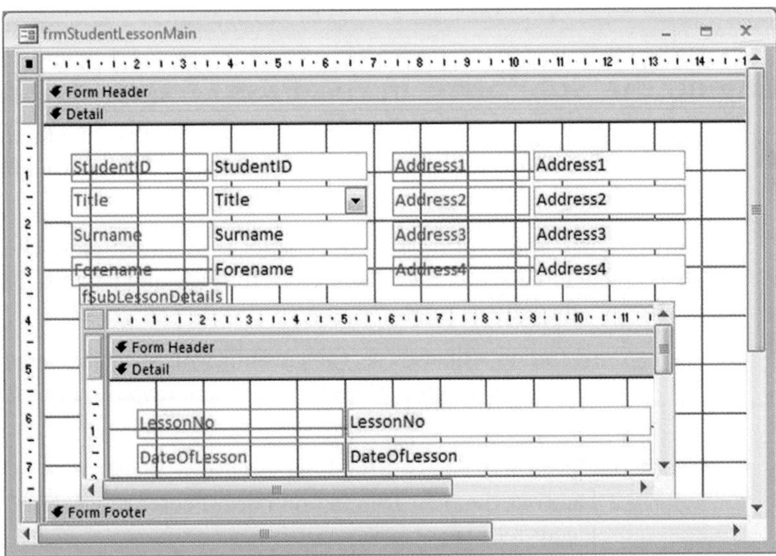

12 Switch back to **Form View**. The SubForm appears by default in **Datasheet View**, from which you can easily change the widths of the columns by dragging in/out the columns as required.

13 In the Navigation Pane, open **fsubLessonDetails** in **Design View** or **Layout View**. Edit the labels and align the text as required. Switch back to **Form View**. Your form should look something like Figure 1.17.17.

Figure 1.17.17 ▶

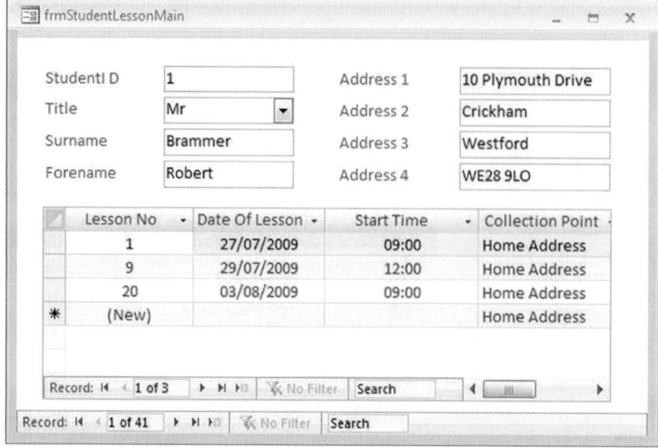

Hint Tidy up the columns by moving the cursor over the border between column headings and double-clicking to give a best fit.

Note: None of the forms developed in this section so far are part of the Pass IT system. To avoid confusion, it is recommended you go into the **Database Window** and delete the forms **frmInstructorMain, fsubLesson, fsubLessonDetails** and **frmStudentLessonMain** by selecting each in turn and pressing DELETE.

Setting up the SubForms in the Pass IT Driving School system

We are going to set up two SubForms in the Pass IT system. Both will be based on queries and both will be accessed and displayed from the main Lesson Booking form at the heart of the system.

When a student rings up to book a lesson, the driving school will want to be able to view lesson availability for that day and perhaps for the week for their attached instructor.

This section will also use Tab controls which were covered in Unit 16. These are particularly useful when the information you want to view is too much for one form.

1 Open the **frmLessonBooking** in **Design View**.
2 Drag out the right margin and **Form Footer** to fill the screen, as shown in Figure 1.17.18.

3 Select the right-hand controls and drag them to a position below the left-hand controls. Move the control panel, logo and rectangle as shown in Figure 1.17.18. This creates room for our tab controls.

Figure 1.17.18 ▶

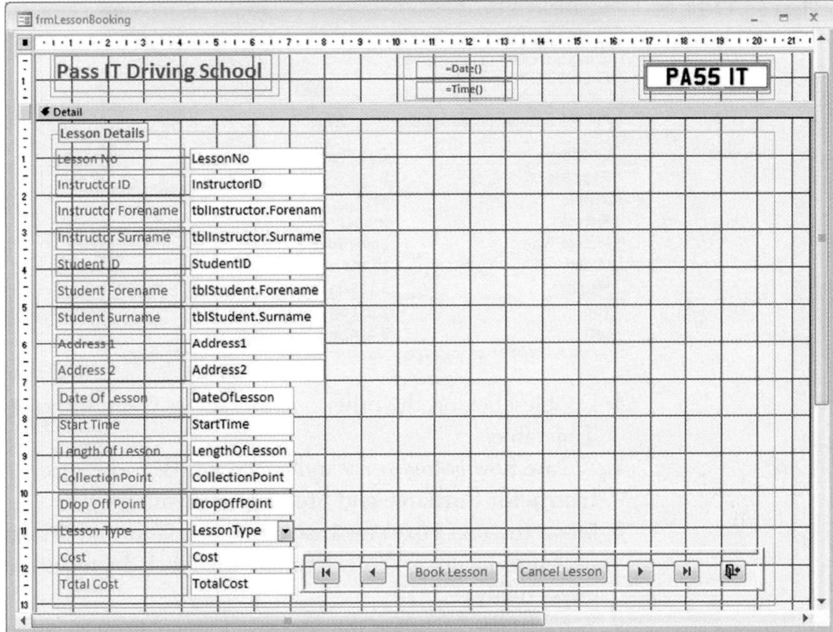

4 On the **Design** tab, click the Tab Control button and drag out a rectangle across the screen about 12cm by 7cm. See Figure 1.17.19

Figure 1.17.19 ▶

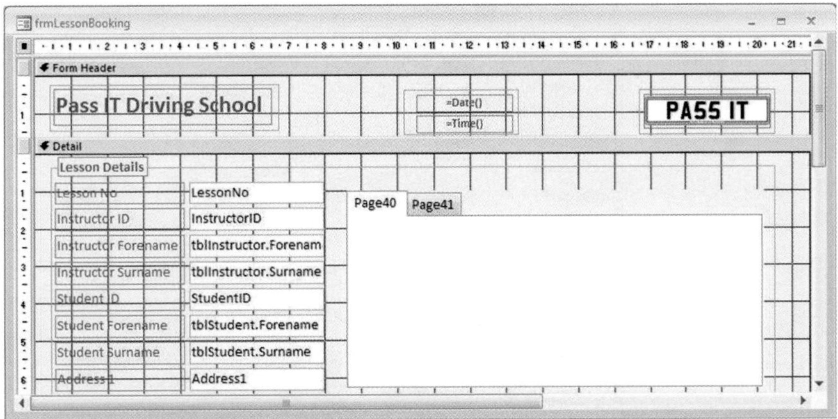

5 The tab control will be headed by some page numbers, as shown in Figure 1.17.19. Double-click on the left one and set its **Caption** property to **Daily Timetable** (see Figure 1.17.20).

Figure 1.17.20 ▶

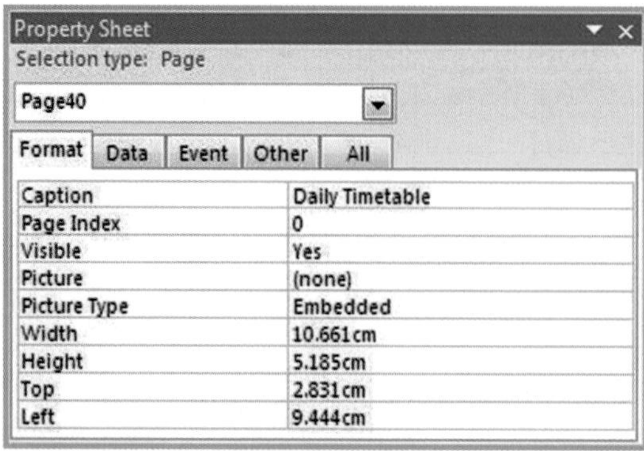

Property Sheet

Selection type: Page

Page40

Format | Data | Event | Other | All

Caption	Daily Timetable
Page Index	0
Visible	Yes
Picture	(none)
Picture Type	Embedded
Width	10.661cm
Height	5.185cm
Top	2.831cm
Left	9.444cm

6 Double-click on the other one and set its **Caption** property to **Weekly Timetable**.

7 We are now going to try and create a little more space. Delete the labels for **Instructor Surname** and **Student Surname**.

8 Move the text boxes for **Instructor Surname** and **Student Surname**, as shown in Figure 1.17.21. Rename the labels **Instructor** and **Student** respectively.

9 You will need to align the controls, format the vertical spacing, resize boxes and edit the labels but your form should appear as below after a little tinkering.

Figure 1.17.21 ▶

Lesson Booking Form
Pass IT Driving School
18 December 2008
20:49:57
PA55 IT
Lesson Details
Lesson No 1
Instructor ID 1
Instructor Derek Jones
Student ID 1
Student Robert Brammer
Address 1 10 Plymouth Drive
Address 2 Crickham
Date Of Lesson 27/07/2009
Start Time 09:00
Length Of Lesson 1
CollectionPoint Home Address
Drop Off Point Home Address
Lesson Type Standard
Cost £24.00
Total Cost £24.00
Daily Timetable
Weekly Timetable
Book Lesson
Cancel Lesson

Adding the SubForm

1 Open the form in **Design View** and click on the **SubForm/SubReport** button. Drag out a rectangle in the tab control area.
2 The **SubForm Wizard** opens. Click on **Use existing Tables and Queries** and click on **Next**.
3 In the next window, choose the **qryFullDetails** and select the available fields as shown in Figure 1.17.22. Click on **Next**.

Figure 1.17.22 ▶

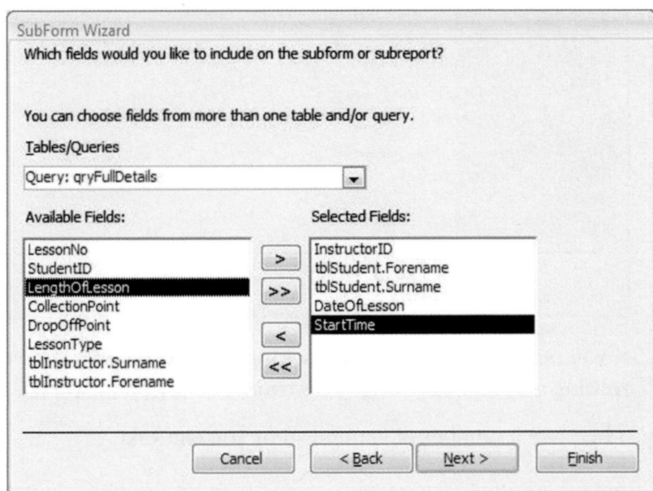

4 You then have to define your linking fields. Check **Define my own** and select **InstructorID** and **DateOfLesson** from the drop-down boxes as shown. Click on **Next** (see Figure 1.17.23).

Figure 1.17.23 ▶

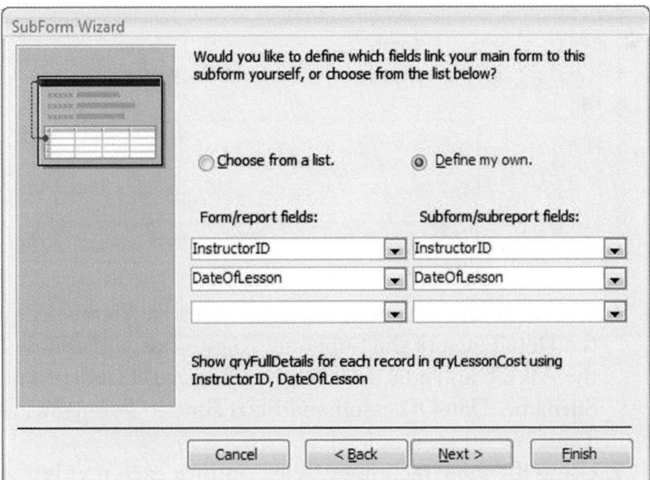

5 Call your SubForm **fsubDailyTimetable** (see Figure 1.17.24). Click on **Finish**.

Figure 1.17.24 ▶

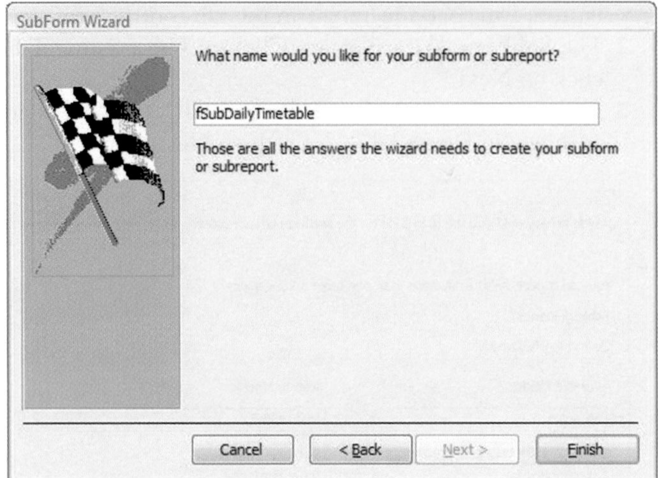

If you now open the Lesson Booking form in **Form View** you will see it needs resizing and repositioning. This can be tricky and can take a lot of patience.

There are a number of general steps you can take.

Figure 1.17.25 ▶

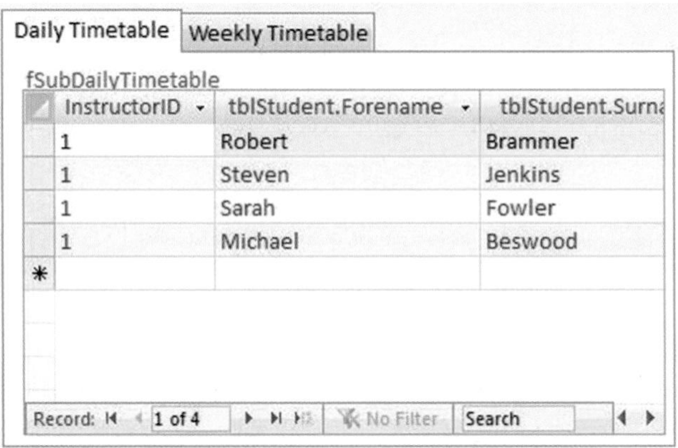

1 To change the column headings, in **Design View** select in turn each label in the **Detail** area of the SubForm. Right-click and choose **Properties**. Click on the **All** tab and edit the caption. Change **tblStudent.Forename**, **tblStudent.Surname**, **DateOfLesson** and **StartTime** to **Forename**, **Surname**, **Date** and **Time**.
2 Using the same technique, select in turn each text box in the **Detail** area of the SubForm and set the **Text Align** property for **tblStudent.Forename** and **tblStudent.Surname** to **Left**. Set the **Text Align** property for **StartTime** and **DateOfLesson** to **Center**.
3 Go into **Form View** and adjust the column widths by dragging out or in the column dividers. Right-click on the InstructorID column header and select **Hide Columns**.

It will take a little time but your form should eventually appear as shown in Figure 1.17.26!

Figure 1.17.26 ▶

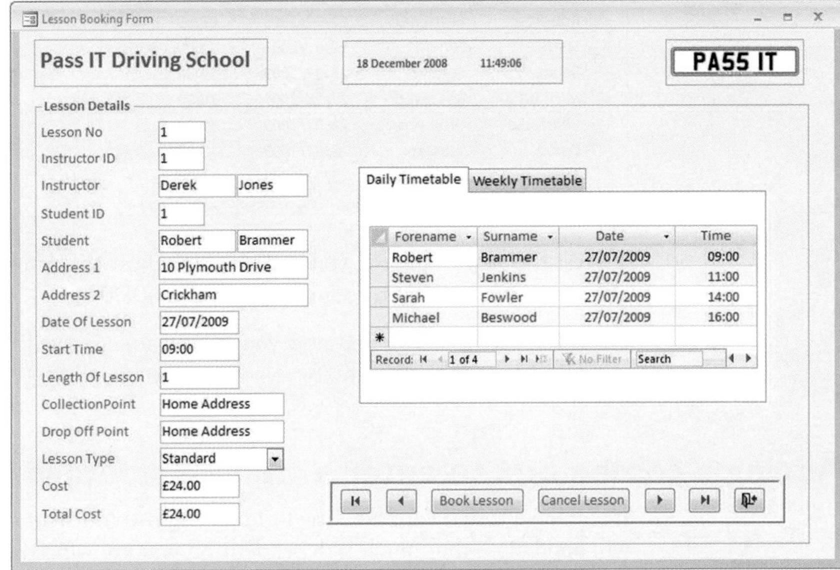

Using your SubForm

1 Open **frmLessonBooking** and ensure the **Daily Timetable** tab is selected.
2 Click on the **Book Lesson** option and book a **Standard** lesson for **Instructor ID 1** with **Student ID 1** on the **27/07/09**.
3 The SubForm will display the available times on that date for that instructor. Press **Escape** to undo the booking.
4 The next stage will allow us to view the available times over a week.

Adding the SubForm to display the weekly timetable

The process is nearly exactly the same as for the daily timetable but you need to base the form on a different query.

You will need to work on the second tab control called **Weekly Timetable**. Drag out a SubForm as before and base it on the query **qryNextWeeksLessons** set up in Unit 8.

Use the fields **InstructorID**, **tblStudent.Forename**, **tblStudent.Surname**, **DateOfLesson** and **StartTime** as before.

When you link the fields in the SubForm, only link the **InstructorID** and not the **Date**. Again you will need to format, resize and reposition the SubForm (see Figure 1.17.27).

Figure 1.17.27 ▶

Forename	Surname	Date	Time
Robert	Brammer	27/07/2009	09:00
Steven	Jenkins	27/07/2009	11:00
Sarah	Fowler	27/07/2009	14:00
Michael	Beswood	27/07/2009	16:00
Charlotte	Williams	28/07/2009	10:00
David	Windsor	28/07/2009	12:00
Mary	Trueman	28/07/2009	14:00

To test the new SubForm, you will need to adjust the dates in your table or adjust the time clock on your computer to 27/07/09.

Enter the data as above and now you will be able to toggle between the **Daily** and **Weekly Timetable** tabs. Save your work.

Adding a combo box to enter a student's details

If you have tested your booking form during the course of these units you will appreciate that much is dependent on you knowing the StudentID or InstructorID. When a student phones the Pass IT Driving School to book a lesson they will quite often forget or not know their Student ID.

The procedure is:

- A student phones the school to book a lesson.
- The operator opens the booking form and clicks on **Book a Lesson**.
- The student cannot remember their ID so the operator ideally needs to be able to call up the student details from a drop-down box.

1 Open **frmLessonBooking** in **Design View**. Select the Student ID control and press DELETE.
2 Click on the **Combo Box** button, in the **Controls** group, on the **Design** tab and drag out a small rectangle where the Student ID control was.
3 The **Combo Box Wizard** dialog box is displayed. Check **I want the combo box to look up the values in a table or query** and click on **Next** (see Figure 1.17.28).

Figure 1.17.28 ▶

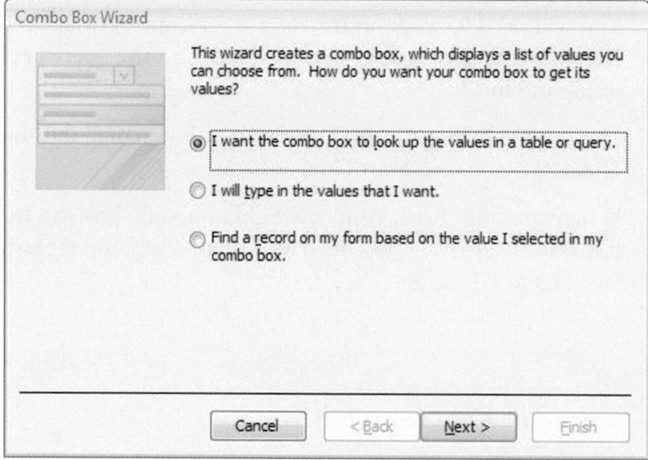

4 Select **Table:tblStudent** from the next dialog box and click on **Next**.
5 Select the fields **StudentID**, **Forename** and **Surname** and click on **Next** (see Figure 1.17.29).

Figure 1.17.29 ▶

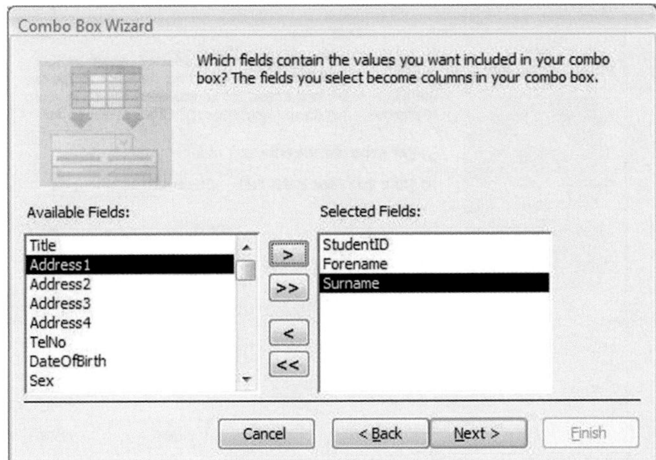

6 From the next dialog box choose to sort on **Surname** and in **Ascending** order. Click on **Next**.
7 The next dialog box shows you how the combo box will display the names. (See Figure 1.17.30.) Uncheck the **Hide key column** box. Click on **Next**.

Figure 1.17.30 ▶

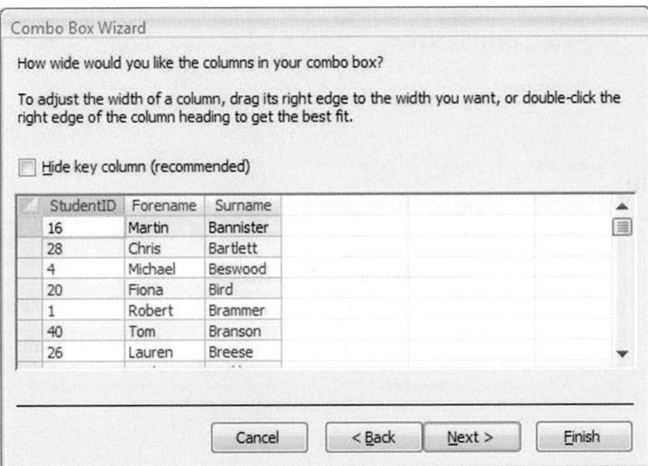

8 Select **StudentID** and click **Next**. Check the **Store that value in this field** option and select **StudentID** from the drop-down. Click on **Next**. (See Figure 1.17.31.)

Figure 1.17.31 ▶

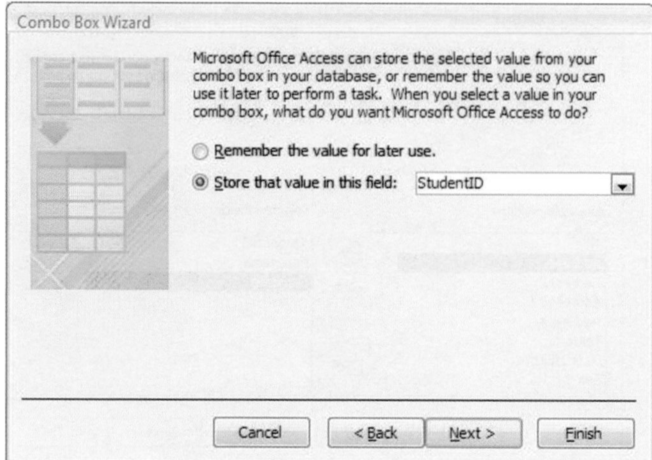

9 Change the Label to **Student ID** and click on **Finish**.

10 Your finished form should appear as in Figure 1.17.32. Repeat the above steps to set up another combo box to select an instructor.

Figure 1.17.32 ▶

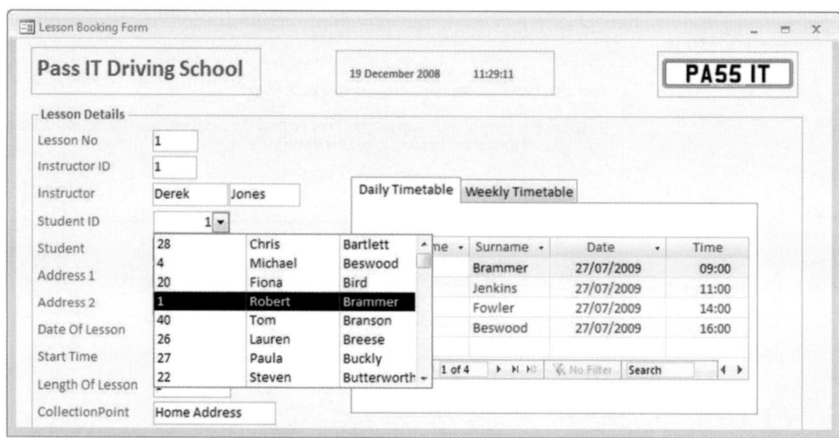

Unit 18: Calculations in reports

The qryLessonCost in Unit 8 set up a calculated field to work out the cost of each lesson.

We are going to set up a report to add up the income from lessons for each instructor.

Calculating totals in a report

1 Create a new report based on the query **qryLessonCost** using the **Report Wizard**.

2 Use the arrow icon (>) to select the following fields in the following order: **InstructorID**, **tblInstructor.Forename**, **tblInstructor.Surname**, **tblStudent.Forename**, **tblStudent.Surname**, **DateOfLesson** and **TotalCost** (see Figure 1.18.1). Click on **Next**.

Figure 1.18.1 ▶

3 If the records are not grouped by InstructorID by default, click on **InstructorID** and click on the right arrow (see Figure 1.18.2). Click on **Next**.

Figure 1.18.2 ▶

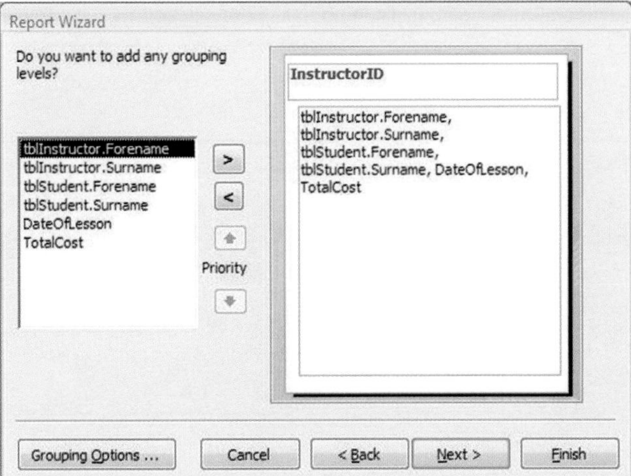

4 Sort by **DateOfLesson** and click on **Next** (see Figure 1.18.3).

Figure 1.18.3 ▶

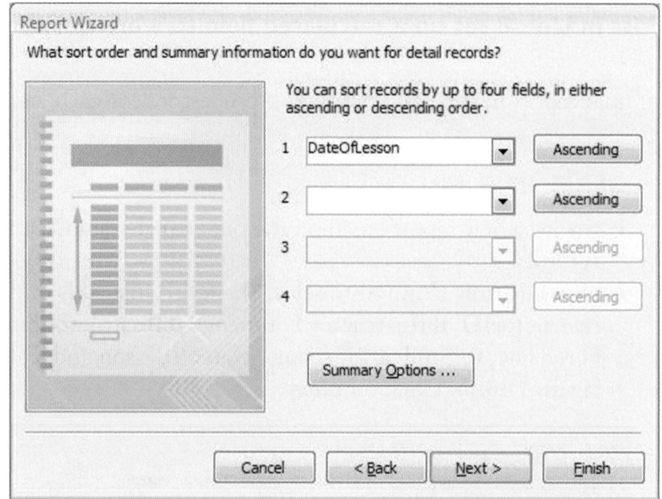

5 Click on **Outline** and click on **Next** (see Figure 1.18.4).

Figure 1.18.4 ▶

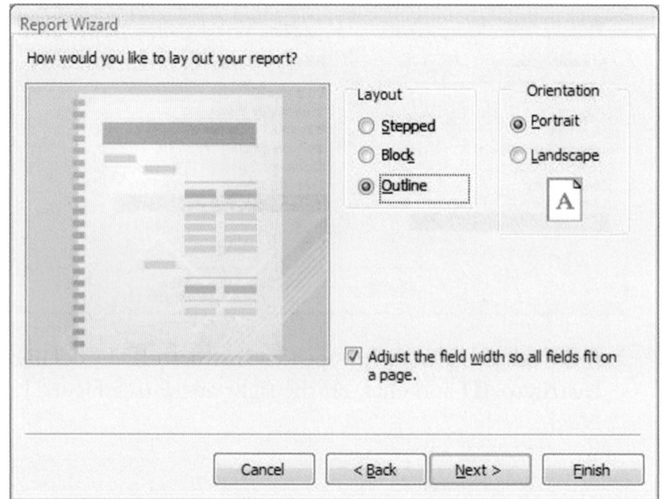

6 Select **Access 2007** style, click on **Next.** Name the report **rptIncome,** click on **Finish**. See Figure 1.18.5.

Figure 1.18.5 ▶

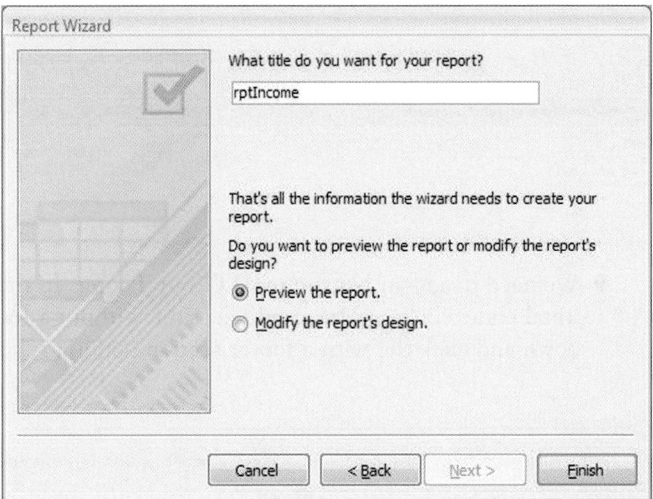

The report opens in **Print Preview** mode and is shown in Figure 1.18.6. You will need to use the page navigation buttons to scroll through the instructors.

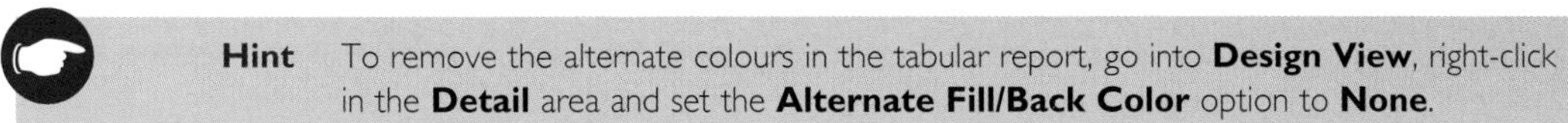

Hint To remove the alternate colours in the tabular report, go into **Design View**, right-click in the **Detail** area and set the **Alternate Fill/Back Color** option to **None**.

Figure 1.18.6 ▶

We are going to add up the total cost of lessons for each instructor, to display the income and total overall income.

7 Close the **Print Preview** window by clicking the **Close Print Preview** button. Switch to **Design View** and click on the **Group & Sort** button in the **Grouping & Totals** group. See Figure 1.18.7.

Figure 1.18.7 ▼

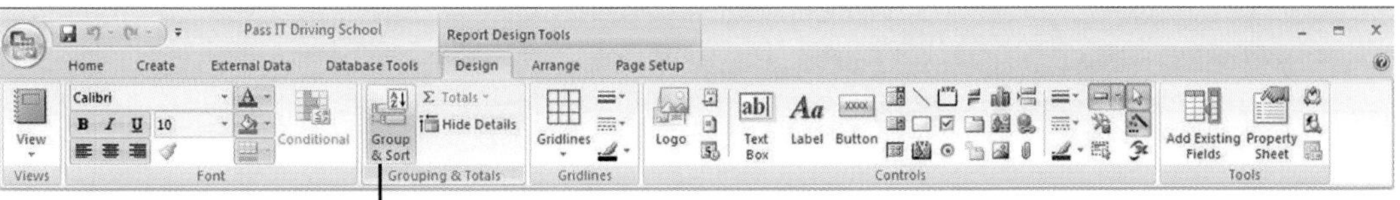

Group & Sort

8 The **Group, Sort and Total** pane is displayed. See Figure 1.18.8. This allows you to easily add grouping, sorts and calculations. The pane tells you that this report is grouped by **InstructorID** and sorted by **DateOfLesson**.

Figure 1.18.8 ▼

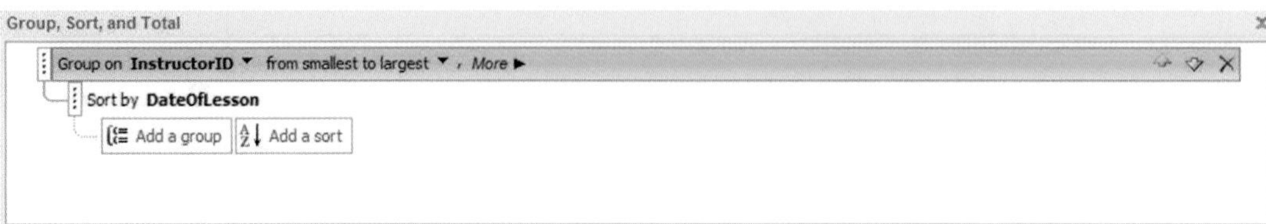

9 We need to add an **InstructorID Group Footer**. In the **Group, Sort and Total** pane, click on **More** and select the **without a footer section** drop-down and click the **with a footer section** option as shown in Figure 1.18.9.

Figure 1.18.9 ▼

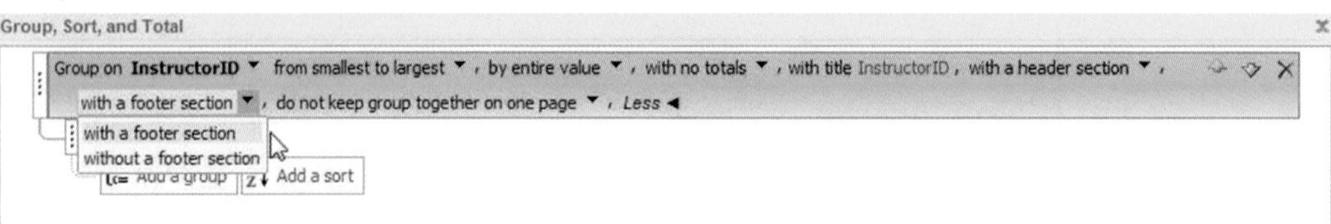

Access inserts an **InstructorID** Footer. See Figure 1.18.10. We will place the income and later the number of lessons for each instructor in this section of the report.

Figure 1.18.10 ▶

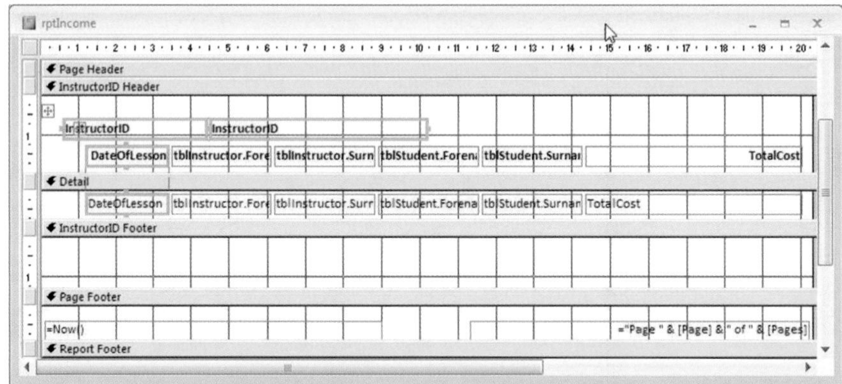

10 Click the **with no totals** drop-down to display the dialog box shown in Figure 1.18.11. Select **TotalCost** in the **Total On** drop-down and select **Sum** in the **Type** drop-down. Check **Show Grand Total** and **Show in group footer**. Close the **Group, Sort and Total** pane.

Figure 1.18.11 ▶

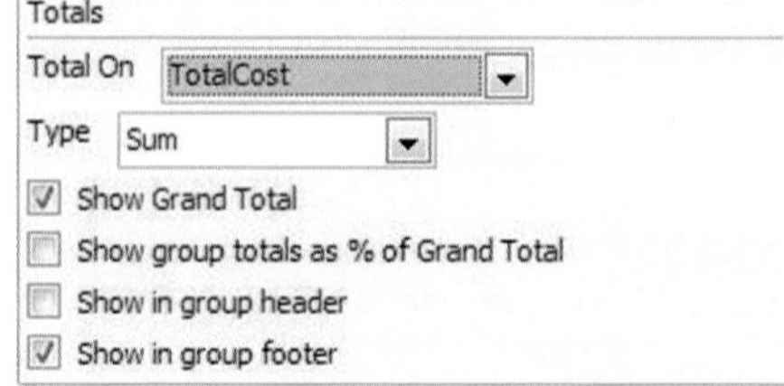

11 Access inserts two text boxes with the formula **=SUM([TotalCost])** Access gives a group total in the **InstructorID Footer** and an overall total in the **Report Footer**. See Figure 1.18.12. Switch to **Report View** to view your report. You will notice we need to format the totals to currency format.

Figure 1.18.12 ▶

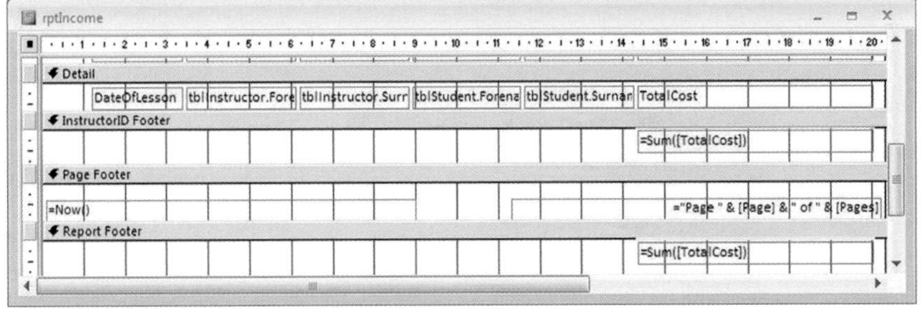

12 In **Design View**, highlight each text box and click on the **Property Sheet** button. Set the **Format** property to **Currency**. See Figure 1.18.13.

Figure 1.18.13 ▶

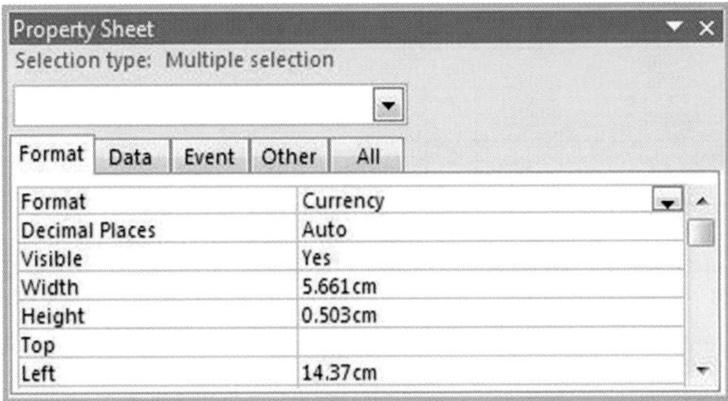

13 Switch to **Report View** and scroll to the bottom of the report to check the totals. See Figure 1.18.14.

Figure 1.18.14 ▶

14 Switch to **Design View** and click on the **Group & Sort** button. Click on **More** and select the **withTotalCost totaled** drop-down. Select **LessonNo** in the **Total On** drop-down and **Count Records** in the **Type** drop-down. Check **Show Grand Total** and **Show in group footer**. See Figure 1.18.15. Close the pane.

Figure 1.18.15 ▶

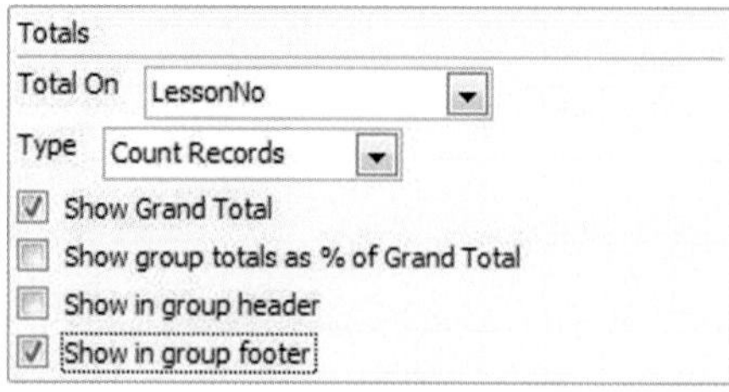

15 Access inserts a **Count** function, returning the total number of lessons for each instructor and the overall number of lessons. Click the **Label** button and add suitable labels to the text boxes as shown in Figure 1.18.16.

Figure 1.18.16 ▼

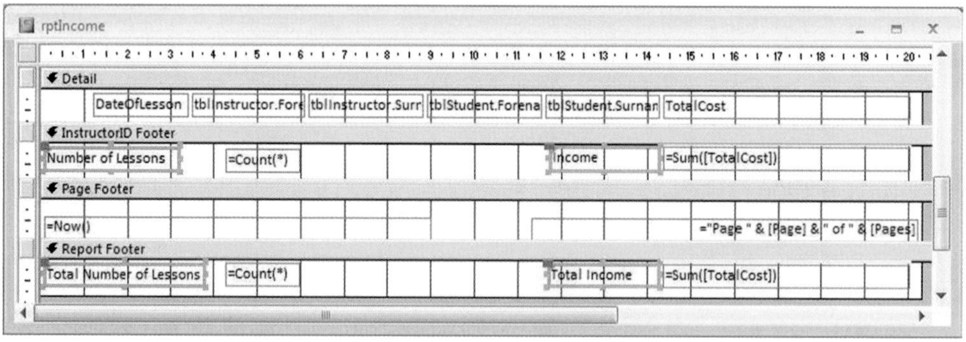

16 Switch to **Report View**. Your finished report should appear as in Figure 1.18.17. As ever, the report will now need tidying up.

Figure 1.18.17 ▼

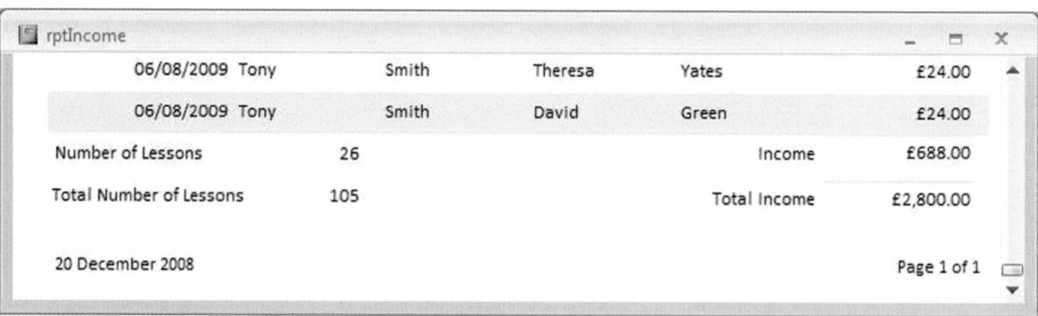

Tidying up the report

1 You will notice from Figure 1.18.17 that the instructor name repeats throughout the report. Drag **tblInstructor.Forename** and **tblInstructor.Surname** from the Detail area into the InstructorID Header as shown in Figure 1.18.18. You will need to remove the Layout Selector.

2 Delete the **tblInstructor.Forename** and **tblInstructor.Surname** column headings.

3 Change the **tblStudent.Forename** column heading to **Name**. Delete the **tblStudent_Surname** column heading and change the title of the report to **Income Report**. See Figure 1.18.18.

Figure 1.18.18 ▼

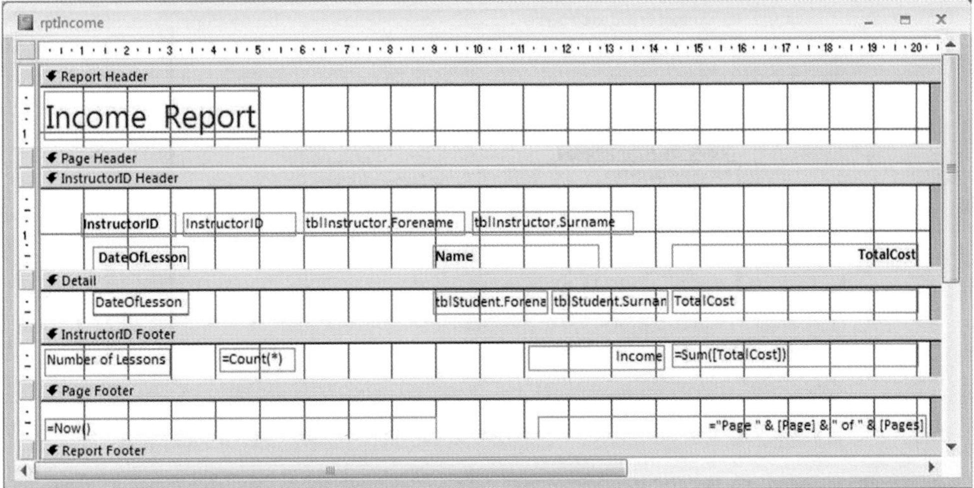

4 Go into **Print Preview** mode and test the report (see Figure 1.18.19). You may wish to format the layout of the report further and add the standard header and style used in Unit 13.

Figure 1.18.19 ▼

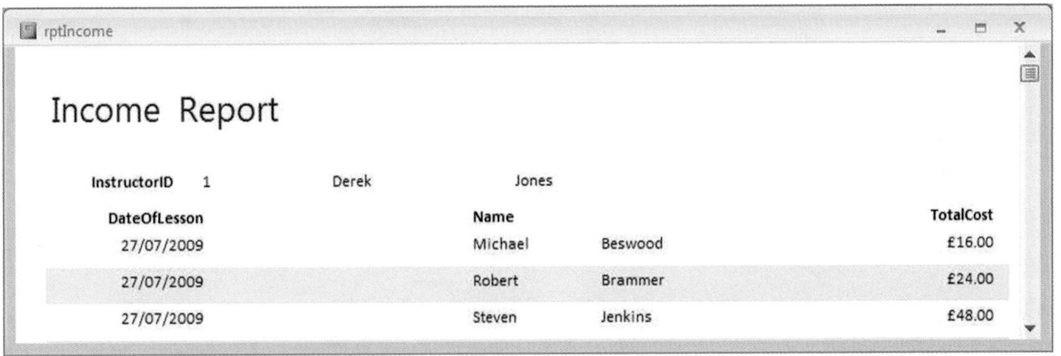

Setting up a lesson analysis report

We are now going to set up a similar report to the previous one using a different method and an improved layout. The report will include two levels of grouping and make use of the summary options. In Unit 20 we will adjust the menus to include this report.

1 Create a new report based on **qryLessonCost** using the **Report Wizard**.
2 Use the arrow icon (>) to select the following fields in the following order: **InstructorID**, **tblInstructor.Forename**, **tblInstructor.Surname**, **StudentID**, **tblStudent.Forename**, **tblStudent.Surname**, **DateOfLesson**, **LengthOfLesson**, **LessonType** and **TotalCost**. Click on **Next**.

3 If the records are not grouped by InstructorID by default, click on **InstructorID** and click on the right arrow (see Figure 1.18.20). Select **StudentID** and click on the right arrow (see Figure 1.18.20). Click on **Next**.

Figure 1.18.20 ▶

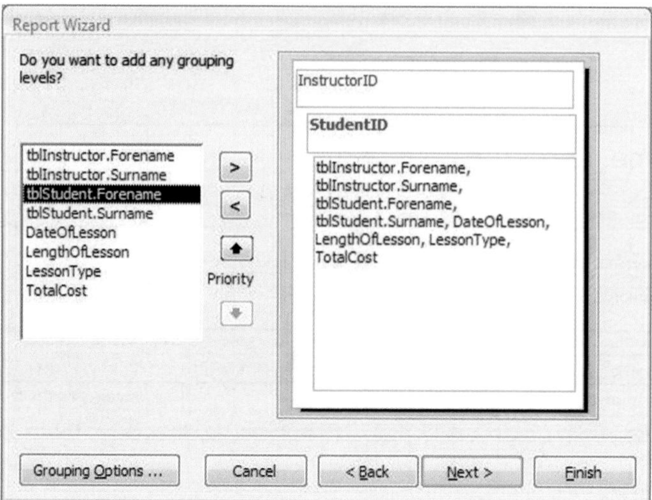

4 Sort by **DateOfLesson** and click on **Summary Options**. (See Figure 1.18.21.)

Figure 1.18.21 ▶

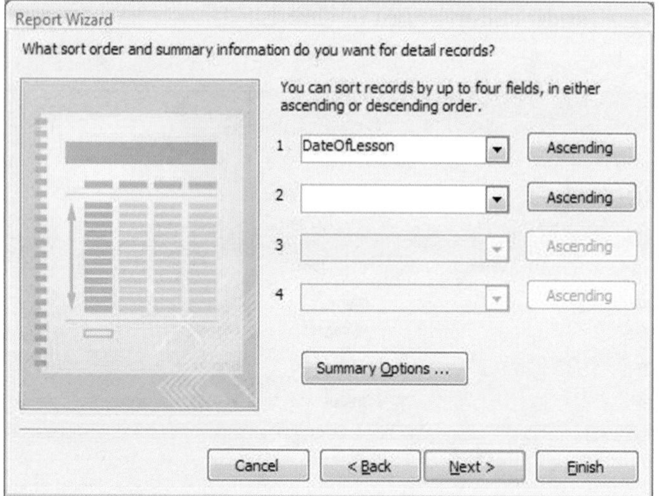

5 The **Summary Options Wizard** displays the fields it can carry out calculations on. Choose to sum **LengthOfLesson** and **TotalCost** as shown in Figure 1.18.22. Click on **OK**. Click **Next**.

Figure 1.18. 22 ▶

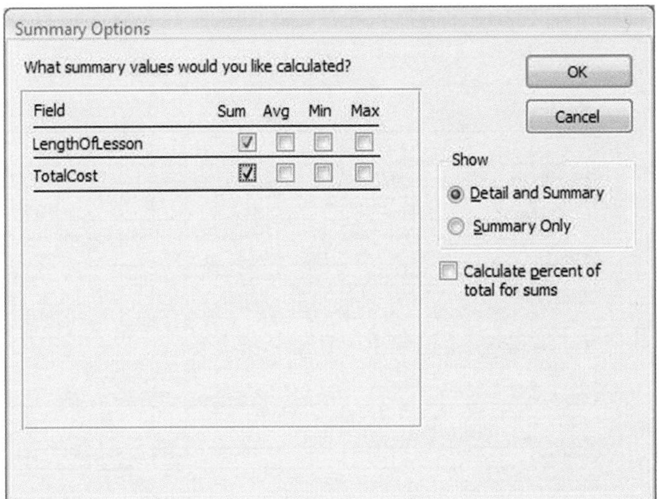

6 Click on **Outline, Landscape** and click on **Next**. Click on **Access 2007** and click on **Next**.

7 Name it **rptLessonAnalysis** and click on **Finish**. Your report should look like Figure 1.18.23.

Figure 1.18.23 ▼

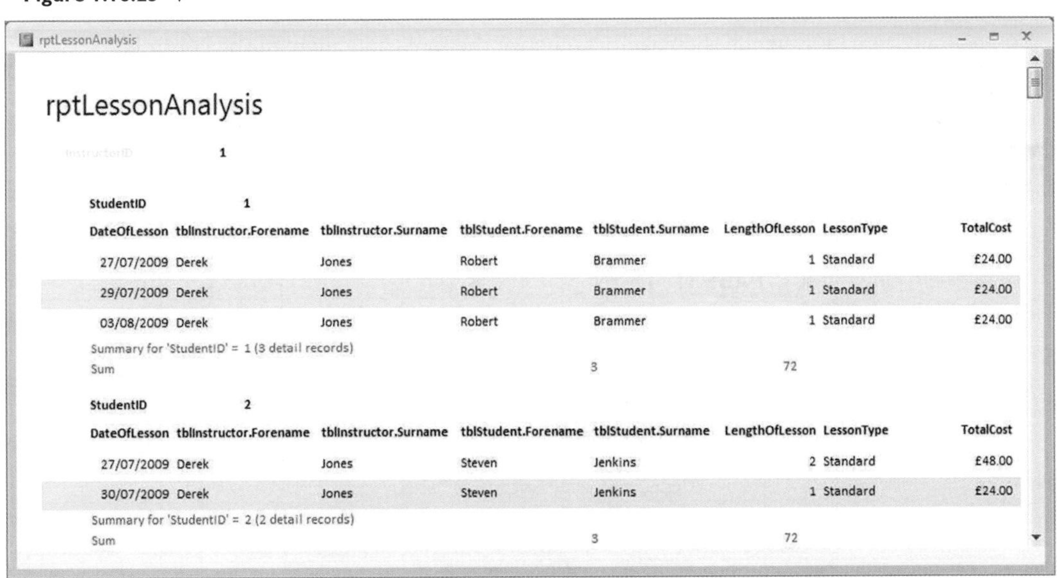

You will notice a number of things. The report is grouped by instructor. Within each instructor group the students for that instructor are grouped also.

The **Summary Options** has added the sum of the **LengthOfLesson** and **TotalCost** fields. The number of records for each student is also displayed.

If you go to the end of the report, you will see **Summary Option** has offered some grand totals.

If you go into **Design View** you will see the **Sum** formulae in the **StudentID Footer, InstructorID Footer** and **Report Footer**. See Figure 1.18.24.

Figure 1.18.24 ▶

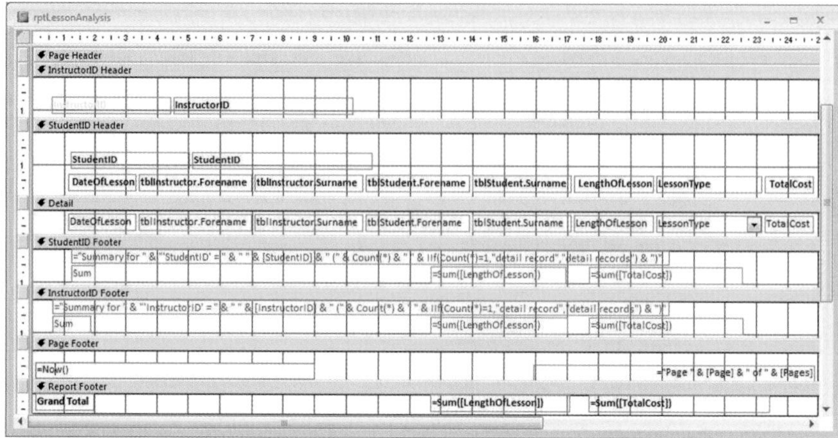

The last stage is to give the report the in-house style developed in Unit 12.

1 Copy and paste the **Report Header** from **rptStudent** in Unit 12. Edit the title to read **Lesson Analysis**.
2 Drag the fields **tblInstructor.Forename**, **tblInstructor.Surname**, **tblStudent. Forename** and **tblStudent.Surname** to the **InstructorID** and **StudentID** headers.
3 Rename the headings, change the fonts and align all the controls.
4 Add the labels **Hours Driven** and **Fees** to the **StudentID Footer** next to the sum controls. Add the labels **Hours Driven** and **Income** to the **InstructorID Footer** next to the sum controls.

Figure 1.18.25 ▶

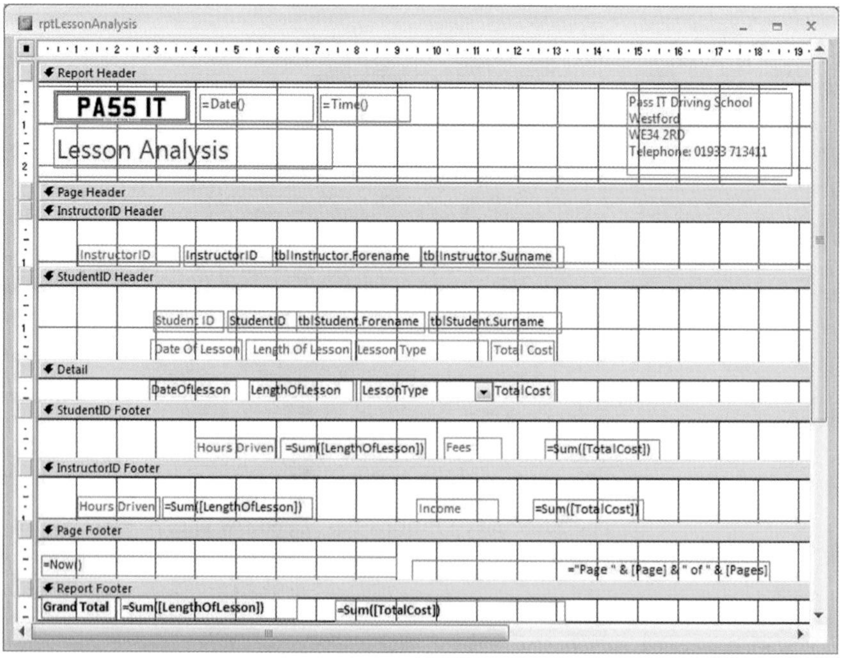

5 Remove the summary controls inserted by Access (optional). Figure 1.18.25 shows how the report may look in **Design View**. Your finished report should appear as in Figure 1.18.26.

Figure 1.18.26 ▶

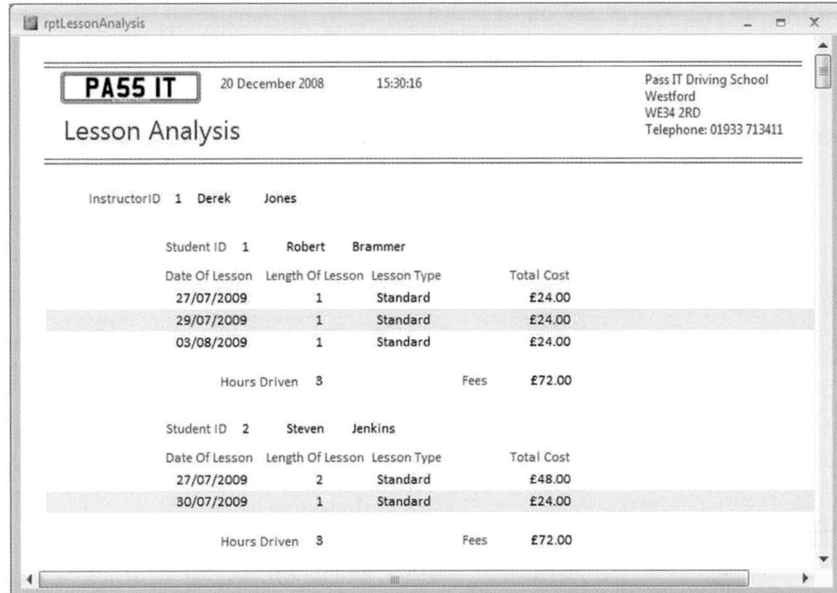

Reports with no records

Some reports have no data in them. For example, you might be searching for lessons on a day when none has been booked. It is possible to check if there is no data in a report and give a warning to the user.

1 Set up a macro called **mcrNoData** that displays this message box (see Figure 1.18.27).

Figure 1.18.27 ▶

The action is **MsgBox.** The arguments are as shown (see Figure 1.18.28).

Figure 1.18.28 ▶

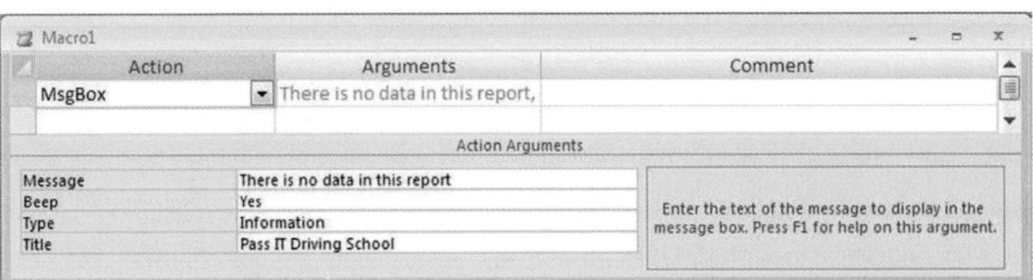

2 Save the macro and test it.

We want to run this macro when we open the **Instructors' Timetable Report**. We can set this up using the report properties.

3 From the Navigation Pane, open **rptInstructorTimetable** in **Design View** and click on the **Property Sheet** button to display the report properties.
4 Click on the **Event** tab (see Figure 1.18.29).

Figure 1.18.29 ▶

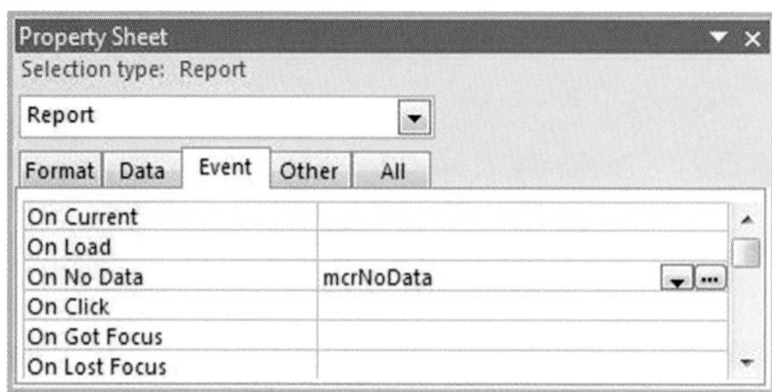

You can now select macros to run at the following points:

On Open	When the report opens.
On Close	When the report closes.
On Activate	When the report becomes the active window.
On Deactivate	When the report stops being the active window.
On No Data	When the report has no data.
On Page	When a page of a report is formatted for printing.
On Error	When there is an error.

5 We want the **mcrNoData** macro to run when there is no data in the report, so set the **On No Data** property to **mcrNoData** using the drop-down list, as shown in Figure 1.18.29.
6 Save the report and test that the macro works when there is no data by opening the report and entering a date when you know that there are no lessons.

Use **Tricks and Tips** numbers 15 and 16 to set up Weekday and Month queries. Set up appropriate reports based on these queries.

Unit 19: Using action queries

In Units 6, 7 and 8 you learned how to use a range of queries to view your data.

In this section you will learn how to use action queries. Action queries actually do something to the data in your system by moving it, changing it or deleting it.

There are four types of action query:

- append query
- delete query
- update query
- make table query (not used in the Pass IT Driving School).

Append queries

An append query will take data from one table and add it to another.

In a club membership system, you might decide to keep details of members who have not renewed their subscriptions rather than delete their records immediately. An append query will enable you to remove their details from the main membership table and transfer them to a table of, for example, expired memberships.

Similarly in a school or college, at the end of each year you could delete all leavers from the system but it is likely you will need to keep records for a period of time. An append query could be set up to transfer leaver details to a table of leavers.

Delete queries

A delete query will remove records from one or more tables according to set criteria.

In the school or college system above you might decide to keep records of ex-students for three years. At the end of each college year you would remove details of all students who left three or more years ago.

Similarly in a video hire/library loans system details of loans will build up. After a period of time you will need to clear old details from the system.

A delete query can be used to carry out these operations.

Update queries

An update query will make changes to data in one or more tables.

In an ordering system you might decide to reduce the prices of all products by 7.5%. At the end of each year in our school system all students will move up a year from Year 7 to Year 8 and so on.

Update queries allow you to make these changes to the data in your tables automatically.

Managing lesson details

In the Pass IT Driving School we need our system to handle information about old lessons. There follows a possible scenario.

- After a lesson has taken place, we will move details to a table of old lessons (append query).
- The details will also need removing from the current table of lessons (delete query).
- After a period of a year we will remove them from the table of old lessons (delete query).

Warning When working with action queries it is a good idea to make a copy of your lesson table because you are going to be moving and changing the data. Making a copy will save you re-entering data at a later stage.

1 In the Navigation Pane, right-click **tblLesson** and click **Copy**.
2 Right-click in the Navigation Pane and click **Paste**.
3 Call the new table **tblLessonCopy** and click on **Structure and Data**. Click on **OK** (see Figure 1.19.1). We will work on **tblLesson**, keeping the copy in case we meet problems.

Figure 1.19.1 ▶

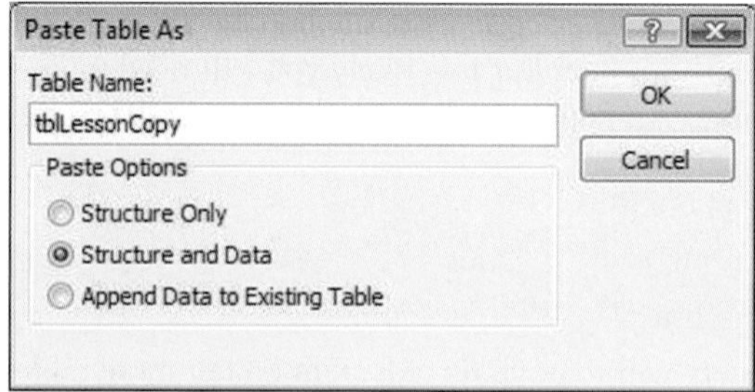

As action queries are often based on dates that clearly change, you will have to edit the lesson dates before you start.

4 Open **tblLesson** and change the dates as follows. Use **Find and Replace** to change all the lessons for one day at once.

- Change the 06/08/2009 lesson to today's date.
- Change the 07/08/2009 lesson to tomorrow's date.
- Change all the 05/08/2009 lessons to yesterday's date.
- Change all the 04/08/2009 lessons to the date exactly one year ago today.

Remove all other lessons by highlighting the rows and pressing **Delete**. Highlight the **DateOfLesson** column and click the **Ascending** button, in the **Sort & Filter** group, on the **Home** tab. This will make it easier. It will leave you with 37 records to work with.

Append query to transfer lesson details

We are going to move details of all old lessons from the Lesson table to a table called Old Lesson.

1 In the Navigation Pane, right-click **tblLesson** and click **Copy**.
2 Right-click in the Navigation Pane and click **Paste**.

3 Name the new table **tblOldLesson** and click on **Structure Only**. Click on **OK**.
4 This has created a new empty table called **tblOldLesson**. Open this table in **Design View**.
5 Set the **Data Type** of the **LessonNo** field to **Number**. (This is vital. It will not work if you don't do this.)
6 Save the table by closing the window.
7 On the **Create** tab, click the **Query Wizard** button**.** Click on **Simple Query Wizard** and click **OK**.
8 Select **tblLesson** from the drop-down. Click on the double arrow to choose all the fields and then click on **Next.**
9 In the **Simple Query Wizard** window, click on **Next** again.
10 Name the query **qryOldLessonAppend** and click on **Finish**.
11 Close the query window and open the query in **Design View**. Set the Criteria row in the **DateOfLesson** column to **<Date()**.
12 On the **Design** tab, click on the **Append** button in the **Query Type** group (see Figure 1.19.2).

Figure 1.19.2 ▼

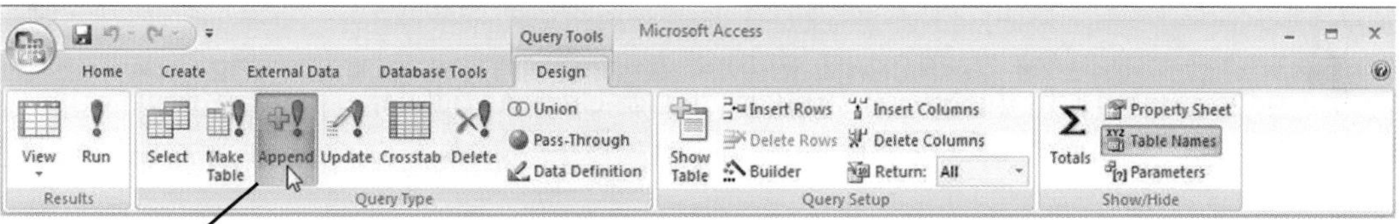

Append

13 The **Append** dialog box is displayed. Choose **tblOldLesson** from the drop-down and click on **OK** (see Figure 1.19.3).

Figure 1.19.3 ▶

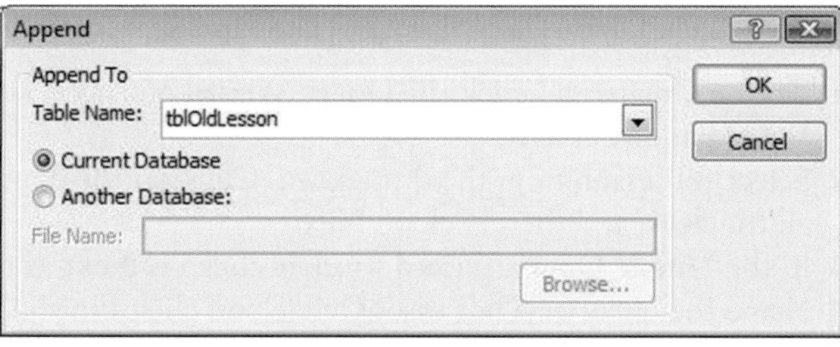

Details of the query are then displayed, as shown in Figure 1.19.4.

Figure 1.19.4 ▶

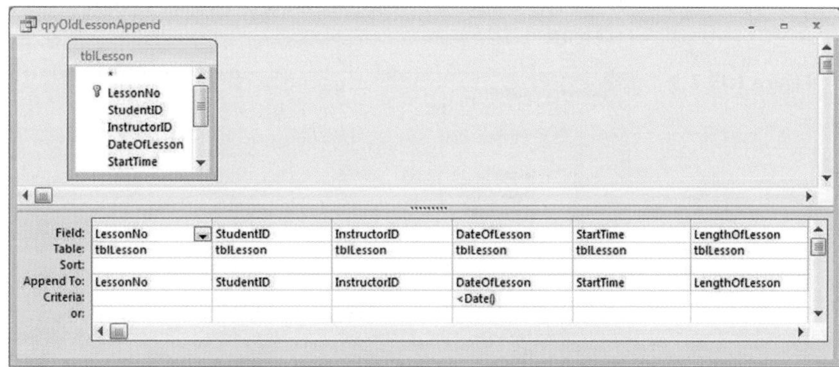

14 Save the query by closing the **Query Design** window.

15 In the Navigation Pane, double-click the **qryOldLessonAppend** icon to run the query.

16 You will be prompted with two warning messages. Click on **Yes** (see Figure 1.19.5).

Figure 1.19.5 ▶

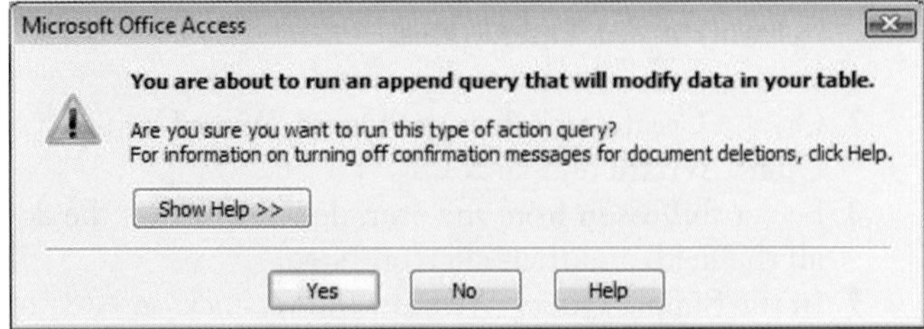

17 Click on **Yes** at the second (see Figure 1.19.6).

Figure 1.19.6 ▶

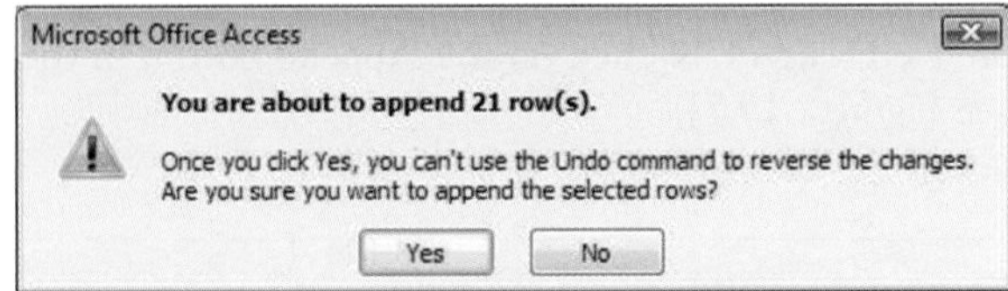

18 In the Navigation Pane, double-click the **tblOldLesson** icon to view the records. 21 records should have been added.

Delete query to remove lesson details from the Lesson table

We now need to clear out the details of all the old lessons which are still stored in the Lesson table. These should be the same 21 records.

1 On the **Create** tab, click the **Query Wizard** button. Click on **Simple Query Wizard** and click **OK**.

2 Select **tblLesson** from the drop-down. Click on the double arrow to choose all the fields and then click on **Next**.

3 In the **Simple Query Wizard** window click on **Next** again.

4 Name the query **qryOldLessonDelete** and click **Finish**.

5 Close the query window and open **qryOldLessonDelete** in **Design View**. Click the **Delete** button, in the **Query Type** group, on the **Design** tab.

6 Set the **Criteria** row in the **DateOfLesson** column to **<Date()** (see Figure 1.19.7).

Figure 1.19.7 ▶

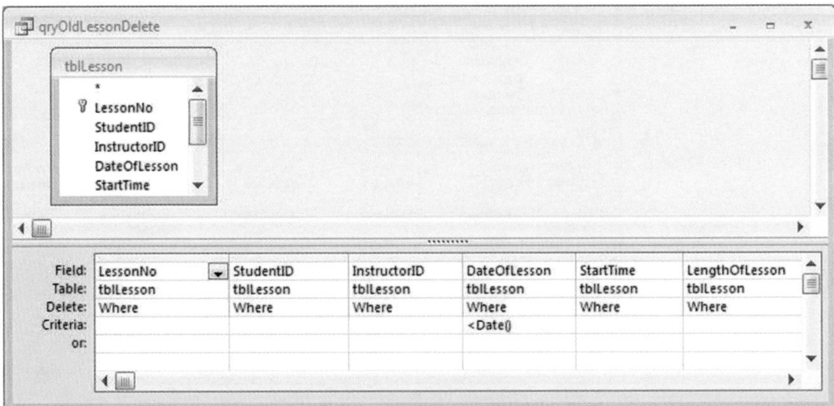

7 Save the query by closing the query window.
8 In the Navigation Pane, double-click the **qryOldLessonDelete** icon to run the query.
9 On running the query you will get the following warning prompts. Just click on Yes (see Figure 1.19.8 and Figure 1.19.9).

Figure 1.19.8 ▶

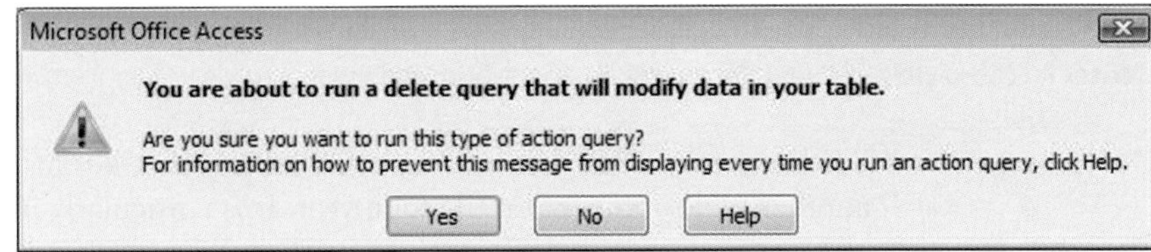

Figure 1.19.9 ▶

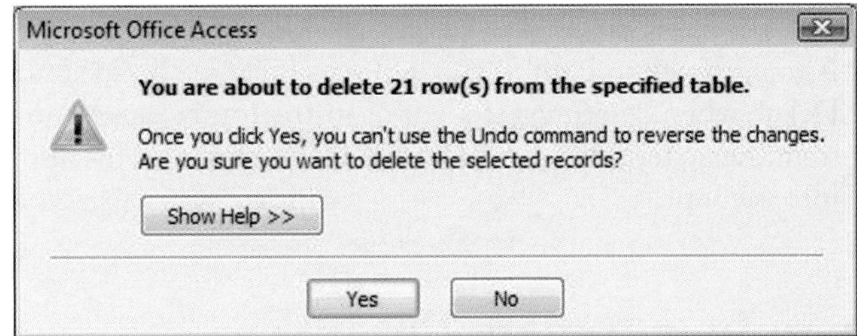

10 In the Navigation Pane, open **tblLesson** and see that the lessons have been deleted. 16 lessons should remain for today and tomorrow.

Delete query to clear out lesson details after a year

We want to delete details of all lessons over a year old.

1 On the **Create** tab, click the **Query Wizard** button. Click on **Simple Query Wizard** and click **OK**.
2 Select **tblOldLesson** from the drop-down. Click on the double arrow to choose all the fields and then click on **Next.**
3 In the **Simple Query Wizard** window, click on **Next** again.
4 Name the query **qryOverOneYearDelete** and click **Finish**.
5 Close the query window and open **qryOverOneYearDelete** in **Design View**. Click the **Delete** button, in the **Query Type** group on the **Design** tab.
6 Set the **Criteria** row in the **DateOfLesson** column to **<=Date()-365** (see Figure 1.19.10).

Figure 1.19.10 ▶

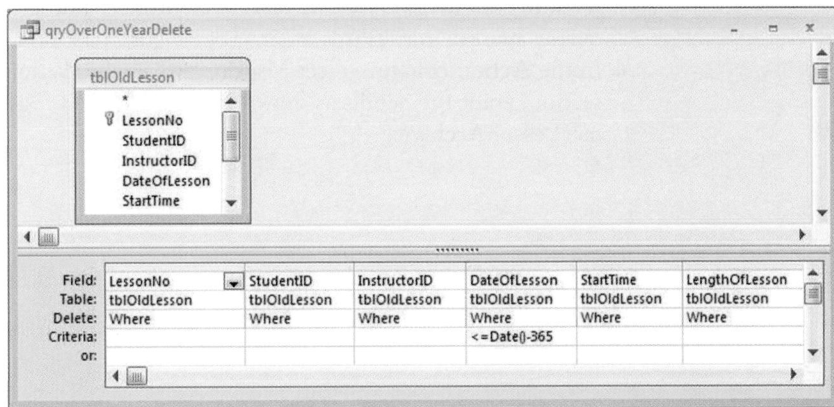

7 Save the query by closing the query window.
8 In the Navigation Pane, double-click the **qryOverOneYearDelete** icon to run the query.
9 Click on **Yes** to accept the warning prompts.
10 Open **tblOldLesson** to check that the year-old lessons have been deleted. 12 should be removed.

Note: It is absolutely vital you think carefully about how and when you clear data from your system.

We have used a daily cycle here, which means that lessons are moved daily to another table and kept on file for a year. It is particularly important to think about your reports and where the data is in the system and at what point it is cleared from the system.

If you go back to Unit 5, you will remember we decided not to set **Cascade Delete** when deleting a student or instructor, because it would clear lessons from the system that would be needed in reports. This also has to be taken into account.

Setting a macro to automate this task

To have to do this every day or every week is an awkward job. We want the user to be able to do it at the click of a button. We will design a macro to do this task and later attach it to a button on the menu.

1 On the **Create** tab, click on the **Macro** button.
2 Click on the drop-down arrow in the **Action** column and click on **SetWarnings**. When you do this the **Action Arguments** section appears in the lower half of the screen. Set the argument to **No** (this will turn off the warning prompts when running the macro).

Note: If the **SetWarnings** command is not available, click the **Show All Actions** button, on the **Design** tab.

3 In the **Action Column**, select **OpenQuery** and in the **Action Arguments** section, choose **qryOldLessonAppend** from the drop-down box.
4 In the **Action Column**, select **OpenQuery** and in the **Action Arguments** section, choose **qryOldLessonDelete** from the drop-down box.
5 In the **Action Column**, select **OpenQuery** and in the **Action Arguments** section, choose **qryOverOneYearDelete** from the drop-down box. (The queries must be run in this order.) (See Figure 1.19.11.)
6 In the **Action** column, select **MsgBox** and in the **Action Arguments** section, enter the details as shown in Figure 1.19.11. Save the macro as **mcrLessonArchive**.

Figure 1.19.11 ▶

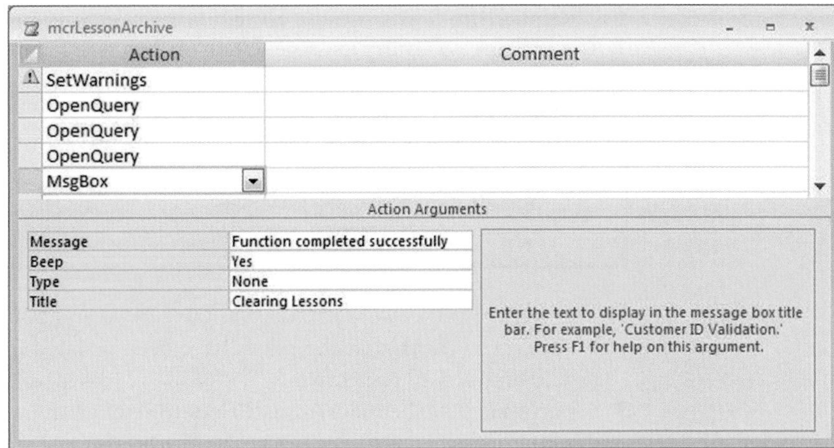

7 Set your data back to the original state and test that the macro moves all the data correctly.

Managing lesson prices

The driving school might occasionally want to increase or decrease its prices. We will use an update query to automate this process.

1 On the **Create** tab, click the **Query Wizard** button. Click on **Simple Query Wizard** and click **OK**.
2 Select **tblLessonType** from the drop-down. Choose **Cost** from the available fields by clicking on the single arrow and clicking on **Next**.
3 In the next **Simple Query Wizard** window, ensure that **Detail** is checked and click on **Next** again.
4 Call the query **qryPriceUpdate** and click **Finish**.
5 Open the query in **Design View** and click the **Update Query** button. In the **Update To** row of the **Cost** column of the QBE grid, enter **[Cost]*1.05.** This increases the value by 5 per cent (see Figure 1.19.12).
To increase by 25 per cent, use the formula **[Cost]*1.25**
To increase by £1, use the formula **[Cost]+1**, etc.

Figure 1.19.12 ▼

6 Click the **Run** button on the **Design** tab.
7 You will get a warning message. Click on **Yes** (see Figure 1.19.13).

Figure 1.19.13 ▶

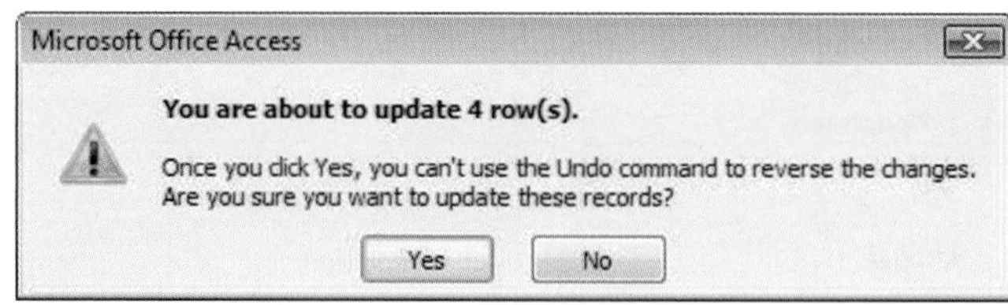

8 The original prices were £16.00, £17.00, £24.00 and £22.00. Click on the **View** icon to check that the prices have been updated to £16.80, £17.85, £25.20 and £23.10 respectively.
9 Set up a macro called **mcrAdjustPrices** to remove the warnings and run this query.

Unit 20: Finishing touches

In this section we will put the finishing touches to our system, including updating the switchboard, tidying up our forms, adding a splashscreen, adding a clock to the switchboard and setting the start-up options.

Updating the switchboard

After completing the additions to the system in Units 16 to 19, it is necessary to edit the switchboard to include the new options.

1 On the **Database Tools** tab, click **Switchboard Manager** and click on **New**. Enter the name of the third switchboard, **System Switchboard** and click on **OK** (see Figure 1.20.1).

Figure 1.20.1 ▶

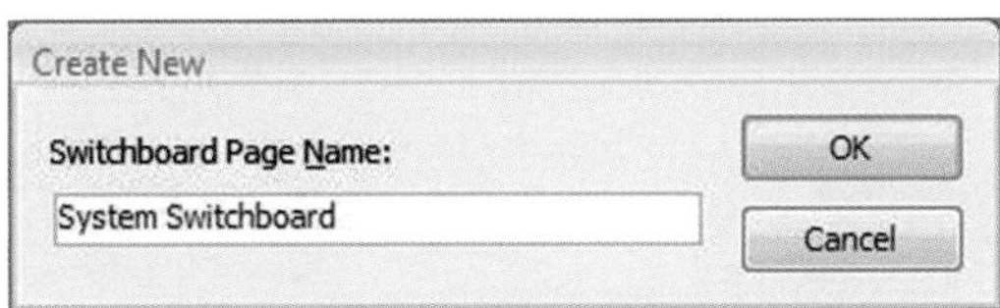

2 Select the **Main Switchboard** and click on **Edit**. Click on **New**. Enter the text **System Functions**. Select the command **Go to Switchboard**. Select the **System Switchboard** (see Figure 1.20.2).

Figure 1.20.2 ▶

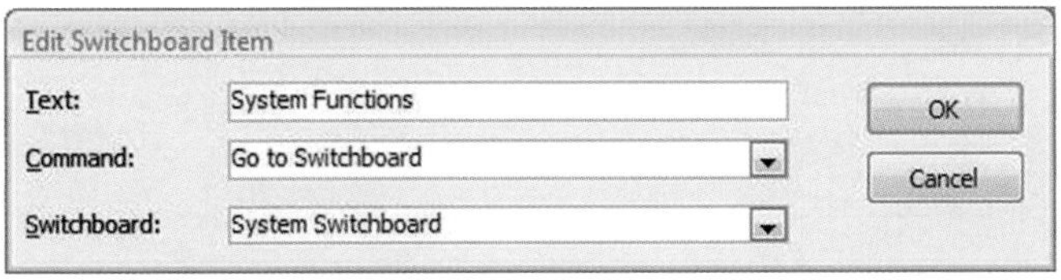

Edit Switchboard Item
Text: System Functions
Command: Go to Switchboard
Switchboard: System Switchboard
OK
Cancel

3 Use the **Move Up** button so that this option is below the **Reports** option (see Figure 1.20.3).

Figure 1.20.3 ▶

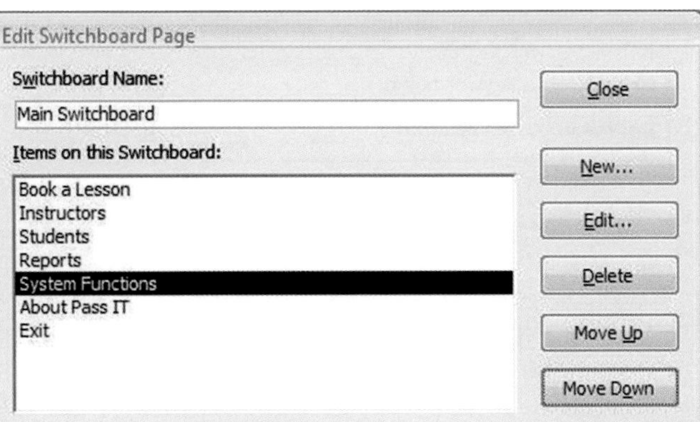

4 Click on **Close** and then select the **Report Switchboard**. Click on **Edit**.
5 Add a new option to open the report **rptLessonAnalysis** (see Figure 1.20.4).

Figure 1.20.4 ▶

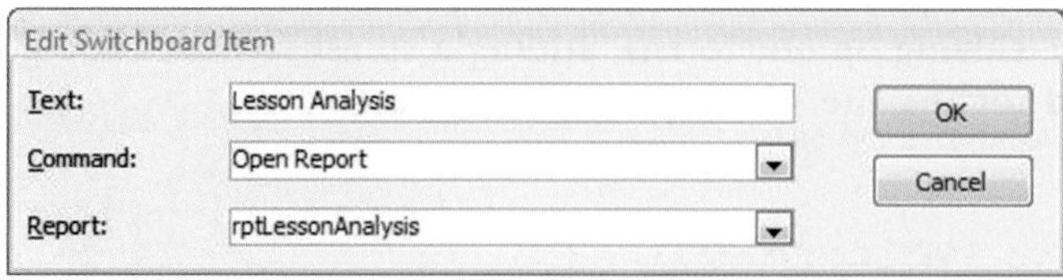

6 Use the Move Up and Move Down button so that the **rptLessonAnalysis** option is above the Main Menu option.
7 Click on **Close** and then select the **System Switchboard**. Click on **Edit**.
8 Add a new option called **Archive Lessons** to run **mcrLessonArchive** (see Figure 1.20.5).

Figure 1.20.5 ▶

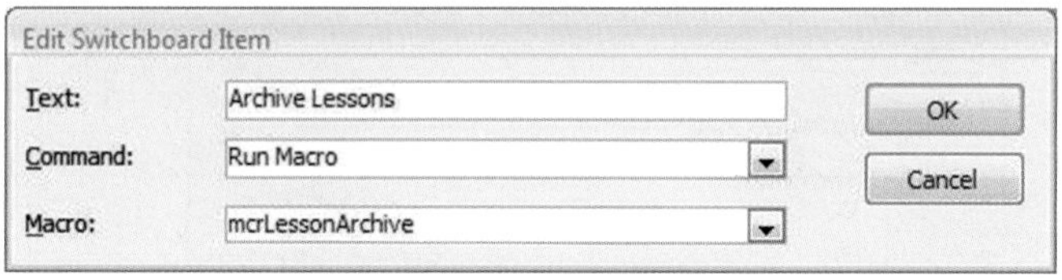

Edit Switchboard Item
Text: Archive Lessons
Command: Run Macro
Macro: mcrLessonArchive
OK
Cancel

9 Add a new option called **Update Prices** to run **mcrAdjustPrices** (see Figure 1.20.6).

Figure 1.20.6 ▶

10 Add a new option named **Main Menu** to return to the **Main Switchboard** (see Figure 1.20.7).

Figure 1.20.7 ▶

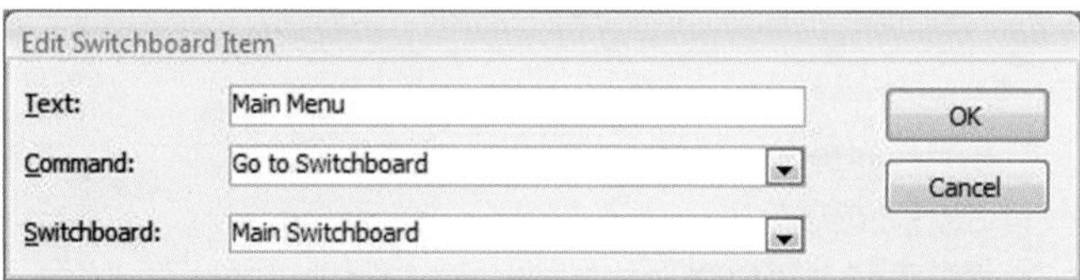

11 Close the **Switchboard Manager**.
12 Open the **Switchboard** from the Navigation Pane. The new main switchboard should now look like that shown in Figure 1.20.8. Test all the buttons to see that they work.

Figure 1.20.8 ▶

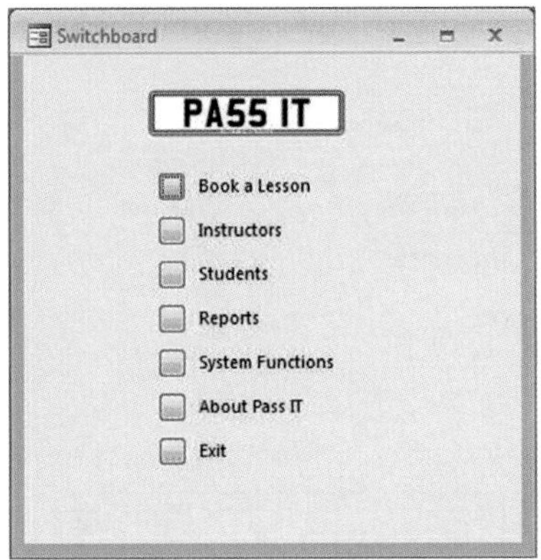

Tidying up forms

The form in Figure 1.20.9 works as expected but is a little untidy. The Student ID control is much too long for a small number. The title control is much too big for a title that is only a few letters long. You can probably see other improvements that could be made.

Figure 1.20.9 ▶

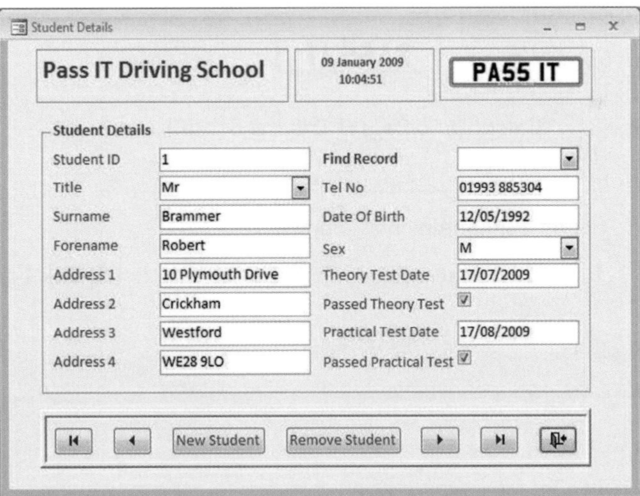

Open all your forms in turn and edit them so that controls are aligned, evenly spaced and the right size as shown in Figure 1.20.10.

Figure 1.20.10 ▶

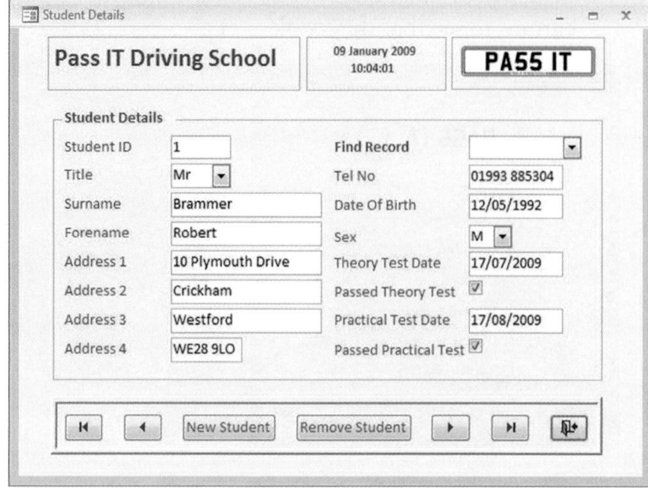

Setting up a splashscreen

A 'splashscreen', like the one shown in Figure 1.20.11, usually loads when the system loads. It appears for a few seconds before the main switchboard loads.

Figure 1.20.11 ▶

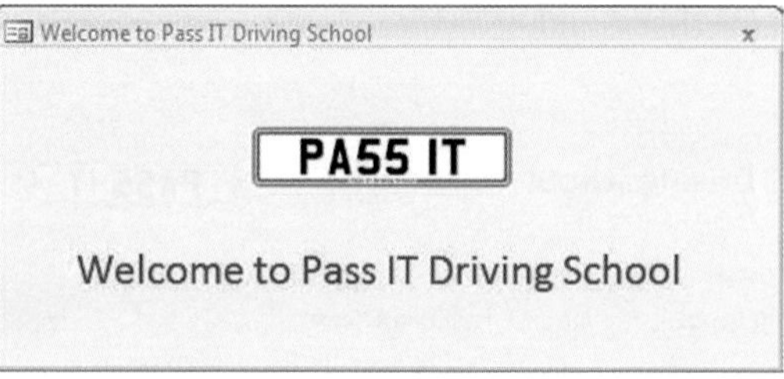

Set up a splashscreen as follows:

1 On the **Create** tab, in the **Forms** group, click **Blank Form**.

2 A blank form appears in **Layout View**. Switch to **Design View** and enlarge it so that it is roughly 12cm by 5cm (see Figure 1.20.12).

Figure 1.20.12 ▶

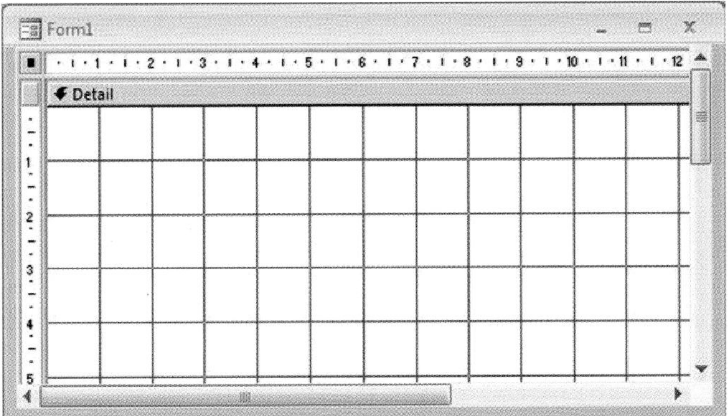

3 Use the **Image** and **Label** buttons to add the logo and display the text as shown in Figure 1.20.13.

Figure 1.20.13 ▶

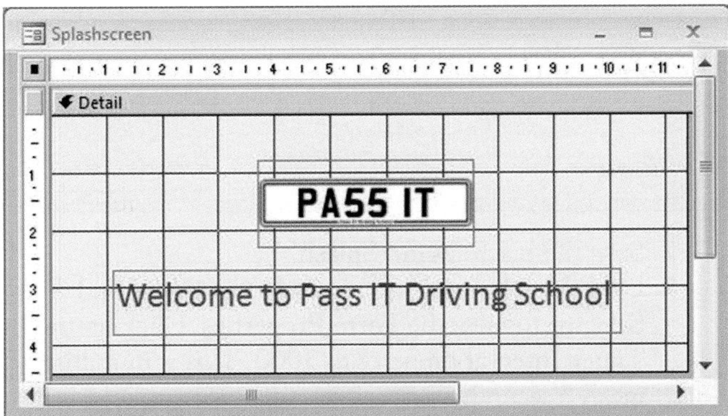

4 Double-click on the **Form Selector** and set the **Form Properties** to remove the scroll bars, record selector, navigation buttons and maximise and minimise buttons. Set the **Border Style** to **Dialog**. Set the **Caption** to **Welcome to Pass IT Driving School**.

5 Save the form as **Splashscreen**. Your form should look like the one shown in Figure 1.20.14.

Figure 1.20.14 ▶

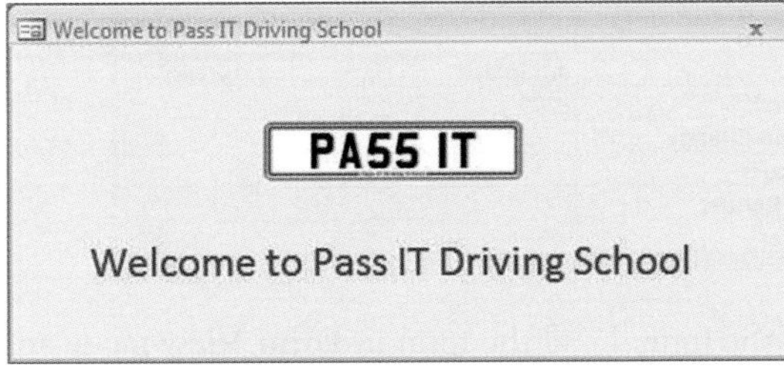

6 On the **Create** tab, click on **Macro** and create a new macro to close the splashscreen form.

- The first **Action** is **Close**. The **Object Type** is **Form**. The **Object Name** is **Splashscreen** (see Figure 1.20.15).

- The second action is to open another form – the **Switchboard** (see Figure 1.20.16).

Figure 1.20.15 ▼

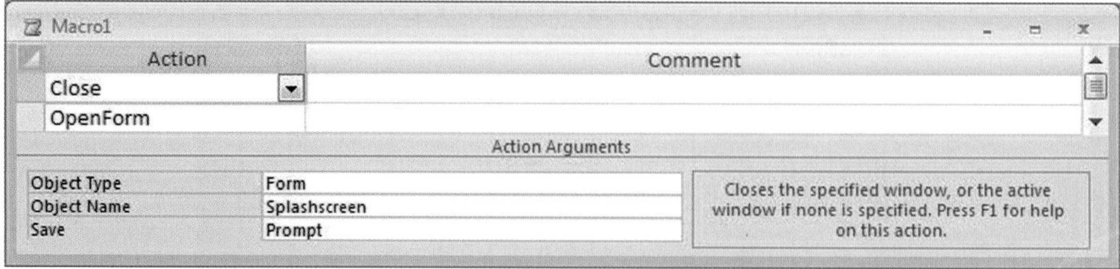

Figure 1.20.16 ▼

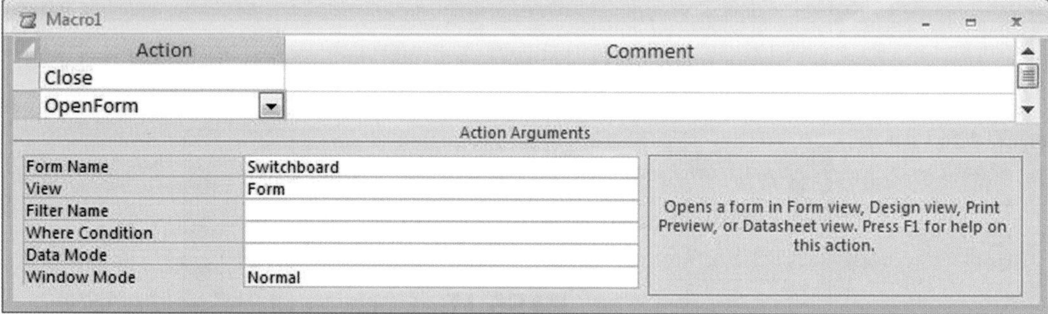

7 Save the macro as **mcrSplash**.

8 Load the splashscreen form in **Design View** and double-click on the **Form Selector** to view the **Form Properties**. Click on the **Event** tab and set the **Timer Interval** property to **3000**. This is in milliseconds, so 3000 would mean 3 seconds.

9 Click on the **OnTimer** property and select **mcrSplash**. You may need to go back to the **Timer Interval** property to adjust your timing a little to get it just right (see Figure 1.20.17).

Figure 1.20.17 ►

Property Sheet

Selection type: Form

Form

Format | Data | Event | Other | All

On Apply Filter	
On Timer	mcrSplash
Timer Interval	3000
On Selection Change	
Before Render	
After Final Render	
After Render	

10 Save the form. Load the form in **Form View** mode and test that it stays on the screen for three seconds before switching to the switchboard.

11 From the **Office Button**, select **Access Options** and click **Current Database**. Set the **Display Form** drop-down to **Splashscreen** to load the splashscreen form when the system loads (see Figure 1.20.18)

Figure 1.20.18 ▼

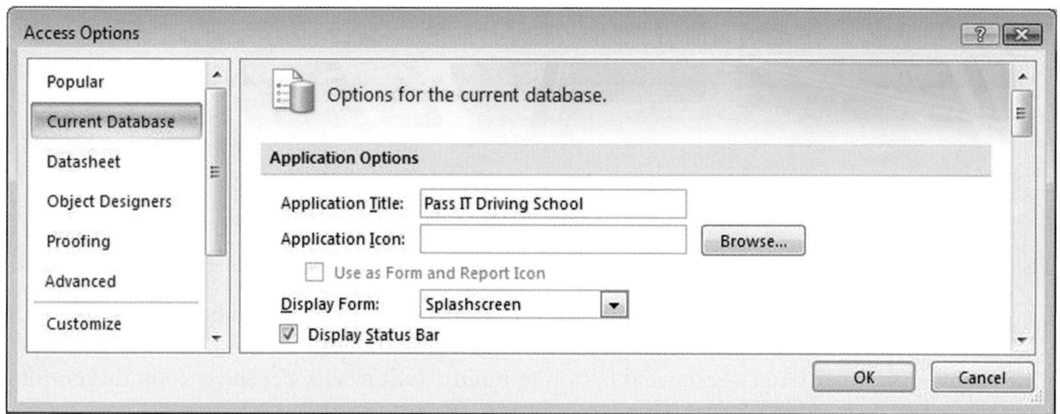

Are you sure?

There is an option on the switchboard to exit from the application. It is a good idea to have an 'Are you sure?' box in case this button is pressed by mistake (see Figure 1.20.19).

Figure 1.20.19 ▶

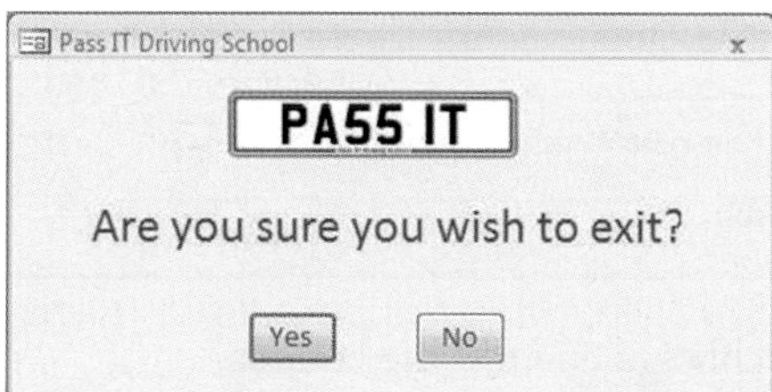

1 Open another blank form in **Design View**.
2 Set the **Form Properties** to remove the scroll bars, record selector, navigation buttons and maximise and minimise buttons. Set the **Border Style** to **Dialog**. Set the **Caption** to **Pass IT Driving School**.
3 Save the form as **frmFinish**.
4 Create a macro called **mcrExit**. The only **Action** is **Quit** with **Arguments** set to **Exit** (see Figure 1.20.20).

Figure 1.20.20 ▼

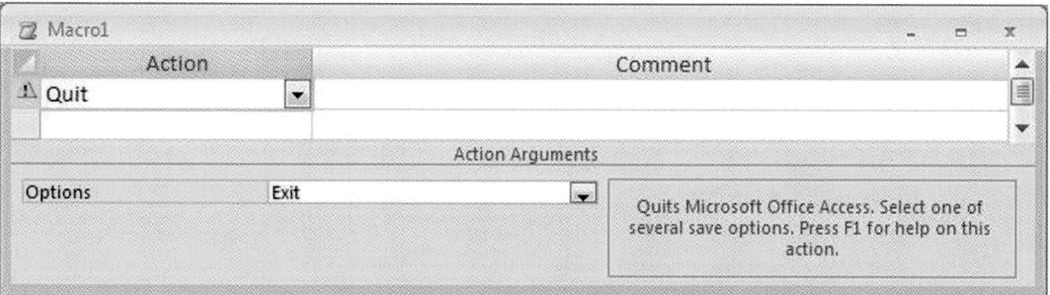

5 Create another macro called **NoExit** to close the **frmFinish** form (see Figure 1.20.21).

Figure 1.20.21 ▼

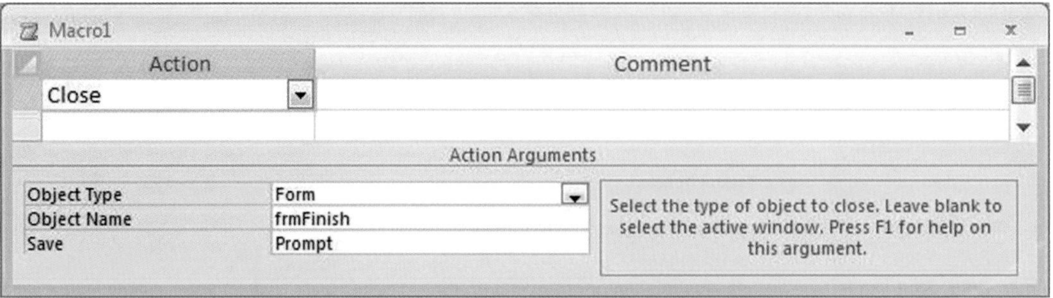

6 Open the **frmFinish** form in **Design View**. Use the **Label** tool to add text similar to the form shown above. Add the logo as shown.

7 Add a command button to run the **Exit** macro. Set the text on this button to **Yes**.

8 Add a command button to run the **NoExit** macro. Set the text on this button to **No**.

9 Save the form and close it.

10 Use the **Switchboard Manager** to edit the **Exit Application** button so that it opens the Finish form in edit mode (see Figure 1.20.22).

Figure 1.20.22 ▶

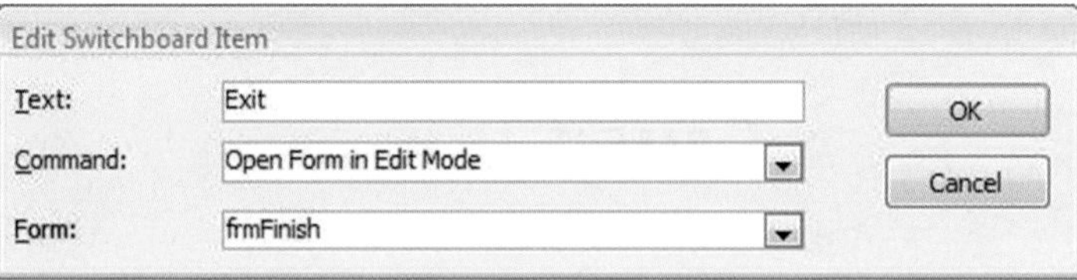

11 Open the switchboard and test the buttons.

Adding a real-time clock to a form

It is possible to add a clock which updates every second to an Access form, such as the switchboard.

1 Open the switchboard in **Design View**.

2 On the **Design** tab, click the **Text Box** button and click in the **Footer** where you want to place your control. The text box will be called something like Text7 (see Figure 1.20.23).

Figure 1.20.23 ▶

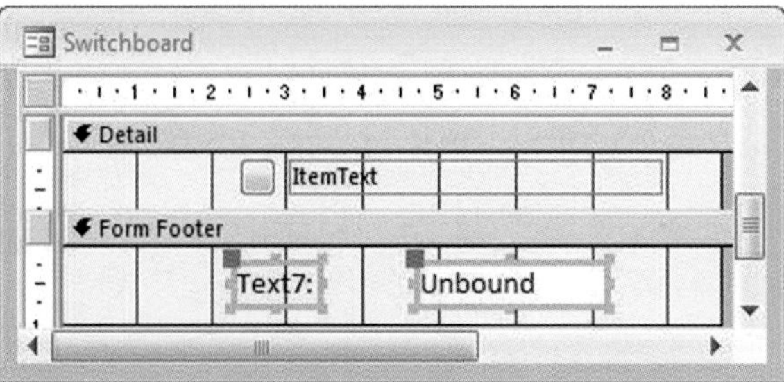

3 Click on the label that says the name (Text7) and delete it (see Figure 1.20.24).

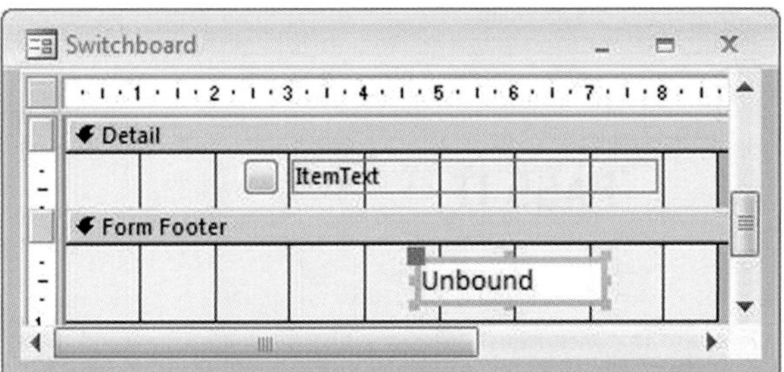

Figure 1.20.24 ▶

4 Click on the text box and click on the **Property Sheet** button or right-click on the text box and choose **Properties**. Click on the **All** tab and edit the name to **Timer1** (see Figure 1.20.25).

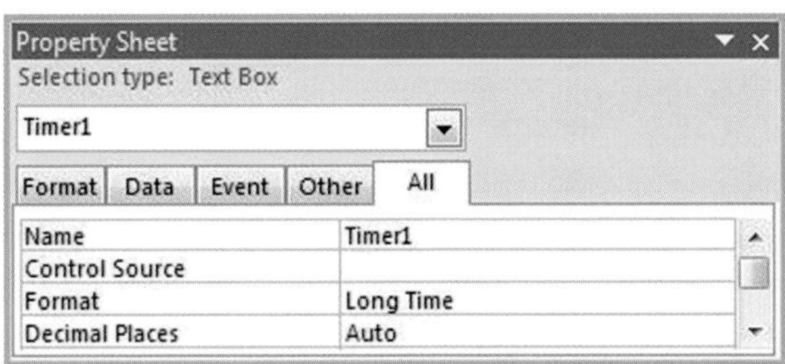

Figure 1.20.25 ▶

5 Click on the **Format** tab and choose the format, **Long Time**.

6 Click on the Form Selector to display the properties for the form. Click on the **Event** tab and set the **Timer Interval** to 1000 (this is one second).

7 Choose the **On Timer** property above **Timer Interval**. Click on the three dots icon and choose **Code Builder**. The **Visual Basic Editor** loads displaying:

```
Private Sub Form_Timer()
End Sub
```

In the middle line type in:

```
[Timer1]=Now
```

See Figure 1.20.26.

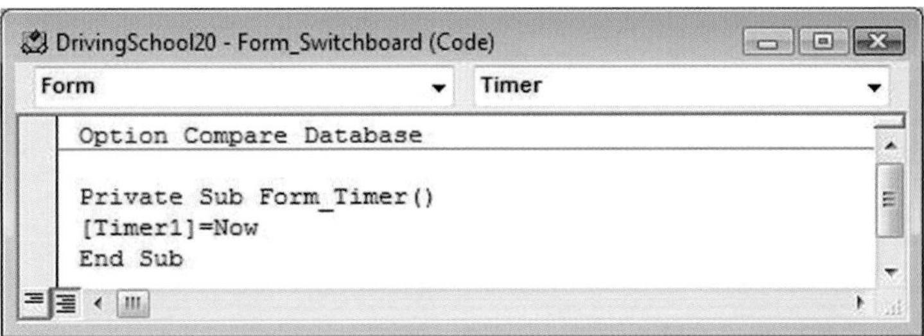

Figure 1.20.26 ▶

8 Close the **Visual Basic Editor** and go into **Form View** to test it (see Figure 1.20.27).

Figure 1.20.27 ▶

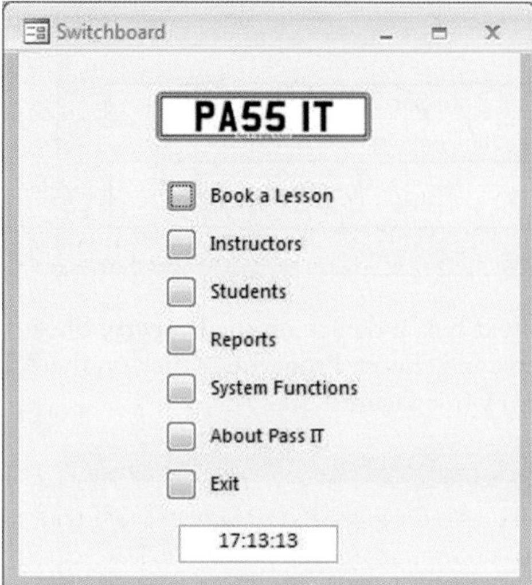

Don't forget that, to disable the start-up options, hold down the SHIFT key as you load the file.

Use **Tricks and Tips** numbers 57–60 to customise your solution further.

2 Access Tricks and Tips

Here are 70 tricks and tips that have been found to be more than useful when implementing Access projects. Website support files are shown in brackets.

Tables

1 Error messages that may occur when setting relationships between tables (Errors)
2 Using the Default Value property to enter a date
3 Adding a Code Prefix to an AutoNumber Field (StationeryCodes)
4 Shortcuts for entering data using the CTRL key
5 Making an AutoNumber field start from 1 again
6 Preventing Duplicate Values in a field
7 Preventing duplicate combinations of data (DoubleBooking)
8 Importing data from Excel (Names)
9 Using copy and paste to take an Excel worksheet into Access (Names)

Queries

10 Finding surnames that begin with a letter or combination of letters (qryWildCardSearch in Queries)
11 Searching for records that contain no values (qryIsNull in Queries)
12 When do you use calculated fields in a query? (qryLessonCost in Queries)
13 Using a query to combine (concatenate) two fields e.g. Forename and Surname (qryConcatenateFullName in Queries)
14 Using a query to calculate initials from a person's forename (qryCalculateInitial in Queries)
15 Calculating the weekday (or month) from the date using Format Properties (qryCalculateWeekday in Queries)
16 Calculating the month name from the date using the Month function (qryCalculateMonthName in Queries)
17 Using a query to calculate the difference between dates – DateDiff function (DateDiffQuery)
18 Using a query to calculate the future dates – DateAdd function (DateAddQuery)
19 Make-Table queries (Queries)
20 Making decisions using the IIf Function in a query (IIfQuery)

Forms

21 Adding a calculated field to a form (frmLesson in Forms)
22 Using the Expression Builder
23 Formatting dates on forms and reports

24 Making a command button the default button (frmLessonBooking in Forms)
25 Changing the properties of a group of controls
26 Preventing users from adding records to a form
27 Creating read-only fields on a form (frmLessonBooking in Forms)
28 Moving the focus to another control on a form (frmLessonBooking in Forms)
29 Borders and special effects (frmLessonBooking in Forms)
30 Designing your own button images
31 Creating a command button from a graphic image (frmLessonBooking in Forms)
32 Customising a Quit or Exit button (frmMainMenu in Forms)
33 Positioning and sizing your form automatically (frmLessonBooking in Forms)
34 Using option buttons or radio controls (frmStudent in Forms)
35 Using option groups (frmInstructor in Forms)
36 Printing a form without the buttons
37 Adding customised tool tips (Screen Tips) to your controls (frmInstructor in Forms)
38 Pop-up and Modal forms
39 Using a Date Picker
40 Starting a form from scratch

Reports

41 Forcing a page break in a report
42 Concatenating text strings on reports (ConcatenateStrings)
43 Replacing check boxes and coded fields with text (Reports)
44 Using Switch to change a coded field
45 Formatting invoice numbers
46 Mailing labels, business and membership cards

Macros

47 Formatting text to bold in a Message Box (mcrNoData in Macros)
48 Putting hard returns in a Message Box (mcrAbout and mcrAbout1 in Macros)
49 The AutoExec macro (mcrAutoexec in Macros)
50 Hiding and unhiding the Navigation Pane from your Autoexec macro
51 Running your system from customised keys (mcrAutoKeys in Macros)
52 Copy (cut) and paste macro (mcrFileAway in Macros)
53 Using Conditions in Macros (mcrTestDateCheck in Macros)
54 Using a Conditional Macro for cross field validation (ConditionalMacro)
55 Control printing multiple copies from a macro (mcrMultipleCopies in Macros)

Others

56 Changing the caption text and other start-up options
57 Changing the application icon

58 Password protecting files
59 Adding a load progress meter to the Status Bar (LoadMeter)
60 Customising information displayed in the Status Bar
61 My Access database is getting very large in size – What do I do?
62 Setting up a Calendar Control to enter dates (CalendarSpinner)
63 Using a Spinner Control to enter dates/numbers (CalendarSpinner)
64 Using SetValue to enter dates
65 Displaying SubForm totals on the Main Form (No65)
66 Customising a Parameter Query dialog box (No66)
67 Print a report from an Option Group control (No67–68)
68 Printing the current record displayed on a form as a report (No67–68)
69 Using conditional formatting to highlight information in a report/form
70 Adding pictures to your database

Tables

1 Error messages that may occur when setting relationships between tables

Error message 1

Figure 2.1.1 ▶

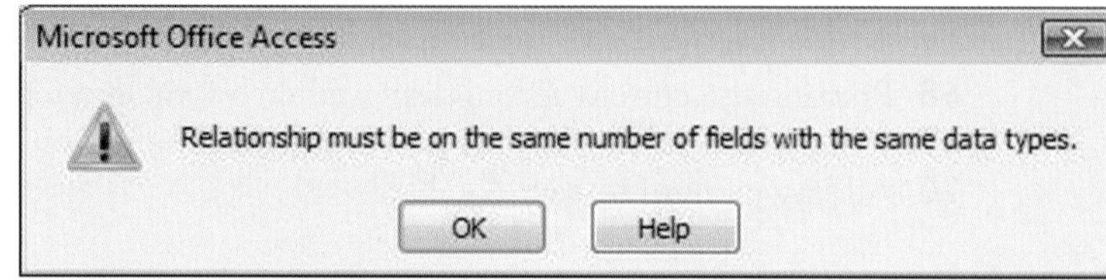
Microsoft Office Access

Relationship must be on the same number of fields with the same data types.

OK Help

Relationships join a field in one table to another field in a second table. These fields should be of the same data type. If one field is set to text then so should the other in the related table. Note that if the primary key field in one table is set to **AutoNumber** and **Long Integer** – e.g. StudentID – then the corresponding field in the other table – e.g. tblLesson – should be set to **Number** and **Long Integer**.

Error message 2

Figure 2.1.2 ▶

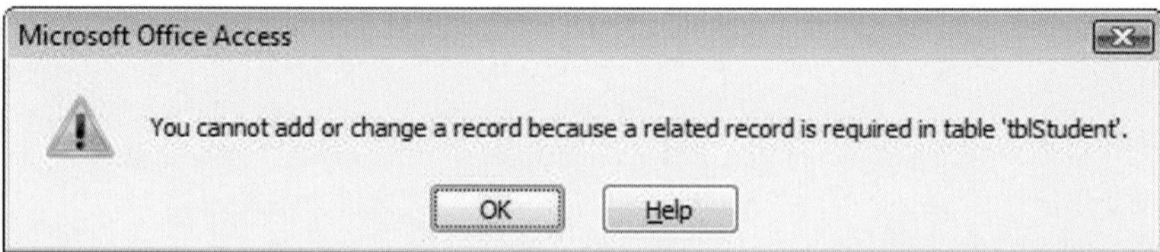
Microsoft Office Access

You cannot add or change a record because a related record is required in table 'tblStudent'.

OK Help

In the Pass IT solution you have worked through, you will get this error message if you try to enter a StudentID (or InstructorID) into the Lesson table when the StudentID does not exist in the related Student table. Referential integrity requires data to be present in both tables. The solution is to enter details of the student (or instructor) in the respective table.

Error message 3

Figure 2.1.3 ▼

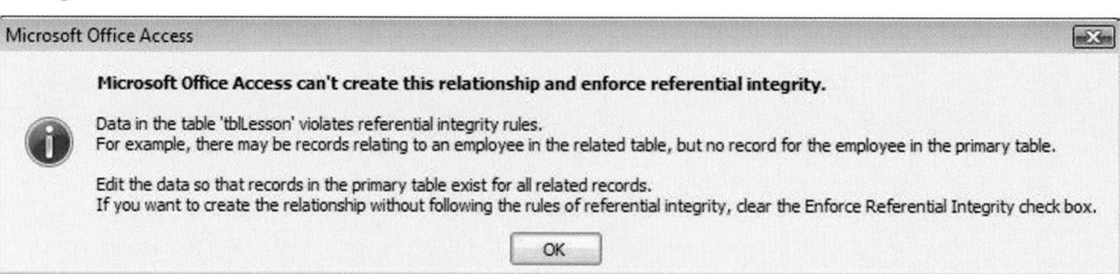
Microsoft Office Access

Microsoft Office Access can't create this relationship and enforce referential integrity.

Data in the table 'tblLesson' violates referential integrity rules.
For example, there may be records relating to an employee in the related table, but no record for the employee in the primary table.

Edit the data so that records in the primary table exist for all related records.
If you want to create the relationship without following the rules of referential integrity, clear the Enforce Referential Integrity check box.

OK

You will get this error message when you enforce referential integrity and already have data in your tables which violates the integrity rule. In other words, in the

Pass IT solution you will have StudentIDs (or InstructorIDs) in the Lesson table which are not present in the linked Student (or Instructor) table.

Error message 4

Figure 2.1.4 ▶

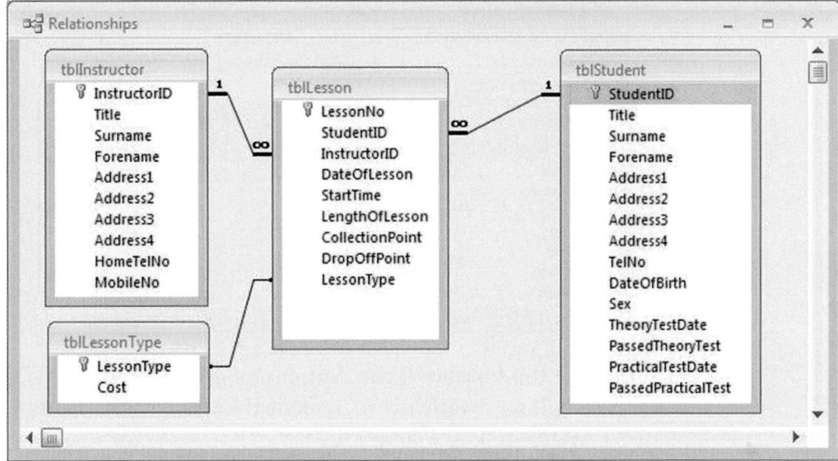

If, when you set your relationships, they just appear as a line, without the **1** and ∞, it is probably because you have not checked **Referential Integrity**. Delete the relationship and set it up again.

If, when you set your relationships, it appears as **1:1** when you were expecting 1 and ∞, it is because you are trying to join a Primary Key (StudentID) to a Foreign Key (StudentID in the Lesson table) with the **Indexed** property of the latter set to **No Duplicates**. The property should be set to **Duplicates OK**.

2 Using the Default Value property to enter a date

In systems such as book or video loaning you invariably will be issuing a loan on today's date and if there is a fixed period of hire, you will know the date of return. In a library, for example, the book will be issued on that day, with a return due in 7 days. You can use the Default Value property in **Table Design View** to do this automatically.

For the field **DateOut** set the Default Value to **=Date()** as shown in Figure 2.1.5 and for **DateOfReturn** set it to **=Date()+7**.

Figure 2.1.5 ▶

General | Lookup

Format	Short Date
Input Mask	
Caption	
Default Value	=Date()
Validation Rule	
Validation Text	
Required	No
Indexed	No
IME Mode	No Control
IME Sentence Mode	None
Smart Tags	
Text Align	General
Show Date Picker	Never

3 Adding a Code Prefix to an AutoNumber Field

When dealing with systems involving sales and stock, products are often coded. For example, stationery products might be coded STA001, STA002, etc.

Figure 2.1.6 ▶

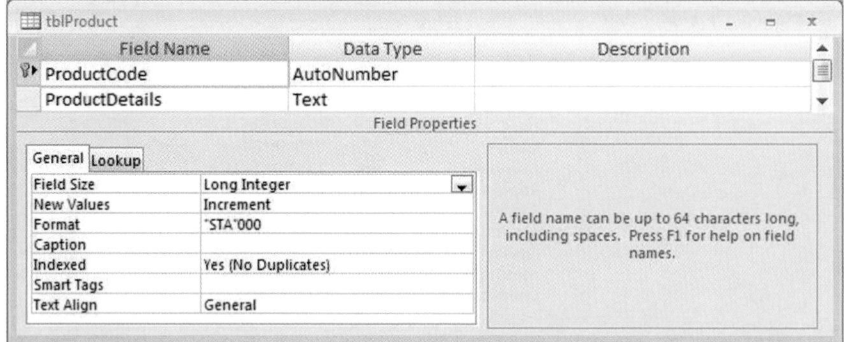

Setting the **Format** of the **AutoNumber** field to "STA"000, as shown in Figure 2.1.6 will automatically increment the value of the field by one – STA001, STA002, etc (see Figure 2.1.7).

Figure 2.1.7 ▶

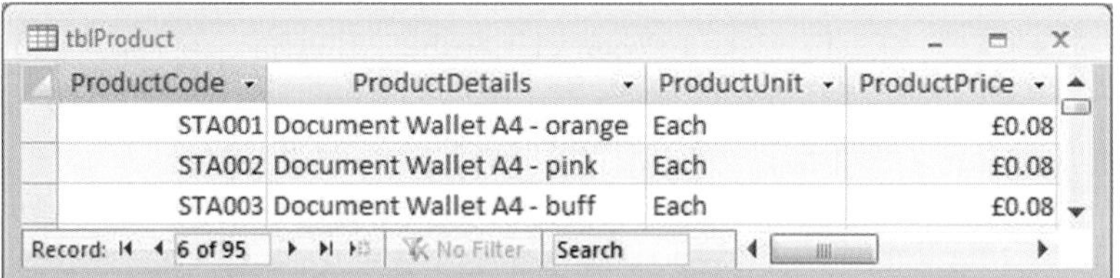

4 Shortcuts for entering data using the CTRL key

- When entering data in a table, you often want to copy the data from the previous record. Do this by simply pressing CTRL and ' (apostrophe).
- You can enter the current time into a table by simply pressing CTRL and : (colon).
- Similarly you can enter the current date into a table by simply pressing CTRL and ; (semi-colon).

5 Making an AutoNumber field start from 1 again

When you first set up the tables in your database the AutoNumber field will automatically increment. While entering data or testing the solution, you will make mistakes and may need to delete rows in the table. You will find you may want to start the numbering from 1 again. To do this:

1. Remove the relationships between all tables.
2. If the **AutoNumber** field is a primary key, click on the primary key icon to unset it.
3. Delete the row for this field.
4. Insert the row again and recreate the field as an **AutoNumber** field.
5. Reset it as a primary key, if appropriate.
6. Set up the table relationships again.

6 Preventing Duplicate Values in a field

Data in a key field cannot be repeated. For example, you could not have two cars with the same registration number. You can prevent two records in the same field having the same value as follows:

1 In the Navigation Pane, open the table in **Design View**.
2 Select the Field Name and set the Field Property **Indexed** to **Yes (No Duplicates)**.

7 Preventing duplicate combinations of data

A theatre uses an Access database to store details of seats sold. A seat such as A1 may be sold many times. Many seats may be sold for a performance on October 12. But any seat can only be sold once for each performance. How can we prevent seats being sold twice?

The theatre has a booking table. The key field is the **BookingNo**. Among the other fields in this table are **SeatNo** and **DateOfEvent**. Once a seat number and date has been entered this combination cannot be entered again.

1 In **Design View** for **tblBooking**, click on the **Indexes** button.

The **Indexes** dialog box is displayed, as in Figure 2.1.8.

Figure 2.1.8 ▶

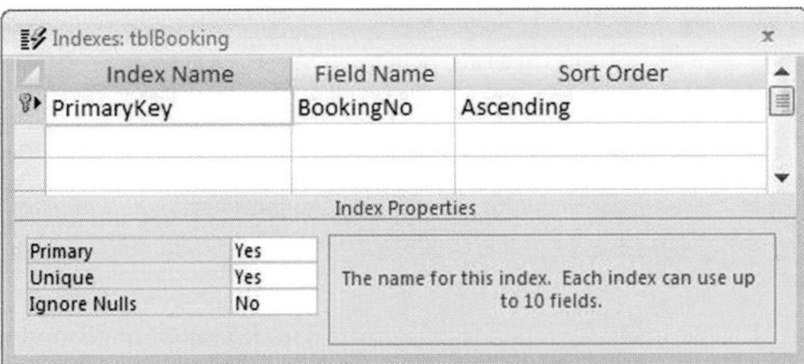

2 Add an **Index Name** such as **DoubleBooking** underneath the Primary Key, as in Figure 2.1.9. The name you choose does not matter.

Figure 2.1.9 ▶

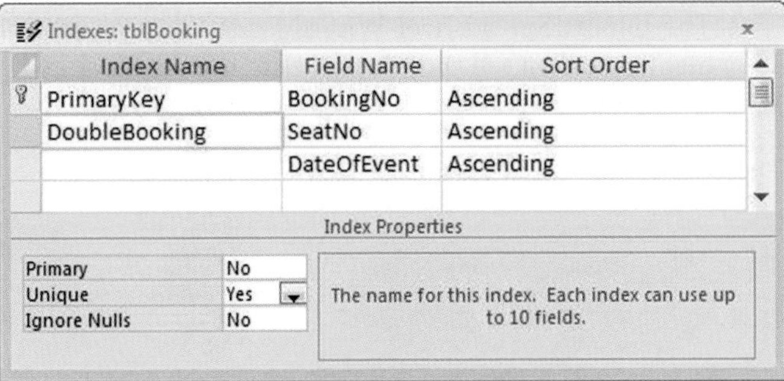

3 In the next column, select the first of the two fields that must not be duplicated. Below it, select the second field. See Figure 2.1.9.
4 Click on **DoubleBooking** and set the **Unique** property to **Yes**, as in Figure 2.1.9.

5 Test it to make sure you get the error message in Figure 2.1.10.

Figure 2.1.10 ▼

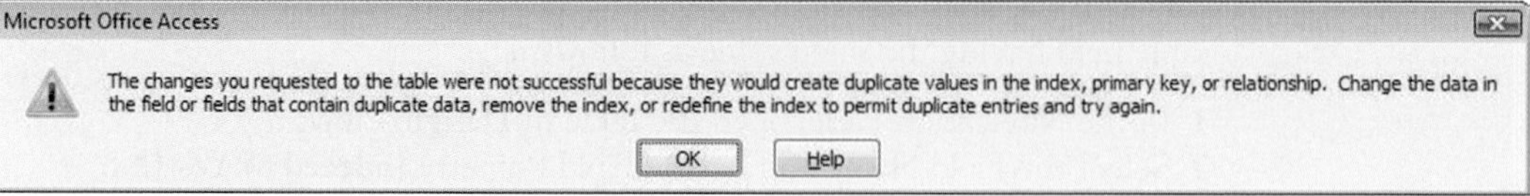

8 Importing data from Excel

Importing data from Excel is easily done in Access using the **Import** options on the **External Data** tab. Suppose we want to import the Excel file of **Names** shown in Figure 2.1.11 into Access.

Note: Row 1 contains the **Field Names** for each column and the names are stored in **Sheet1**.

Figure 2.1.11 ▶

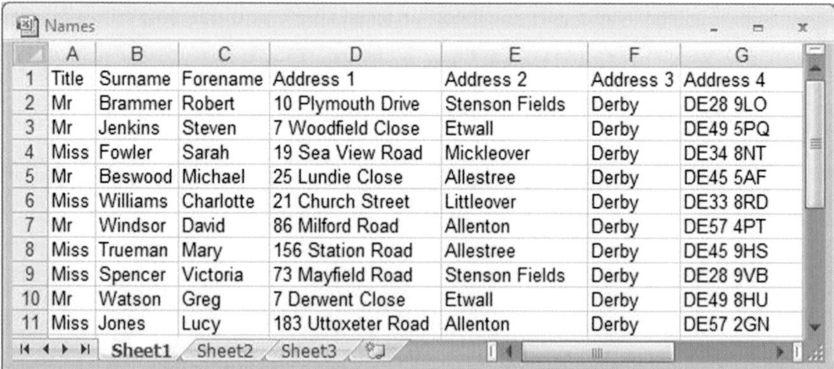

Names

	A	B	C	D	E	F	G
1	Title	Surname	Forename	Address 1	Address 2	Address 3	Address 4
2	Mr	Brammer	Robert	10 Plymouth Drive	Stenson Fields	Derby	DE28 9LO
3	Mr	Jenkins	Steven	7 Woodfield Close	Etwall	Derby	DE49 5PQ
4	Miss	Fowler	Sarah	19 Sea View Road	Mickleover	Derby	DE34 8NT
5	Mr	Beswood	Michael	25 Lundie Close	Allestree	Derby	DE45 5AF
6	Miss	Williams	Charlotte	21 Church Street	Littleover	Derby	DE33 8RD
7	Mr	Windsor	David	86 Milford Road	Allenton	Derby	DE57 4PT
8	Miss	Trueman	Mary	156 Station Road	Allestree	Derby	DE45 9HS
9	Miss	Spencer	Victoria	73 Mayfield Road	Stenson Fields	Derby	DE28 9VB
10	Mr	Watson	Greg	7 Derwent Close	Etwall	Derby	DE49 8HU
11	Miss	Jones	Lucy	183 Uttoxeter Road	Allenton	Derby	DE57 2GN

Sheet1 Sheet2 Sheet3

1. Open the Access database into which you want to import the file called **Names**. On the **External Data** tab in the **Import** group, click on the **Excel** button.
2. The **Get External Data** dialog box appears. Click on **Browse** to locate your file **Names**, double-click the file and click **OK**.
3. The **Import Spreadsheet Wizard** loads. Click on **Sheet1** (if it is not already highlighted) to tell the wizard where the data is stored. Click on **Next**.

4 In the next **Import Spreadsheet Wizard** dialog box, check **First Row Contains Column Headings**, as shown in Figure 2.1.12 (Access will use these as field names in the table). Click on **Next**.

Figure 2.1.12 ▶

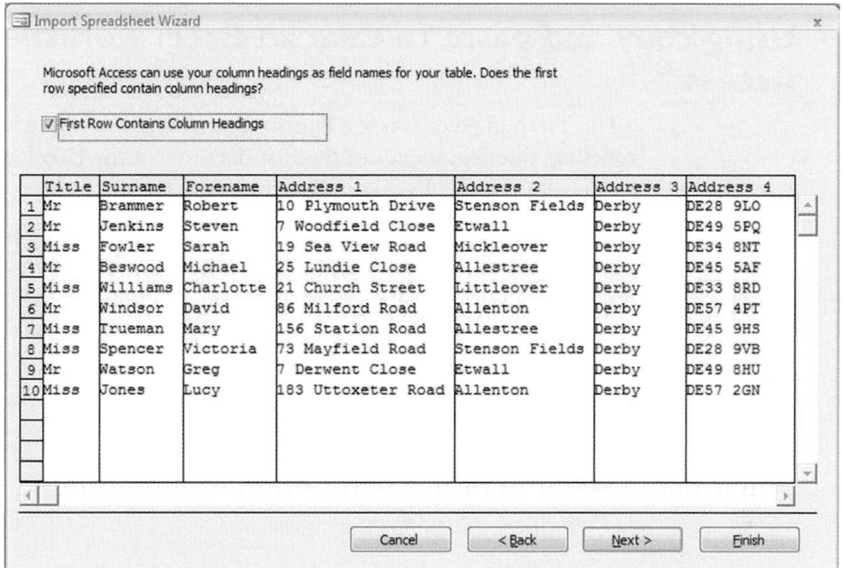

5 The next **Import Spreadsheet Wizard** dialog box gives you the option to specify information about the data. Click on **Next**.

6 In the next dialog box you are given some primary key options. Select **Let Access add primary key** (see Figure 2.1.13). You will notice Access inserts a Primary Key ID. Click on **Next**.

Figure 2.1.13 ▶

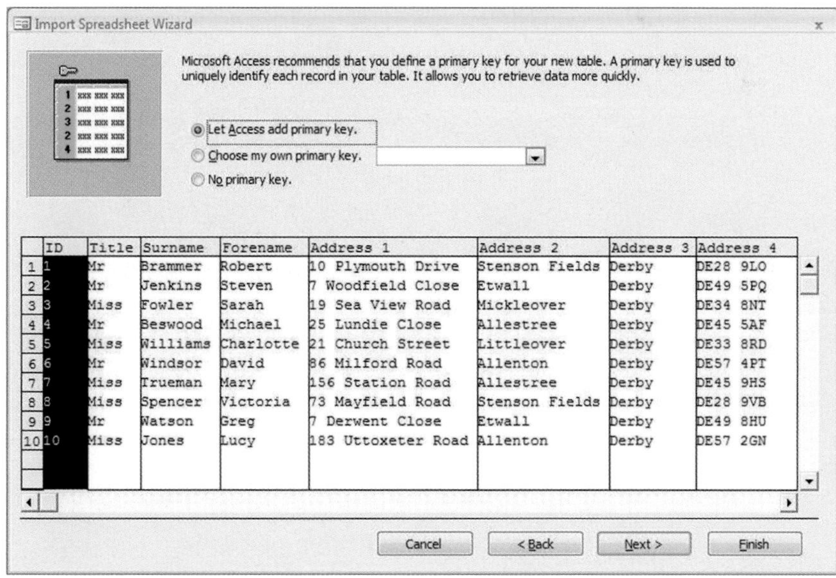

7 In the final dialog box click in the **Import to Table** box and type **tblNames**. Click on **Finish** and then on **Close**. In the Navigation Pane, open **tblNames** to check the import has been successful.

9 Using copy and paste to take an Excel worksheet into Access

This method gives you less control than Tip 8 but is quick and easy. It helps to include the field names in the first data row of the Excel worksheet. To try it you will need the Excel file called Names used in Tip 8.

1 Open the Excel file **Names** and select the data (including column headings) that you want to paste into Access. Click on **Copy**.
2 In Access, in the Navigation Pane, click on **Paste**.
3 Access will ask you if the first row of data contains column headings. Answer **Yes**.
4 Open the table to view your data. Access calls the table **Sheet1**. Switch to **Design View** and edit as you need.

Queries

10 Finding surnames that begin with a letter or combination of letters

You can use the asterisk (*) as a wildcard in searches and queries. For example, a query searching on a postcode equal to **WE34*** will find all the postcodes beginning with WE34.

We want to set up a query so that when we enter a letter or combination of letters, the query will return all surnames beginning with those letters. For example, if we enter **Ste** the query would return Stebbins, Stephenson and Stevens, etc.

Create a parameter query in the normal way, based on **tblStudent**, using the **LIKE** operator and the wildcard symbol (*). Use this statement in the query, as shown in Figure 2.2.1. **Like [Enter the first letter of the surname:] & "*"**

Figure 2.2.1 ▼

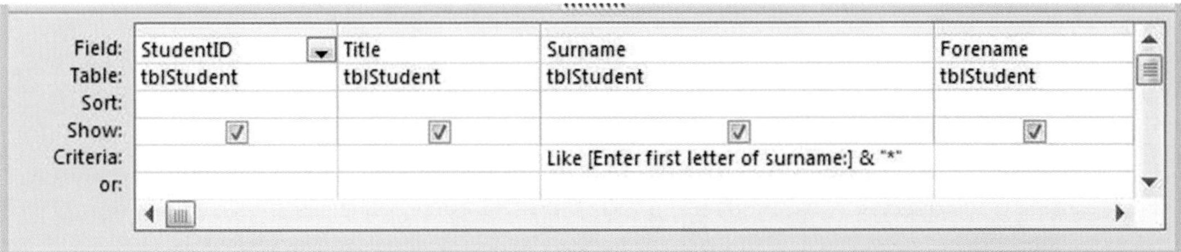

11 Searching for records that contain no values

In the Pass IT system, suppose you wanted a list of students who hadn't arranged a theory test date. You need to set up a query using the **Is Null** operator which returns missing or unknown data.

Set up a query based on **tblStudent** and in the **Criteria** cell for the **Field**; **TheoryTestDate** enter **Is Null** (see Figure 2.2.2).

Figure 2.2.2 ▼

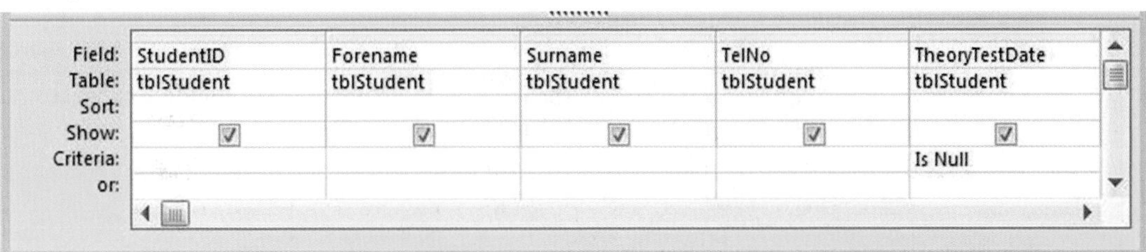

The operator **Is Not Null** would return all records containing any value.

12 When do you use calculated fields in a query?

In Unit 8 you added a calculated field to a query. The query created a new field based on the data from two other fields. In this case the new field **TotalCost** which was the result of **[LengthOfLesson] * [Cost]**.

Figure 2.2.3 ▼

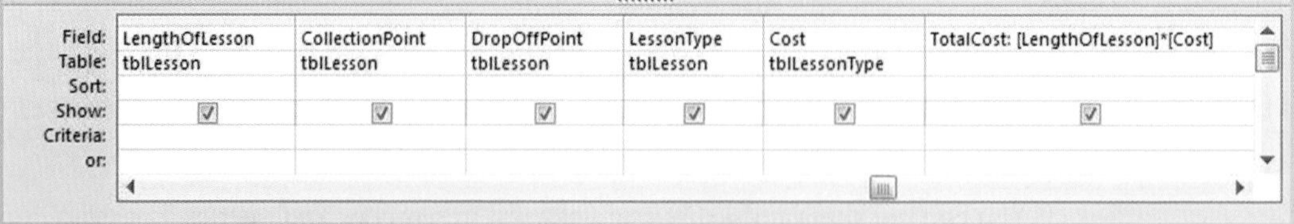

Field:	LengthOfLesson	CollectionPoint	DropOffPoint	LessonType	Cost	TotalCost: [LengthOfLesson]*[Cost]
Table:	tblLesson	tblLesson	tblLesson	tblLesson	tblLessonType	
Sort:						
Show:	☑	☑	☑	☑	☑	☑
Criteria:						
or:						

This query forms the basis of forms and reports. Calculated fields are created by using a blank column of the QBE grid and entering the formula in the Field row as shown in Figure 2.2.3. Other examples are:

Purpose	Example
Multiply a field by a number	VAT: [Cost]*17.5/100
Add one field to another	Total: [Cost]+[VAT]
Add 7 days to a date	ReturnDate: [DateOfLoan]+7
Calculate the number of years since a date	Age: DateDiff("yyyy",[DateOfBirth],Now())

13 Using a query to combine (concatenate) two fields e.g. Forename and Surname

You can join together the text from two fields by using a calculated field in a query.

Set up a query based on **tblStudent** with the fields as shown in Figure 2.2.4. Add a new column to the QBE grid and set up the new field: **Full Name: [Forename] & " " & [Surname]**

Figure 2.2.4 ▶

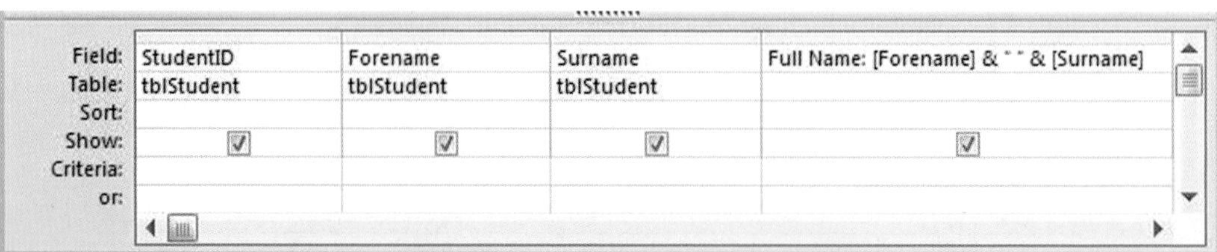

Field:	StudentID	Forename	Surname	Full Name: [Forename] & " " & [Surname]
Table:	tblStudent	tblStudent	tblStudent	
Sort:				
Show:	☑	☑	☑	☑
Criteria:				
or:				

When you run the query it concatenates **Surname** and **Forename** to give the field **Full Name**, as shown in Figure 2.2.5.

Figure 2.2.5 ▶

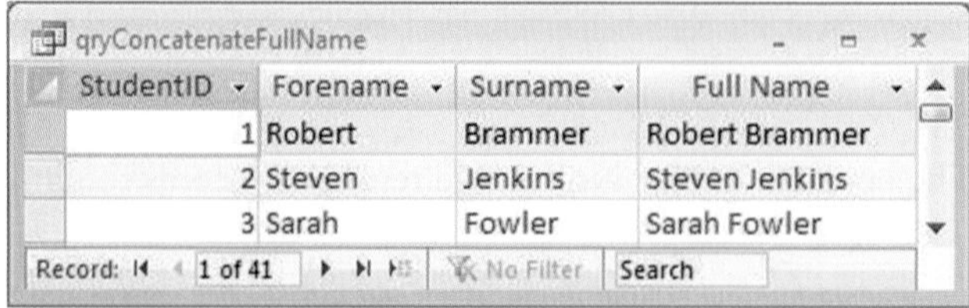

qryConcatenateFullName

StudentID	Forename	Surname	Full Name
1	Robert	Brammer	Robert Brammer
2	Steven	Jenkins	Steven Jenkins
3	Sarah	Fowler	Sarah Fowler

Record: 1 of 41 No Filter Search

14 Using a query to calculate initials from a person's forename

Using the principles in the tip above set up a query based on **tblStudent** with the fields as shown. Add a new column to the QBE grid and set up the new field:

Initial: Left([Forename],1)

This will return one character from the left of the field **Forename** – i.e. the initial. Add another column to the QBE grid and set up the new field:

Full Name: [Title] & " "& [Initial] & " " & [Surname]

Figure 2.2.6 ▼

Field:	StudentID	Title	Forename	Surname	Initial: Left([Forename],1)	Full Name: [Title] & " " & [Initial] & " " & [Surname]
Table:	tblStudent	tblStudent	tblStudent	tblStudent		
Sort:						
Show:	☑	☑	☑	☑	☑	☑
Criteria:						
or:						

When you run the query, it concatenates the fields **Title** and **Surname** with the calculated field **Initial** to give the field **Full Name** as shown in Figure 2.2.7.

Figure 2.2.7 ▶

qryCalculateInitial

StudentID	Title	Forename	Surname	Initial	Full Name
1	Mr	Robert	Brammer	R	Mr R Brammer
2	Mr	Steven	Jenkins	S	Mr S Jenkins
3	Miss	Sarah	Fowler	S	Miss S Fowler
4	Mr	Michael	Beswood	M	Mr M Beswood

Record: 1 of 41 No Filter Search

15 Calculating the weekday (or month) from the date using Format Properties

The following method is a simple way of giving the name of the weekday from a date. It can easily be adapted to give the month name.

1 Set up a query based on **tblLesson** with the fields as shown. Add a new column to the QBE grid and set up the new field: **DayOfTheWeek: DateOfLesson**.

Figure 2.2.8 ▼

Field:	LessonNo	StudentID	InstructorID	DateOfLesson	DayOfTheWeek: DateOfLesson
Table:	tblLesson	tblLesson	tblLesson	tblLesson	tblLesson
Sort:					
Show:	☑	☑	☑	☑	☑
Criteria:					
or:					

2 Right-click on this field and select **Properties**.
3 In the **Format** box, type **dddd**, as in Figure 2.2.9.

Figure 2.2.9 ▶

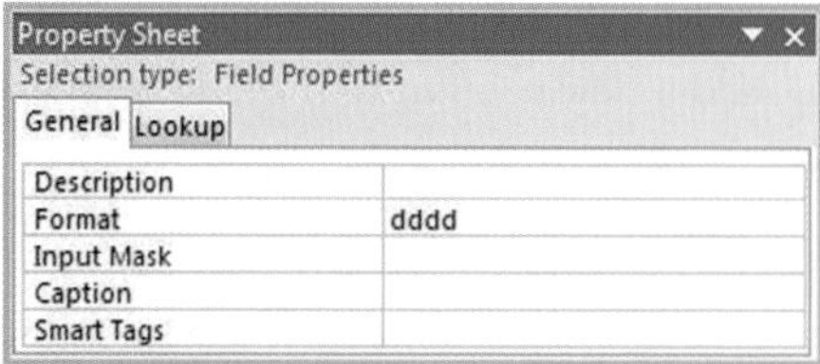

Property Sheet
Selection type: Field Properties
General | Lookup

Description	
Format	dddd
Input Mask	
Caption	
Smart Tags	

4 Run the query to test it. You should get the results in Figure 2.2.10.

Figure 2.2.10 ▶

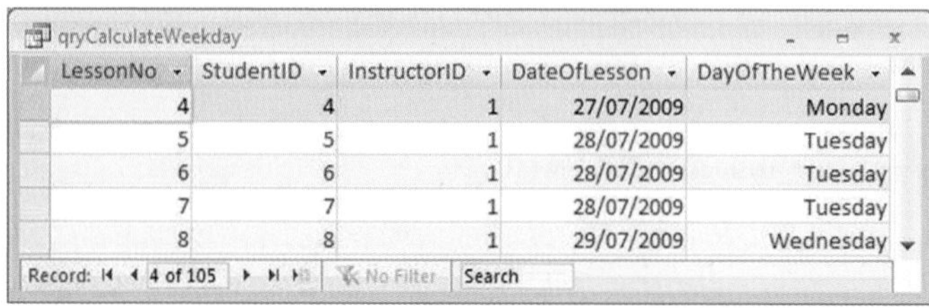

qryCalculateWeekday

LessonNo	StudentID	InstructorID	DateOfLesson	DayOfTheWeek
4	4	1	27/07/2009	Monday
5	5	1	28/07/2009	Tuesday
6	6	1	28/07/2009	Tuesday
7	7	1	28/07/2009	Tuesday
8	8	1	29/07/2009	Wednesday

Record: 4 of 105 No Filter Search

In the same way a field **MonthName** could be set up with **Properties** set to **mmmm**.

16 Calculating the month name from the date using the Month function

Set up a query based on **tblLesson** with the fields as shown in Figure 2.2.11. Add a new column to the QBE grid and set up the new field:
Month: MonthName(Month([DateOfLesson]))

Figure 2.2.11 ▼

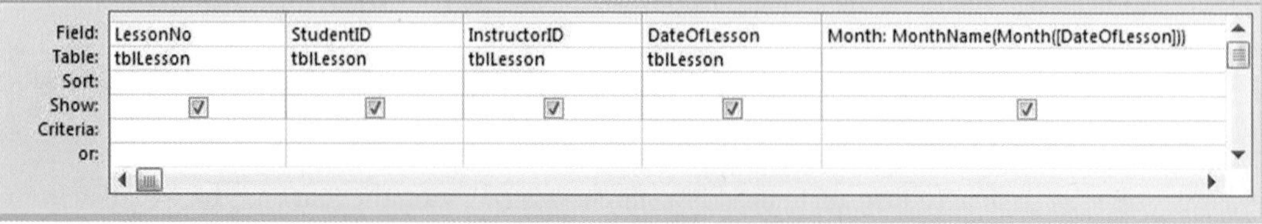

Field:	LessonNo	StudentID	InstructorID	DateOfLesson	Month: MonthName(Month([DateOfLesson]))
Table:	tblLesson	tblLesson	tblLesson	tblLesson	
Sort:					
Show:	☑	☑	☑	☑	☑
Criteria:					
or:					

The function **Month** returns a month number from the date. The function **MonthName** returns the name of the month from the month number, as shown in Figure 2.2.12.

Figure 2.2.12 ▶

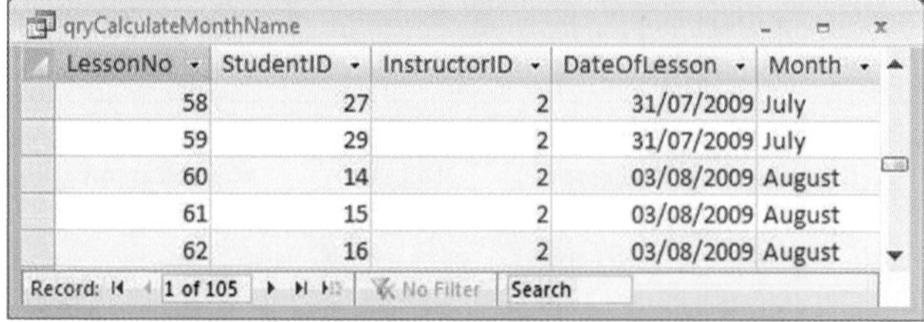

qryCalculateMonthName

LessonNo	StudentID	InstructorID	DateOfLesson	Month
58	27	2	31/07/2009	July
59	29	2	31/07/2009	July
60	14	2	03/08/2009	August
61	15	2	03/08/2009	August
62	16	2	03/08/2009	August

Record: 1 of 105 No Filter Search

In the same way, the built-in Access functions **Weekday** and **WeekdayName** can be used to return the day name.

17 Using a query to calculate the difference between dates – DateDiff function

If you have two date fields, you may need to calculate the time between them. This can be done by adding a calculated field to the query.

In the example shown in Figure 2.2.13, the calculated field **DaysOnLoan** is added, which returns the value from the calculation **[DateBack]–[DateOut]**

Figure 2.2.13 ▼

Field:	BookNo	DateOut	DateBack	DaysOnLoan: [DateBack]-[DateOut]	DaysOut: DateDiff("d",[DateOut],[DateBack])
Table:	tblLoan	tblLoan	tblLoan		
Sort:					
Show:	☑	☑	☑	☑	☑
Criteria:					
or:					

There is also a **DateDiff()** function, which uses an argument to determine how the time interval is measured. Use "m" to calculate date differences in months, "ww" to calculate in weeks, "yyyy" for years and "d" to calculate in days.

Figure 2.2.13 also shows the calculated field **DaysOut** using the **DateDiff()** function to return the difference between fields **DateOut** and **DateBack**.

18 Using a query to calculate the future dates – DateAdd function

If you have a date field and a period of time, you may need to calculate a future date, such as the date of return from number of days on hire. This can be done by adding a calculated field to the query.

In the example shown in Figure 2.2.14 the calculated field **DateOfReturn** is added, which returns the value from the calculation **[DateOut]+[NoOfDays]**

Figure 2.2.14 ▼

Field:	BookNo	DateOut	NoOfDays	DateOfReturn: [DateOut]+[NoOfDays]	DateDueBack: DateAdd("d",[NoOfDays],[DateOut])
Table:	tblDaysOut	tblDaysOut	tblDaysOut		
Sort:					
Show:	☑	☑	☑	☑	☑
Criteria:					
or:					

There is also a **DateAdd()** function, which is used in much the same way as the **DateDiff()** function. Figure 2.2.14 also shows the calculated field **DateDueBack**, using the **DateAdd()** function to return the sum of the fields **NoOfDays** and **DateOut**.

19 Make-Table queries

In Unit 19 you were introduced to action queries and shown how to move data with append and delete queries. A **Make-Table** query does just that, it creates a new table from the results of a query.

The following example searches the student table and makes a table of students who have passed their practical test.

1 Set up a query in the usual way, based on **tblStudent**. Select the fields **StudentID**, **Forename**, **Surname**, **Address1**, **Address2**, **Address3**, **Address4** and **PassedPracticalTest**.

Figure 2.2.15 ▼

Field:	StudentID	Forename	Surname	Address1	Address2	Address3	Address4	PassedPracticalTest
Table:	tblStudent	tblStudent	tblStudent	tblStudent	tblStudent	tblStudent	tblStudent	tblStudent
Sort:								
Show:	☑	☑	☑	☑	☑	☑	☑	☑
Criteria:								Yes
or:								

2 In the field **PassedPracticalTest** set the criteria to **Yes**.
3 On the **Design** tab, click the **Make Table** button and click **OK**.
4 You will be prompted for a table name. Type **tblPassedTest**.
5 Run the query. You will receive the warning that a number of rows are to be pasted into a new table. Click on **Yes**.
6 In the Navigation Pane, open your new **tblPassedTest** and check the data has transferred correctly.

Figure 2.2.16 ▼

tblPassedTest

StudentID	Forename	Surname	Address1	Address2	Address3	Address4	PassedPracticalTest
1	Robert	Brammer	10 Plymouth Drive	Crickham	Westford	WE28 9LO	-1
6	David	Windsor	86 Milford Road	Pilton	Westford	WE49 4PT	-1
7	Mary	Trueman	156 Station Road	Pilton	Westford	WE49 9HS	-1
8	Victoria	Spencer	73 Mayfield Road	Crickham	Westford	WE28 9VB	-1
35	Tom	Heaney	6 Cavendish Way	Blakeway	Westford	WE44 3W	-1
37	Lee	Giles	4 Devonshire Drive	Crickham	Westford	WE28 6YR	-1

Record: 1 of 6 No Filter Search

Note: You will notice that the new table does not inherit the field properties or primary key settings from the original table. Go into Table Design View and set the Format for the PassedPracticalTest field to Yes/No.

20 Making decisions using the IIf Function in a query

You can use the **IIf** function in a query when you want to do a calculation on some records in one way and in another for others. The syntax is:
IIf (condition,true,false).

For example, in the Pass IT Driving School, students with a valid NUS card can get 10% discount off the usual cost of lessons. We want to be able to click a check box if a student discount applies and automatically re-calculate the discounted cost as shown below.

Figure 2.2.17 ▶

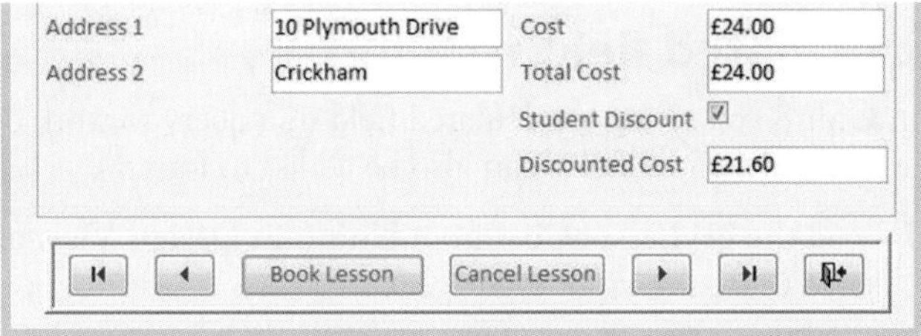

A Yes/No field called **Discount** is added to **tblLesson** and the **qryLessonCost** set up in Unit 8 as shown in Figure 2.2.18. A calculated field:

DiscountedCost: IIf([Discount]=True,[TotalCost]*0.9,[TotalCost])

is added, as shown in Figure 2.2.18.

Figure 2.2.18 ▼

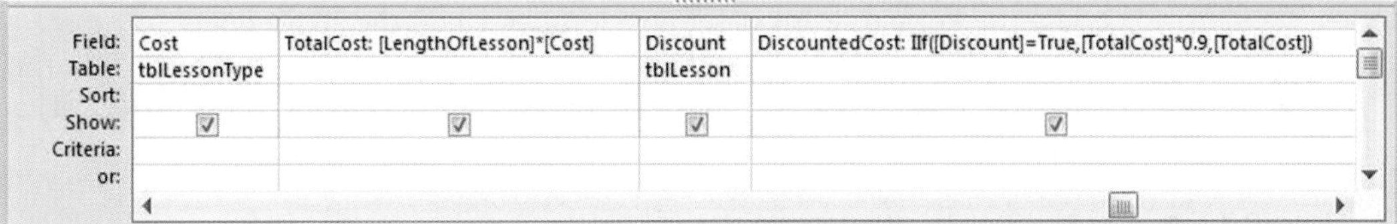

The **IIf** function looks to see if the **Discount** field is checked (True), if it is, it sets the **DiscountedCost** to **90%** of the **TotalCost** else it leaves the **DiscountedCost** at the value of **TotalCost**.

The same technique can be used for adding where applicable, VAT, delivery charges, postage, etc.

Forms

21 Adding a calculated field to a form

In Unit 8 you set up a calculated field in a query to work out the cost of a lesson. Calculated fields can also be added to forms.

1 Load the **qryLessonCost** from Unit 8 in **Design View** and delete fields to leave those shown in Figure 2.3.1.

Figure 2.3.1 ▼

Field:	LessonNo	StudentID	InstructorID	DateOfLesson	StartTime	LengthOfLesson	LessonType	Cost
Table:	tblLesson	tblLesson	tblLesson	tblLesson	tblLesson	tblLesson	tblLesson	tblLessonType
Sort:								
Show:	☑	☑	☑	☑	☑	☑	☑	☑
Criteria:								
or:								

2 Use the **Form Wizard** to set up a form based on the above query.

3 Switch to **Design View** and add a Text Box at the foot of the form. Edit the label to read **TotalCost**. In the Text Box type **=[LengthOfLesson]*[Cost]** (see Figure 2.3.2).

Figure 2.3.2 ▶

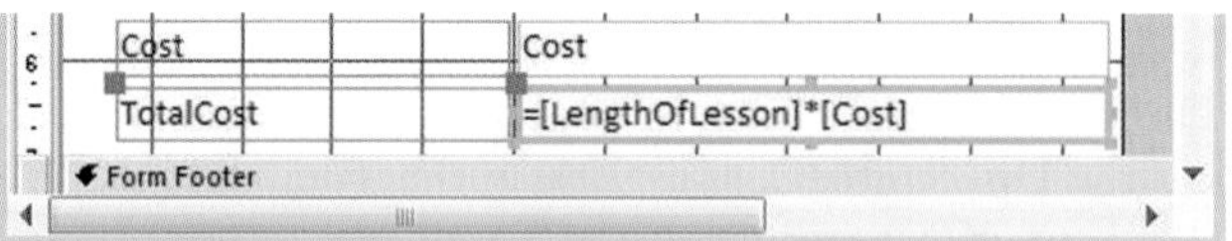

4 Display the **Properties** for the Text Box, set the **Format** to **Currency.** Switch to **Form View** to see the form, as shown in Figure 2.3.3. Save your form as **frmLesson**.

Figure 2.3.3 ▶

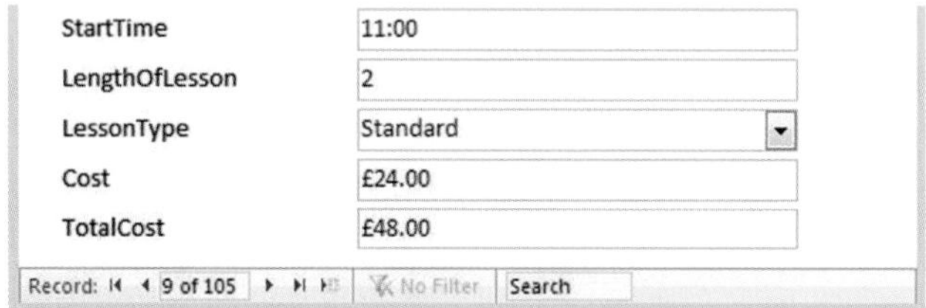

22 Using the Expression Builder

The Expression Builder shown in Figure 2.3.4 helps you easily set up expressions in Access, such as when setting up calculated fields in a query or calculated controls on a form.

Figure 2.3.4 ▶

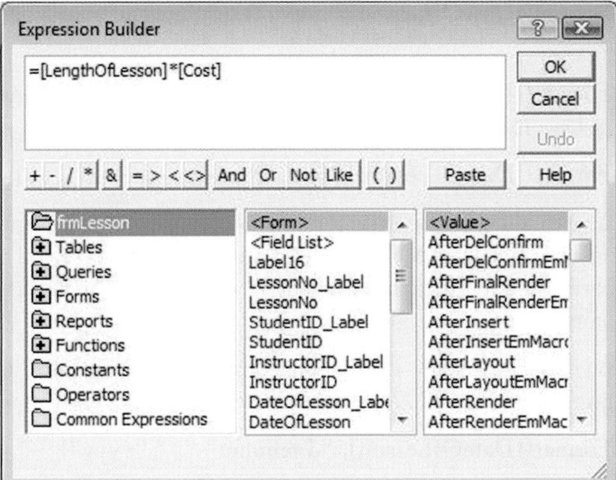

1 Load the form from the previous tip called **frmLesson** in **Design View**.
2 Highlight the **TotalCost** text box and delete the formula.
3 Right-click to call up its properties, select the **Data** tab and, in the **Control Source**, click the three dots to load the **Expression Builder**.
4 Build your expression by pasting the symbols and field names from the dialog box.

23 Formatting dates on forms and reports

You can use the **Format** function to display different dates in different formats or different date components on a form or a report.

For example, suppose you have a field called **DateOfLesson**.

Set up a new Text Box called **Day of the Week** and set the **Control Source** property to:

=Format([DateOfLesson],"dddd")

Figure 2.3.5 ▶

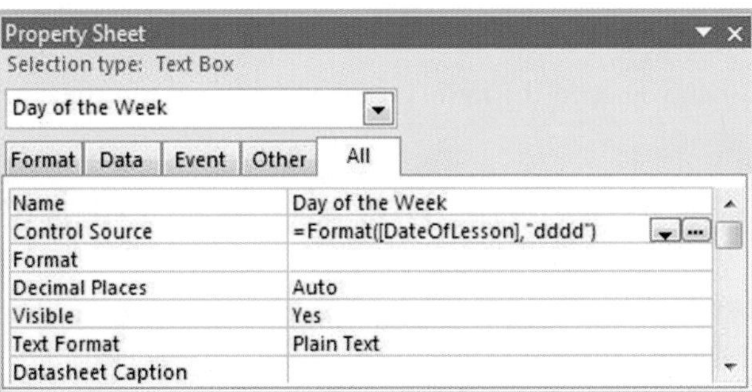

This will display the date's day, e.g. Monday if the date was 27/07/09.

=Format([DateOfLesson],"m") displays the month number, e.g. 12.

=Format([DateOfLesson],"yy") displays the abbreviated year number, e.g. 01.

=Format([DateOfLesson],"mmm") displays the abbreviated month name, e.g. Dec.

=Format([DateOfLesson],"mmmm") displays the full month name, e.g. December.

=Format([DateOfLesson],"yyyy") displays the full year number, e.g. 2009.

You can also combine the formats to create your own format, e.g. **=Format([DateOfLesson],"dmmmyy")** which would display the day, the abbreviated month, and a two-digit year value, with no spaces in between each component.

You can also display a literal character, such as a comma and space in a date to make it 17 June, 2009. Just use this format:

=Format([DateOfLesson], "d mmmm" ", " "yyyy")

24 Making a command button the default button

When you open a form you can make a command button the default and respond by just pressing ENTER. Typically, this might be the most commonly used operation, such as Book a Lesson on the Lesson Booking form.

1 Open the form in **Design View**, right-click on the button you want to respond to ENTER and choose **Properties**.
2 Click the **Other** tab and set the **Default** property to **Yes**.

Figure 2.3.6 ▶

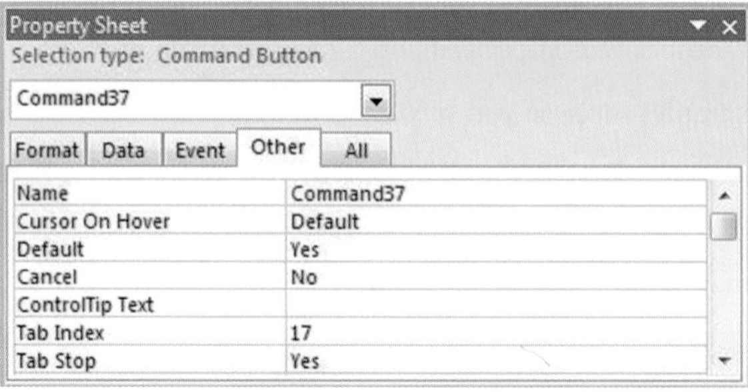

When you open the form, pressing ENTER will run the command button action.

25 Changing the properties of a group of controls

1 Open a form in **Design View**.
2 Select the first control whose property you want to change. Hold down SHIFT and select the other controls you want to change.
3 Right-click on any of the controls and choose **Properties**.
4 The **Property Sheet** opens with the title **Multiple selection**. From here any property you select will be applied to all selected controls.

Figure 2.3.7 ▶

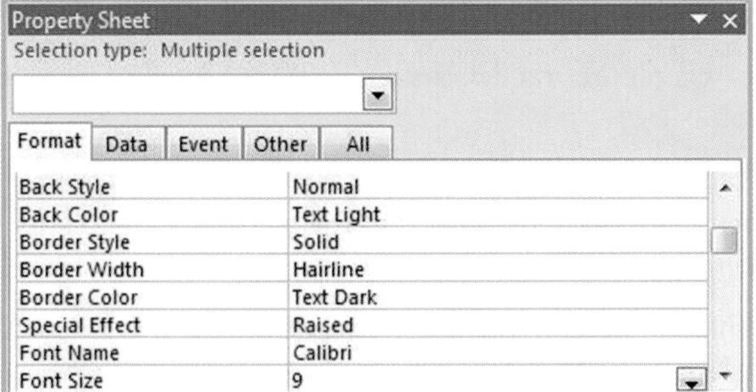
Property Sheet

Selection type: Multiple selection

Format | Data | Event | Other | All

Back Style	Normal
Back Color	Text Light
Border Style	Solid
Border Width	Hairline
Border Color	Text Dark
Special Effect	Raised
Font Name	Calibri
Font Size	9

26 Preventing users from adding records to a form

1 Load the form in **Design View** and choose the **Form Properties**.
2 Click on the **Data** tab and set the **Allow Additions** property to **No**. When the form is opened, the **New Record** icon is greyed out.
3 To further control access set the **AllowDeletions** and **AllowEdits** properties to **No** as well.

27 Creating read-only fields on a form

Sometimes you may want to make a field available but not allow it to be changed by the user.

1 Load your form in **Design View** (we have used **frmLessonBooking**). Select the fields and click on the **Property Sheet** button. Click on the **Data** tab.
2 Set the **Enabled** property to **No** and the **Locked** property to **Yes**. The field will not receive the focus and the user will not be able to change it.
3 If you set the **Enabled** property to **No** and the **Locked** property to **No**. The field will not receive the focus and will appear dimmed, as shown in Figure 2.3.8.

Figure 2.3.8 ▶

Lesson Booking Form

Pass IT Driving School

28 December 2008
15:31:40

PA55 IT

Lesson Details

Lesson No	1		
Instructor ID	1	Date Of Lesson	27/07/2009
Instructor Forename	Derek	Start Time	09:00
Instructor Surname	Jones	Length Of Lesson	1
Student ID	1	CollectionPoint	Home Address
Student Forename	Robert	Drop Off Point	Home Address
Student Surname	Brammer	Lesson Type	Standard
Address 1	10 Plymouth Drive	Cost	£24.00
Address 2	Crickham	Total Cost	£24.00

Book Lesson | Cancel Lesson

28 Moving the focus to another control on a form

Often, when entering data into a form, you need to move the cursor to another control.

For example, when booking a lesson in the Driving School, you need to automatically move the cursor to the StudentID field after entering the InstructorID. You can do this with a macro.

1 In the **Action** column select **GoToControl** and set the **Control Name** to **StudentID**.

Figure 2.3.9 ▶

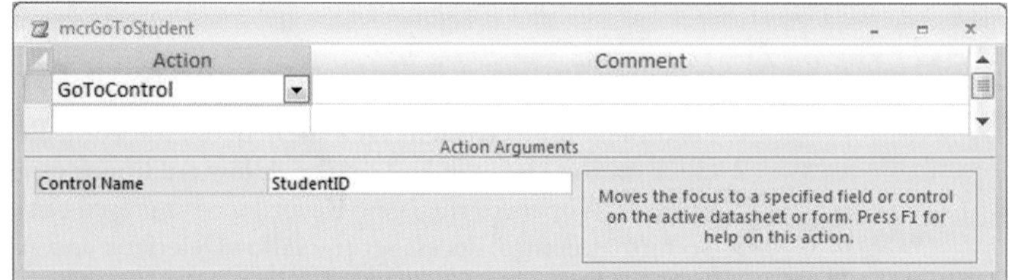

2 Name the macro **mcrGoToStudent** and attach it to the **After Update** property of the **InstructorID** control.

Figure 2.3.10 ▶

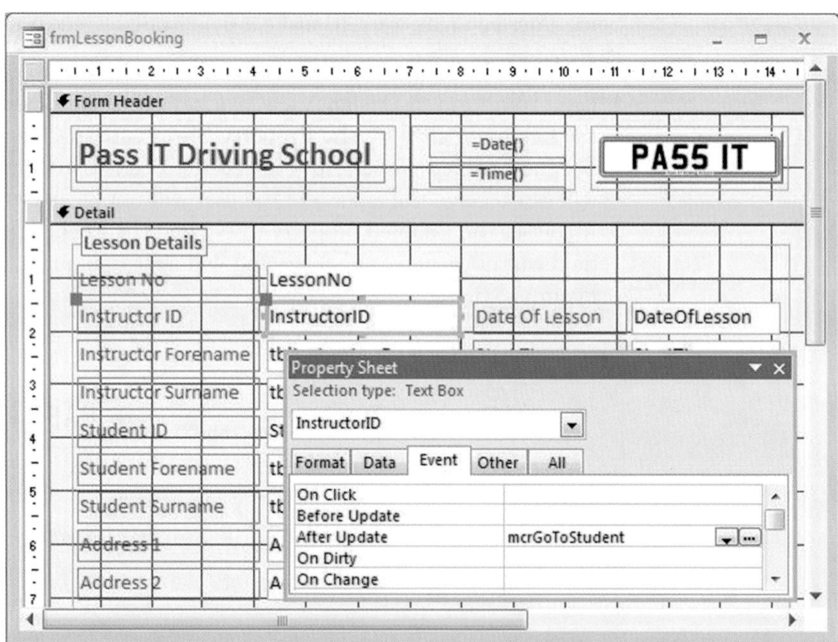

Another way of achieving this is using the **Tab Stop** property. Simply group the controls you want the cursor to skip (e.g. **InstructorForename** and **InstructorSurname**) and set the **Tab Stop** property to **No**.

Figure 2.3.11 ▼

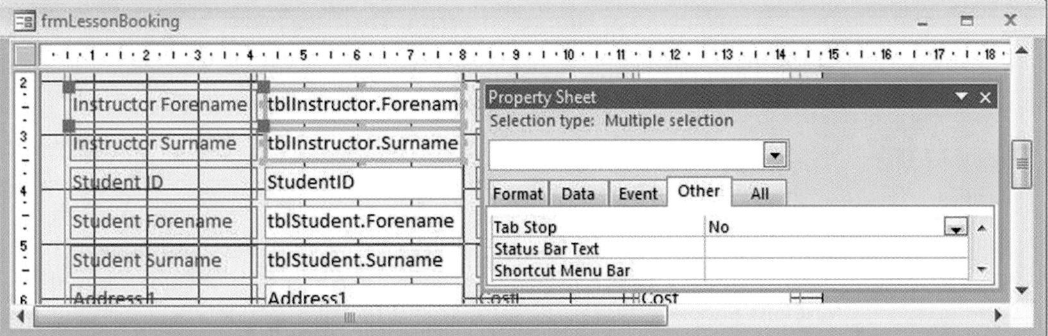

29 Borders and special effects

Borders can be added to controls using the rectangle tool. Special effects can then be applied to controls using the control's properties.

Figure 2.3.12 ▶

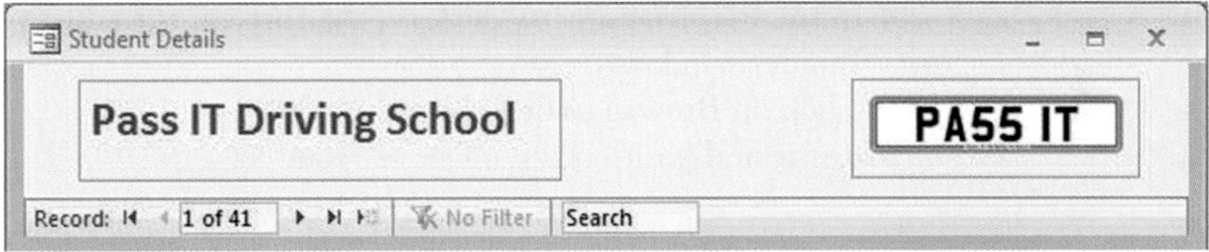

1 Right-click the logo in **Design View** and click on the **Property Sheet** button.

Figure 2.3.13 ▶

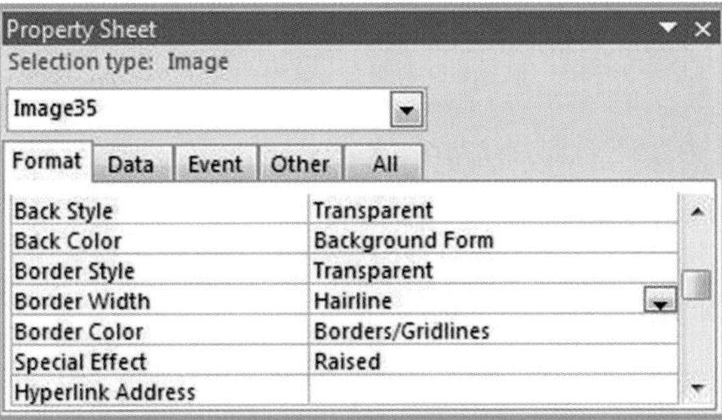

2 Click the **Format** tab and set the **Border Style** to **Transparent**.
3 Set the **Special Effect** property to **Raised** (see Figure 2.3.13).
4 Select the other controls and set their **Special Effect** property to **Raised**.

Figure 2.3.14 ▶

30 Designing your own button images

You can use images as buttons on a form. There are two ways to get started:

- Use Paint or a similar program to design your image.
- Find an image via a clip art library or the Internet.

Figure 2.3.15 ▶

It is important to resize your image to the size of an Access button (about 39x39 pixels). This is easily done in an image editor such as Paint, Photoshop or Paint Shop Pro.

1 Open a form in **Design View** and use the **Command Button** tool to set up a button, choosing picture when asked if you want text or a picture on your button.
2 Select the button and right-click on it to display its properties.
3 Click on the **Format** tab.
4 In the **Picture** property click on the three dots to display the **Picture Builder** window.
5 Click on **Browse** to find the image.
6 Resize and position the image as required.

31 Creating a command button from a graphic image

You can create buttons from graphic images with just a little Visual Basic. In Unit 11 you added the simple Pass IT graphic to the menu. You can turn any graphic into a command button. This example shows you how to make the graphic run a macro.

Figure 2.3.16 ▶

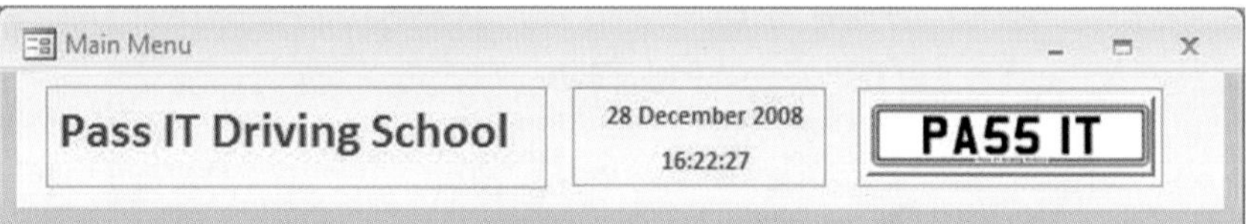

1 In **Design View**, click on the graphic and display the **Property Sheet**.
2 Change the **Name** property to **Logo**, it will be something like Image20. Set the **OnClick** property, on the **Event** tab, to run the macro **mcrAbout**.

Figure 2.3.17 ▶

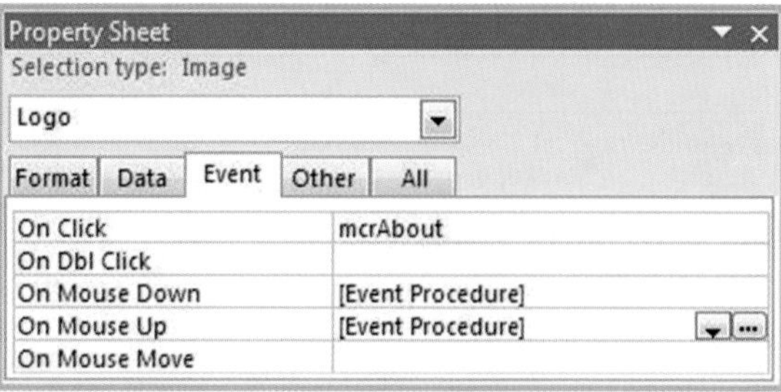

3 Go to the **On Mouse Down** property, choose **Code Builder** by clicking the three dots and add the line of code: **Logo.SpecialEffect = 2**

4 Repeat for the **On Mouse Up** property, as shown in Figure 2.3.18.

Figure 2.3.18 ▼

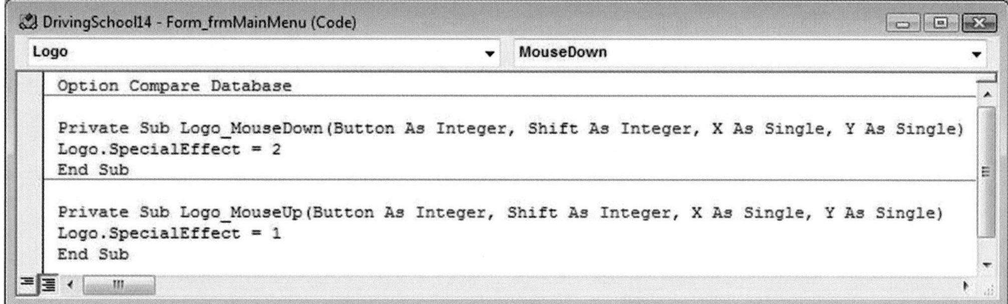

5 Test the button runs the macro **mcrAbout**.

32 Customising a Quit or Exit button

If you design a button to **Quit Application** using the wizards it doesn't give you an **Are you sure?** option. This can easily be achieved with a simple few lines of Visual Basic.

Figure 2.3.19 ►

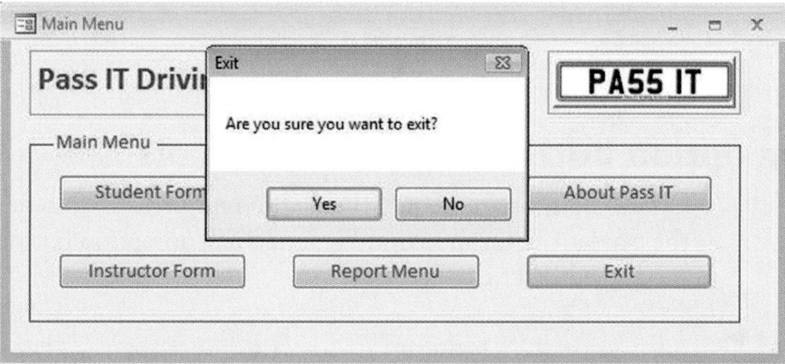

1 Go into **Design View** and display the **Property Sheet** of the **Quit/Exit** command button.

2 View the **Event Procedure**, attached to the **OnClick** property and enter the five lines of code shown below.

Figure 2.3.20 ▼

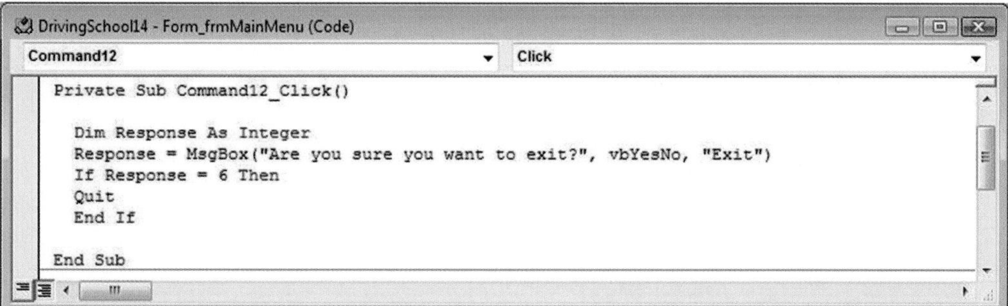

3 On clicking the **Exit** button, you will be given the message box shown in Figure 2.3.19 with **Yes** and **No** buttons. If you press **No** nothing happens, if **Yes** is pressed then the quit procedure takes place.

33 Positioning and sizing your form automatically

It is easy to position your form using its **Form Properties**. To open your form centred and sized to display a complete record, set the properties as follows:

1 Open the form in **Design View** and click the **Property Sheet** to view its **Properties**.
2 Click the **Format** tab on the **Properties Sheet**.
3 Set the **Auto Center** property to **Yes**.
4 Set the **Auto Resize** property to **Yes**.

Figure 2.3.21 ▶

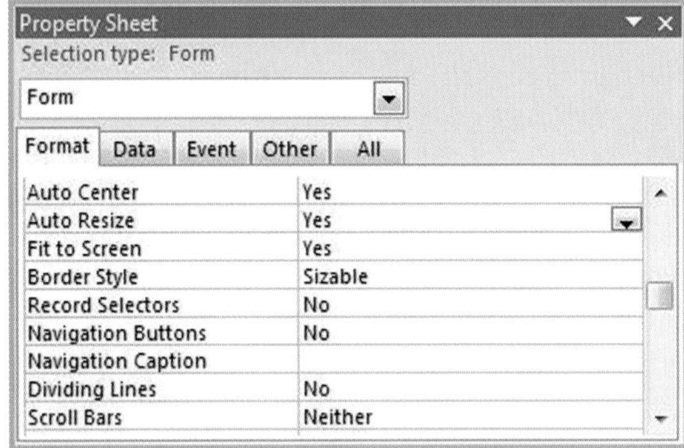

34 Using option buttons or radio controls

Option buttons are frequently used to represent Yes/No fields. For example, on the Student Form shown in Figure 2.3.22, an option button could be used for the Passed Practical Test field.

Figure 2.3.22 ▶

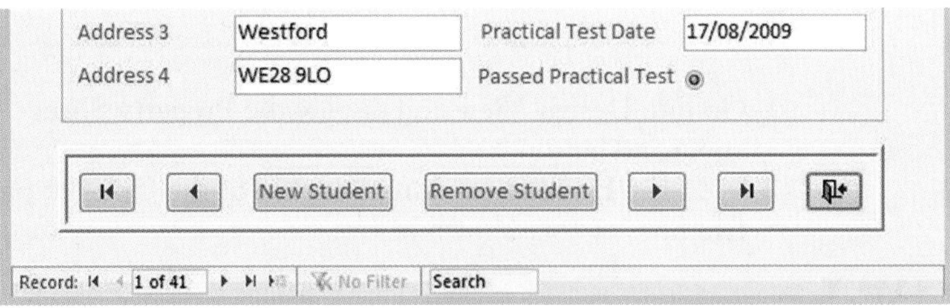

1 Open **frmStudent** in **Design View** and delete the PassedPracticalTest field check box.

Figure 2.3.23 ▼

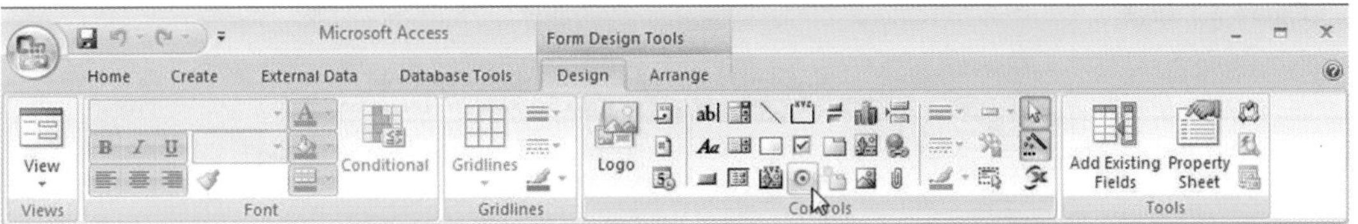

2 On the **Design** tab, in the **Controls** group, click on the **Option Button** control and click on the form where you want to place the button. Set the label to **Passed Practical Test**.

3 Select the control and right-click to view its properties. Click on the **Data** tab and set the **Control Source** to the **PassedPracticalTest** field, as shown in Figure 2.3.24.

Figure 2.3.24 ▶

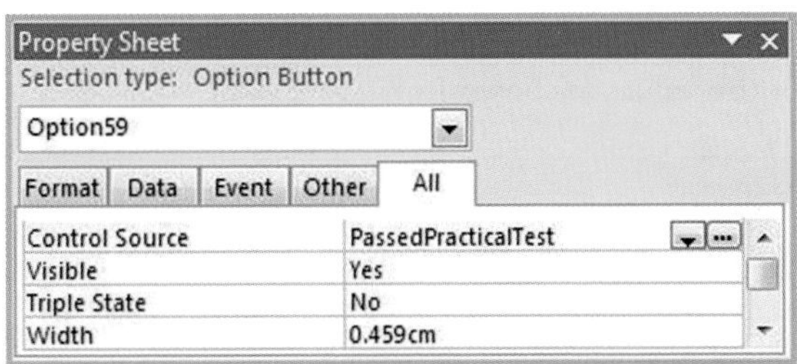

Toggle buttons and check boxes can be set up in the same way but it is important when designing forms to be consistent.

35 Using option groups

Option groups let the user choose one option from a list of alternative values. For example, the Title field on the Instructor Form shown in Figure 2.3.25 could be entered using option buttons in a group. It is important to note Access stores the data as a number e.g. 1 = Mr, 2 = Mrs, etc.

Figure 2.3.25 ▶

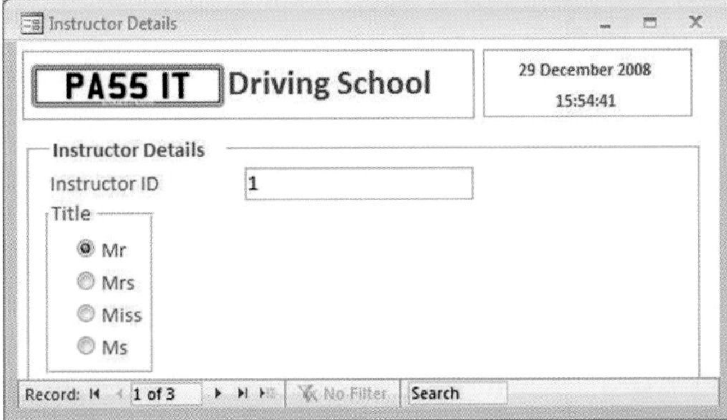

1 Open the **frmInstructor** in **Design View**, delete the **Title** field and create some room for the option group.

2 On the **Design** tab, in the **Controls** group, click on the **Option Group** control and drag out a rectangle. In the **Option Group** dialog box, set the labels as shown in Figure 2.3.26 and click on **Next**.

Figure 2.3.26 ▶

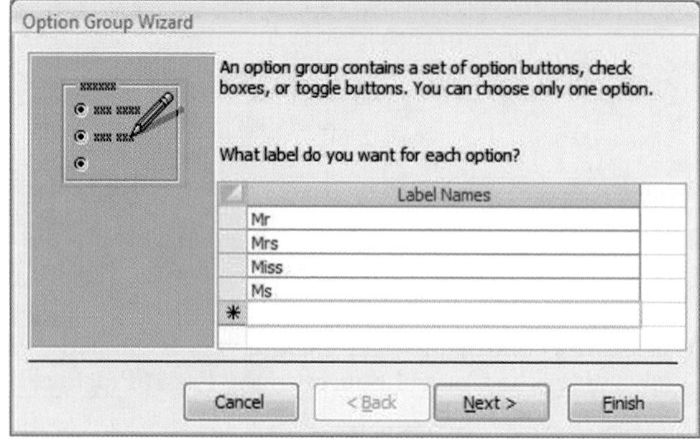

3 Select the default value required and click on **Next**. Click on **Next** again to accept the values as shown in Figure 2.3.27.

Figure 2.3.27 ▶

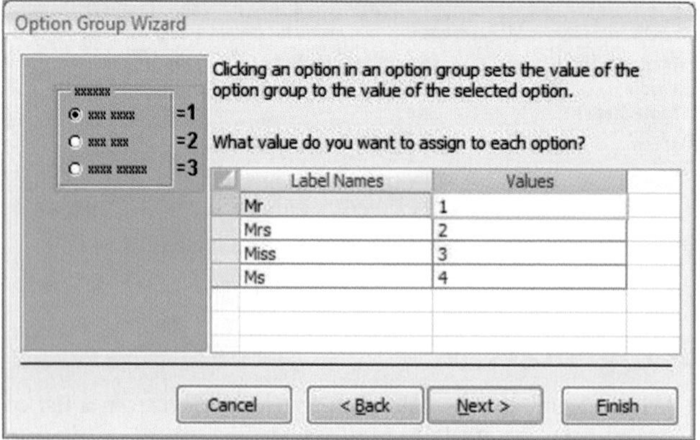

4 Click on **Store the value in this field** and select **Title** from the drop-down. Click on **Next**.

5 Choose your control style, click on **Next** and set the **Caption** to **Title**. Click on **Finish**.

36 Printing a form without the buttons

You may want to print an on-screen form without printing the buttons and other objects, such as images. We will use the Instructor Form set up in the Driving School system as an example.

1 Open the **frmInstructor** in **Design View**. Highlight the objects you don't want to print, in this case the control panel.

Figure 2.3.28 ▶

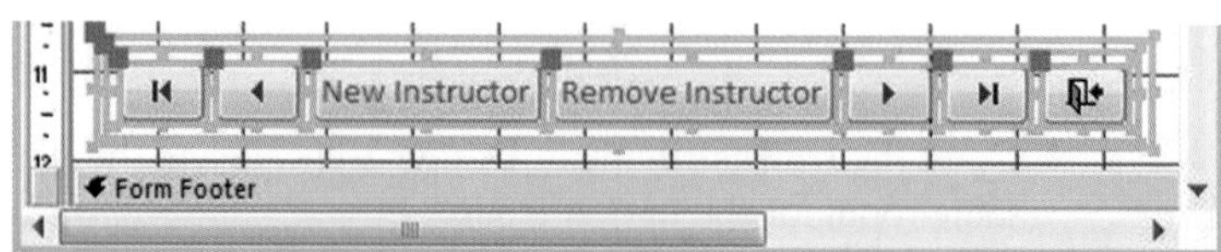

2 Click the **Property Sheet** button and set the **Display When** property to **Screen Only**. Save the form and return to **Form View**.

Figure 2.3.29 ▶

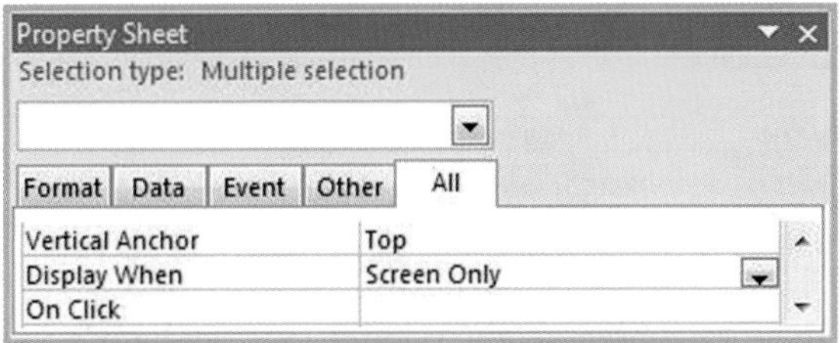

If you chose to print now you would get all the forms printing without the objects. We only want the currently displayed record to print.

3 On the **Create** tab, click the **Macro** button.

4 In the **Action** column, select the **PrintOut** command. In the **Action Arguments**, click in the **Print Range** box and choose **Selection**. Name the macro **mcrPrintForm**.

Figure 2.3.30 ▶

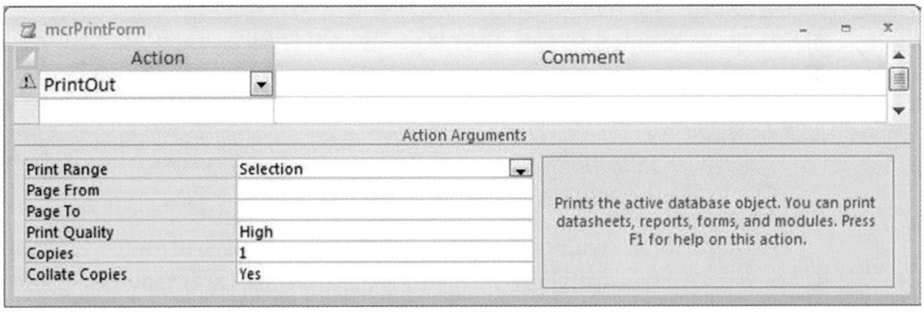

mcrPrintForm
Action | Comment
PrintOut
Action Arguments
Print Range: Selection
Page From
Page To
Print Quality: High
Copies: 1
Collate Copies: Yes
Prints the active database object. You can print datasheets, reports, forms, and modules. Press F1 for help on this action.

5 Set up a command button on the Instructor Form to run the **mcrPrintForm**.

37 Adding customised tool tips (Screen Tips) to your controls

When you move the mouse pointer over a button you get a Screen Tip explaining what the button does, as shown in Figure 2.3.31.

Figure 2.3.31 ▶

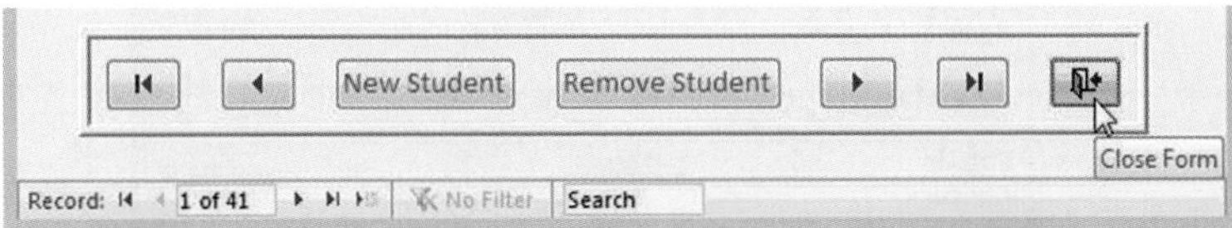

In Access it is easy to customise these tips and make them more user-friendly.

1 Open a form in **Design View**. We have chosen **frmStudent** in the Driving School system.

2 Right-click on the **New Student** button to view its Properties. Click on the **Other** tab. Set the **ControlTip Text** property to **Add a New Student** (or whatever you choose). See Figure 2.3.32.

Figure 2.3.32 ▶

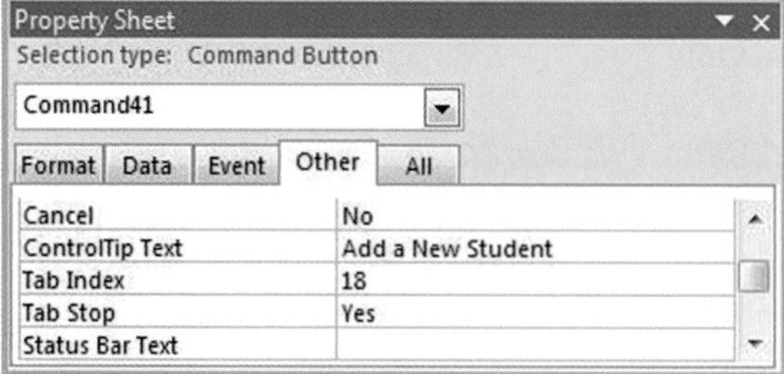

3 Save the form and move the pointer over the button to view your tip.

Figure 2.3.33 ▶

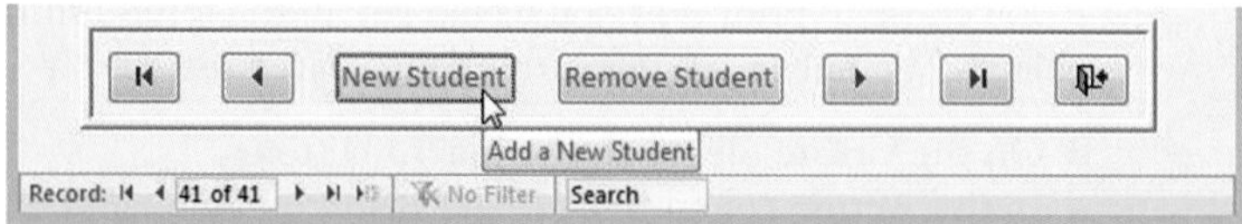

38 Pop-up and Modal forms

When a **modal** form is open, you cannot move to another object such as another form. This is important if you want data to be entered into the form before moving on.

A **pop-up** form always remains on top of other Microsoft Access windows when it is open.

When we open the Student Form or the Instructor Form to paste in details, we may want these forms to remain on top and may not want to allow the user to choose any other object. In other words, these forms will be pop-up modal forms.

We can set this up in Form Design View.

1 Load each form in turn in **Design View**.
2 Double-click on the **Form Selector** to show the **Form Properties**.
3 Click on the **Other** tab and set the **Modal** and **Pop Up** properties to **Yes**.

Figure 2.3.34 ▶

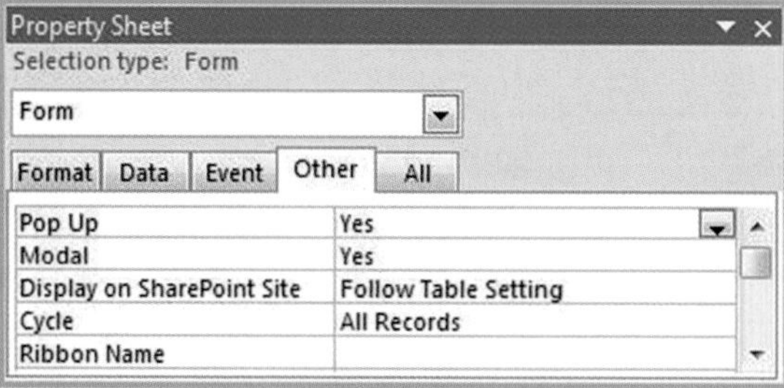

4 Switch to **Form View** and test that you cannot click on objects outside the form window.

39 Using a Date Picker

If your database requires a user to enter dates, then Access supplies a pop-up calendar, as shown in Figure 2.3.35.

Figure 2.3.35 ▶

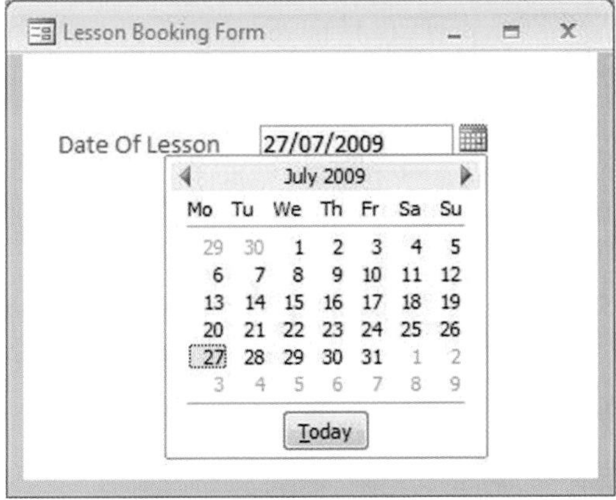

In **Design View**, display the properties of your **Date/Time** field. The **Show Date Picker** property must be set to **For Dates**.

40 Starting a form from scratch

Throughout the study units we used the wizards to set up our forms. Of course, as ever, you could choose to ignore the wizards and set up the form manually.

1. On the **Create** tab, click **Blank Form**.
2. A blank form will open in **Layout View** with the **Field List** window, as shown in Figure 2.3.36.

Figure 2.3.36 ▶

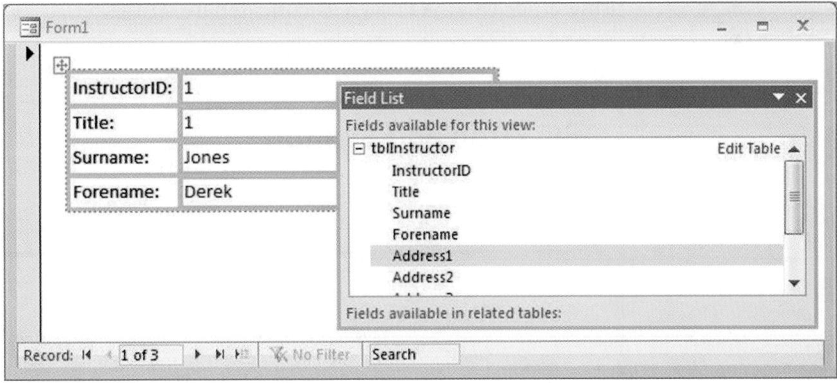

3. Drag and drop the fields needed as required.

Note: If the **Field List** is not displayed, then click the **Add Existing Fields** button on the **Format** tab.

Reports

41 Forcing a page break in a report

Typically at setup a report would be grouped by customer, supplier or order number. This produces a header section on the report – e.g.an order number header.

Ensure the header has a footer by clicking on the **Group & Sort** button to show the **Group, Sort and Total** pane. Under the **More** options select **with a footer section.**

Right-click in the footer to display the **Property Sheet** and set the **Force New Page** property to **After Section.**

Figure 2.4.1 ▶

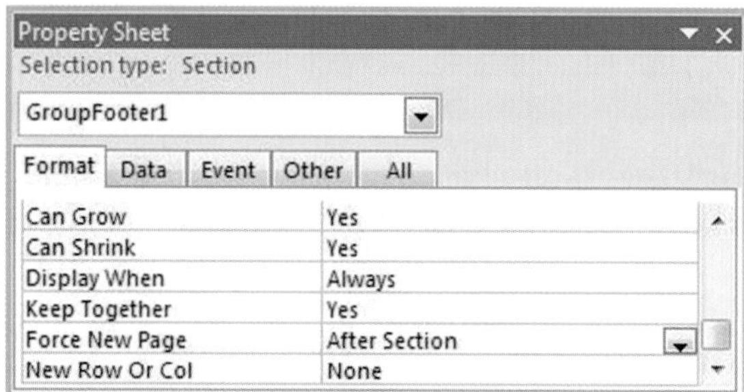

42 Concatenating text strings on reports

It can often be difficult on reports to align text properly, as shown in Figure 2.4.2 with the customer name. It can be easier to combine data fields using &, or what is known as concatenate strings.

Figure 2.4.2 ▶

For example, remove the fields Title, Surname and Forename from your report and replace with an unbound text box. Enter into the text box or set its control source as shown: **=[Title] & " " & [Forename] & " " & [Surname]**

Figure 2.4.3 ▼

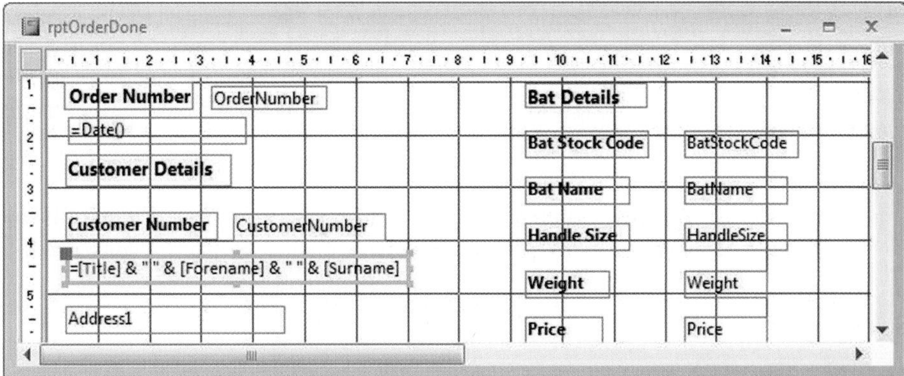

This will join the three fields and insert a space between them. You might need to display the initial only. Using **Left([Forename],1)** will do just that.

You can add text in much the same way on a report. For example, in the footer of an order/invoice to be completed on **[CompletionDate]**, simply add a text box and again enter the following:

="Order to be completed by" & " " & [CompletionDate]

="Payable within 28 days from completion of order" & " " & [CompletionDate]+28

43 Replacing check boxes and coded fields with text

Using a check box for a Yes/No field returns a -1 for Yes. The check box itself can look a little meaningless on reports. Remove the check box field and replace with an unbound text box.

The IIf statement can be used as shown. Enter the statement into the text box or via its control source to change the check box or code as shown. If the check box field is called status:

=IIf([status]=-1,"Yes","No")

=IIf([status]=-1,"Order Paid","Order Unpaid")

or, for a field called Gender:

=IIf([Gender]= "M","Male","Female")

or, for the field PassedPracticalTest in the Pass IT Driving School:

=IIf([PassedPracticalTest]=-1,"Passed","Not yet taken")

Figure 2.4.4 ▼

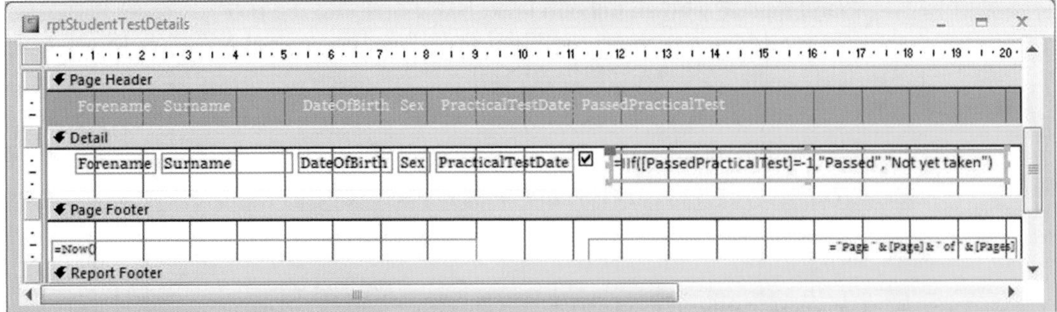

In this example we have left the check box but added an unbound text box to display the meaning of the check box, as shown in Figure 2.4.4. The output is shown in Figure 2.4.5.

Figure 2.4.5 ▼

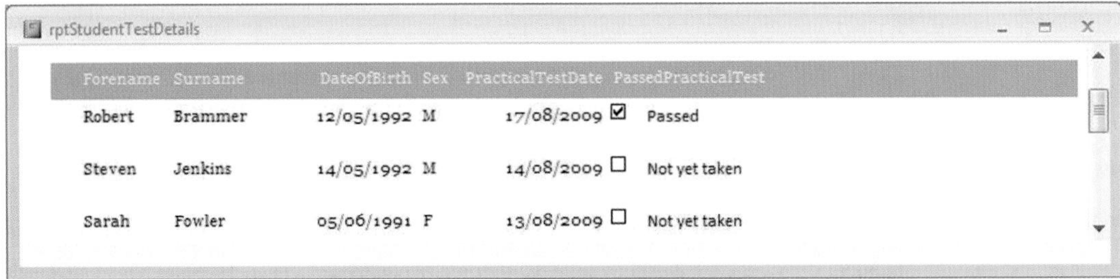

44 Using Switch to change a coded field

If a field is coded then the **Switch** command can be used in the same way. In this example, a field called Status is coded **A**, **Pd** and **P**. Switch is used to convert to **Active**, **Paid** or **Pending**. The statement is:

=Switch([Status]="A","Active",[Status]="Pd","Paid",[Status]="P", "Pending")

45 Formatting invoice numbers

If you are using **Autonumber** or **Numeric** for an OrderNumber field, you might want the report to display preceding zeros. For example, to display **OrderNumber 1** as **OrderNumber 000001**, simply use the following code:

=Format([OrderNumber]),"000000"

46 Mailing labels, business and membership cards

If you have a list of names and addresses, as in the Student table of the Driving School system, you can easily customise and print mailing labels for them, as follows.

1 In the Navigation Pane, select **tblStudent**.
2 On the **Create** tab in the **Reports** group, click the **Labels** button.

3 Select your label manufacturer, label size and other options, as shown in Figure 2.4.6.

Figure 2.4.6 ▶

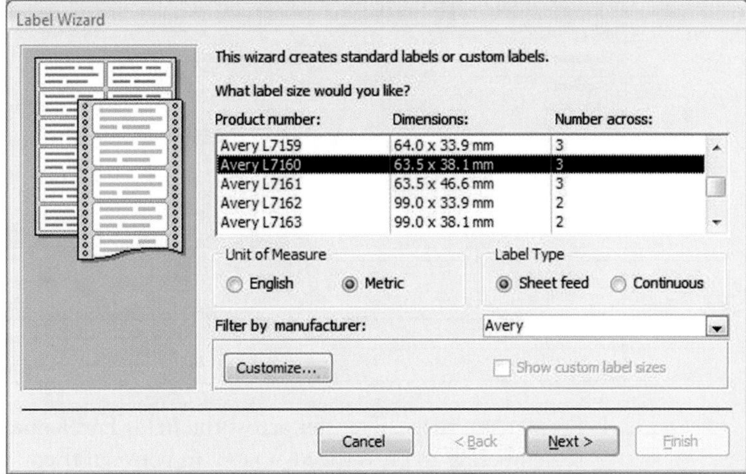

4 Choose the **Font name**, **Font weight**, **Font size** and **Text color**, as shown in Figure 2.4.7, and click on **Next**.

Figure 2.4.7 ▶

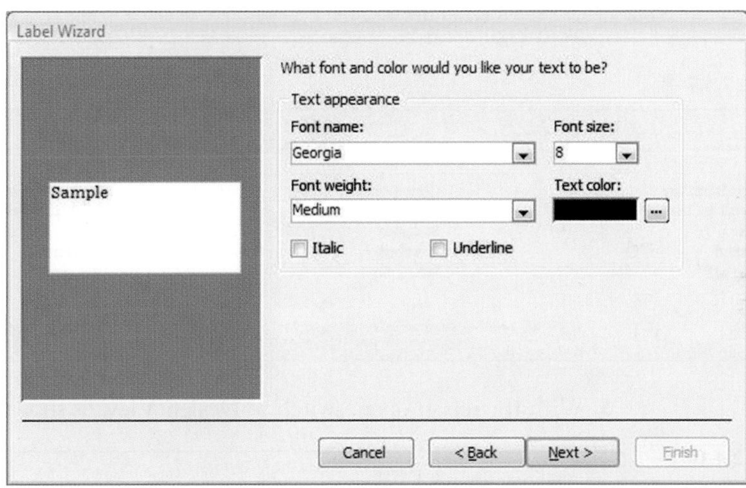

The next stage is to position the text and fields on the Prototype label.

Figure 2.4.8 ▶

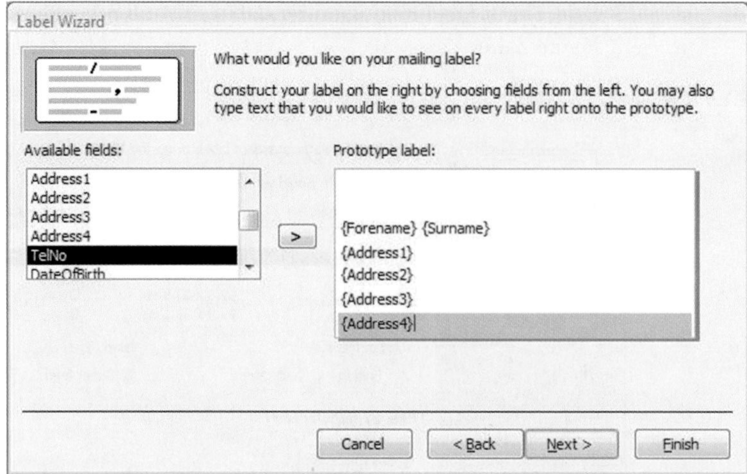

1 Press ENTER twice. Transfer across the fields **Forename** and **Surname**, remembering to press the SPACEBAR in between them. Press ENTER.
2 Continue to transfer the fields **Address1**, **Address2**, **Address3** and **Address4**. Click on **Next**.
3 Choose to sort by **Surname**. Click on **Next**.
4 Name the report **rptLabels** and click on **Finish**. The labels should appear as in Figure 2.4.9.

Figure 2.4.9 ▼

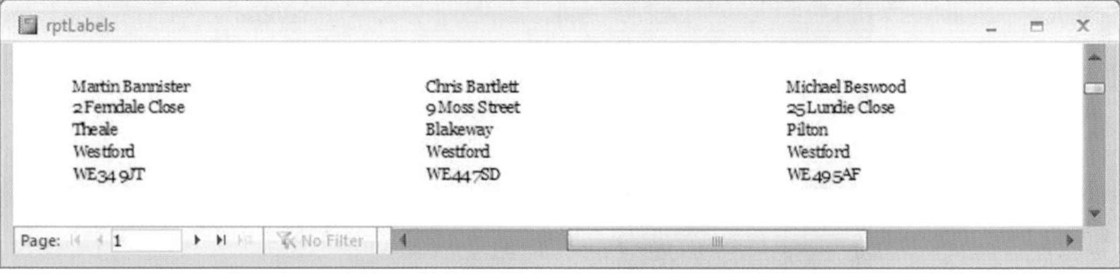

5 With the report open, switch to **Design View** as shown in Figure 2.4.10.

Figure 2.4.10 ▶

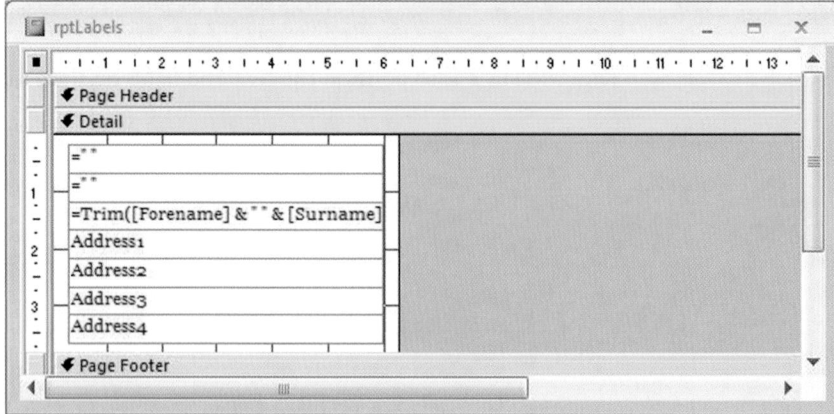

6 On the **Design** tab, click the **Rectangle** button and carefully position a rectangle around the label. On the **Arrange** tab, click the **Send to Back** button.

7 With the rectangle still selected, set its **Border Width** property to **1pt** (see Figure 2.4.11).

8 On the **Design** tab, click the **Logo** button and import the Pass IT logo (or use copy and paste). Position the logo as shown.

9 Add a **Label** with the text **Driving School**. Set the **Font Name** to **Georgia**.

Figure 2.4.11 ▶

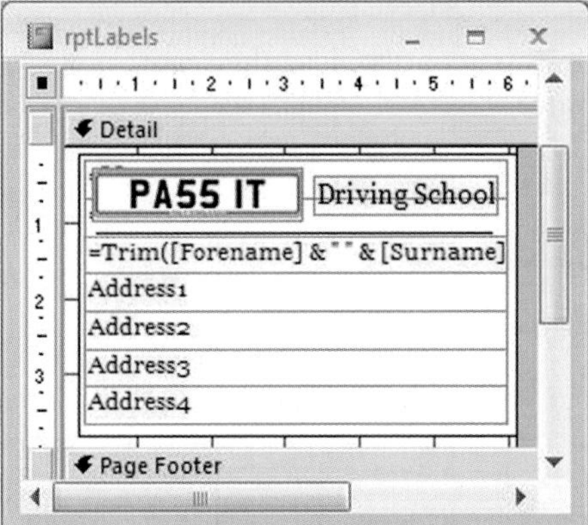

10 Switch to **Print Preview** to view the mailing labels, as shown in Figure 2.4.12. We have added a line using the Line tool. Save the report as **rptLabels**.

Figure 2.4.12 ▼

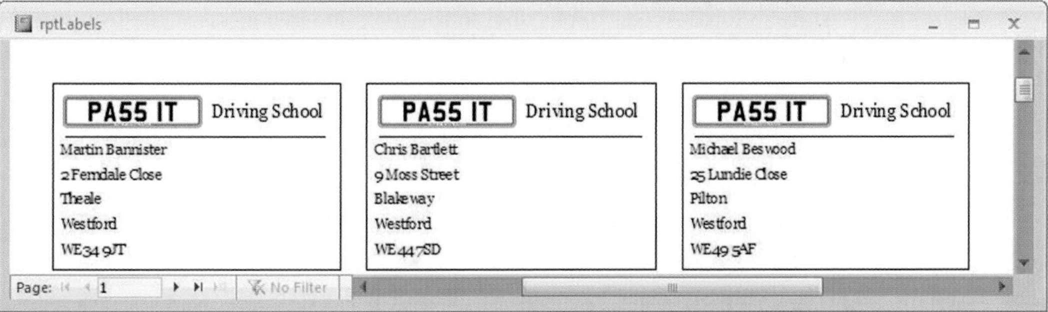

Macros

47 Formatting text to bold in a Message Box

You can set text to bold in a Message Box using the @ symbol. Access allows three sections in a Message Box separated by @. The first is displayed in bold.

For example, in the **No Data** macro used in the Pass IT system, set the message as follows:

There is no data in this report@Close the report now@Check with your System Administrator

Figure 2.5.1 ▶

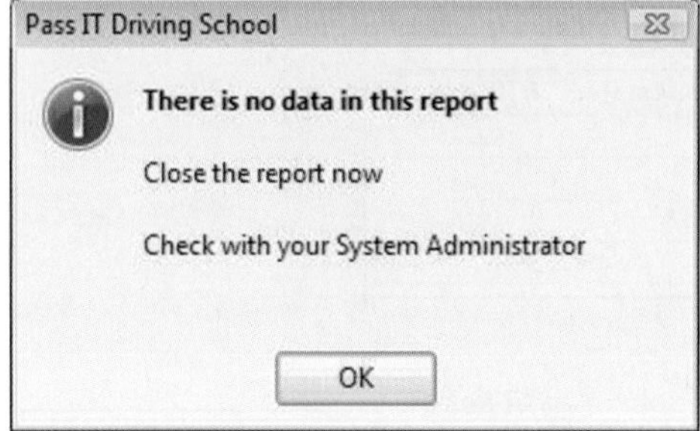

Run the macro and the message box is displayed as in Figure 2.5.1.

48 Putting hard returns in a Message Box

You can force Access to put text on the next line in a message box by using the ASCII code for a carriage return: **Chr(13)**.

1 Set up a new macro and choose the **Action**: **MsgBox**.
2 In the **Action Arguments**, click in the **Message** box and enter: **="The Pass IT Driving School"& Chr(13) & "by" & Chr(13) & "Ian Rendell"**

Figure 2.5.2 ▶

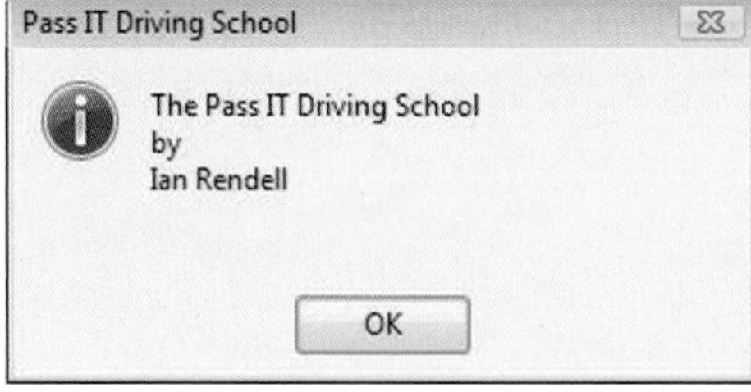

You can improve the presentation of your message box further by using the code **Chr(9)** for a tab space and **Chr(32)** for a space.

The Message Box shown in Figure 2.5.3 uses this statement:

=Chr(9) & "The Pass IT Driving School" & Chr(13) & Chr(9) & Chr(9) & "by" & Chr(13) & Chr(9) & Chr(32) & Chr(32) & Chr(32) & Chr(32) & Chr(32) & Chr(32) & Chr(32) & Chr(32) & "Ian Rendell"

Figure 2.5.3 ▶

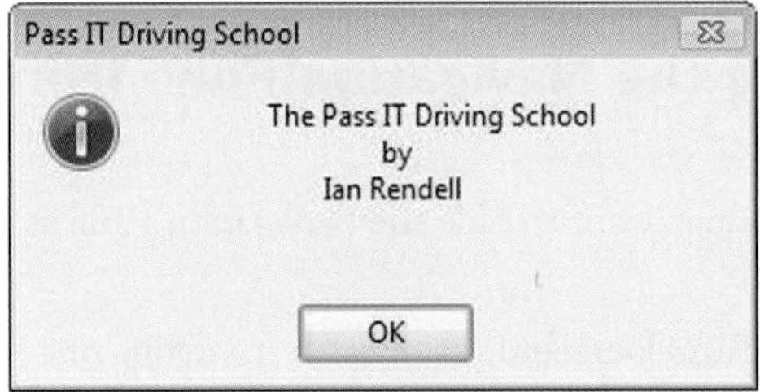

Don't forget that, by pressing SHIFT and F2, you can zoom and see all the text in a Message Box.

49 The AutoExec macro

A macro saved as **AutoExec** automatically runs when the database is opened. You can control start-up options from this macro.

Create a new macro, as shown in Figure 2.5.4, with the following actions and arguments. Save the macro as **mcrAutoexec**. To run it automatically, rename it as **AutoExec**.

Action	Argument	Comment
Echo	No	Hides events
Hourglass	Yes	Pointer displayed as hourglass
RunCommand	WindowHide	Hides the Navigation Pane
OpenForm	Switchboard	Opens the Switchboard or Main Menu

Figure 2.5.4 ▶

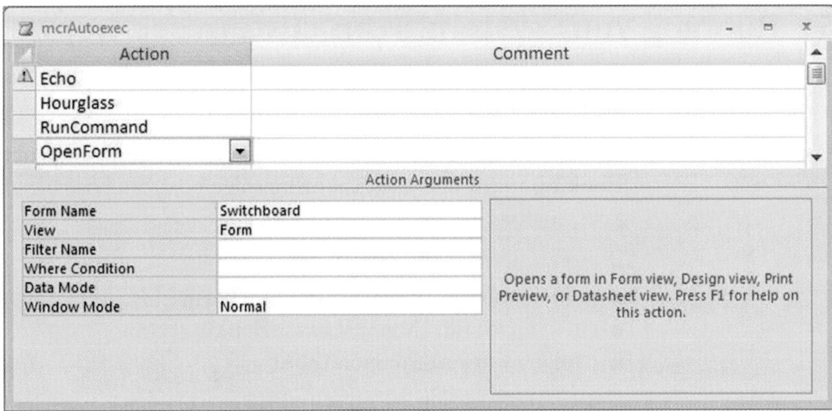

Note: Use **F11** to display the Navigation Pane again.

Note: If you don't want the **AutoExec** macro or the start-up options to run, hold down the SHIFT key when you open the database.

50 Hiding and unhiding the Navigation Pane from your AutoExec macro

On start-up you may want to hide the Navigation Pane as part of your **AutoExec** macro.

Simply use the **RunCommand** action with its argument set to **WindowHide** as shown below. Then use the **OpenForm** action to open your switchboard or front-end menu.

Figure 2.5.5 ▶

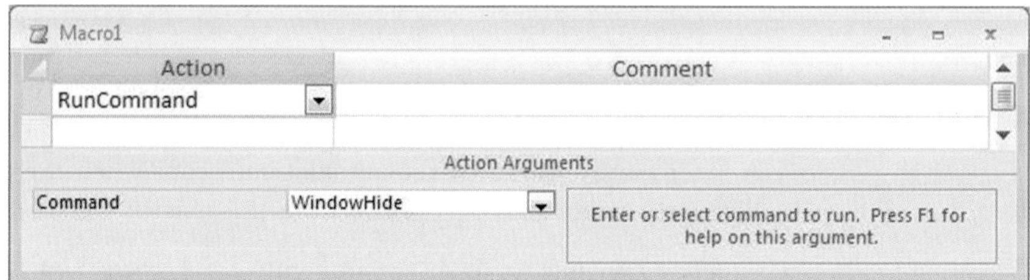

If you have fully customised your solution to hide Access from the user you might offer a **System Design** or **Maintenance** option from your switchboard. This would be a command button that ran the reverse of the above macro and allowed the user access to the Navigation Pane.

Use the **RunCommand** action with its argument set to **WindowUnhide**.

There is also a Macro action **LockNavigationPane**, which offers further security.

51 Running your system from customised keys

An **Autokeys** macro allows you to customise keys, typically to run frequently used actions.

In Unit 14 we set up macros to open the **Student**, **Instructor** and **Lesson Booking** forms and the **About** message box. Suppose we want to set up hot-keys, such as:

- CTRL + S to run **mcrStudentForm**
- CTRL + I to run the **mcrInstructorForm**
- CTRL + L to run the **mcrLessonBookingForm**
- CTRL + A to run the **mcrAbout**.

(Choose your hot-keys carefully as CTRL + A is already used for **Select All** and CTRL + S for **Save**. You might prefer, therefore, to use another combination of keys. The key combination you choose replaces that used by Access.)

1 On the **Create** tab, click the **Macro** button.
2 In the **Action** column, select **RunMacro**.
3 In the **Macro Name** box, at the bottom, select **mcrStudentForm**.
4 Click on the **Macro Names** button. A new column appears, headed **Macro Name**. In the first row of this new column enter the key combination ^S (press CTRL + S).
5 Set up the other key combinations as shown in Figure 2.5.6.

Figure 2.5.6 ▶

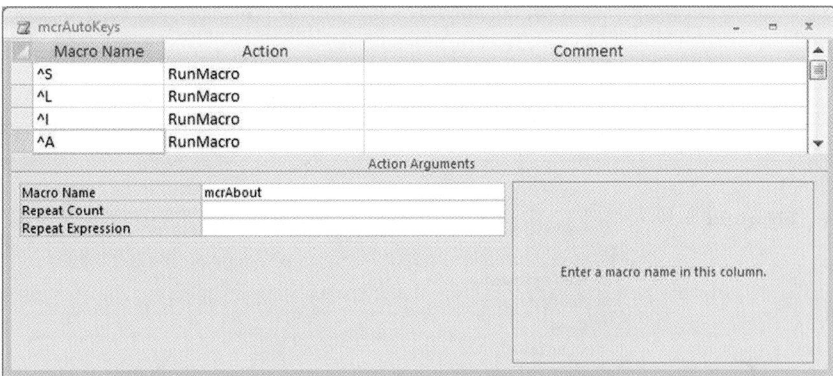

6 Save the macro as **mcrAutokeys**. To run it automatically, rename it as **Autokeys**.

The new keys are in effect as soon as you save the macro and each time you open the database. Search Microsoft Access Help for more on key combinations.

52 Copy (cut) and paste macro

A macro can be used to cut or copy a record from one table and paste it into another.

Imagine the scenario in the driving school system when a driving instructor leaves the school. You don't want to delete the record entirely from the Driving School system but just move it into a table of Ex-Instructors so that you have a record of their details.

1 Load the **Driving School** database and in the Navigation Pane, highlight **tblInstructor** and click on **Copy**.

Figure 2.5.7 ▶

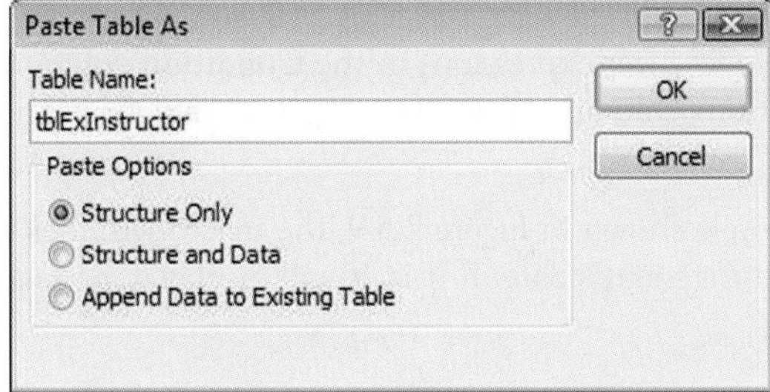

2 Click on **Paste** and, in the **Paste Table As** dialog box, name the table **tblExInstructor** and select **Structure Only**. Ensure the InsructorID field has data type **Number**.

3 Create a new macro using the following commands:

Action	**RunCommand**	Command	**Select Record**		
Action	**RunCommand**	Command	**Cut**		
Action	**Close**	Object Type	**Form**	Object Name	**frmInstructor**
Action	**Open Table**	Table Name	**tblExInstructor**		
Action	**RunCommand**	Command	**Paste Append**		
Action	**Close**	Object Type	**Table**	Object Name	**tblExInstructor**
Action	**OpenForm**	Form Name	**frmInstructor**	View	**Form**

Figure 2.5.8 ▶

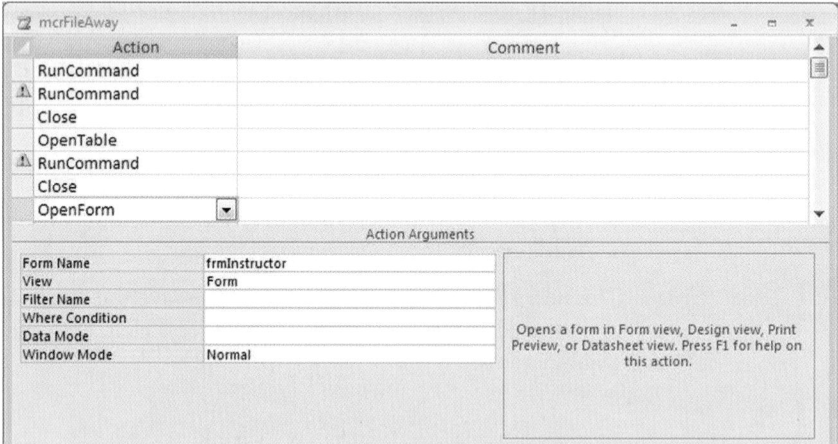

4 Name the macro **mcrFileAway**. Open **frmInstructor** in **Design View** and place a command button on the form to run the macro.

5 Open **frmInstructor** in **Form View** and test the macro. You will need to ensure also that **Cascade Delete Related Records** is checked between **tblInstructor** and **tblLesson**.

53 Using Conditions in Macros

On the **Create** tab, click the **Macro** button. In the **Macro Design** window, click the **Conditions** button to insert the **Condition** column.

It is possible to enter expressions in the **Condition** column. When the value in the **Conditions** column is true, the action to its right in the **Action** column is performed.

In the example shown in Figure 2.5.9, the macro will look to see if a student's practical test is today's date. If it is, it will display a message box reminding them.

Open **frmStudent** in the Driving School system in **Design View** and attach the macro to the **On Current** event of the form.

Figure 2.5.9 ▼

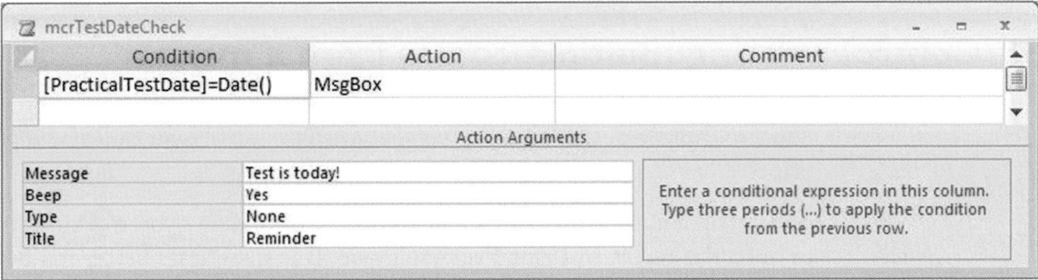

Using conditions in macros is an immensely powerful tool. Use **Microsoft Help** to explore further possibilities.

54 Using a Conditional Macro for cross field validation

A conditional macro can be used to ensure that if **Mr** is chosen, **Male** is stored in the **Sex** field. If **Ms**, **Mrs** or **Miss** is chosen, **Female** is stored in the **Sex** field.

Figure 2.5.10 ▶

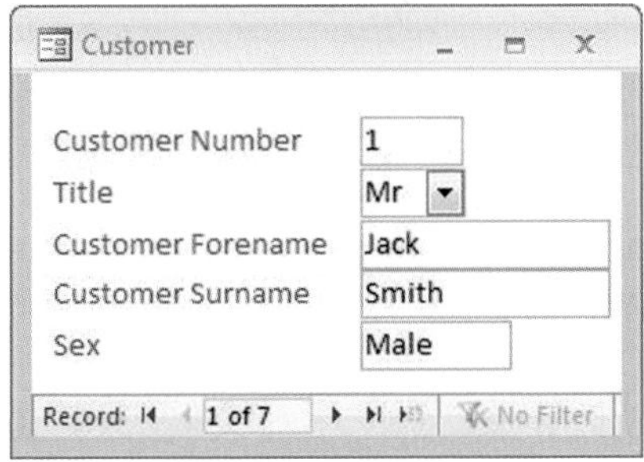

When you run the macro Access evaluates the first condition and, if **True**, uses the **SetValue Action** to set **[Sex]** to **Male**.

Figure 2.5.11 ▼

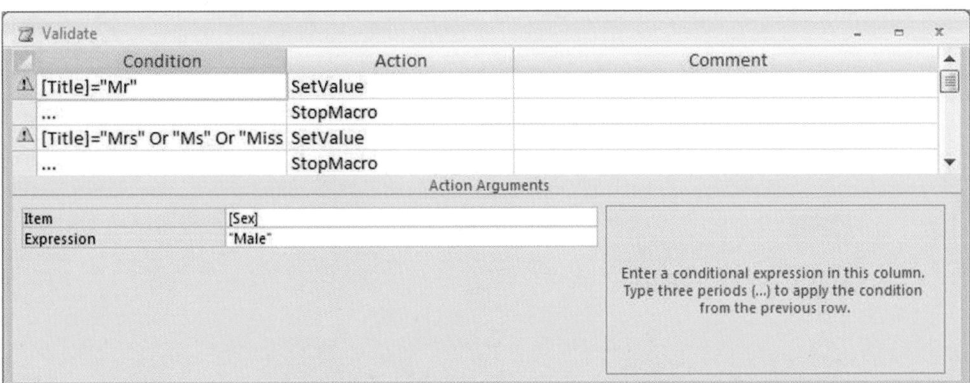

If the condition is **False**, Access ignores the action and any following actions preceded by an ellipsis. The macro is attached to the **AfterUpdate** property of the field **Title**.

55 Control printing multiple copies from a macro

It is easy to use the wizards to set up a command button to run a report. Using a macro, however, will always give you greater control over how the report prints.

Setting up a macro using the **OpenReport** action allows you to **Print** directly or open the report in **Print Preview** mode. It is sometimes better to offer both options to the user.

Figure 2.5.12 ▼

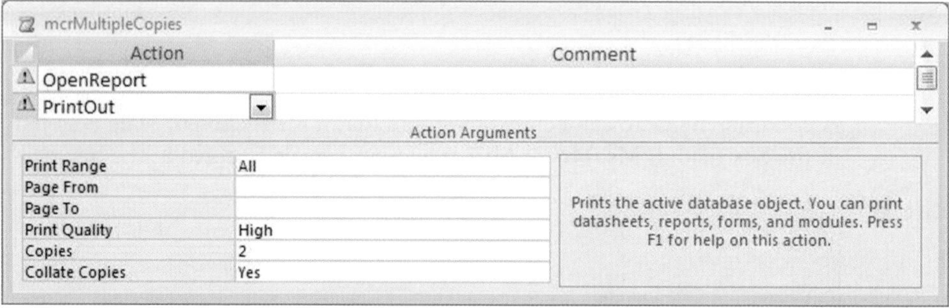

By adding the macro action **PrintOut**, it is possible to control the number of copies and the pages printed.

Others

56 Changing the caption text and other start-up options

The caption appears at the top of the screen in the Title bar. It normally gives you the version and name of the database, as shown in Figure 2.6.1.

Figure 2.6.1 ▼

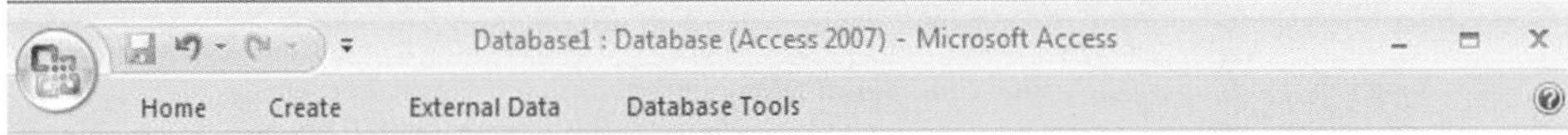

You can customise the caption to include your own text by clicking on the **Office Button** and selecting **Access Options**. Click on **Current Database** and under **Application Options**, enter the text **Pass IT Driving School** in the **Application Title** box.

Figure 2.6.2 ▼

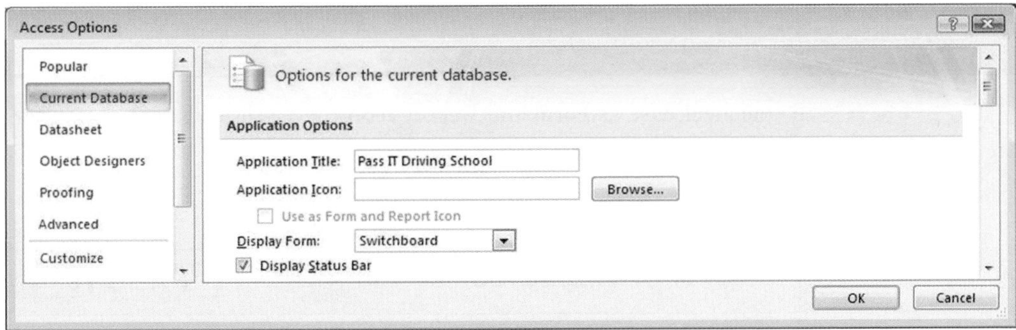

Your caption will now appear as shown in Figure 2.6.3.

Figure 2.6.3 ▼

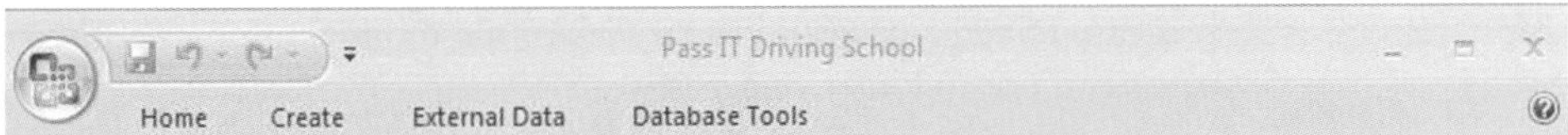

It will also appear in the Task Bar as shown in the next tip.

It is possible here to explore other options that can be controlled from this point. The Status Bar and Navigation Pane can be hidden. You can set which form should display at start-up, typically a menu or switchboard.

57 Changing the application icon

The application icon is the small graphic normally displayed in the Task Bar, as shown in Figure 2.6.5. By default Access displays the Access program icon.

The first stage in replacing this icon is to create your own Icon (*.ico) file. It is important that your file has an **ico** file extension.

There are many sources of freely available icons on the Internet, or you can use programs such as **Paint** to create your own. Set the width to **32 pixels** and the height to **32 pixels**.

Click on the **Office Button** and select **Access Options**. Click on **Current Database** and in the **Application Icon** box click **Browse** to locate your icon. Our example is **Minicar.ico**.

Figure 2.6.4 ▼

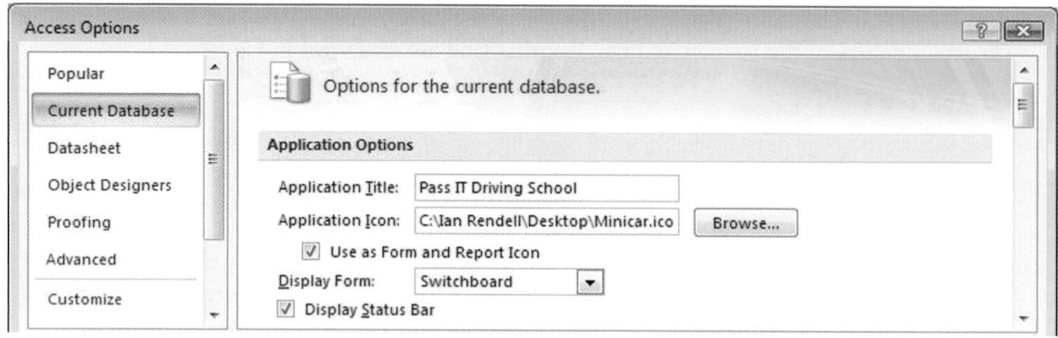

The icon is displayed in the Task Bar, as shown in Figure 2.6.5.

Figure 2.6.5 ▼

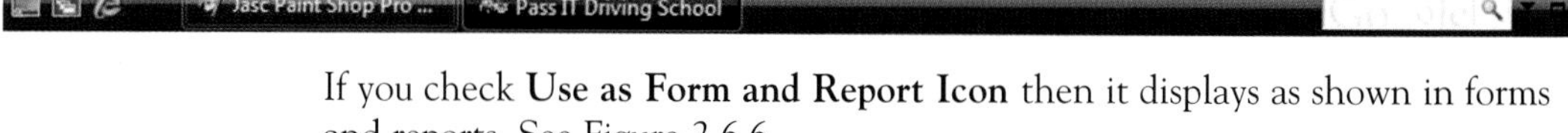

If you check **Use as Form and Report Icon** then it displays as shown in forms and reports. See Figure 2.6.6.

Figure 2.6.6 ▶

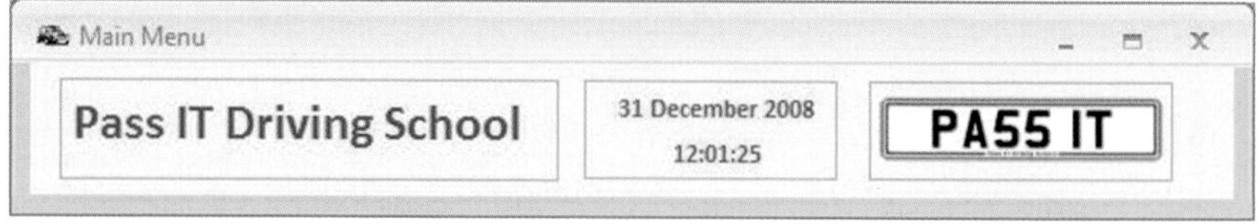

58 Password protecting files

It is easy to add a password to an Access file to prevent unauthorised access but be careful not to forget your password.

You won't be able to set a password in Access unless you have opened the database exclusively. Click the **Microsoft Office Button** and use the **Open** command to load your database.

1 In the **Open** dialog box, click the drop-down by the **Open** box and select **Open Exclusive**.
2 On the **Database Tools** tab, click the **Encrypt with Password** button.

Figure 2.6.7 ▶

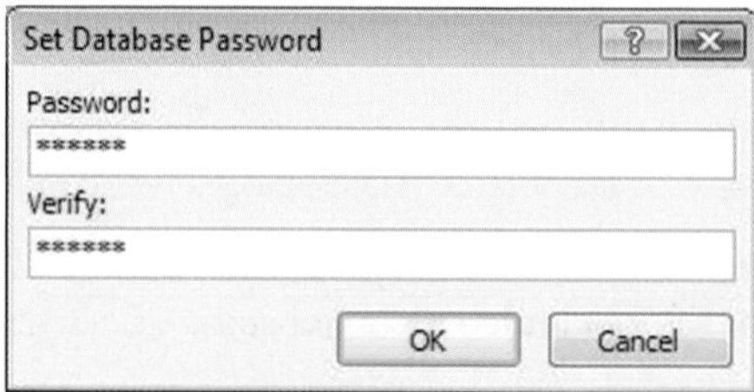

3 In the **Password** box, type your password.

4 In the **Verify** box, confirm your password by typing the password again, and then click **OK**.

The password is now set. Passwords are case-sensitive. The next time you open the database, a dialog box will be displayed requesting the password.

Figure 2.6.8 ▶

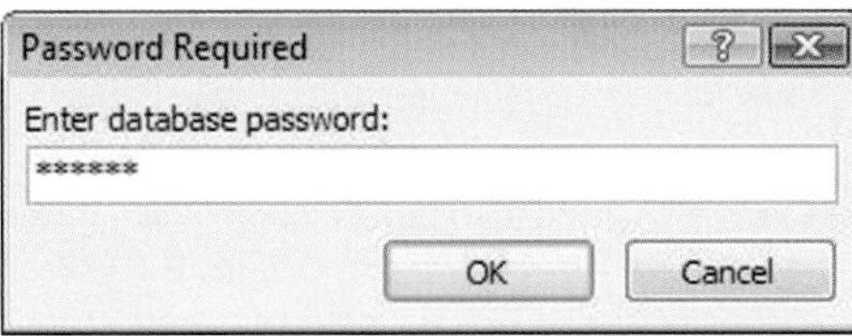

You can reset passwords by opening your database exclusively and using the **Decrypt Database** option, on the **Database Tools** tab.

59 Adding a loading progress meter to the Status Bar

1 Load your database. On the **Database Tools** tab, click the **Visual Basic** button.
2 Type in (or copy and paste) this function called **meter**.

```
Function meter()
Dim counter1, counter2
Action = SysCmd(acSysCmdInitMeter, "Loading the Pass IT
Driving School", 1000)
For counter1 = 1 To 1000
For counter2 = 1 To 200000
Next counter2
Action = SysCmd(acSysCmdUpdateMeter, counter1)
Next counter1
Action = SysCmd(acSysCmdSetStatus, "Ready")
End Function
```

Figure 2.6.9 ▼

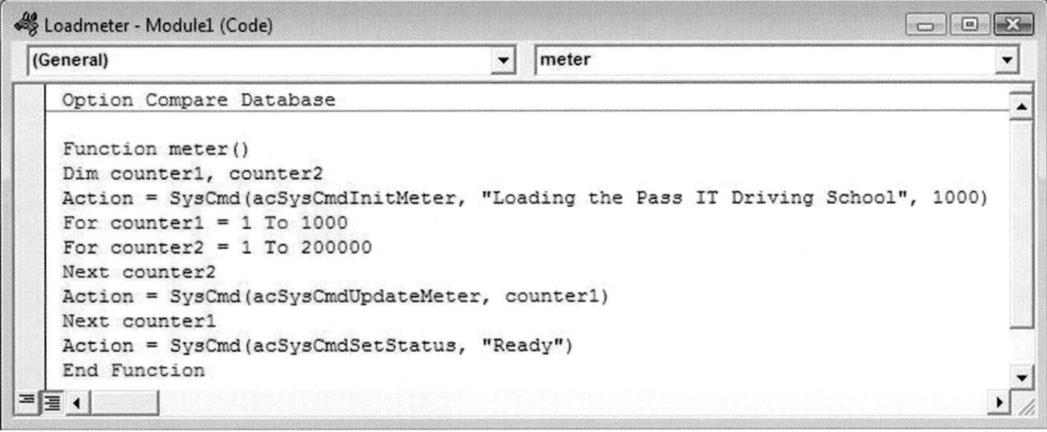

3 Press ALT + F11 to close the **Visual Basic** window.
4 Set up a new macro. The only command is **Run Code** and the function is **Meter()**.
5 Run the macro when loading the switchboard or attach the command to an **Autoexec** macro.

Note: It is easy to edit the displayed text or timing of the loading bar by editing the above code.

60 Customising information displayed in the Status Bar

If you want to display information in the Status Bar, then you can use **SysCmd** to do so:

```
Dim varStatus As Variant
varStatus=SysCmd(acSyscmdSetStatus,"The Pass IT Driving
School")
```

Simply attach the code to the **On Load** property of the Switchboard.

Figure 2.6.10 ▼

And you can clear the Status Bar by using a different Access constant:

```
Dim varStatus As Variant
varStatus=SysCmd(acSyscmdClearStatus)
```

However, there are several problems with using the Status Bar. The user might have used the Access options to turn off the Status Bar. As Access also uses the Status Bar to display information, you might find that your text is overwritten.

61 My Access database is getting very large in size – What do I do?

Figure 2.6.11 ▼

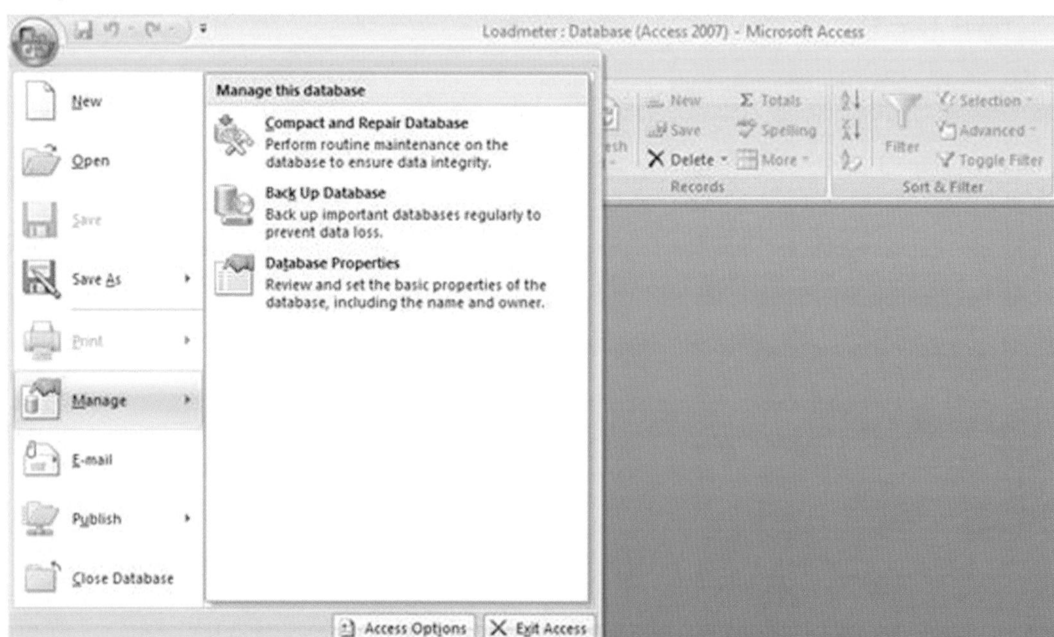

As you work on your database, the file size will get bigger. As you add, edit and delete objects, particularly graphics, then the file can become fragmented and use disk space inefficiently.

From time to time you should ensure that you run the **Compact and Repair** option. Compacting your database can reduce the size of the file by up to a third.

Open the database you would like to perform the **Compact and Repair** on and click on the **Office Button**, select the **Manage** options and click on **Compact and Repair Database**.

62 Setting up a Calendar Control to enter dates

1 Open your form in **Design View**. In the **Controls** group, click on the **Active X Controls** button. In the dialog box select the **Calendar Control 12.0** and click on **OK**.

Figure 2.6.12 ▶

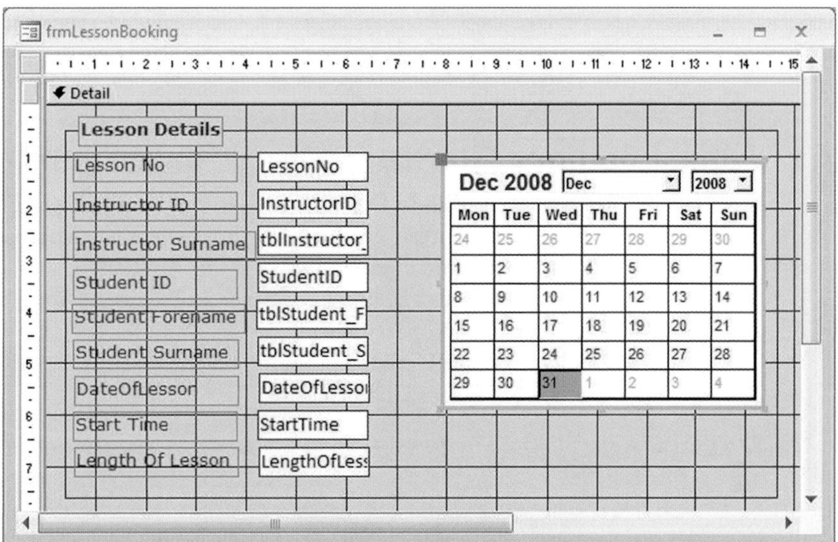

2 This will insert a **Calendar** as shown. Click on the **Property Sheet**. Note the name of the calendar control. It will probably be something like **Calendar5.**

3 Select the **On Updated** property on the **Event** tab and click on the three dots icon. Select **Code Builder**.

4 The **Visual Basic Editor** screen will load. In the top right is a drop-down box labeled **Updated**. Click on it and choose **Click**.

5 Type in **Me.DateOfLesson = Calendar5.Value**

Figure 2.6.13 ▼

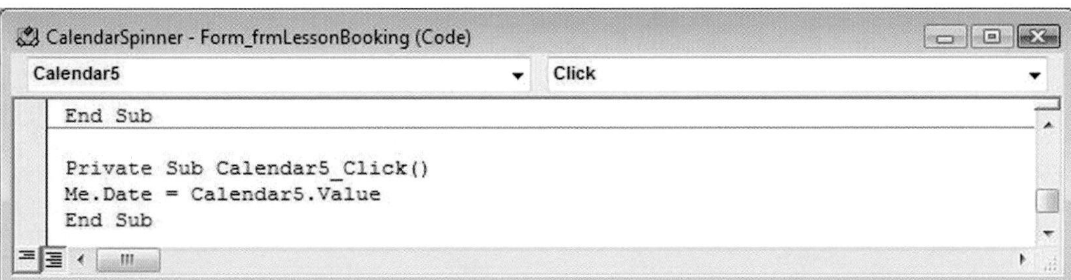

6 Save and close the **Visual Basic Editor**. Go into **Form View** and test that when you click on a date, it appears in the **DateOfLesson** text box as shown below.

Figure 2.6.14 ▶

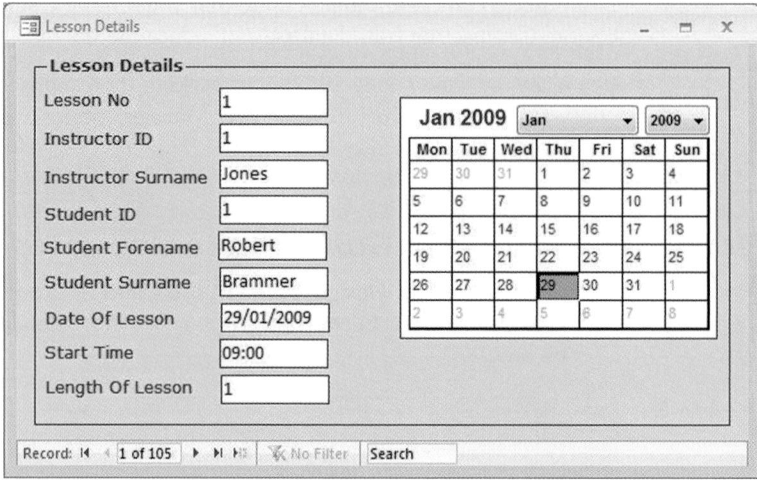

63 Using a Spinner Control to enter dates/numbers

1 Open your form in **Design View**. In the **Controls** group, click on the **Active X Controls** button. In the dialog box, select the **Microsoft Forms 2.0 SpinButton** and click on **OK**.
2 This will insert a Spinner, as shown in Figure 2.6.15. Select the control and click on the **Property Sheet**.
3 Select the **On Updated** property, on the **Event** tab and click on the three dots icon. Select **Code Builder**.

Figure 2.6.15 ▶

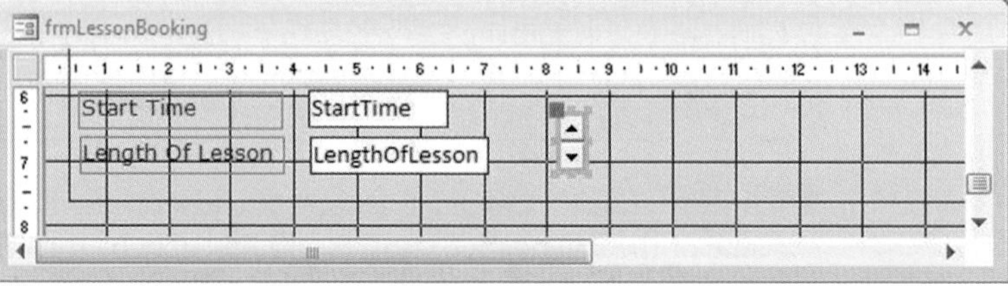

4 The **Visual Basic Editor** screen will load. In the top right corner is a drop-down box labeled **Updated**. Click on it and choose **SpinDown**.
5 The coding for a field called **LengthOfLesson** will be **Me.LengthOfLesson. Value = Me.LengthOfLesson.Value – 1**

6 Repeat for SpinUp, as shown in Figure 2.6.16.

Figure 2.6.16 ▼

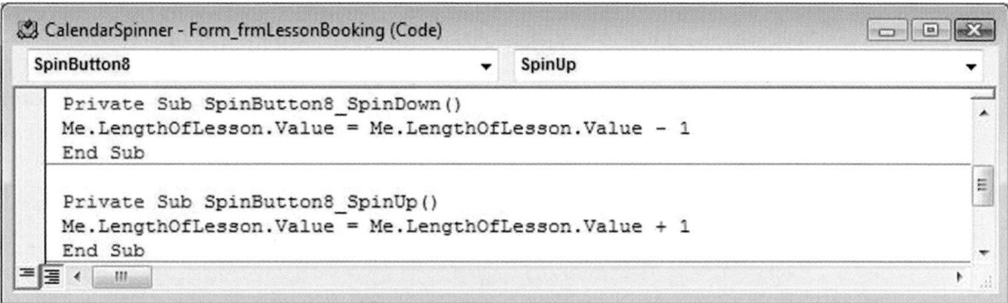

7 Save and close the **Visual Basic Editor**. Test your spin control increases or decreases the Length of Lesson.

Figure 2.6.17 ►

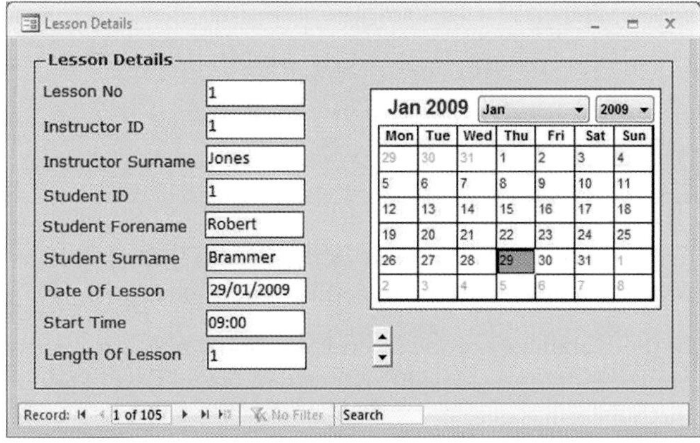

64 Using SetValue to enter dates

The **SetValue** action can be used in a macro to enter a date easily.

Assuming you have a field called, for example, **[DateOfLoan]**, set up a macro using the action **SetValue** with **Item** set to **[DateOfLoan]** and **Expression** set to **Date()**.

Figure 2.6.18 ▼

Call the macro **mcrSetDate** and attach it to a command button.

Another button could be set using Date()+1, Date()+3 etc for Date of Return.

65 Displaying SubForm totals on the Main Form

It is not possible in Access to add a control to the main form which directly totals data in a SubForm. You have to create a control in the SubForm to total the data and then reference the control on the main form.

In the stationery store example we added a text box to the **Form Footer** of the SubForm and set its **Control Source** property to **=Sum([Cost])**.

Figure 2.6.19 ▶

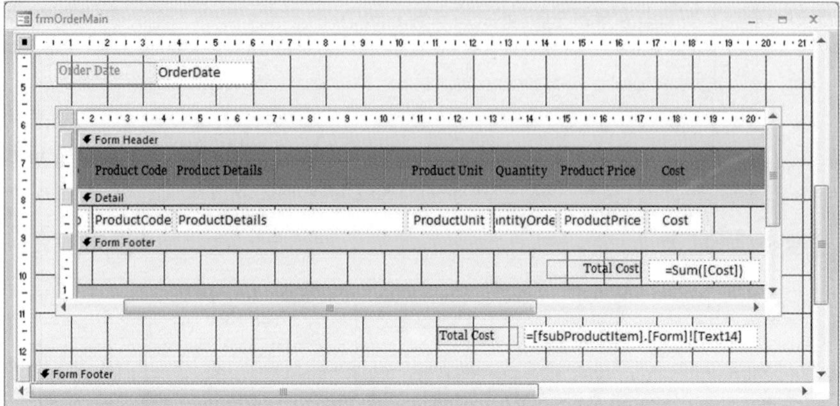

This gives us the **Total Cost of the Products**. You need to make a note of the text box name; it will be something like **Text14**.

In the **Detail** area of the Main Form, add a text box control and set its **Control Source** property to **=fsubProductItem.Form!Text14** where fsubProductItem is the SubForm name.

Set the **Format** property to **Currency** and **Text Align** as needed. Click on the text box control in the SubForm and set its **Visible** property to **No**.

The finished main form will appear as in Figure 2.6.20.

Figure 2.6.20 ▶

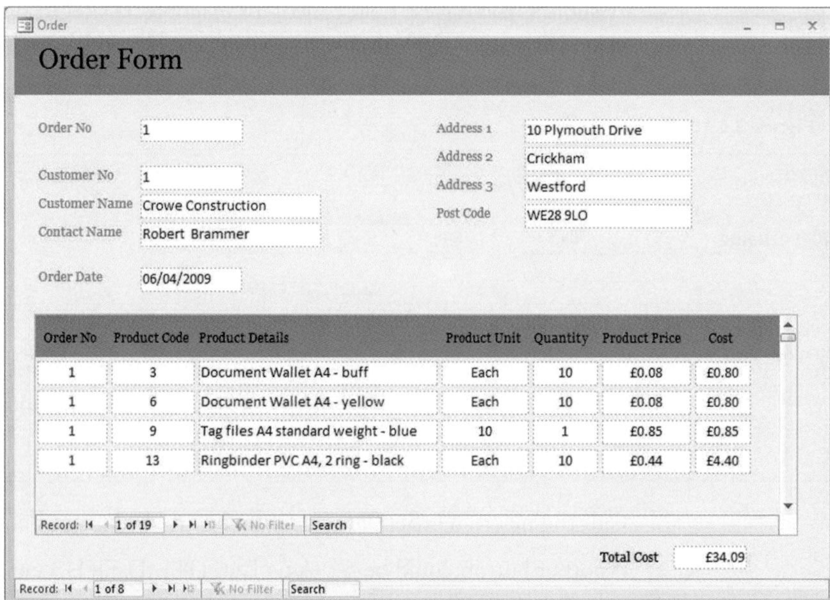

66 Customising a Parameter Query dialog box

In Unit 7 you set up a number of simple parameter queries in the Driving School system, including **qrySearchLessonDate**. When you run the query it produces a dialog box.

You can set up your own dialog box by designing a blank form and using form referencing. Open a new **Blank Form** in **Design View** and add an unbound text box to receive the date. Note the name of the control; it will be something like Text0.

Figure 2.6.21 ▶

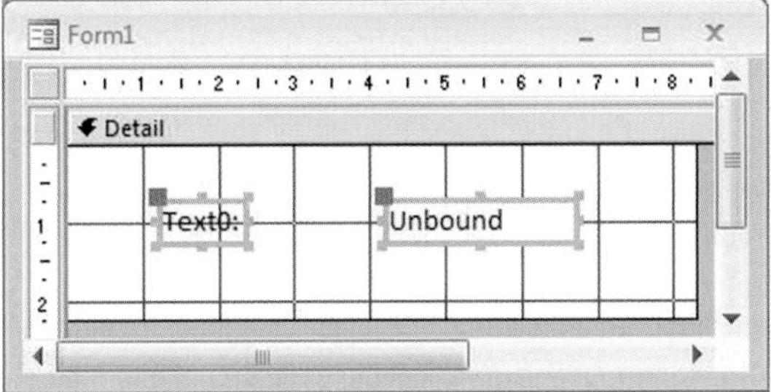

Add a logo, change the background colour, remove the Scroll Bars, Record Selector and Navigation Buttons and change the Properties of the form as required. Save your form as **frmEnterDate**.

Figure 2.6.22 ▶

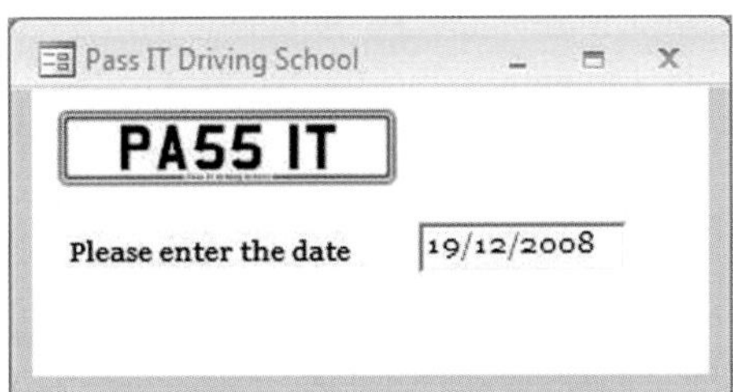

Form referencing allows you to identify an object on the form in the format **Forms![Form Name]![Name of Field]**. In this case the date will be stored as the value **Forms![frmEnterDate]![Text0]**.

Figure 2.6.23 ▼

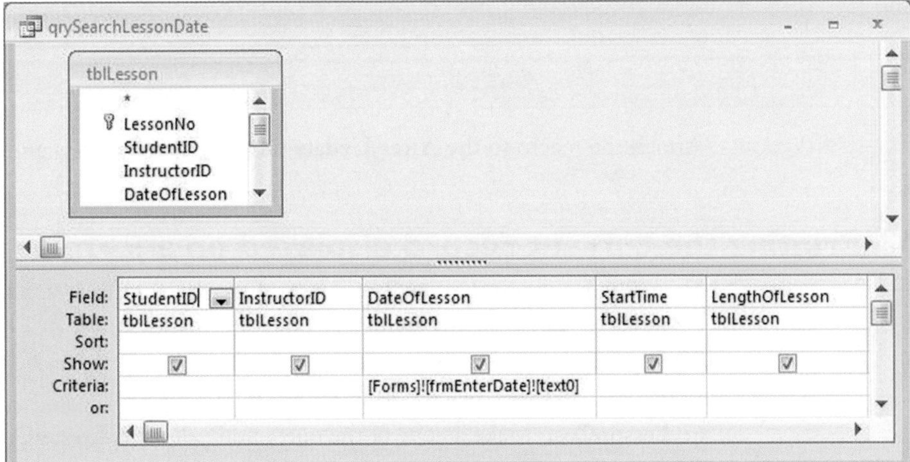

You can now use this expression in the query criteria, as shown in Figure 2.6.23. You will need to set up a macro to first run the form and then open the query.

67 Print a report from an Option Group control

On a new form or existing form add an Option Group. Use the **Option Group Wizard** to list the reports you want to display as options, as shown in Figure 2.6.24.

Figure 2.6.24 ▶

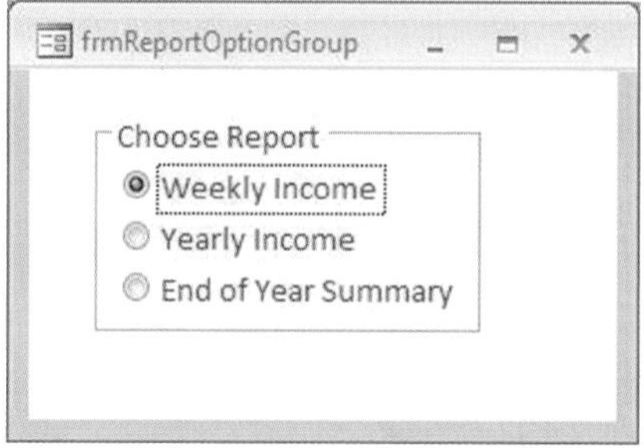

Make a note of the Option Group name; it will be something like **Frame0**. The name of the form in this case is called **frmReportOptionGroup**.

Set up a macro, as shown in Figure 2.6.25 below, which references the option chosen on the named form and prints the report selected, depending on the condition met.

Figure 2.6.25 ▼

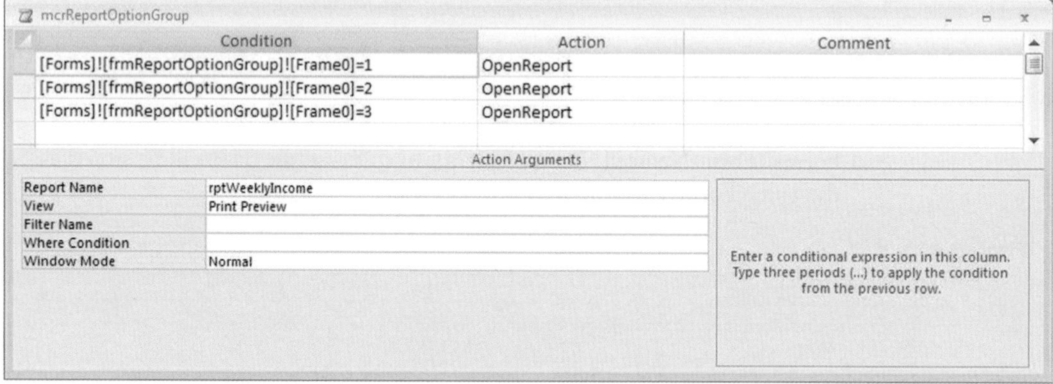

Attach the macro to the **After Update** property of the option group control.

68 Printing the current record displayed on a form as a report

Normally in systems there will be a form through which orders, sales, quotes, bookings or appointments are made. The form will be based on a multi-table query.

In the Pass IT Driving School the Lesson Booking form is based on the **qryLessonCost**. Make a copy of the query and call it **qryLessonConfirmation**.

Figure 2.6.26 ▼

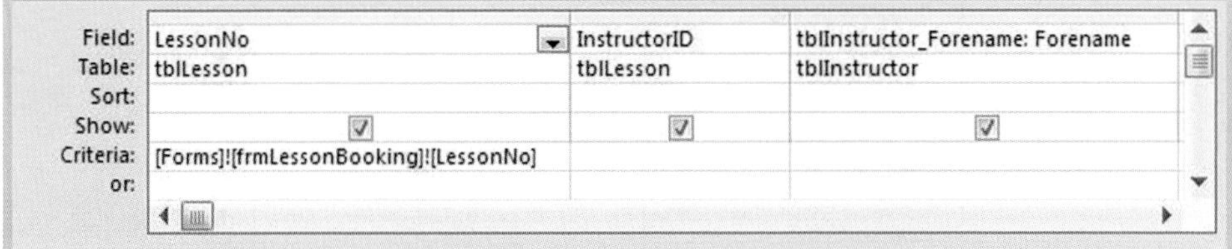

Field:	LessonNo	InstructorID	tblInstructor_Forename: Forename
Table:	tblLesson	tblLesson	tblInstructor
Sort:			
Show:	☑	☑	☑
Criteria:	[Forms]![frmLessonBooking]![LessonNo]		
or:			

Add the criteria **[Forms]![frmLessonBooking]![LessonNo]** as shown in Figure 2.6.26, referencing the control **LessonNo** on **frmLessonBooking**. Base a report on this query and call it **rptLessonConfirmation**.

Use the Form Wizards to add a command button to the Lesson Booking form to run **rptLessonConfirmation**. Select the **Report Operations** category and the action **Preview Report**.

Figure 2.6.27 ▼

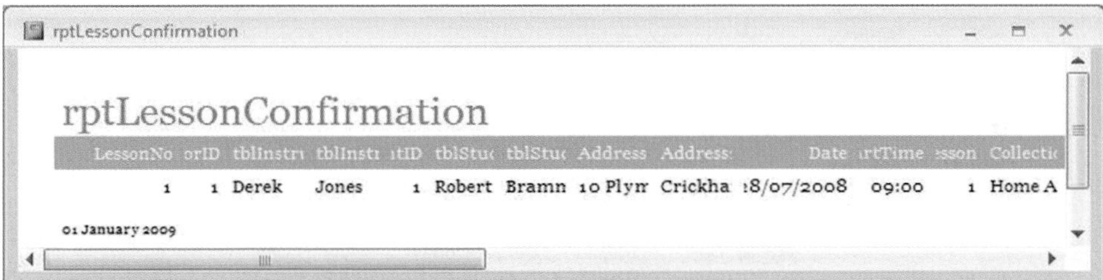

The report will need a lot of customising, but will always show the current record displayed on the form.

69 Using conditional formatting to highlight information in a report/form

Conditional formatting allows you to highlight data in forms and reports according to certain conditions.

For example, in our Student Lesson Details report developed in Unit 13 we could highlight afternoon or perhaps two-hour lessons. In the example here we are going to highlight lessons not requiring pick up at the home address.

Figure 2.6.28 ▼

rptStudentLessonDetails

tblStudent.Forename Header

tblStudent. tblStudent.Surname

Detail

DateOfLesson StartTime tblInstructor tblInstructor.Surname LengthOfLesson CollectionPoint

Page Footer

1 Open the report in **Design View** and select the required control, in this case **Collection Point**.
2 On the **Design** tab, in the **Font** group, click the **Conditional** button.

Figure 2.6.29 ►

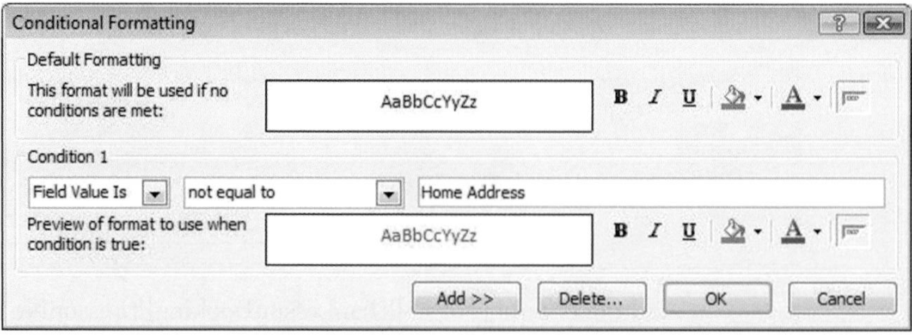

3 This displays the **Conditional Formatting** dialog box. From the drop-down, select **not equal to** and enter **Home Address**. Select a red font. The report will display all pick-ups in red.

Figure 2.6.30 ▼

You can apply more than one condition and across a number of controls.

70 Adding pictures to your database

In Part 3 of this book you will see a file of Bouncy Castles set up with images of each castle.

Add a field to the table, called **PictureOfCastle** and set its **Data Type** to **Attachment**.

Open the table in **Datasheet View**, the attachment field is shown by the paper clip icon.

Figure 2.6.31 ▼

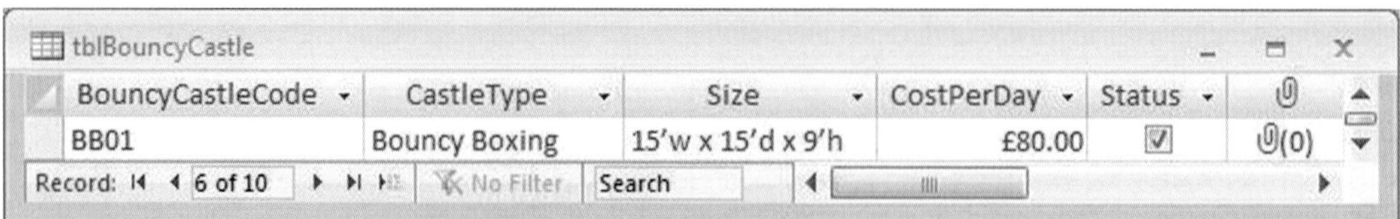

Double-click the icon to open the **Attachments** dialog box. Click **Add** to locate your image and click **OK**.

Figure 2.6.32 ▶

Use the **Form Wizard** to set up your form in the usual way.

Figure 2.6.33 ▶

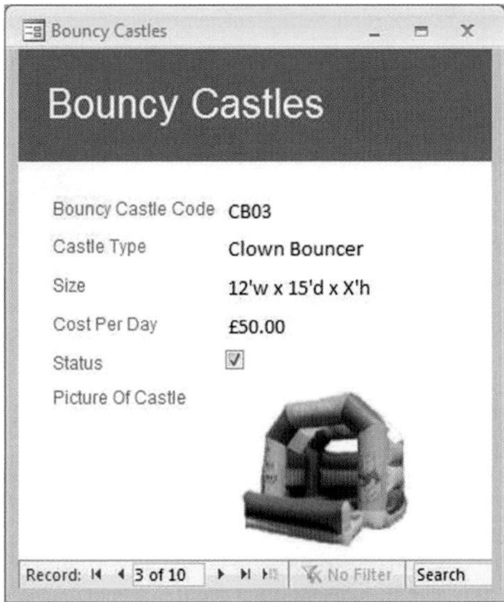

You can add multiple attachments. Attachments can be documents and images.

3 Starting Points

1: Bouncy Castle Hire

Bounce-a-Lot is a bouncy castle hire company based in Westford.

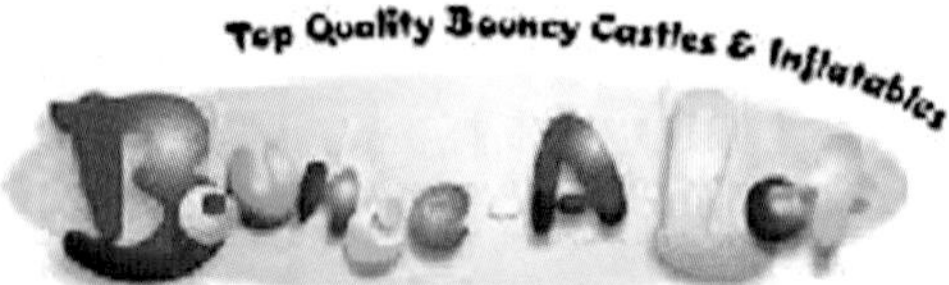

The owner Kerry Williams hires out bouncy castles to companies, children's birthday parties, weddings and other large social events.

She currently has ten different bouncy castles available for hire. Details of castles and costs are shown below. Delivery is free and the castles are erected by the delivery team. Hires can be from 1 to 14 days.

Castle Code	Castle Type	Size	Cost/Day
BB01	Bouncy Boxing	15'w x 15'd x 9'h	£80.00
BR02	Bungee Run	12'w x 35'd x 12'h	£150.00
CB03	Clown Bouncer	12'w x 15'd x 10'h	£50.00
FB05	Flintstone Bouncer	15'w x 15'd x 9'h	£45.00
FB06	Forest Bouncer	13'w x 16'd x 8'h	£45.00
G07	Gladiators	15'w x 20'd x 9'h	£80.00
GS08	Giant Slide	15'w x 25'd x 35'h	£125.00
JB09	Jungle Bouncer	15'w x 16'd x 10'h	£45.00
KB010	Kangaroo Bouncer	10'w x 12'd x 10'h	£40.00
RB11	Rainbow Bouncer	12'w x 10'd x 12'h	£35.00

Kerry currently keeps her records in a notepad and issues little in the way of paperwork with each hire. Kerry has found business increasing steadily and feels the need to computerise her record keeping, to deal with hiring, keeping timetables and providing professional invoices with each hire.

Setting up the solution

The solution will consist of the three tables as shown: **tblBouncyCastle**, **tblCustomer** and **tblHire**.

The **Bouncy Castle** table contains the seven fields shown. It includes a Picture of the Castle, a brief Description of the Castle to help the customer and a Status field set to Yes/No which will be used to indicate if the castle is available or not. The castles are coded as above with **BouncyCastleCode** as the key field.

Figure 3.1.1 ▼

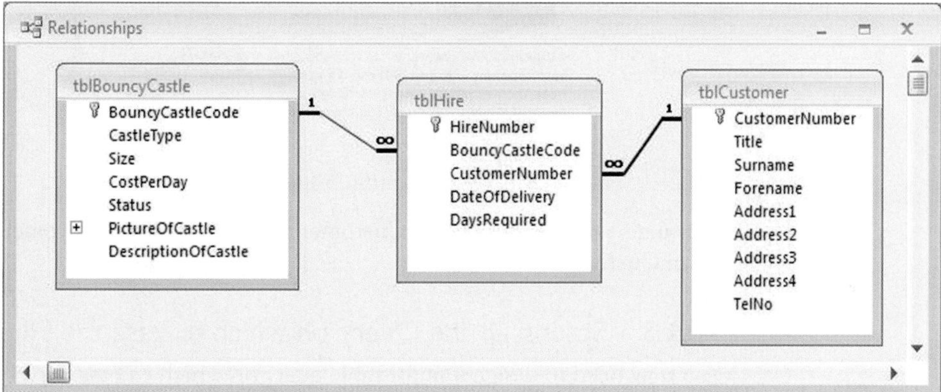

The **Customer** table contains the usual fields **Title**, **Forename** and **Surname** with **Address Lines 1** to **4** and **Tel No**.

The **Hire** table contains details of **Hire Number**, **Customer Number** and **Bouncy Castle Code** which will link to the other tables.

The **Hire** table also contains the fields **DateOfDelivery** and **DaysRequired**.

Task 1 – Setting up the Relationships

1 Load the file **BouncyCastle** from the **Access Support website**. The file contains the tables and data already set up. You will need to set up the relationships as shown above.

Task 2 – Setting up the Forms for Customers and Bouncy Castles

1 Use the **Form Wizard** to set up a **Bouncy Castle Form** based on **tblBouncyCastle**. Save the form as **frmBouncyCastle**.
2 Use **Layout View** to quickly edit and adjust the size of the labels. Resize the text box controls to fit the data. You may need to remove the layout to develop it further.
3 In **Design View**, go into the **Form Properties** and remove the Scroll Bars and Record Selectors. Edit the **Caption** property to **Bouncy Castles** and the **Title** label. On the **Design** tab, use the **Logo** tool to add the **Bouncy Castle** logo from the Access Support website.

Figure 3.1.2 ▶

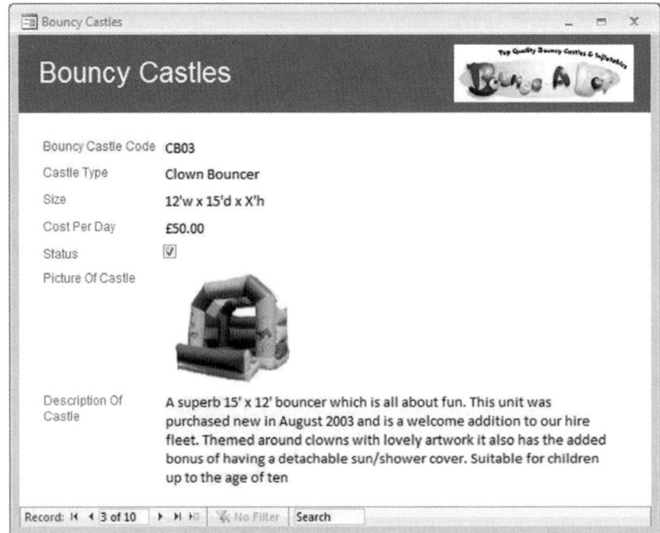

4 You also need to set up the **Customer** form based on **tblCustomer**. Save it as **frmCustomer**.

Task 3 – Setting up the Query on which to base the Hire Form

You now need to design a multi-table query on which to base the **Hire Form**.

1 Set up the **qryHire** as shown below. Select the **HireNumber** and **BouncyCastleCode** from **tblHire** and then the fields **CastleType**, **Size**, **CostPerDay** and **Status** from **tblBouncyCastle**.

Figure 3.1.3 ▼

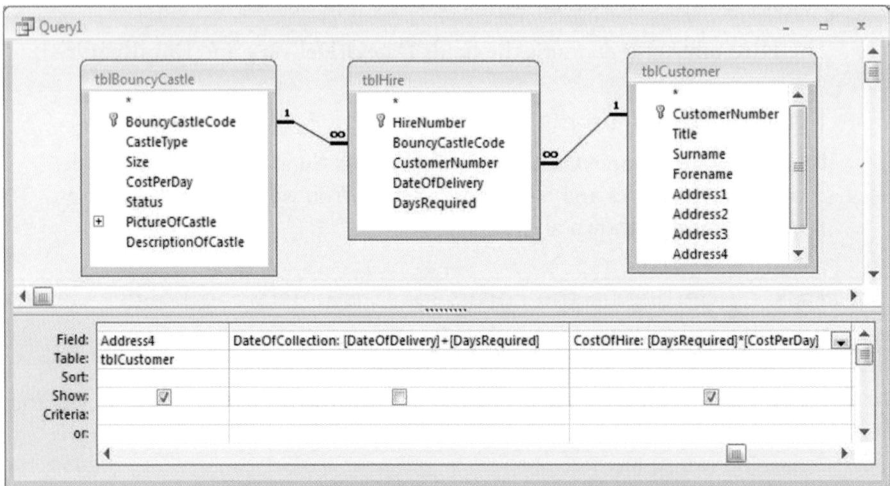

2 Select **DateOfDelivery** and **DaysRequired** from **tblHire**. Select the **CustomerNumber** from **tblHire** and then the fields **Title** to **Address4** from **tblCustomer**.

3 You will need to add two calculated fields as shown above.
DateOfCollection: [DateOfDelivery]+[DaysRequired]
and
CostOfHire: [DaysRequired]*[CostPerDay]

Task 4 – Setting up the Hire Form

1 You now need to set up the **Hire Form** based on **qryHire**. Use the **Form Wizard** and select all fields. It will look a little untidy. Use **Layout View** to quickly edit and adjust the size of labels and text boxes. Customise further in **Design View**. Save as **frmHire**.

Figure 3.1.4 ▶

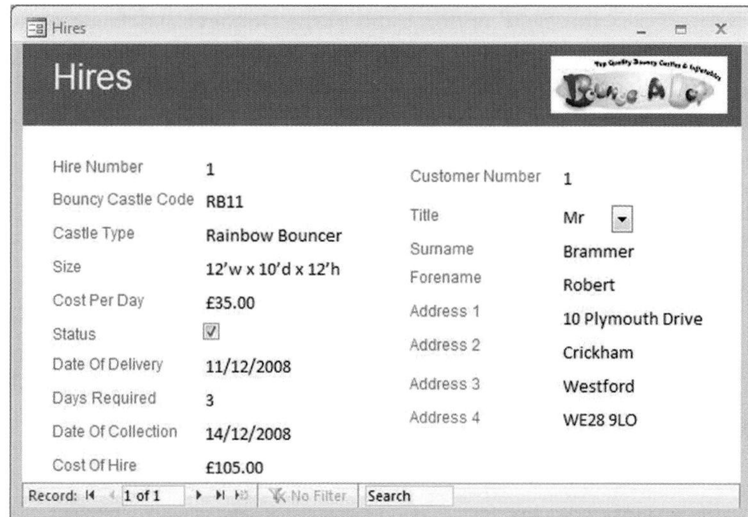

2 Book out castle RB11 to Customer 1 for 3 days and check all the features are working.

The next stage is to make data entry a little easier by adding a combo box to drop down just the castles that are available for hire.

3 Set up a query based on **tblBouncyCastle** using the fields **BouncyCastleCode, CastleType** and **Status**. Add the criteria **-1** to the **Status** field. Save as **qryAvailable**. The query is shown below.

Note: -1 is the way Access stores "Yes" in a Yes/No field, showing whether the castle is available.

Figure 3.1.5 ▶

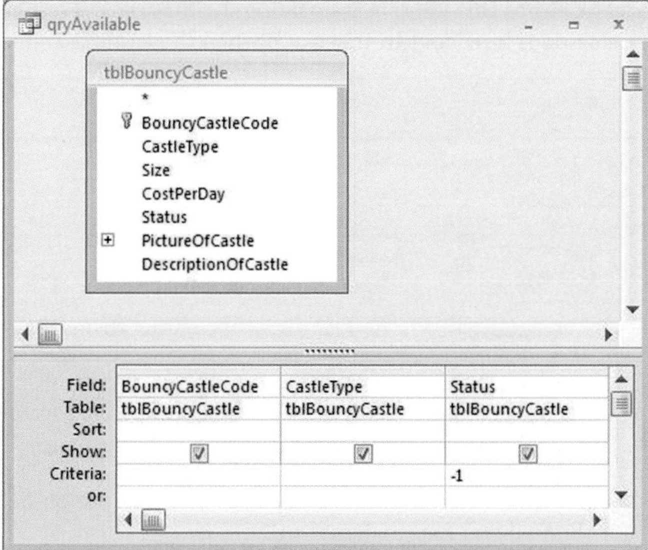

4 Open **frmHire** in **Design View** and add a combo box based on **qryAvailable** between the **Hire Number** and **Bouncy Castle Code** fields. You will need to drag down the controls a little.
5 Follow the **Combo Box Wizard** steps, choosing to include all three fields in your combo box. Ignore sorting and hide options.
6 Select the key field **BouncyCastleCode** and select the '**Store that value in this field'** option to fill in the **BouncyCastleCode** on your form. Set the label to **Select Castle**.
7 In much the same way, add another combo box based on **tblCustomer** to drop down the customer numbers, forenames and surnames. We have hidden the customer number.
8 Choose to sort on **Surname** and remember to select the **'Store that value in this field'** option, choosing to fill in the **CustomerNumber** on your form. Your finished form will appear as below. We will add the **Confirm Hire** button later.

Figure 3.1.6 ▶

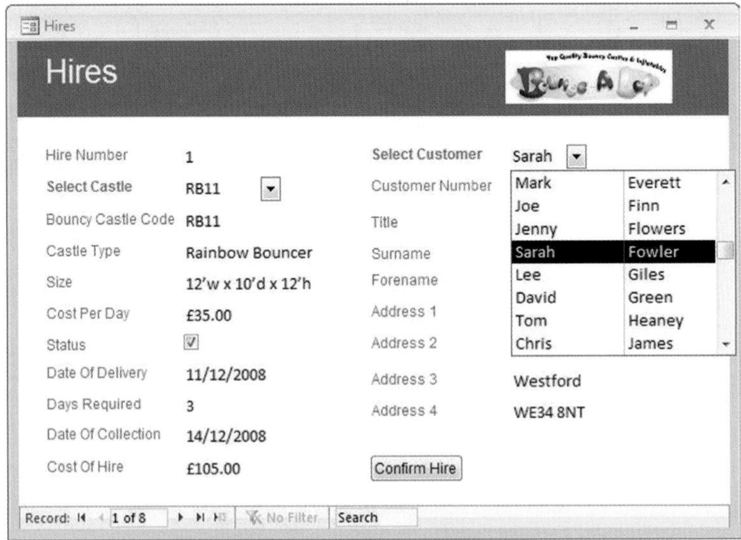

Task 5 – Dealing with the Hire Process

The key to this solution is updating the **Status** field to **Out** (unchecked) when a castle is hired and **In** (checked) when the castle is collected and returned.

Figure 3.1.7 ▶

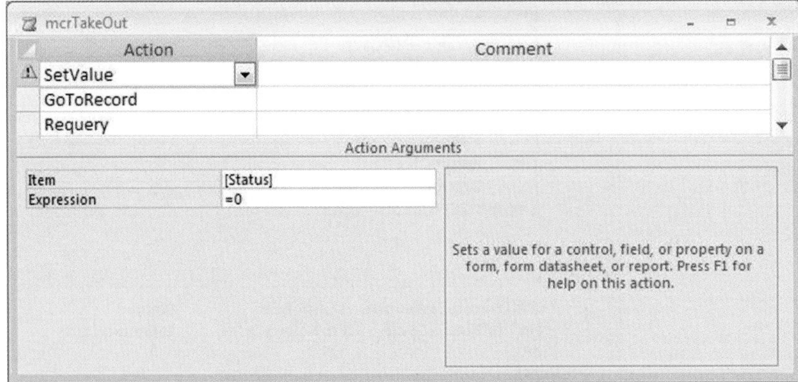

1 Set up a macro called **mcrTakeOut** using the action **SetValue**. Set **Item** to **[Status]** and **Expression** to **=0**.

2 Add the action **GoToRecord** ready for adding a new hire. Set **Record** to **New**.
3 Add the action **Requery** and set the **Control Name** to the name of your combo box; it will be something like **Combo39**. This will refresh and update the records it drops down.
4 Add a command button to the Hire Form with the label **Confirm Hire** to run the macro when a castle is hired. See Figure 3.1.6 on page 272.

Task 6 – Dealing with the Return Process

We now need to set up a form to deal with returns. We want to be able to call up the hire and set the status of the castle back to -1 to show that it has been returned and is available for hire again.

1 To save time, make a copy of **qryHire** and call it **qryReturn.** Set up a Returns Form called **frmReturn** based on **qryReturn**.
2 Use the wizard to add a combo box to **"Find a record on my form based on the value I selected in my combo box"**. Choose to drop down the fields **HireNumber**, **CastleCode** and **Surname**. Label the combo box **Select Hire Number** as shown.
3 Set up a macro called **mcrReturn** using the action **SetValue**. Set **Item** to **[Status]** and **Expression** to **= -1**.
4 Add a command button called **Confirm Return** to run the macro from the **Returns** form. Test your solution by hiring a castle, checking its status and then returning it.

Figure 3.1.8 ▶

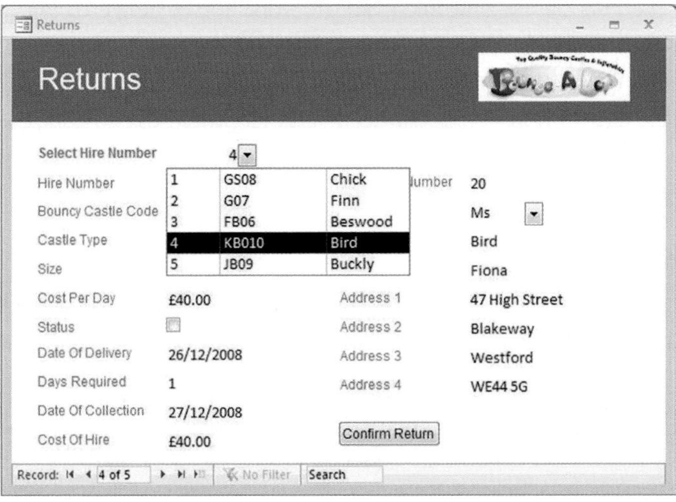

Note: There are a number of issues at this point that we leave to the reader to solve. At this point you clearly need to know the hire number to enable the return. There are certainly ways we could make that easier.

On the returns form it might be a way forward to just drop down the hires that are out on loan, in the same way that we dropped down the castles available for hire on the hire form.

Clearly the hires will build up over a period of time. A possible key to the solution is to clear hires from the solution on their return in a way that keeps track of active hires and returned hires.

2: Cricket Bat Orders

John Spalton makes handmade cricket bats from the finest English willow. He has worked for Buckston and Spalton in Somerset for 15 years.

Each bat is handmade to the purchaser's precise specification. He makes cricket bats on request by taking orders from local cricketers and cricket clubs.

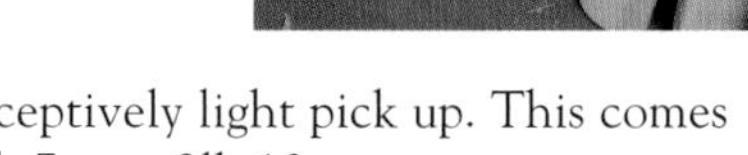

He produces two styles of bat.

The Excalibur: a shape designed with a deceptively light pick up. This comes in short or long handle and weighs from 2lb 7oz to 2lb 10oz.

The Sword: a shape designed for the player who likes a heavier bat. This comes in short or long handle and weighs from 2lb 11oz to 3lb 4oz.

In addition a **Bat Cover** can be supplied for £8.99.

Bats can be collected from the workshop or delivered via courier with a **Postage & Packing** charge of £10.00.

John currently stores all information about orders in a hand-written diary and post-it notes on his notice board. He would like to computerise his jobs, sales and orders to improve his record keeping and build up a customer database.

Setting up the Solution

The solution will consist of three tables: **tblBat**, **tblCustomer** and **tblOrder**.

The **Bat Table** contains the five fields shown. The data for the bat table is also shown.

Rather than use a number as a key field we have decided to code each type of bat. For example, **ELH207** is a **Long Handle**, **Excalibur** weighing **2lb 7oz**.

Figure 3.2.1 ▶

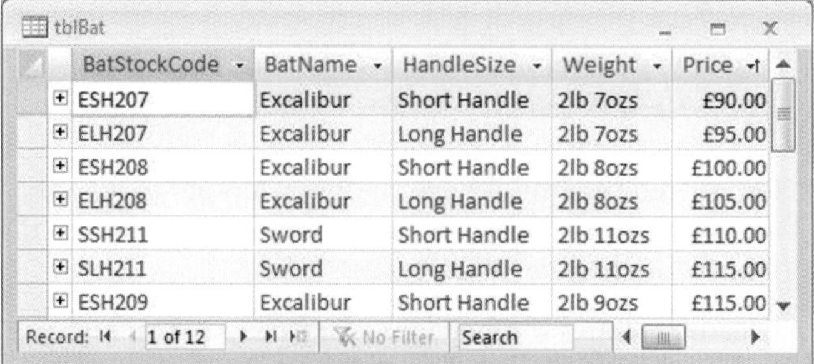

tblBat

BatStockCode	BatName	HandleSize	Weight	Price
ESH207	Excalibur	Short Handle	2lb 7ozs	£90.00
ELH207	Excalibur	Long Handle	2lb 7ozs	£95.00
ESH208	Excalibur	Short Handle	2lb 8ozs	£100.00
ELH208	Excalibur	Long Handle	2lb 8ozs	£105.00
SSH211	Sword	Short Handle	2lb 11ozs	£110.00
SLH211	Sword	Long Handle	2lb 11ozs	£115.00
ESH209	Excalibur	Short Handle	2lb 9ozs	£115.00

Record: 1 of 12 No Filter Search

The **Customer** table contains the usual fields **Title**, **Forename** and **Surname** with **Address** lines **1** to **4** and **TelNo**.

The **Order** table contains the fields **OrderNumber**, **CustomerNumber** and **BatStockCode** which will link to the other tables.

Figure 3.2.2 ▼

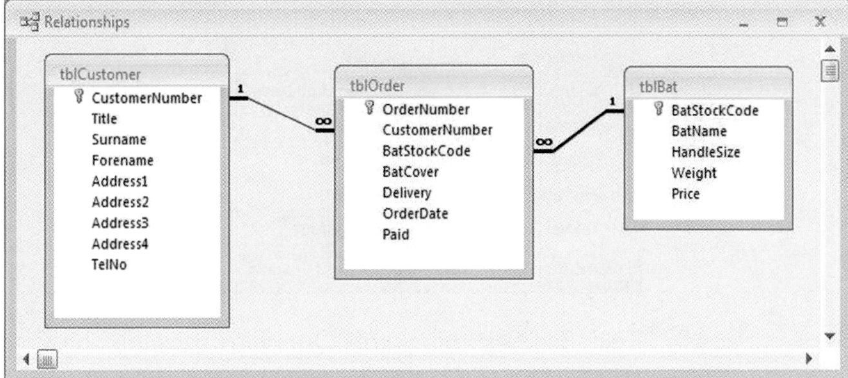

The fields **BatCover** and **Delivery** have been set to **Yes/No**, depending on whether it is required or not.

A **Paid** field has been added, which also uses **Yes/No** to determine when payment is made for the bat.

Task 1 – Setting up the Relationships

1 Load the file **Bats** from the **Access Support website**. The file contains the tables and data already set up. You will need to set up the **Relationships** as shown.

Task 2 – Setting up the Customer and Bat Forms

1 Use the **Form Wizard** to set up a **Bat Form** based on **tblBat**. We have used the Access 2007 style. Go into its **Form Properties** and remove the Scroll Bars and Record Selectors. Edit the **Caption** property to read **Bats**.
2 You also need to set up the **Customer Form** based on **tblCustomer**. Save your forms as **frmBat** and **frmCustomer**.
3 Customise the forms further by editing and aligning the labels and text boxes. Your completed forms should appear something like those shown.

Figure 3.2.3 ▶

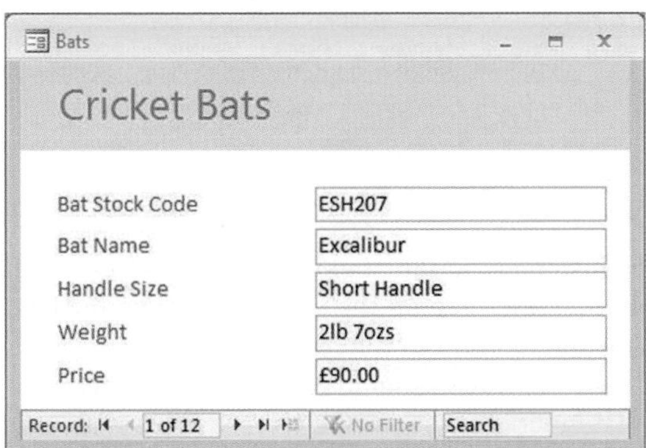

Figure 3.2.4 ▶

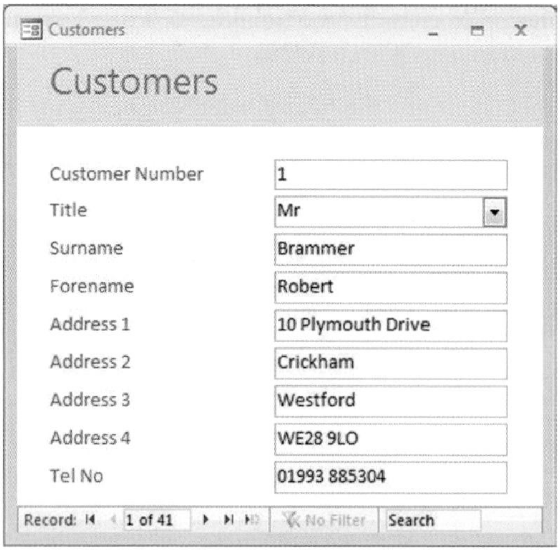

Customers

Customers

Customer Number 1
Title Mr
Surname Brammer
Forename Robert
Address 1 10 Plymouth Drive
Address 2 Crickham
Address 3 Westford
Address 4 WE28 9LO
Tel No 01993 885304

Record: 1 of 41 No Filter Search

Task 3 – Setting up the Query to develop the Order Form

You now need to design a multi-table query on which to base the **Order Form**.

You have seen how queries have been used to make calculations; in this example we are going to use the **IIf** function to make decisions. If you look ahead to the completed order form, you will see, for example, the cost of postage being calculated if delivery is required.

1 Set up the query as shown with **OrderNumber** and **CustomerNumber** from **tblOrder**. It is vital you select the fields from the correct table and in the right order.

Figure 3.2.5 ▼

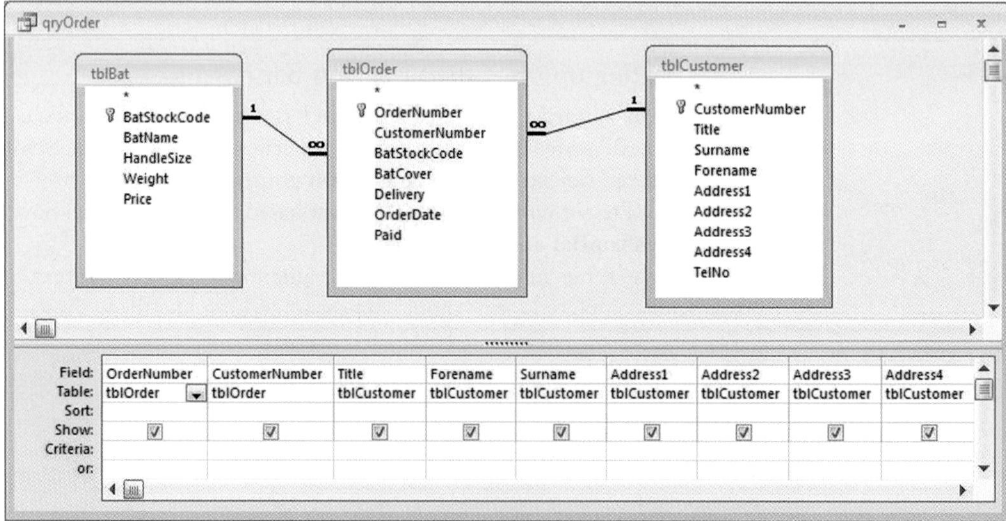

2 From **tblCustomer**, add the fields **Title** to **Address4**. Select **BatStockCode** from **tblOrder** and then all the other fields from **tblBat**. Add all the remaining four fields from **tblOrder**.

3 You will need to insert columns after the field **BatCover** and **Delivery** to add the **IIf** function as shown below.

Figure 3.2.6 ▶

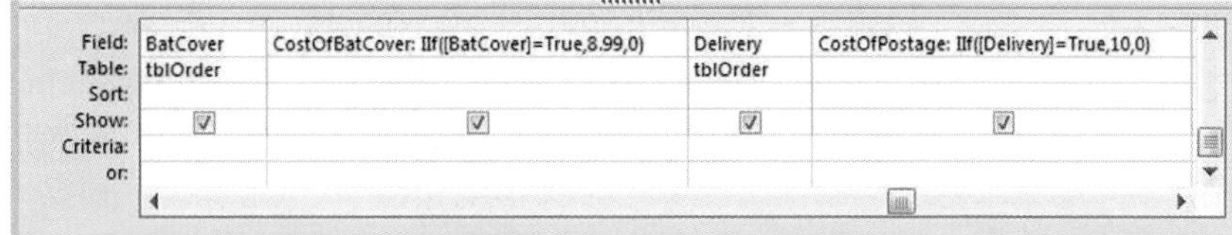

Field:	BatCover	CostOfBatCover: IIf([BatCover]=True,8.99,0)	Delivery	CostOfPostage: IIf([Delivery]=True,10,0)
Table:	tblOrder		tblOrder	
Sort:				
Show:	☑	☑	☑	☑
Criteria:				
or:				

4 The **BatCover** field has been set to **Yes/No**. The **IIf** function will look to see if the **BatCover** field is checked (True) and set **CostOfBatCover** to £8.99 else leave it at £0.00. The function deals with **Delivery** and **CostOfPostage** in the same way as shown below.

Figure 3.2.7 ▶

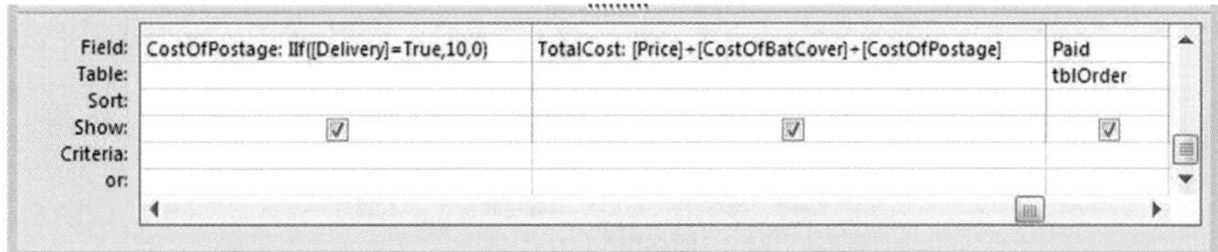

Field:	CostOfPostage: IIf([Delivery]=True,10,0)	TotalCost: [Price]+[CostOfBatCover]+[CostOfPostage]	Paid
Table:			tblOrder
Sort:			
Show:	☑	☑	☑
Criteria:			
or:			

5 Set up the **CostOfBat Cover** and **CostOf Postage** fields as shown above. Add a calculated field **TotalCost: [Price]+[CostOfBatCover]+[CostOfPostage]**.

6 Save the query as **qryOrder**.

Task 4 – Setting up the Order Form

1 You now need to set up the **Order Form** based on **qryOrder**. Use the **Form Wizard** and select all fields from **qryOrder**. Choose the fields in the order you want them to appear on the form.

2 You will need to use **Form Properties** to remove the Scroll Bars and Record Selectors. You will need to go into the **Properties** of some of the text boxes and set **Format** to **Currency** and **Text Align** as required.

3 Labels and text boxes will need aligning, positioning and re-sizing to produce the **Order Form** as shown below. Save as **frmOrder**.

4 Enter an order to check it is working – e.g. Customer 2 – Bat ESH207 with all extras chosen. It is not easy to enter data as you need to know the **BatStockCode** and **CustomerNumber**. In the next stage, we will set up a combo box to drop down this information.

Figure 3.2.8 ▶

Orders

Orders

Order Number	1	Bat Stock Code	ESH207
Customer Number	2	Bat Name	Excalibur
Title	Mr	Handle Size	Short Handle
Forename	Steven	Weight	2lb 7ozs
Surname	Jenkins	Price	£90.00
Address 1	7 Woodfield Close	Bat Cover	☑
Address 2	Pilton	Cost Of Bat Cover	£8.99
Address 3	Westford	Delivery	☑
Address 4	WE49 5PQ	Cost Of Postage	£10.00
Order Date	28/07/2009	Total Cost	£108.99
		Paid	☑

Record: 1 of 40 No Filter Search

Task 5 – Making Data Entry easier

1 Set up a simple select query based on **tblBat** using all fields, name it **qryDropDown**. We will use this query to select the fields the combo box drops down.

Figure 3.2.9 ▶

2 Remove the **BatStockCode** field from **frmOrder** and replace it with a combo box based on **qryDropDown**. Follow the wizard steps through. Remember to click **Store that value in this field** and select the **BatStockCode** field.

Figure 3.2.10 ▼

3 In the same way, a combo box can be set up to drop down the **Customer** details.

Task 6 – Producing the Hard Copy Order

To produce a hard copy order, we would normally design a parameter query to ask for the order number and then base a report on that query.

We are going to use a technique called **Form Referencing**, which makes the process a little slicker. You can refer to the value of any control on a form using form referencing.

For example, the identifier: **Forms![frmOrder]![OrderNumber]** refers to the value of the **OrderNumber** control on the **Form** named **frmOrder**.

1 In the Navigation Pane, make a copy of **qryOrder** and call it **qryPrintOrder**.

Figure 3.2.11 ▼

Field:	OrderNumber	CustomerNumber	Title	Forename	Surname	Address1	Address2
Table:	tblOrder	tblOrder	tblCustomer	tblCustomer	tblCustomer	tblCustomer	tblCustomer
Sort:							
Show:	☑	☑	☑	☑	☑	☑	☑
Criteria:	[Forms]![frmOrder]![OrderNumber]						
or:							

2 Add the form reference as shown above in the **OrderNumber** field: **[Forms]![frmOrder]![OrderNumber]**

3 Now use the **Report Wizard** to set up a report based on **qryPrintOrder**. Select all fields except **Paid** and follow the wizard default choices. We used **Outline** layout and **Access 2007** style. Call it **rptOrder**.

4 The report will try to run by asking for a parameter value. Click **OK** and close the window. The report will only run from the **Order Form**. Set up a **Command Button** on **frmOrder** to run the report in **Preview**. You may wish to add a **Print Order** button later.

Figure 3.2.12 ▶

Address 4	WE49 5PQ	Cost Of Postage	£10.00
Order Date	28/07/2009	Total Cost	£108.99
View Order	Print Order	Paid	☑

Record: 1 of 40 No Filter Search

When **frmOrder** is open, the reference takes the value of the **OrderNumber** and returns that to the report.

Figure 3.2.13 ▼

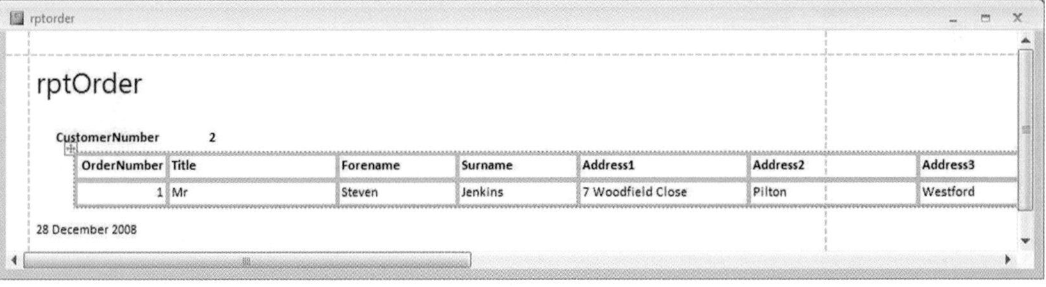

5 The report (shown in Layout View) will need tidying up. Use Layout View to edit and adjust the size of the controls to fit the data. The report will probably spread across two or three pages. You will need to get everything on one page and drag the margins in.

6 Go into **Design View**, remove the Layout and drag and drop the controls needed for the report into the Detail area. Remove any headers, leaving just the Report Header and Footer. We have removed the Customer detail labels and placed the controls under a heading called Customer Details.

Figure 3.2.14 ▼

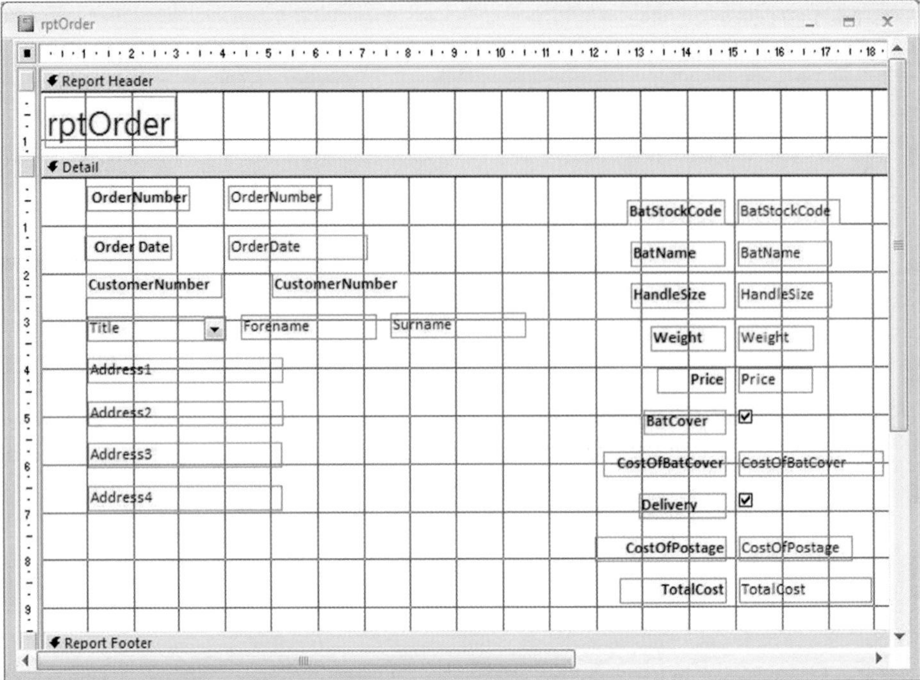

7 Select a suitable font (e.g. Segoe UI) for the controls in the **Detail** area. Add the company details (use the Label tool) and logo to the **Header**, as required. We have used the **Line** tool to add two lines and edited the **Width** and **Color** properties.

Figure 3.2.15 ▶

Hint Use **Concatenate** found in **Tricks and Tips** number 42 to further tidy up the layout.

3: The Stationery Store

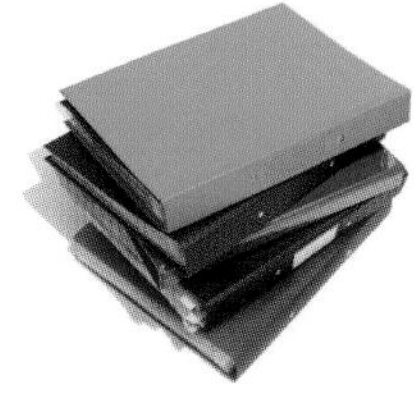

The Irongate Copy and Stationery Store, situated in the centre of Westford provides a comprehensive range of stationery, office supplies and computer consumables to local businesses.

Customers are able to phone orders through to the store and expect free delivery within 24 hours.

At present customers phone up and make an order. The shop assistant writes down the customer and order details in the shop diary.

The store would like to improve their ordering process. They would like an easier and more efficient way to store details of customers and orders.

Setting up the Solution

The table for the stationery products is set out as shown. Each product has a product code.

Details of the products are stored along with typical units and the price – e.g. pens come in packs of 10 @ £0.73 per pack.

Figure 3.3.1 ▶

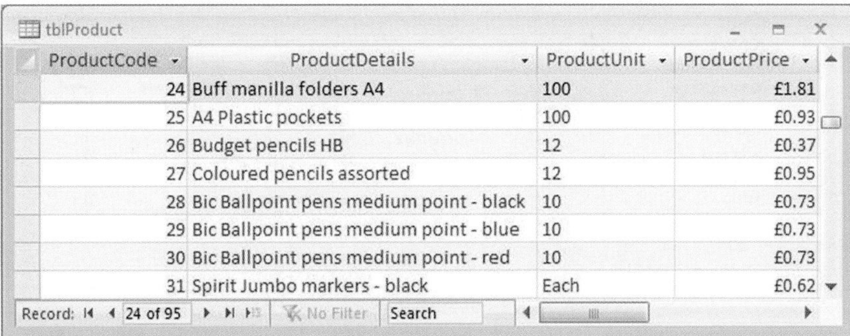

tblProduct

ProductCode	ProductDetails	ProductUnit	ProductPrice
24	Buff manilla folders A4	100	£1.81
25	A4 Plastic pockets	100	£0.93
26	Budget pencils HB	12	£0.37
27	Coloured pencils assorted	12	£0.95
28	Bic Ballpoint pens medium point - black	10	£0.73
29	Bic Ballpoint pens medium point - blue	10	£0.73
30	Bic Ballpoint pens medium point - red	10	£0.73
31	Spirit Jumbo markers - black	Each	£0.62

Record: 24 of 95 No Filter Search

A table, **tblOrder**, stores details of the **OrderNo**, **CustomerNo** and **OrderDate**. For example, Order 4 is for Customer 7.

Figure 3.3.2 ▶

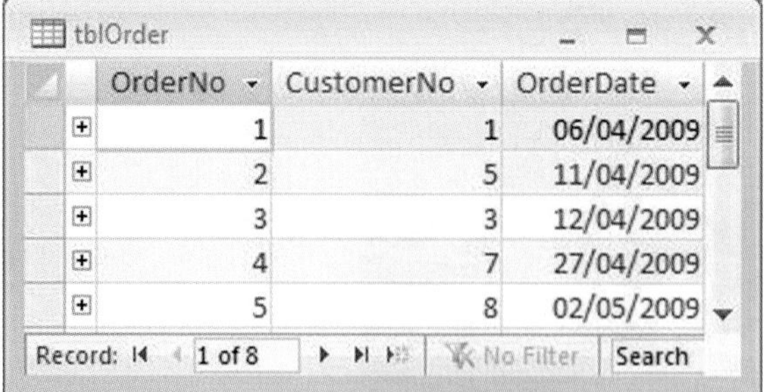

tblOrder

OrderNo	CustomerNo	OrderDate
1	1	06/04/2009
2	5	11/04/2009
3	3	12/04/2009
4	7	27/04/2009
5	8	02/05/2009

Record: 1 of 8 No Filter Search

Another table, **tblOrderedProduct**, is used to store details of the products attached to each order. For example, Order 4 has three products listed.

Figure 3.3.3 ▶

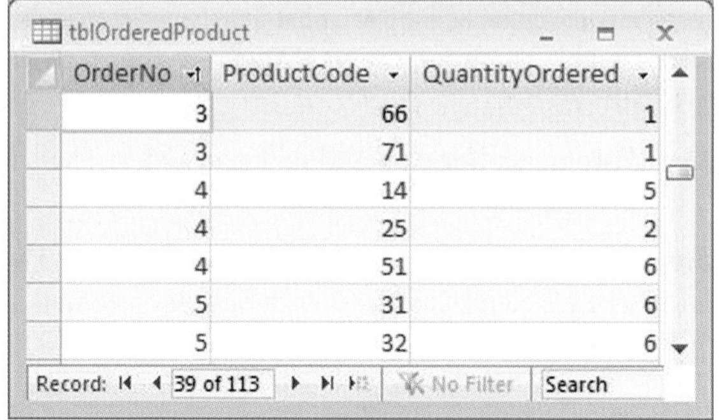

tblOrderedProduct

OrderNo	ProductCode	QuantityOrdered
3	66	1
3	71	1
4	14	5
4	25	2
4	51	6
5	31	6
5	32	6

Record: 39 of 113 No Filter Search

The relationships are set up as shown below.

Figure 3.3.4 ▼

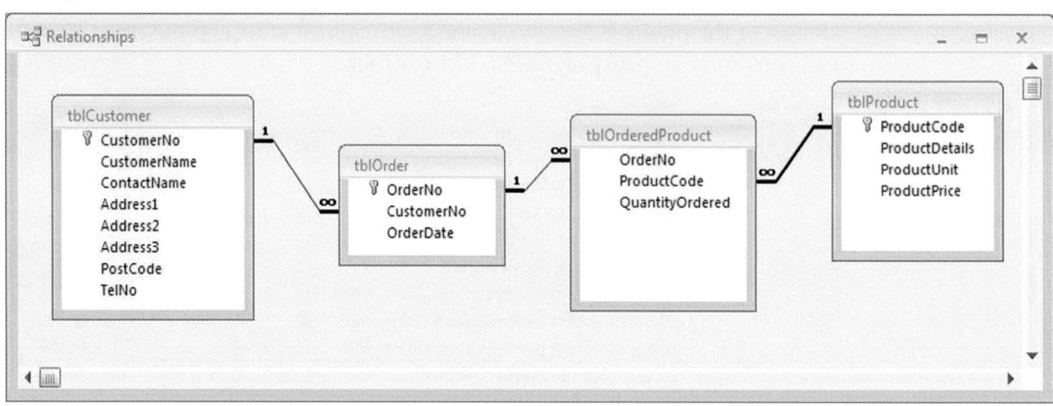

Task 1 – Setting up the Relationships and Product and Customer Forms

1 Load the file **StationeryStore** from the Access Support website. The file contains the tables and data already set up. Set up the relationships as shown previously.

2 Use the **Form Wizard** to set up a **frmProduct** based on **tblProduct**. We have chosen **Civic** style.

Figure 3.3.5 ▶

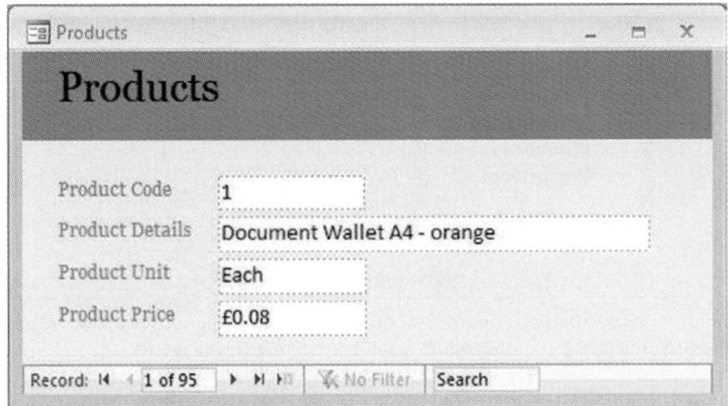

3 In **Layout View** edit and resize the controls as shown above.
4 In **Design View** use the **Form Properties** to remove the Scroll Bars and Record Selector. Change the **Caption** to **Products**.
5 You also need to set up **frmCustomer** based on **tblCustomer**. Your completed form should appear something like the one shown below.

Figure 3.3.6 ▶

Customers

Customers

Customer No	1
Customer Name	Crowe Construction
Contact Name	Robert Brammer
Address 1	10 Plymouth Drive
Address 2	Crickham
Address 3	Westford
Post Code	WE28 9LO
Tel No	01993 885304

Record: 1 of 40 No Filter Search

Task 2 – Setting up the SubForm

To set up the **frmOrder** we need to use a Main Form/SubForm approach.

The Main Form will be based on **tblCustomer** and **tblOrder**. The SubForm will display the products ordered with each order.

1 To set up the SubForm, design a query using the tables **tblOrderedProduct** and **tblProduct**.
2 Select the fields **OrderNo**, **ProductCode** and **QuantityOrdered** from the **tblOrderedProduct**.
3 Select all the fields from **tblProduct**, except **ProductCode**. Arrange them as shown below.

Figure 3.3.7 ▼

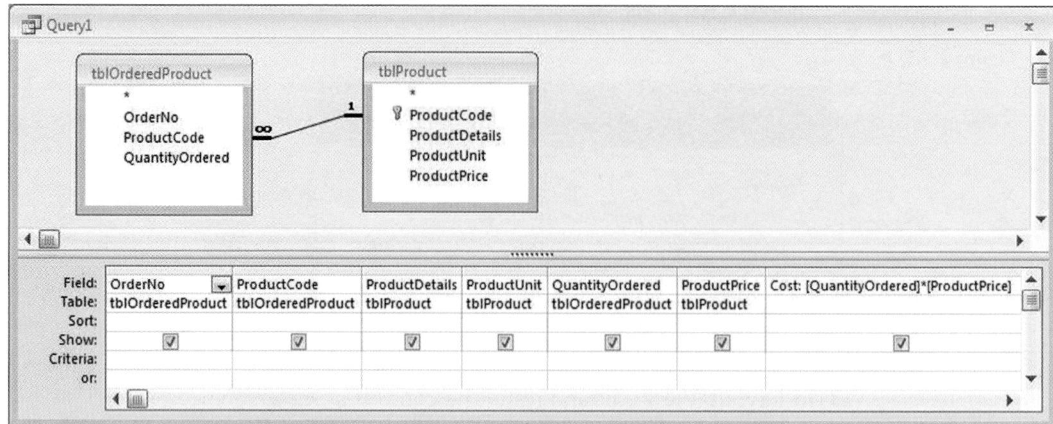

4 We need to calculate the cost of each product ordered, so add a calculated field to the query:

Cost: [QuantityOrdered]*[ProductPrice]
Save the query as **qryOrderedProduct**.

Task 3 – Setting up the Main Form

1 Use the **Form Wizard** to set up a form based on **tblOrder**. Select the fields **OrderNo** and **CustomerNo**. Switch to **tblCustomer** and select all fields except **TelNo** and **CustomerNo**. Then select the **OrderDate** field from **tblOrder**.
2 Do not click **Next** but, from the drop-down, select the **qryOrderedProduct**, select all fields and then click on **Next**.
3 Access detects this is a form with SubForm(s). Click **Next**. Select **Tabular** and a suitable style (we have chosen **Civic**) from the dialog boxes and name the forms **frmOrderMain** and **fsubProductItem**.

Your completed order form should appear as below.

Figure 3.3.8 ▼

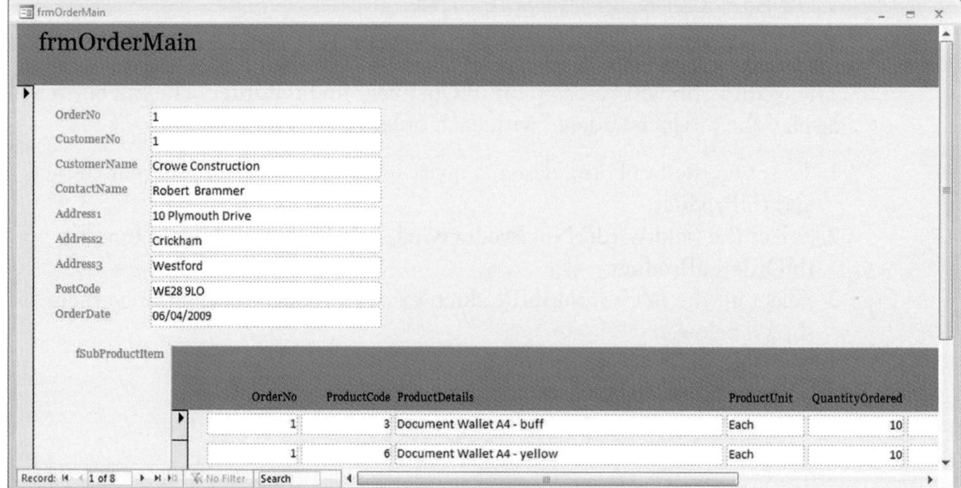

Test the solution by setting up an order. You do not have to enter the OrderNo in the SubForm. Access will do that for you after you have entered a ProductCode.

Note: You do not need display the OrderNo in the SubForm. It has been left in to show the relationships.

Task 4a – Tidying up the Main Order Form

You will notice immediately that the Main Form and SubForm need tidying up.

1 Working in **Layout View**, move the controls so that the address is grouped together on the right. Some controls will need resizing and aligning – e.g. Order No and Customer No.

2 Drop into **Design View**, go into the **Form Properties** of the Main Form and remove the Scroll Bars and Record Selectors. Change the Caption to **Order.** Edit the Title label to **Order Form**.

3 Edit the control labels with spaces as shown. Remove the SubForm label and drag the SubForm across to align with the Main Form.

Figure 3.3.9 ►

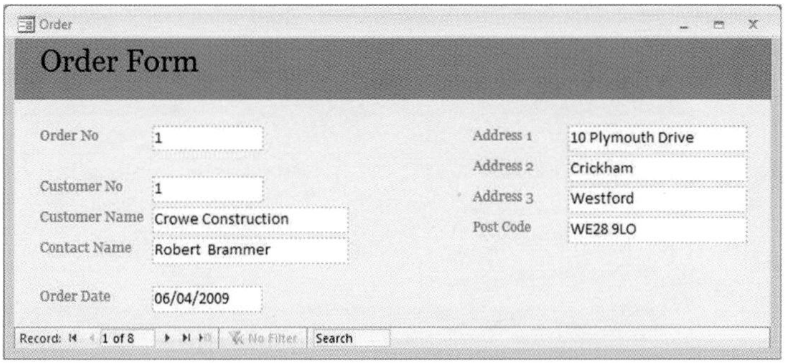

Order

Order Form

Order No 1

Customer No 1

Customer Name Crowe Construction

Contact Name Robert Brammer

Order Date 06/04/2009

Address 1 10 Plymouth Drive

Address 2 Crickham

Address 3 Westford

Post Code WE28 9LO

Record: 1 of 8 No Filter Search

Task 4b – Tidying up the Order SubForm

1 Open the SubForm from the Navigation Pane. A number of controls need to be centre-aligned, resized and positioned under their heading labels.

Figure 3.3.10 ▼

2 Go into **Layout View** as shown below. Resize, edit and centre align the controls as shown.

Figure 3.3.11 ▼

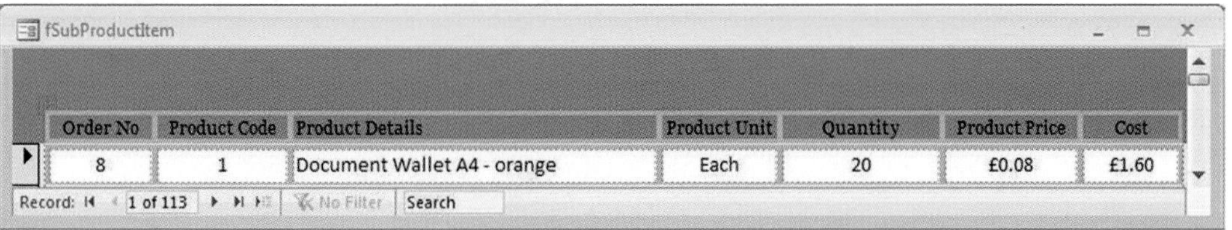

3 In **Design View**, select **Form Properties** and remove the Record Selector and horizontal Scroll Bar.

We need to add a calculated field to the **Form Footer** area of the SubForm.

Figure 3.3.12 ▼

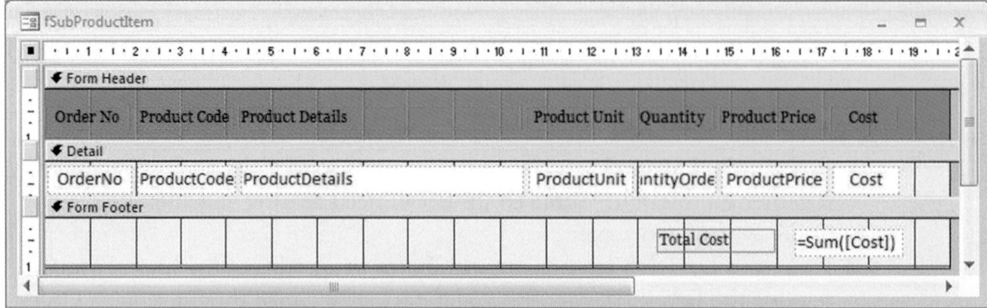

4 Add a Text Box to the **Form Footer** and enter the formula **=Sum([Cost]). Format** to **Currency**. Edit the label to read **Total Cost**. Align the controls with the **Cost** column.

Figure 3.3.13 ▶

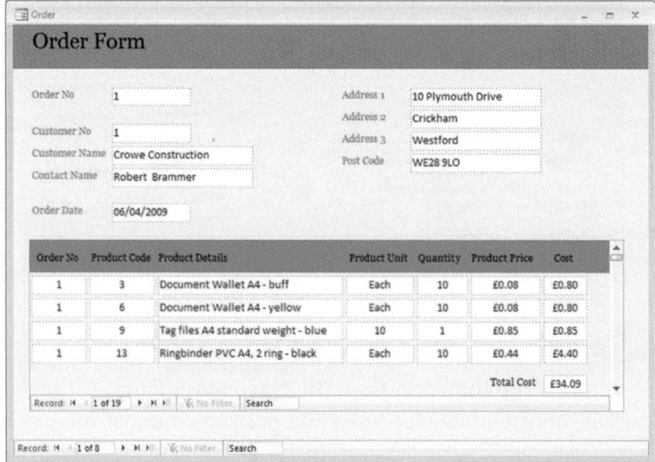

Task 5 – Producing and Printing the Order

Presenting the final order takes a lot of patience! Set up a multi-table query using all the tables.

1 Select the **OrderNo**, **CustomerNo** and **OrderDate** from the **tblOrder** and the **Customer** details (not **CustomerNo** and **TelNo**) from **tblCustomer**.
2 Select the fields **ProductCode** and **QuantityOrdered** from **tblOrderedProduct** and the remaining fields in **tblProduct**.
3 Add the calculated field **Cost: [QuantityOrdered]*[ProductPrice]**

Figure 3.3.14 ▼

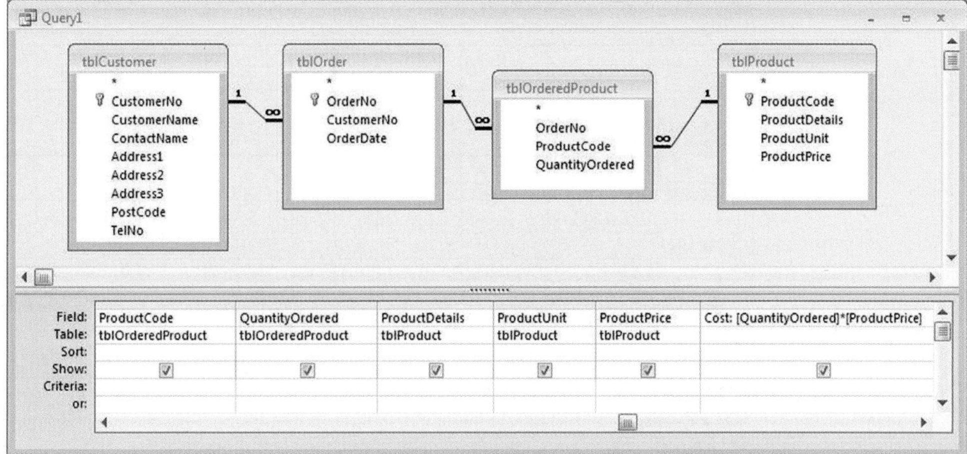

4 Save the query as **qryOrder**. Use the **Report Wizard** to set up a report based on this query.

5 Select all fields. Group by **OrderNo** (not **CustomerNo**) and select **Outline** style, **Civic** layout. Save the report as **rptOrder**. The report will print all the orders in the format shown below.

Figure 3.3.15 ▼

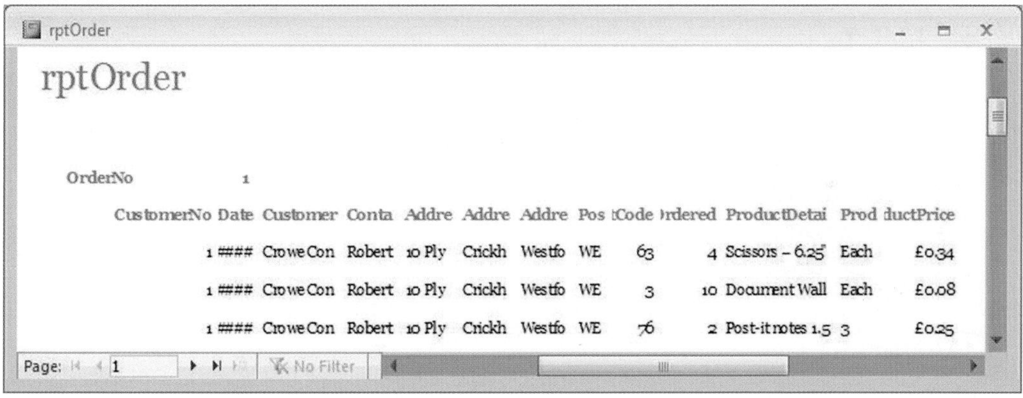

6 The next step is to get each order on a new page. In **Design View**, click the **Group & Sort** button**.** In the **Group, Sort and Total** pane, click on **More** and select **with a footer section**.

7 This will insert an **OrderNo Footer**. Right-click in the **Footer** and select **Properties**. Set **Force New Page** to **After Section**. If you scroll through the records in **Print Preview** you will see each order starts on a new page, but a lot of editing is needed yet!

Figure 3.3.16 ▶

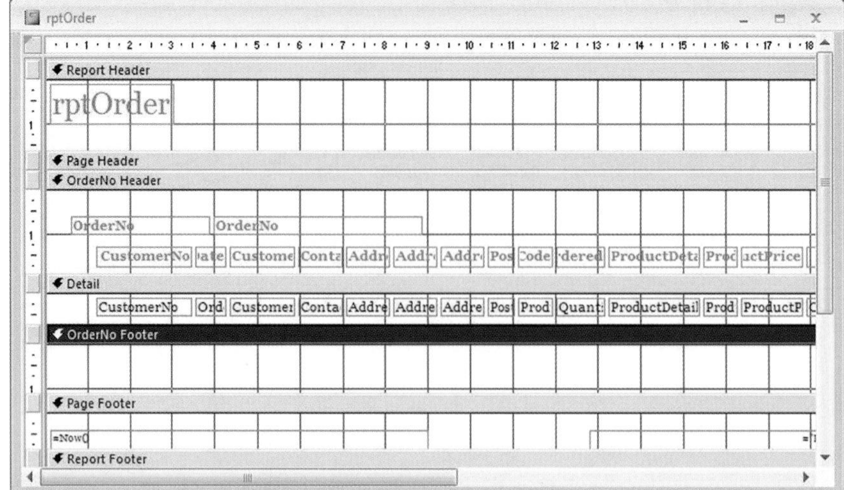

8 Right-click in the **Report Header** and, from the menu, choose to remove the **Report Header/Footer**. This will remove any controls in the **Header/ Footer** as well.

9 Expand the **Page Header** a little to add the company logo found on the Access Support website. Add a Label and enter the company details as shown. Add two lines to separate the **Header** from the **Detail** section. We have removed the **Back Color**.

Figure 3.3.17 ▼

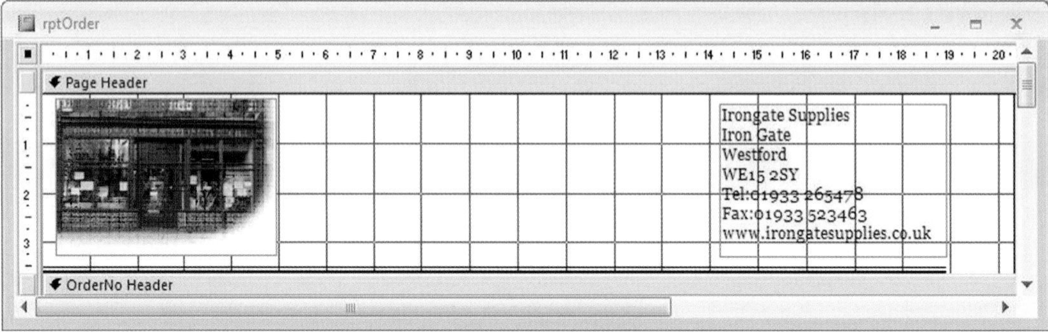

10 Expand the **OrderNo Header** by about 4 or 5cm. Move the **Customer** details, **Order Date** and **Order No** to the **OrderNo Header**.

11 Position the **Product** labels above the **Detail** section with their associated text boxes in the **Detail** section, as shown.

Figure 3.3.18 ▶

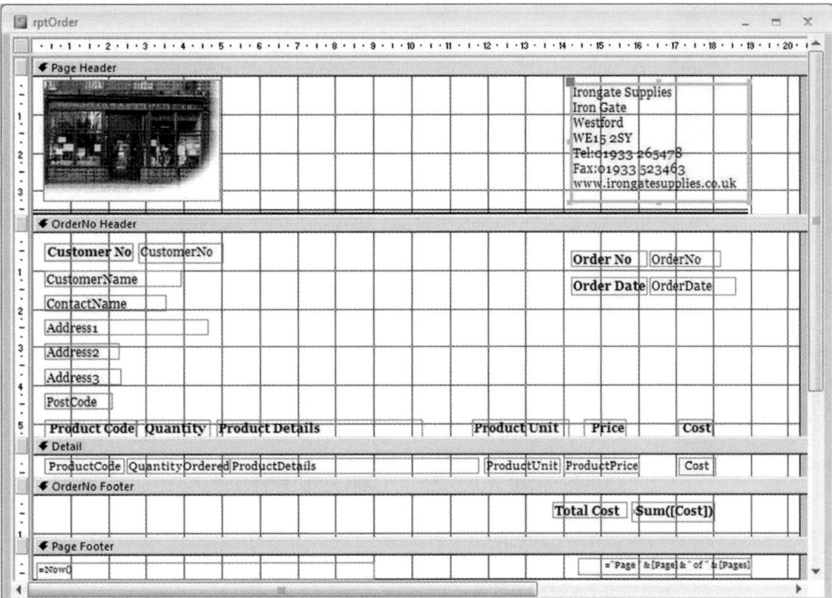

12 In the **OrderNo Footer** add a Text Box. Edit the Label to read **Total Cost**. Add the formula **=Sum([Cost])** to the control and set the format to **Currency**. Switch to **Print Preview**.

Figure 3.3.19 ▼

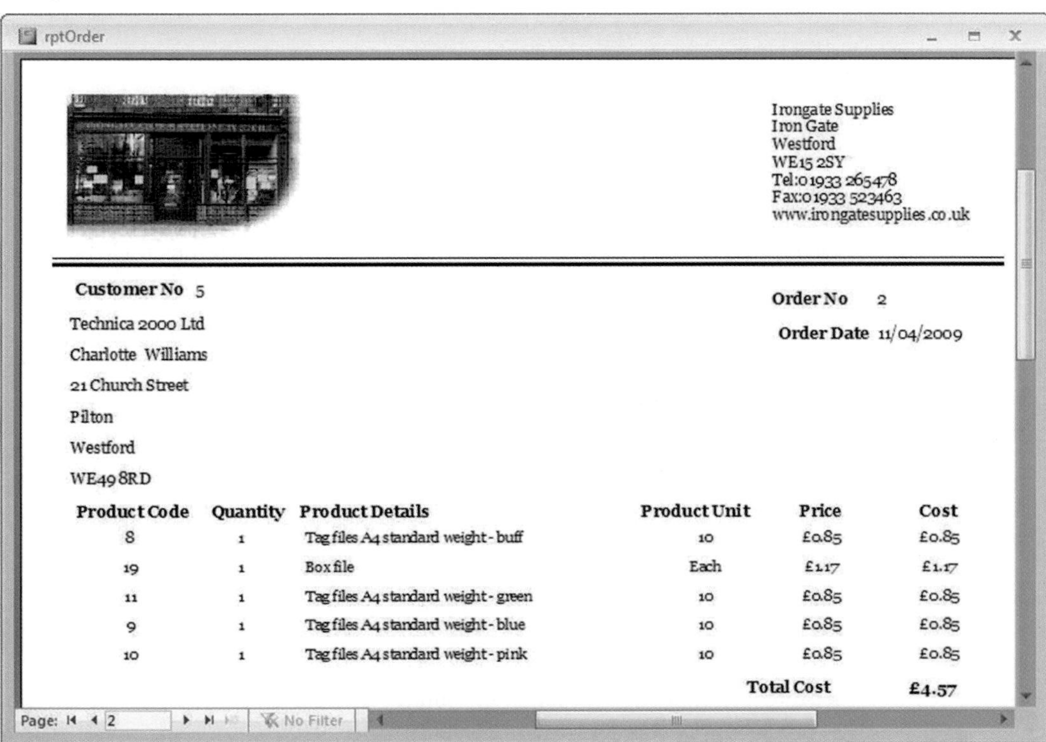

Note: If you want to just print the current order on screen you will need to use the form referencing techniques previously shown and add a button to the main order form.

4 Project Ideas

1: Abbey Window Cleaning Services

Kate Reeves organises her husband Ken's window cleaning business from home.

Two other window cleaners are employed as the business grows.

The business serves two or three small villages on the outskirts of a large East Midlands town. Ken is always on the lookout for new business and adding properties to his rounds.

He does this by calling door to door or distributing flyers. A number of customers are added by word of mouth. He bases his charges on the size of property, which in turn reflects the number of windows.

Category	House Type	Charge
A	Large Detached	£9.50
B	Detached	£8.00
C	Bungalow	£5.00
D	Semi-Detached	£6.00
E	Cottage	£5.00
F	Other	TBN

He tries to categorise jobs as simply as possible to help the customer. He reserves category F for individually negotiated prices.

Details of rounds are held in a file. Each round is numbered and contains the addresses of the properties in each round along with their charge category. Some properties contain additional notes detailing special requirements or requests – e.g. conservatory.

Rounds are allocated to window cleaners weekly, each receiving a photocopied work list. A calling card is left, requesting payment and letting the customer know the window cleaner has been. If payment is received on the day, the work list is updated and handed back to Kate. She updates records and then produces work lists to collect payments.

Kate wants to computerise the system. She wants to be able to:

- store and easily update details of rounds
- produce work lists for window cleaners
- store details of payments and jobs
- produce payment request lists
- issue payment requests
- produce income reports.

2: Albion Away Travel

Dave Shaw organises the away travel for supporters of Burton Albion Football Club.

He lays on coaches for all 23 league games and FA Cup games, as required. Usually only one 60-seater coach is needed for a game, but there will be occasions in a season when he needs to lay on two or more coaches.

He keeps a chart of the fixtures over the season. Two or three weeks prior to each game he discusses with the coach company the estimated price, departure and return times for each trip.

He then sets the price of the journey and publishes details in the match day program and club shop as shown below.

Match No	Opponents	Date	Dept Time	Return Time	Price
1	Halifax Town	16/08/08	4.30 pm	12.30 am	£10.00
2	Woking	20/08/08	10.30 am	8.00 pm	£12.00
3	Southport	29/08/08	11.00 am	7.30 pm	£10.00

Supporters book their places by phoning Dave and requesting seats for their chosen match. Dave keeps a seating plan for each coach, takes down names and contact numbers, the number of seats required and pencils in details on his plan. Payment is made on the day. Any profit made goes to the supporters club and helps keep the cost of travel down.

Dave wants to computerise this job and provide an improved service to the customer.

He would like to:

- store details of bookings and seat allocation
- have quick access to seat availability
- produce reports on bookings and income for each match
- produce reports on income over the season
- develop a customer mailing list.

3: Bouncy Castle Hire

Bounce-a-Lot is a bouncy castle hire company based in Westford.

The owner Kerry Williams hires out bouncy castles to companies, children's birthday parties, weddings and other large social events.

She currently has ten different bouncy castles available for hire. Details of castles and costs are shown below. Delivery is free and the castles are erected by the delivery team. Hires can be from 1 to 14 days.

Castle Code	Castle Type	Size	Cost/Day
BB01	Bouncy Boxing	15'w x 15'd x 9'h	£80.00
BR02	Bungee Run	12'w x 35'd x 12'h	£150.00
CB03	Clown Bouncer	12'w x 15'd x 10'h	£50.00
FB05	Flintstone Bouncer	15'w x 15'd x 9'h	£45.00
FB06	Forest Bouncer	13'w x 16'd x 8'h	£45.00
G07	Gladiators	15'w x 20'd x 9'h	£80.00
GS08	Giant Slide	15'w x 25'd x 35'h	£125.00
JB09	Jungle Bouncer	15'w x 16'd x 10'h	£45.00
KB010	Kangaroo Bouncer	10'w x 12'd x 10'h	£40.00
RB11	Rainbow Bouncer	12'w x 10'd x 12'h	£35.00

Kerry currently keeps her records in a notepad and issues little in the way of paperwork with each hire. Kerry has found business increasing steadily and feels the need to computerise her record keeping.

She wants her computerised solution to:

- improve her record keeping and manage the castle hires
- book out castle hires
- issue daily delivery and collection details
- issue an invoice with each hire
- develop a customer database
- manage income and hire statistics
- produce a catalogue of bouncy castles.

4: Cake Making

Kirsty Wright makes a variety of cakes for all occasions, such as birthdays, anniversaries and weddings. If it is possible then she can make it.

She has been trading since 2003 and has many satisfied customers, who return to her again and again.

Cakes come in set sizes and prices as shown below.

The prices shown are inclusive of VAT, packaging, stands and delivery.

Kirsty keeps details of all her prices and customers in a diary.

Sponge Cakes	**Basic Price**
Round (6" or 10")	£2.00,£3.00
Square (6" or 10")	£2.50,£3.50
Fruit Cakes	
Round (6" or 10")	£2.50,£3.50
Square (6" or 10")	£3.00,£4.00

At present, customers phone up and make an order. Kirsty writes down the customer details, the cake they require and the delivery date in her diary.

Kirtsy would like to improve her current cake-ordering process. She would like an easier and more efficient way to store details of her customers and orders.

She has a new PC and would like a solution provided to offer her:

- quick access to a customer database and contact numbers
- quick access to a pricing catalogue for customer mailing
- a diary of cakes to be made and delivered
- access to orders past and present
- a professional-looking receipt to accompany payment for each cake
- an order history to help her with her future planning.

5: Charity Xmas Cards

Jane Sanders is a Breast Cancer Care volunteer.

Each year, in the run-up to Christmas, she delivers catalogues of charity Christmas cards to families in and around the village of Twerton.

She bases some of her deliveries on a mailing list of families registered with Breast Cancer Care and individual requests from local volunteer groups who help promote the charity.

She keeps a record of her deliveries and details of collection times so she can pick up unwanted catalogues and/or orders.

Customers requiring cards are invited to complete an order form enclosed in the catalogue and return to Jane.

Jane compiles her orders on a spreadsheet grid, as shown below.

Customer	Address	Cat No	Description	Quantity	Price	Date
Wenn	21 Heathway	A456	Snowmen	2	£3.99	11/11/09
		C387	Xmas Trees	3	£2.75	
Pedley	37 Station Rd	A233	Assorted	5	£4.99	13/11/09
		C546	Snow Scenes	2	£3.75	
		A463	Baubles	1	£2.75	

Jane wants to enter her orders on to her PC and organise her collection and deliveries.

She would like the system to:

- help her build up a committed customer mailing list
- track unwanted catalogues
- keep details of orders and requests
- monitor money raised for returns to the charity.

6: Conferences @ The Bird in the Hand Hotel

The Bird in the Hand Hotel is situated in South West Derbyshire. It offers conference facilities for local business.

It has three conference rooms available: Suite 1, Suite 2 and Suite 3. Daily hire charges are shown below.

Room	Price per day	Max no of Delegates
Suite 1	£150	15
Suite 2	£150	20
Suite 3	£200	30

Rooms can be arranged by request in classroom or U-shape style. Further equipment can be hired for the day at the rates shown below.

Equipment	Price per day	Equipment	Price per day
TV	£30	Flip Chart	£10
OHP	£15	Data Projector	£40
Screen	£15	Lectern	£10

Catering is charged @ £21.00 per delegate. This includes hot/cold buffet and tea/coffee/mineral water throughout the day.

Andrew Corbett is the conference manager. Requests for conference facilities are taken by phone or letter.

Andrew takes down the customer details, the conference date, the number of delegates and the facilities they require. He allocates a suite for the conference and confirms by letter the details and costs. On the day of the conference the client is given an invoice which they are expected to pay within 28 days.

Although it is a small business, Andrew wants to run the operation from a computer. He wants to be able to:

- store details of bookings and issue letters of confirmation
- invoice the company on the day of the event
- produce weekly/daily rotas and suite requirements for the hotel staff
- build up a customer database of local businesses
- produce management reports on use and income
- issue flyers with updated details of facilities offered.

7: Cricket Bat Orders

John Spalton makes handmade cricket bats from the finest English willow.

He has worked for Buckston and Spalton in Somerset for 15 years.

Each bat is handmade to the purchaser's precise specification. He makes cricket bats on request by taking orders from local cricketers and cricket clubs.

He produces two styles of bat.

The Excalibur: a shape designed for the ultimate in power, with a deceptively light pick up. This comes in short or long handle and weighs from 2lb 7oz to 2lb 10oz.

The Sword: a shape designed for the player who likes a heavier bat with a great pick up. This comes in short or long handle and weighs from 2lb 11oz to 3lb 4oz.

In addition, a toe guard can be fitted to each bat for £5.00 and a bat cover supplied for £8.50.

Bats can be collected from the workshop or dispatched via courier with a postage and packing charge of £10.00.

John currently stores all information about orders in a hand-written diary and post-it notes on his notice board. He would like to computerise his jobs, sales and orders to improve his record keeping and build up a customer database. He needs to be able to:

- store and access orders
- issue delivery notes and order details
- provide information on jobs to be completed this week
- develop a customer database
- circulate all customers pre-season with flyers and price lists
- keep track of paid and unpaid orders
- produce details of annual income.

8: The Derwentdale Fun Run

Sue Spalton organises an annual Fun Run in May of each year, called the Derwentdale Dash. It is in aid of the National Trust and Marie Curie Cancer Care.

The venue is the picturesque area around the village of Thorpe and Dovedale in the south of the Derbyshire Peak District.

It is a series of cross-country races of between 1 and 5 miles, run by about 600 people of all abilities.

There are three race categories. There is a 1-mile fun run for children under the age of 12, scheduled to start at 10am. It is followed by a 3-mile fun run for people of all ages at 10.30am and then, starting at 11.30am, is the 5-mile event for serious runners.

Each runner must pay an entrance fee. The fees for this year are shown in the table below.

Under 12 Yrs	12–18 Yrs	OAP	Adult
£5	£7	£9	£12

All runners are invited to fill in an application form.

Applicants are invited to enter for one of three race categories.

For each runner, the organising committee needs to know their name, date of birth, gender, telephone number, date of application, race category and category of payment (Under 12, 12–18, 'Old Age Pensioner' (OAP), Adult).

A unique four-digit number is allocated to each runner.

If the application is received before 1 April then a £1.00 discount is applied.

Sue wants to use her PC to computerise the organisation of the event. She wants to be able to:

- store details of entry and entry fees
- issue confirmation of entry automatically
- issue race lists
- enter results and times
- invite runners to the following year's event.

9: Hair On The Move

Hair On The Move is a mobile hairdressing service run by Karen Sirrel in rural Derbyshire.

She employs two trainees and offers a wide range of services in the comfort of your home at convenient times and affordable prices.

Karen's business is expanding and demand is high. She is adding to her customer base on a weekly basis.

Customers ring Karen to arrange an appointment and service. Karen takes down their details and allocates a hairdresser to the service. Customers tend to want to keep the same hairdresser.

Her prices are shown below. Additional services, such as coloring, are available on request.

Service	Price
Ladies Cut & Finish	£20.00
Ladies Wet Cut	£10.00
Gents Cut & Finish	£15.00
Gents Wet Cut	£10.00

Karen wants a solution set up on her PC to deal with the appointments, income and services.

She would like to be able to:

- keep records of her customers to provide a better service
- organise her appointments more efficiently
- keep records of payments and income
- manage the work of her assistants.

10: Hotel Room Booking @ The Broadway Hotel

The Broadway Hotel is situated in South West Derbyshire. It offers bar, catering, conference facilities and room booking.

The hotel has eleven bedrooms numbered 101 to 111. Rooms 101 to 107 are twin, 108 to 111 are double en-suite.

A twin room can be booked at £44.95 per night, with a £10.00 supplement for a second person.

A double en-suite costs £54.95 per night with a £15.00 supplement for a second person. Breakfast is included in the cost.

Bookings are made by phone, letter or email.

The hotel manager, Alan Currie, records the customer details, along with dates, room number and the number of nights required.

A letter of confirmation is sent to the customer. On departure, the customer receives an invoice detailing the costs. Payment is made on departure.

During the stay at the hotel all meals, drinks at the bar, newspapers and telephone calls are charged to the customer's bill and added to the invoice.

Alan wants to computerise this part of the hotel operation. He wants to be able to:

- store details of bookings and issue letters of confirmation
- have quick access to room availability
- invoice the customer on departure, to include details of all additional expenditure
- produce daily lists of arrivals for the cleaning staff
- build up a customer database
- produce management reports on use and income
- produce daily lists of departures for the cleaning staff.

11: Peak Cycle Hire

Richard James has been hiring out cycles in the Peak District National Park for many years.

He runs the hire business from a small café he owns near the entrance to the park. He has cycles to suit all sizes, ages and abilities.

Pumps, puncture repair kits, locks, carriers and a map are available and are included in the cost of hire.

A deposit of £20 is required on all bikes. A £50 deposit is payable on a tandem.

Deposits are withheld in the event of damage or late return.

The hire charges are shown below. Payment is by cash only.

Type of Bike	Up to 3 hours	Whole Day	No. of Bikes
Mountain/Trails Bike	£9.00	£13.00	10
Junior Bike	£6.50	£8.50	10
Tandem	£22.00	£30.00	2

Availability is from 9.30 am to 4.30 pm, later in summer. Last hire 2 hour 30 minutes before closing. It is not possible to reserve bikes in advance; they are available on a first come first served basis.

10% discount is offered for students and OAPs.

Richard keeps details of hires in a diary on a daily basis. He writes down the customer details, the type of bike hired, the time it was hired and the payments due.

Increasingly, during the summer months, he is very busy and all bikes are out on hire regularly.

He wants to computerise his record keeping to:

- store details of daily hires and times
- record details of deposits and payments
- issue a receipt to the customer on payment
- produce reports on daily hires, demand and income
- produce reports on bike usage.

12: School Stationery Orders

Christine Taylor works at Westford School and is in charge of ordering stationery from suppliers. Stationery can include anything from paper and document wallets to sticky tape and board pens.

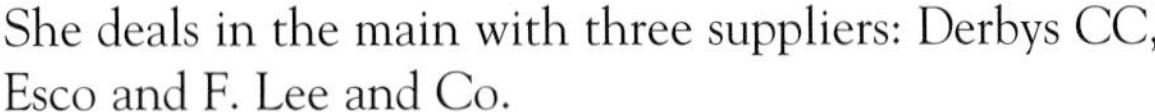

She deals in the main with three suppliers: Derbys CC, Esco and F. Lee and Co.

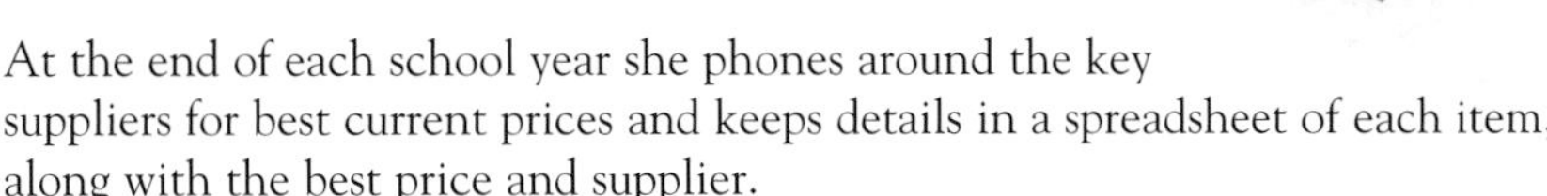

At the end of each school year she phones around the key suppliers for best current prices and keeps details in a spreadsheet of each item, along with the best price and supplier.

The school has nine faculties: Maths, English, Science and so on. Each faculty has a budget holder who is responsible for completing stationery orders. Usually there is a major order at the start of the year and then a number of minor ones throughout the school year.

At the start of the new school year the budget holder for each faculty is allocated a sum of money for stationery, based on numbers. Christine issues a stationery price list and order form to all budget holders. This has to be completed before the start of the school year.

Christine currently keeps all her records on a spreadsheet but thinks a database solution may improve processing. She wants to:

- maintain a database of suppliers
- maintain a database of products and best prices
- keep track of faculty ordering and improve her record keeping
- produce reports analysing faculty expenditure
- produce reports analysing usage – e.g. paper
- use the information to better plan needs
- provide better information to faculties and management on expenditure.

13: Village Hall Auctions

Stanton on the Hill Village Hall runs 80:20 auctions every three months. Items are submitted for auction, the customer takes 80% of the sale price and 20% goes to the Village Hall Fund. The organiser is Beryl Hartley.

Typically, auctions are attended by 200 or so people offering over 400 lots.

At the auction you will find furniture, household items, memorabilia and objets d'art, as well as many other items, all at knock-down prices.

Sellers wanting to offer lots for auction are invited to submit details by at least 28 days before the next published auction date. This enables Beryl to publish catalogues.

Sellers offering lots give Beryl their name and contact details. They also provide details of the lot and requested reserve price. Beryl logs these details into a spreadsheet as shown.

Lot No	Lot Details	Reserve	Seller	Contact No
00017	Beatles Yellow Submarine	£100	Don Buxton	01283 734562
00018	Smokers' items and pipes	£40	Charles Alman	01283 534892
00019	Brass Carriage Clock	£20	Marie Thomas	01332 775344
00020	Wind-up Gramophone	£90	Don Buxton	01283 734562

On the day of the auction, bidders pay a small entry fee, give their contact name and phone number to Beryl and in turn are issued with a Bidder ID Number.

When a lot is sold, the auctioneer notes the Lot No, the winning Bidder ID Number and the actual selling price. Collection and payments are then dealt with while the auction continues.

Beryl wants to run the auctions from her PC. She would like to:

- store details of lots and sellers
- produce pre-auction catalogues
- store details of bidders and issue ID numbers
- record sales and issue confirmation receipts
- access records and reports on sales, sellers and income.

14: Westford Community Bus

David Griffiths is responsible for the Westford Community Bus Scheme in Mid-Somerset. The 20-seater bus is funded by the local parish council. It provides a weekly service for the local community to the three major towns in the area.

The bus leaves on the same day each week, at the same time and picks up and drops off at the home of the passenger. A nominal fee is charged.

David keeps a register of volunteers who are trained in driving the bus. He allocates a driver to each journey, each week.

Day	Date	Destination	Cost	Driver
Tuesday	21/11/08	Taunton	£1.00	David Griffiths
Wednesday	22/11/08	Street	£0.50	Pete Wilson
Thursday	23/11/08	Weston-Super-Mare	£1.00	Claire Griffiths

To take advantage of the scheme, residents have to register for a permit with the local council for which a fee of £2.00 is charged annually. David keeps a file of residents who participate in the scheme.

To book a seat on the bus, residents have to phone David and simply give their name, the bus service required and pick-up point. David keeps a seating plan for each trip and merely allocates a customer to a seat on a first come first served basis. The service is immensely popular and David feels a computer solution will improve the service and his record keeping.

He would like the solution to offer the following features:

- store details of residents with permits
- store details of volunteer drivers
- improve the booking process
- give quick access to seat availability
- produce timetables and seating plans
- produce annual reports on income and use for the local parish council.

15: Westford Toy Library

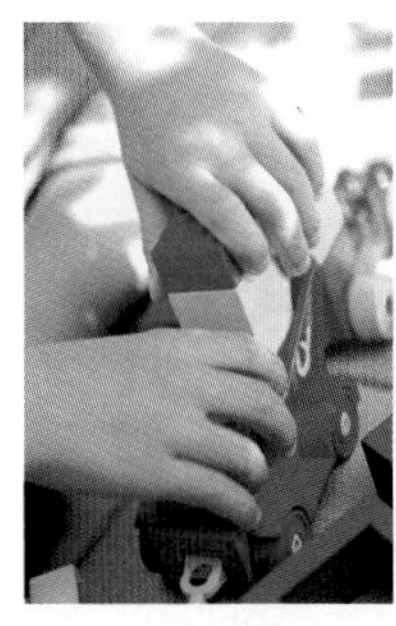

Westford Toy Library is based in the local community centre in Westford. The library is affiliated to the Early Years Library Network. It hires out toys to parents, childminders and playgroups.

It has built up a stock of over 1000 toys, details of which are stored in a ring bound folder.

Toys are coded and allocated a category: Activity, Basic, Co-ordination, Electronic, Fun and Games, Jigsaws, Music, Special Needs. Toys are also catalogued by a target age range 0–1, 2–3, 4–5 and 6–7 years old.

Toy Code	Description	Category	Age Range	Value £
T1	Farm playmat	Activity	2–3 yrs	10.00
T29	Flutterfly	Activity	2–3 yrs	7.50
T67	Super Scribbler	Co-ordination	0–1 yrs	15.00
T156	Coloured Clown	Basic	2–3 yrs	10.00
T234	Crazy Guitar	Electronic	6–7 yrs	25.00
T256	Train Set	Electronic	6–7 yrs	35.00

To join the library, there is an annual subscription fee, as shown below. Toys can be borrowed on a weekly basis for up to a month at 30p per toy per week. Members can borrow as many toys as they like. Fines are paid on a basis of 30p per day overdue.

Type	Fees
Parents	£2.00
Childminders	£3.00
Playgroups	£5.00

The library is run by volunteers who feel a computerised solution would improve record keeping. The solution should:

- provide a detailed and up-to-date catalogue of toys
- store details of members and fees payable
- record details of loans and overdue items
- manage loan and overdue payments
- provide a range of reports on loans, members and income.

Index